Alexander Balloch Grosart

Songs of the Day and Night

Or, Original Hymns for Public and Private Praise and Reading

Alexander Balloch Grosart

Songs of the Day and Night
Or, Original Hymns for Public and Private Praise and Reading

ISBN/EAN: 9783744781930

Printed in Europe, USA, Canada, Australia, Japan

Cover: Foto ©Lupo / pixelio.de

More available books at **www.hansebooks.com**

FAME.

1 *The fame I seek is* GRATITUDE,
That all vanity doth exclude;
Lord, may this gather round me, gone,
My life fulfill'd and my work done;
Thro' these my *"Songs of Day and Night,"*
Lord, may some few souls find Thy light.

2 *The fame I seek is* GRATITUDE,
Abiding—no mere interlude;
O Lord! Wilt Thou admit my claim,
And use me to nurture Thy flame?
Reviving still, the life divine,
With oil pour'd in,— not mine but Thine.

3 *The fame I seek is* GRATITUDE,
From elect souls, who know no feud;
Fain—fain would I Thy Singer be
Unto a late posterity;
Rose would I place above each thorn,
Bearing Thy cheer to hearts forlorn.

4 *The fame I seek is* GRATITUDE,—
As sweet gums from pierc'd branch exude;
Lord, grant that words which I have writ
May be Thy balm to hearts sin-smit;
Yea, be Thy Hand to softly guide
Poor wand'rers to THE CRUCIFIED.

5 *The fame I seek is* GRATITUDE,—
As swells on sight of the red Rood;
Lord, may my Song enkindle LOVE,
With Hope and Joy from Thee above;
My Master, I for this appeal;
This FAME wilt Thou unto me seal!

6 *The fame I seek is* GRATITUDE,
That magnifies "the precious blood";
I'd draw sad souls to Thee Lord Christ,
Still keeping Thy peace-bringing tryst;
May some hearts grateful be I've sung,—
My name Thy minstrels plac'd among!

SONGS OF THE DAY AND NIGHT

OR

ORIGINAL HYMNS

For Public and Private Praise
and Reading;

THE LIFE-STORY OF JESUS CHRIST—A CANTATA
with other sacred poems

BY THE

Rev. ALEXANDER B. GROSART, D.D.
LL.D. (Edin.), F.S.A. (Scot.)
St. George's, Blackburn, Lancashire.

BLACKBURN:
D. E. Rothwell, Art Printer, Salford Bridge
London:
Elliot Stock, Paternoster Row

All Rights of Translation and Reproduction reserved

1891

PROGRESS.

1 As rivers to the OCEAN flow,
Whether rushing, or moving slow ;
So would I, Lord, have my life be
A ceaseless PROGRESS unto Thee.

2 A ceaseless PROGRESS unto Thee,
Thro' Time unto Eternity;
My life's current pure and strong,
Nor banks without or flowers or song.

3 Nor banks without or flowers or song,
Onward, still onward borne along ;
Ever an influence for good,
Tho' no mighty careering flood.

4 Tho' no mighty careering flood,
Sanctified in every mood ;
Forward, still forward 'gainst all foes
Valiant in Him whate'er oppose.

5 Valiant in Him whate'er oppose,
Kept in beginning and in close ; [more
Deep'ning, widening, brightening
As I voyage to GOLDEN SHORE.

6 As I voyage to GOLDEN SHORE,
That shall lost Paradise restore :
So would I, Lord, have my life be
A ceaseless PROGRESS unto Thee.

To
MY DEAR WIFE AND OUR FOUR BOYS;

WITHOUT WHOM THESE

"SONGS OF THE DAY AND NIGHT"

WOULD NEVER HAVE BEEN WRITTEN:

This Book is re=dedicated,

LOVINGLY AND GRATEFULLY

ALEXANDER B. GROSART.

AN ALLEGORY OF THE GOD-PROTECTED CHILD OF GOD.

1 ONCE on a time in an ancient close
  Of a grey old Norman town;
Where through the whole week scarce
    any one goes
  Save a priest with a shaven crown;
I saw a hawk dash at a cagèd bird
  As it warbled tuneful song;
Songster and loving mistress scar'd,
  But the hawk could do them no wrong;
For the cage was hung and softly swung
  Within a window wide;
That crystal wall of protection flung
  Around the songster inside;
The bird of prey in defeated rage
  Dash'd again and again;
But vain the warfare it sought to wage;
  It but struck the window pane;
Bru's'd and bleeding, and with shatter'd
    wing
  At length it flew away;
And there the canary you hear sing
  In that old close to-day.

2 Is not all this sweet ALLEGORY
  Of our own Christian life?
Vain the assaults of the Adversary,
  As vain his vengeful strife;
He dreams that the lonely child of God
  Unguarded before him lies;
He dashes on him with smiting rod;
  But to meet a strange surprise;
For a crystal wall, unseen yet strong,
  Circleth God's humblest child;
Faith's eye beholds it, with trustful song;
  And the enemy is foil'd:
Praise to our God, and confession low
  If pulse of fear be started;
For stronger than he who aims the blow
  Is Jesus the loving-hearted:
And the dear Lord grant that you and I,
  May never be put to shame;
But unfearing stand as beneath His eye,
  And strong in HIS GREAT NAME.

CONTENTS.

Those marked † appeared originally in a tiny privately-printed vol. (1866) of which under 100 copies were issued; those marked * appear for the first time herein; the rest are reproduced—with revision—from "Three Centuries of Original Hymns" (1890) and several periodicals.

Fame	ii.
Progress	iv.
Dedication	v.
An Allegory of the God-protected Child of God	vi.
Contents	vii-xiv
My Nook and Emblems of Saints	xv
Preface	xvi-xx
I. GOD THE FATHER	1-13
1. Father-God Reverence	1
2. Worship	1-2
3. The Glory of God in Creation	2
4. God's Fairness	2-3
5. The Hiding of God's Power	3
6. God's Hand	3
7. The Everlasting Arms underneath	3-4
8. Most hidden and most manifest	4
9. Grandeur of Man's Soul	4-5
10. Host and Guest	5-6
11. Dark Thoughts of God	6
12. God's Keeping Silence	6-7
13. I know their Sorrows	7
14. The Broken Heart	7
15. Losing by leaving God	7-8
16. Distance from God	8
17. Dwelling with God	8
18. Ever at work and ever at rest	8-9
19. Our God a consuming Fire	9
20. The Unchanging God	9-10
21. God's Loving-kindness	10
22. The Earth not God-forsaken	10
23. Man proposes, God disposes	10-11
24. God turning the bed	11
25. Judgment and Mercy	11
26. Gentle Guidance	11-12
* 27. Upbraideth not	12
* 28. The Weaker Side	12
29. The Ever-loving God	12-13
* 30. Lean Hard	13
* 31. God near and far	13
My Heart	14
II. GOD THE SON	15-47
* 32. The Messiah expected	15
33. Bethlehem	15
34. Birth of Christ	16
35. Bethlehem and Calvary	16
* 36. The Burning Bush	16-17
37. Immanuel	17
38. God unmanifest in flesh	17-18
† 39. "He comes," "Until He comes"	18
40. The Scape-goat	18
41. The Divine Child	19
42. Twelve Years old	19
43. Child	19-20

CONTENTS.

44.	Temptation	20
45.	"Suffer the little Children to come unto Me"	20
46.	Jesus and Children at play	20-21
47.	Ephphatha	21
48.	Talitha Cumi	21
49.	He stood still	21-22
50.	Sea of Galilee	22
51.	Tears	22
52.	Seeker who seeketh nothing	22-23
53.	Tempted to forsake	23
54.	The Hands of Jesus	24
55.	Faith not Sight	23-24
56.	Rest after toil	24
57.	The Two Sleeps—Tabor and Gethsemane	24-25
58.	Emmaus: fellowship with Jesus	25
59.	Moriah and Calvary	26
60.	By His Stripes we are healed	26-27
61.	Victim-victor, Victor-victim	27
62.	The once Marred Face	27
63.	The King on His Cross-throne	27-28
64.	The Cross ("bitter tree") foreshadowed	28
65.	Stabat Mater, and in Latin	28-29
66.	It is Finished	29
67.	Mystery of Sin counterworked	29-30
68.	Shame changed to Glory	30
69.	The Shed Blood	30
70.	The Risen Saviour	31
71.	The Abiding Presence	31
72.	The Resurrection	32
73.	The Stone rolled away	32
74.	Ascension and Pentecost	33
75.	Christ's Word	33
76.	Jesus Reigns	34
77.	Longing for Christ's Second Coming	34-35
78.	Cross-bearing after Christ	35
79.	Unseen yet loved	35
80.	Safety and Comfort	35-36
81.	The divineness of the Christian	36
82.	Jesus—Sun and Shield	36
83.	Leader and Guide	36
84.	Heart-surrender	37
85.	Rose of Sharon	37
86.	Everlasting Love	38
87.	Love of God in Christ	38
88.	Boundlessness of Christ's Love	38-39
89.	Love of God—God of Love	39
90.	Heart-keeping by Jesus	39
91.	Serenity	40
92.	Imputed Righteousness	40
93.	Not Graces but Christ	40-41
94.	The Names of our Blessed Redeemer	41
95.	The Living Way	41
96.	Power from on High	41-42
97.	Unrest	42
98.	Full supply for utmost need	42
99.	Christ all in all	43
100.	Indwelling—Dwelling in	43
101.	I, yet not I, but Christ	43-44
*102.	The Door	44
*103.	Direct Access	44
*104.	The Saviour, not His Cross	44
*105.	Worship refused to Mary	45
106.	Triumph	45
*107.	Advance to triumph	46
108.	Vision of Glory	46
109.	The Final Judgment	27†
	III. GOD THE HOLY SPIRIT	48-53
110.	God the Holy Spirit	48
111.	The Love of the Spirit	48
112.	The Holy Spirit our strength	48
113.	Serenity under the Spirit's reproof	49
114.	Symbols of God the Holy Spirit	49
115.	The Holy Spirit invoked	50
116.	Grace perfecting	50
*117.	Fire of the Spirit	50-51
*118.	The Temple restored	51
*119.	Breathing	51
*120.	Man	51-52
*121.	The Trinity	53
	IV. THE HOLY SCRIPTURES	54-56
122.	The Bible in all Languages	54
123.	Symbols of Holy Scripture	54-55

CONTENTS.

	PAGE.
124. The Guiding Lamp	55
125. The English Bible	55
*126. The first Japanese convert to Christianity	55-56
V. THE SABBATH	57-59
127. The Resurrection — Sunday morning	57
128. Sunday "made" of God	57-58
129. Sunday first day of the seven	58-59
130. The Lord's Day	59
131. Sabbath Prayer-song	59
VI. THE CHURCH OF CHRIST IN ITS WORK AND SERVICES	60-90
132. The House of God	60
133. One in Christ	60-61
*134. The Church	61
135. Wonder	61
136. Longings for a Revival	61-62
137. On Joining the Church	62
138. Preparation for the Communion	62-63
139. The Lord's Supper	63
140. After the Lord's Supper	63
*141. At the Table of the Lord	63
142. Gethsemane and the Judgment-Hall	64
143. Unworthy, Unworthily	64
144. Evangelisation	65
145. Home-Missions	65-66
146. Evangelizing in the Streets	66
147. Weeds—Waifs	66-67
*148. A day in the country with "Street Arabs"	67-68
*149. Waifs at the Sea-Side	68
150. The Salvation Army	68
151. Evangelization of the World	69
152. Ultimate Christianisation of the World	69
153. Always Morning somewhere	69-70
*154. Triumph	70
*155. Thy Kingdom come	70-71
156. Advance	71
157. Ordination of Foreign Missionaries	71-73

	PAGE.
158. The Missionaries at Sea	72
*159. Martyrs of our day	72-73
160. The Jews	73
161. The Church and Sunday School	73-74
162. The Sunday School Teacher	74
*163. Sunday School Teacher	74
164. Children's debt of love to their Christian Parents	74-75
165. Parents debt of love to Children	75
166. Prayer Meeting, "two or three"	75-76
167. The Mid-week Service	76
168. Sunday-school Anniversary	76
*169. Marriage "in the Lord"	76-77
170. Marriage	77
171. Marriage	78-79
*172. Marriage	78
173. Baptism of Children	78
174. Baptism	79
175. The first Cradle of the First-born	79
*176. Baptism	79-80
*177. Reminiscences of Baptism	80
*178. Shiloh	80
*179. The Church asleep	81
*180. One	81
*181. Saints	81-82
*182. More Saints	82
*183. The Harvest of Light	82-83
184. The Cross of Christ	83
*185. The Cross	83-84
*186. The uplifted Redeemer	84
*187. The good fight of Faith	84-85
*188. Error	85
*189. Not Peace but Truth	85-86
*190. Creeds	86
*191. On laying Foundation-stone of a Church	86-87
*192. Opening and Dedication of a Church	78
*193. Looking up	87-88
*194. Powers of the World to come	88

CONTENTS.

		PAGE
*195.	Liberty and Love	88
*196.	Spoken Truth	88-89
*197.	Extra Ecclesiam nulla salus	89
*198.	Mocking Agnostics	89
*199.	The Latter Days	89
200.	Of the increase of His Government, no end	90

VII. LIGHTS AND SHADOWS OF SPIRITUAL EXPERIENCE ... 91-164

201.	Watching by a death-bed	91
202.	He leads round, but He leads right	92
203.	"The blue of Heaven is larger than the cloud"	92-93
204.	The Furnace of Affliction	93
205.	The Light not self to shine	93
206.	Growth in grace	93-94
207.	Love is cold	94
208.	Joy in Sorrow	94
209.	Heart-surrender	95
*210.	Reading	95
211.	Angelic Ministry	95-96
212.	The one talent improved	96
213.	The unrenewed heart	96-97
214.	After a long illness	97
215.	Little Faith	97
216.	Weariness	97-98
217.	Divine choosing	98
218.	Unrest	98
219.	Rest	100
220.	Castaway	99
221.	Despondency	99
222.	Rest	100
223.	Heavenly use of earthly things	100
224.	God's chosing for us	100-101
225.	The God of Patience	101
*226.	The Daisies	101-102
227.	Deadly sweet	102-103
228.	Divine and Human Love	103
229.	Compensations	103
230.	Impatience	103-104
231.	Joy born of Pain	104
232.	Returns	104-105

		PAGE
*233.	Victory by defeat	105
234.	"It is well"	105-106
235.	Remaining Sin	106
236.	Mary, Sister of Lazarus	106-107
237.	Ruins	107
238.	Faith without a perhaps	107
239.	The bending bough or song and wings	107-108
240.	The choice	108
241.	Longings	108
242.	Loveliness	108
243.	A Jubilee Royal saying	109
244.	Cup running over	109-110
†245.	The Bow in the Cloud	110
246.	Wakefulness and unrest	110
247.	The Cup of Consolation	110-111
248.	The rod that budded and blossomed	111
249.	Rooted by the River	111-112
250.	"We are tired, my heart and I"	112
251.	Sons and Daughters of God	112-113
252.	In the far country by the swine-troughs	113-114
253.	The uplifted Serpent	114
254.	Litany	114
255.	Penitence	115
256.	The Penitent	115-116
257.	Penitent return	116
258.	Contrition	116
259.	Each day the evening comes at last	116-117
260.	God of Peace	117
261.	The Shining Face	117-118
262.	Lily and Cedar	118
263.	Laid aside	118-119
264.	Unity and Diversity	119-120
265.	Divine Teaching	120
266.	"Thy will be done"	120
267.	Fading Leaf	120
268.	The blessings of Sadness	120
269.	Dignity of the body	121
270.	Compunction not Conversion	121

CONTENTS.

	PAGE.
271. Help in the Day of Grace	122-123
272. The spent Bottle and Well revealed	123
273. There's a bright side to darkest things	124
274. The Future	124
275. Aimlessness	125
276. Longing	125
277. Fretting	126
278. Fear cast out by Love	126
279. Progress and Fidelity	127
280. "Oh not this, anything but this"	127
*281. Cradle Songs	127-128
282. The Garment of Praise	128
283. Praise	129
284. Morning Hymn of Praise	129-130
285. Within and Without	130
286. Experience sanctified	130
287. Darkness	130
288. Sleep—God's gift	131
289. A Bright Christian	131-132
290. Sweet Longings	132
291. Barrenness	132
292. Mizpah	132
293. Trembling	133
294. Discipline	133
*295. It is toward evening	134
*296. Strokes	134
*297. QUI SE PLAINTE PECHE	135
*298. Friends	135-136
†299. Heavenly and Earthly Life in one	136
*300. Days of Heaven upon the Earth	
301. Anguish of Spirit	136-137
*302. Cords of a Man	137
*303. Todmüdt	137
*304. Grafted	137-138
*305. John Bunyan and his own heart	138
*306. Chief of Sinners	138-139
*307. Through much tribulation	139
*308. Second Coming	139
*309. Heaven on Earth	140
*310. Overflowing Grace	140

	PAGE.
*311. Trust not thyself, but thy God trust	141
*312. The Choice	141
*313. Wonder and no wonder	141-142
*314. Love's enigma	142
*315. Kept	142
*316. If it be possibe	142
*317. Perfection on Earth	163
†318. Lullaby	143
*319. In the Woods	143
*320. Staying Power	144-145
*321. "Strong Crying"	145
*322. The Burning Heart	145
*323. Conversion	145-146
*324. New Birth	166
*325. "Neglect the root to trim the Flower"	146
*326. Crown of Thorns, and "Thorn in the Flesh"	147
*327. " Lord, a thorn from Thy Cross"	147
*328. The Crucified	147
*329. My Body is My Cross	147
*330. The Abandoned	148
*331. Heart-searching	148
332. *Mergere sed non submergere Christus*	149
333. *In la sua voluntade è nostra pace*	149-150
334. Love without measure	150
335. Sanctified ills	150
*336. Thankfulness	151
337. Despair and God	151
*338. Despondency	151-152
339. The Rich Young Man	152
340. Genuineness	152-153
341. Necesstty and freedom	153
*342. Wearying for the Second Coming of the Lord	153
*343. Revival	154
*344. "God forgot me, and I fell"	154
345. Conscience or short work with Unbelief	155
*346. Purity	155-156

CONTENTS.

	PAGE.
347. Holy Madness	156
348. Ecstasy	156-157
349. Life, a Mystery	157-158
350. Despondency	158
351. Patience	158
352. Self-emptiness, "the precious blood"	159
353. "Noblest things find vilest using"	154-160
354. "Lord, I believe, help mine unbelief"	160
355. Chi fa cose di Cristo	160
356. Halting	161
357. Bubble	161-162
358. Mystery of Being	162
359. Das Unbewusste (The Unconscious)	162-163
360. A Backslider Awakened at Keswick Convention	163
361. The Secret of the Lord	164
362. Worth of Human Life	164
363. Christ's Freedman	164
XVIII. CHRISTIAN GRACE	165-178
364. Holiness	165
365. Hatred of Sin	165
366. God of Hope	166
367. Peace	166
368. Faith	166-167
369. Patient Waiting	167
370. Forgivingness	167
371. The Meek	168
372. Song of Joy	168
373. Purity	168-169
374. Obedience, or the "New Cart," v. "The New Heart"	169
375. To-day and not To-morrow	169
376. Content	170
377. Pleasing	170
378. "Be Courteous"	171
379. Unfearing	171
380. Sympathy	171-172
381. The Three Sisters—Faith, Hope and Love	172

	PAGE.
382. Faith, Hope and Love	172-173
383. Love	173
384. Seen through unseen	173-174
385. Character	174
386. The Heart an alabaster box of Ointment	174
387. Garment of Salvation	174
388. Desire and Power	175
389. Finding Fault	175
390. Restfulness	175-176
391. Fear and not Fear	176
392. Unclothed	176
393. Imperfection	176
394. Strength with Light	176
395. Longing	177
396. Infirmities	177-178
IX. WORK, WORKERS, AND WITNESS.	
397. Christmas	179
398. Work while it is Day	179
399. Angels	179-180
400. Count One For Christ	180
401. Every Christian bound to be a Worker	180-181
402. Kindness in Giving	181
403. "God Bless You"	181-182
404. "If we can't all gather a sheaf"	182
405. Go, Not Send	182-183
406. Using	183
407. Liberality	183
408. Known and Unknown	183-184
409. Simulation	184-185
410. Never Despair	185
411. Erring	185
412. Unshared Pleasure	185-186
413. Missed	186
414. Humble Usefulness	186
415. Peu et Bien	187
416. Frailty	187
417. "Forgive her and don't give over trying"	187-188
418. "God Buries His Workman"	188-189
419. Life Sufficient	189

CONTENTS

		PAGE			PAGE
420.	The Stronger than the Enemy	273	455.	Soothing Thought	205
*421.	Life not too hard	189	*456.	Christ in the under-world	205
*422.	"She hath done what she could"	189-190	*457.	Resurrection—One Unopened Grave	206
423.	Highways and Hedges	190	458.	The Resurrection	206-207
424.	No Retreat	190	*459.	O death where is thy sting?	207
425.	"If you want a thing well done"	191	*460.	Glory to glory	207-208
426.	Enduring to the End	198	461.	Types of Resurrection	207-208
427.	Work and Rest	191-192	462.	Gone before	208
*428.	Unadvised Speaking	192	*463.	Roses on our Family-graves	208-209
*429.	Praying and Working	192	XI.	PRAISE, PRAYER, AND SEASON-THANKSGIVING	210-221
*430.	The Lord's Handmaiden	192-193		A godly peasant home in Scotland	210
*431.	Rights and Duties	193-194	464.	Prayer	211
*432.	Keep at thy Post	194	465.	The Wrestling at Jabbok	212
*433.	Labour and Rest	194	466.	Sustained Prayer	212-213
*434.	God's "Little Ones"	195	467.	Restraint in Prayer	213-214
*435.	Yes	195	468.	"Prayed, and spake the same words"	214
*436.	Little Helpers	196	469.	The "shut door"	214-215
437.	The Ten Commandments	196	470.	Prayer is the dew of Faith	215
X.	CHRISTIAN VIEWS OF DEATH AND ETERNITY	197-209	*471.	Prayer for Purity	215-216
438	Our Dead First-Born and other two "Little Ones"	195	472.	"No more, no more"	216
*439.	Submission Our Firstborn	198	473.	"Lux in tenebris"	216-217
440.	Sorrowful yet Rejoicing	198	*474.	Family-prayer	217
441.	A Christian's Death-bed	198-199	475.	Christ Jesus my crucified Love	217
442.	The Dying Conqueror	199	*476.	The All-ruling Father	217-218
443.	Crossing to the other side	199	477.	Winter	218
444.	Longings for Departure	200	478.	Spring	218-219
445.	Mi disse:—"Non cercar, l'ho sotterato"	200	479.	Summer	219
446.	The Good die not	201	480.	Harvest-Festival	219-220
447.	Death Dethroned	201	*481.	Floods in Harvest	220
448.	No more Death nor Pain	201-202	*482.	Late Autumn	220-221
449.	No More Pain	202	†483.	Earth is no desert drear	221
450.	The Christian's Gain by Death	202-203	*484.	Every fête has a to-morrow	221
451.	Christ with me or I with Christ	203	XII.	NATIONAL HYMNS	222-225
452.	"Not dead, but just beginning to live"	203-204	485.	For our England	222
453.	The Tear-dimmed Lamp	204	486.	For England	222-223
454.	Tears but Hope	204-205	487.	For Sailors	223
			*488.	A Christian sailor's hymn at Sea	223
			489.	After a storm at Sea	223-224
			490.	"In the desired haven"	224
			491.	The Sea	224

CONTENTS.

	PAGE
492. Shipwreck	225
493. The Miner's Song	225
XIII. OLD AND NEW YEAR SERVICES	226-226
494. Looking back—old and New Year	226
494. Onward—Upward—Heavenward	226-227
496. The New Year Born	227
497. Another Year	227-228
498. A New Year's Hymn	228
499. Transcient and Permanent	228
500. The Judgment	228-229
XIV. THE LIFE-STORY OF JESUS CHRIST OUR LORD	230-238
XV. NATURE'S FIELD OF CLOTH OF GOLD	239-242
XVI. "SUNNY MEMORIES" OF THE "DEAD IN CHRIST"	243-249
XVII. IN MEMORIAM—THOMAS ASHE, M.A.	248-249
PAIN	250-252
XVIII. THE SNOWSTORM	253-257
THREE BIRTHDAY GIFTS TO A LITTLE GIRL—A Life-story	259-261

	PAGE
STORY OF THE LOST SHEEP	261-262
*THE LITTLE MAID AND THE LITTLE LADS OF HOLY SCRIPTURE	262-265
*THE SLAVE-MARTYR	265
*HOLY SCRIPTURE	265-266
*THE BIBLE	266
*The Light of the World	266-267
*"But some doubted"	267-268
A Little Boy's Prayer	268
A Child's Song-prayer and Prayer-song	268
A very little Child's Prayer	269
*"It is enough to have deserved"	270
*"Dead I sing more than when I was alive"	270
DROPPED NOS.	271-272
*109 The Final Judgment.	271
*420 The Stronger than the Enemy.	271-272
*429 Prayer and Working (substituted).	272
Notes and Illustrations	273-281
Other Books by Dr. Grosart	283-285
A Last Request	286

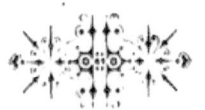

MY NOOK.

Won from Lakeside by the dredge;
Tongue of land, shap'd like a wedge,
Peb bled to the very edge,
'Neath a great cliff's shelt'ring ledge;

2 'Neath a great cliff's shelt'ring ledge;
Golden lilies 'mongst the sedge,—
Fair as vi'lets by lane hedge;
Haunt, too, where the wild-fowl fledge.

3 Haunt, too, where the wild-fowl fledge,
Nor hold it thou for sacrilege,
That oft here I plead His pledge—
No mere vain chance sortilege.

4 No mere vain chance sortilege,
But His promises allege;
Claiming "two three's" privilege,
Far from the World's hammering sledge.

5 Praise, O God, that 'tis my lot
To know this secluded spot—
Still and cool as sea-wash'd grot;
Near it there's not ev'n a cot.

6 Near it there's not e'vn a cot,
Here I go when brain is hot,
Sore-perplexed by many a knot;
Still may it remain forgot.

7 Still may it remain forgot,
Nor Improvement ever blot,—
That 'gainst God's green earth doth plot:
Save it from e'er being "a lot."

8 Save it from e'er being "a lot,"
By the highest bidder got;
And "my Nook" town's smoke know not;
I shall of hope bate no jot.

FLOWERS BIRDS—GEMS—
EMBLEMS OF THE SAINTS.

1 Flower of white Pureness,
   All-stainless Lily;
  Flower of glad Sureness
   Gold Daff-down-Dilly;
  Flower of the Martyrs,
   Love's red red Rose:
  Faith never barters
   For joy her woes.

2 Bird of the Red Breast,
   Sheath'd in sweet bale;
  Bird of sore unrest,
   Thy note a wail;
  Bird of the great wings
   Sunward uplifted;
  Bird that the Night brings
   Song, sorrow-sifted.

  Gems of the dark mine,
   Mystic your shining;
  Round the Great Vine,
   Memories twining:
  In the days olden—
   Lustrous tho' hoary;
  Wrought with art golden,
   Sacred your story.

4 Flowers of the green Earth,
   Birds of the air;
  Gems of thrice-rare worth
   Far 'bove compare;
  Thought of sin you taint,
   Flawless and pure;
  Emblems of Christ's saints
   Aye ye endure.

PREFACE.

In publishing—as distinct from the original edition for 'private circulation only'—the present enlarged contribution to our Hymnology, I must again leave my Hymns to speak for themselves and vindicate their right of recognition. I trust they will be found in line (so-to-say) with our great national Hymnology, in all the fundamental truths of evangelical Christianity, whilst presenting them in new settings and as having regard to aspects and experiences not exhaustively represented therein. I make my own the profound words of VINCENT OF LERINS, "what has been believed by all, always, everywhere.": (*Quod semper, quod ubique quod ab omnibus*).

In my former Preface I reprinted a Paper on Praise. I do not deem it needful to reproduce it here in full. But it may not be without advantage to summarise its arguments:—

a. Praise must be more than mere singing or playing. The singing or playing cannot be too 'skilful' or cultured or painstaking. "*Sing* unto Him a new song; *play* SKILFULLY with a loud noise" (Psalm xxxiii. 3.) But besides, we must pray King David's prayer—"*O Lord open Thou my lips*, and my mouth shall shew forth Thy praise" (Psalm li. 15). That is, it needs the same grace of God and the very same ministry of the Holy Spirit to 'open' our lips and purify our hearts for Praise as for Prayer.

b. Praise to be really Praise must be consciously addressed to God. When St. Paul instructs on praise through "psalms and hymns and spiritual songs" he is careful twice over to remind the Ephesians (v. 19) and Colossians (iii. 16) and all of us, that it is to be "*to the Lord.*" It will keep us from preoccupation about our own voices or 'parts' or our own skill and our own selves altogether, if we only stedfastly remember that our singing and playing are the vehicles of Praise and that God Himself is in the assemblies of His people to hear and accept, to own and be glorified by their worship.

c. *Praise has also its human side.* I recur to the apostolic teaching already referred to—"Speaking *to yourselves* in psalms and hymns and spiritual songs, and making melody in your hearts to the Lord"——"Let the word of Christ dwell in you richly in all wisdom, *teaching and admonishing one another* in psalms and hymns and spiritual songs, singing with grace in your hearts to the Lord." We may place beside these, the earlier counsel of the Psalmist (c.v. 2) "Sing unto Him; sing Psalms unto Him; *tell* ye of all His wondrous works."

In my judgment these several portions of Holy Scripture ought to set our Churches and Sunday-schools a-thinking as to whether our Praise is not impoverished of its function and purpose by failure to carry out what I have designated its human side. I feel strongly that this enjoined "speaking *to yourselves*" and "*teaching and admonishing one another*" through "psalms and hymns and spiritual songs" would broaden and deepen and enrich our Praise immeasurably. Specifically, were Praise thus given its full scope and function we would not be perplexed with fears and doubts about our joining in given hymns. Necessarily there are those for "babes in Christ," for beginners, for the little experienced in the spiritual life and beyond whom the advanced Christian is far ahead. But retrospectively, the most advanced Christian may and ought to sing such hymns; and not only so, but this very advance may be turned into gracious "teaching and admonishing of *one another.*" Similarly with the awfulness and anguish of certain "psalms and hymns and spiritual songs." Many Christians know no such conviction or pungency of distress; they have gratefully to sing rather "Thy *gentleness* hath made me great" (Psalm xviii. 35) or of "life for a look." But "no man liveth *to himself*" only. By the unity of Christian fellowship, we owe it to exchange experiences and to turn to account these and those as the other, and so when we are called upon to join in hymns that are not behind us but beyond us, as telling of faith and love, glow and rapture, consecration and surrender that are to us an ideal only, we will wrong ourselves if we hesitate through them to "make melody in our hearts." As a Christian I have no objection to sing a hymn that is better than I am any more than I have objection to the company of a fellow-Christian better than I am, who knows more, feels more, does more than I. Such singing of the greater hymns may be blessed as an excitant to rising higher than I have hitherto attained.

Holding these convictions I have to a large extent in my Hymns looked to their being used, after singing and playing, in fulfilling the apostolic injunction "speaking to yourselves" and "*teaching and admonishing* ONE ANOTHER."

Having regard to my own Hymns in another aspect, it must be permitted me to observe that I have found that wherever actual human experience has been truly told, responses have been found. The human heart and human lives are so alike all the world over, that even the most personal and seeming unique experiences prove to be in touch with others. In this edition I would accentuate that our Hymn Books speaking broadly, have been prepared too much as Praise, not only for Christians merely, but for Christians at their best and highest. The matter of fact is that no actual or conceivable congregation or assembly, answers to this basis. Human and Christian experience is progressive; and in my Hymns I have kept before myself the steps and stages of the process and progress corresponding with human and Christian fluctuations and as mediums whereby to "speak to *one another*," and "teach and admonish one another" in mutual sympathy, forbearance and teachableness. It is possible that some of my Hymns may be condemned as revealing and recording a spiritual or unspiritual condition that ought not to exist. I am prepared for such heartless criticism. I can only anticipatively protest that just as in the prayer the dear Lord most values—prayer that is the very utterance of the moment's emotion—this type of Hymn is the truest of the true to actual facts. I have had pathetic evidence that the saddest even most awful of my Hymns have been helpful to others similarly, "walking in darkness and *seeing no light*." And it had been strange if it had proved otherwise. For alike in Praise and Prayer, it being the fact that I am in doubt and dread, in darkness and despair, I am bound by integrity of conscience thereby to tell my heavenly Father through Jesus Christ that it is so with me. I must not, at the peril of my spiritual life, cover up my state with orthodox unrealities. Hence on the one hand "a beautiful prayer" (as the poor phrase runs) is not the ideal of prayer any more than is mere dulcet verse conformable to the creeds, a hymn. I quote here the following suggestive and confirming words from Besant's very striking story of the "Children of Gibeon." "I can sing,"

PREFACE.

said Valentine. "I will sing you a hymn, mother." She hesitated, and then for some fancied appropriateness—I know not what, perhaps it existed only in her imagination—of the place and the time with the *motif* of the hymn,—she chose an old Puritan hymn which has now dropped out of use and been forgotten since the Churches resolved to stifle the sadness of life and to simulate the voice of one who continually rejoices and is not afraid, and has neither doubt nor question. The hymn had very little joy in it, save that of a faith, humble and resigned, with an undercurrent of an unexpressed feeling of sorrow, and even perhaps of humble remonstrance, that things had been ordered otherwise from the beginning. This hymn begins with the words, "We've no abiding city here," and as Valentine sang them, the blessed old woman joined her hands as one who prays, and the tears gathered in her eyes."—(Book II. c. iii.)

Subsidiary to these observations, it will be noted that I sometimes place as heading and sometimes take for refrain golden words or apt saying or deep utterance of the spiritual life of others. I may be pardoned in affirming that these are probably the most original of my Hymns. For just as the greatest and most enduring Sermons owe their immortality to their unfolding of the mind of God in the portion of His Word chosen for text, so these inspiring words meeting the actual experience of the Hymn-writer quickens him to his best.

As to the FORMS of my Hymns, I have so chosen these as that the vast majority will be interpretable by well-known tunes agreeably to the measure-markings prefixed to each. In a thorough revision of all formerly printed, I have kept this in view, albeit I would call attention to my title-page before and now, as declaring that my Hymns are for "private reading" as well as "private and public praise."

I am profoundly thankful for the many "good words" that have reached me from far and near since the privately-printed edition was issued. Alas! Even in this brief interval I have had to mark out of my surely remarkable select and spontaneous list of Subscribers (with all modesty be it so declared) names such as these—H. E. CARDINAL NEWMAN—BISHOP OF DURHAM—(LIGHTFOOT) CANON H. PARRY LIDDON—EDWIN HATCH, D.D.—DEAN CHURCH (friend of long years)—Professors ELMSLIE and DAVID DUFF and T. G. ROOKE—DR. MACFADYEN—JAMES BROWN, D.D.—JOHN ADAM, D.D.—ALEXANDER MCLEOD, D.D.—and of my literary circle ROBERT BROWNING and THOMAS ASHE. It will not be held ambitious (I hope) if I covet the passing of some of my Hymns into the Hymnology of the Church Universal. The bloom and fruitage of elect moments of a life-time, these Hymns may perhaps thus live after me. (See 'Fame' facing title-page).

I cannot close this Preface, without as before and with added emphasis, acknowledging my obligations to various literary and musical friends who have given me the benefit of reading my printed books and MSS. More or fewer have been thus read by Professor F. T. Palgrave of Oxford: and the late Thomas Ashe, M.A. and Rev. J. H. Clark, M.A., of East Dereham, Norfolk. But most of all am I under obligation to my 'brethren beloved' the Rev. Canon Wilton, M.A., poet of "Wood-notes and Church-Bells," Rector of Londesborough; Rev. Samuel McNaughton, M.A., Preston, and Principal G. C. H. Moule, M.A., Cambridge, who have severally transmuted task into labour of love by sympathetic and painstaking helpfulness and suggestions. These three are all "Sweet Singers" themselves, as my readers will do well to find out.

ALEXANDER B. GROSART.

N.B. I shall hold it as a special favour if the Reader *at once* correct the Printer's *errata* recorded below. Others in literals, punctuation and the like, will be readily put right without being noted; also a few measure-figures that have been omitted.

Page 15 'come' place on first line of 2nd column instead of last line of first column.
",, 16 Hymn 35, st. 8, l. 4 read 'Laud.'
,, 22 ,, 50, st. 2, l. 1 read 'Sea of Galilee.'
,, 27 ,, 61, st. 2, l. 3 read 'Victor, yet Victim.'
,, 35 ,, 80, st. 4, l. 2 read 'mine.'
,, 38 ,, 87, st. 5, l. 1 read 'this.'
,, 47 ,, 108, st. 6, l. 7 read 'From' and for 'aprise' read 'praise.'
,, 78 ,, 173, st. 6, l. 1 read 'parental."
,, 86 ,, 190, st. 2, l. 5 read 'book.'
,, 87 ,, 192, st. 12, l. 4 read 'hear.'
,, 126 ,, 277, st. 8, l. 2 read 'values.'

In 255, st. 7, l. 2, read 'alone' for 'lone.'

Omitted in Contents—Christ for all the World—The Marys at Christ's Tomb. Page xxii.

☞ Persons desirous of using any of the Hymns and Poems in this book will please communicate with myself.

CHRIST FOR ALL THE WORLD: ALL THE WORLD FOR CHRIST: *I John ii 2.* 6s

1 The wideness of the sky,
  The fulness of the sea;
  To Faith's clear-seeing eye,
  Shew, Lord, Thy love to me;
  To me, and all mankind,
  Where 'er the Gospel goes;
  For all who seek do find,
  Cure for Sins deepest woes:
    O Cross of Calvary!
    May the round world thee see.

2 The myriad-numbered stars,
  The sands that line the shore;
  Lo! clear o'er all Earth's jars
  Sound out, "Weep ye no more;"
  For the sav'd multitude
  By these rich-symbol'd be;
  That Grace in plentitude
  Seeks all condemn'd to free:
    O Cross of Calvary!
    May the round world thee see.

3 Behold as light of Day
  Rolls on from pole to pole,
  So His Truth speeds its way—
  The Truth that saves the soul;
  Rejoice! rejoice! all Lands,
  Your hour shall soon be born;
  When ye with clapping hands
  To Christ the Lord shall turn:
    O Cross of Calvary!
    May the round world thee see.

4 The Word of God is pass'd;
  The oath of God is sworn;
  And tho' the sky's o'er cast
  Our Hope undimm'd doth burn;
  That, trav'lling in His might,
  The Lord as King of Men
  Darkness shall change to light,
  Nor Sin triumph again:
    O Cross of Calvary!
    May the round world thee see.

THE MARYS AT CHRIST'S TOMB.
St. Matthew xv. 47. xvi. i. 8s.

1 With their erst FAITH brought to a stand,
  LOVE sent the Marys to His tomb;
  Spices the rarest in their hand, [gloom.
  Though they went on in grief and

2 They had forgot the GREAT THIRD DAY
  Was pledg'd to free the awful dead;
  That the strong GRAVE must yield its prey
  Even as the Lord Christ had said.

3 Came the CROSS,—crown of woe and shame,—
  Branding HIM aye THE CRUCIFIED;
  Where, like a lamb, 'midst altar flame,
  Jesus, the victim-victor died.

4 But it was life by death achiev'd,
  As the great Resurrection flash'd;
  Ah! had the Marys ALL believ'd,[dash'd.
  Their FAITH and HOPE had not been

5 Nor to the tomb would they have gone,
  There to weep all disconsolate;
  But they had waited—His work done—
  Him to meet in first high estate.

6 Give me, Saviour, the Marys LOVE,
  And FAITH that sees THEE still alive;
  Upward draw me, HEAVENLY DOVE,
  That against Thee no more I strive.

FATHER-GOD—REVERENCE.—WORSHIP.

1. God the Father.

1. FATHER-God—REVERENCE. *Ps. xxxiii. 8.*
8.8.8.8.8.8.4.6.

1 O FATHER-God, fill me with awe,
Like Moses, when THY FACE he saw;
Or Peter, as in his amaze
'Fore THEE he did himself abase;
   That I may rev'rence more and more,
   And THEE in very deed adore;
     More and still more,
     Thee rev'rence and adore.

2 O Father-God, I seek that Thou
May'st my whole inmost being bow;
Great God, forbid that I should be
Forgetful of THY MAJESTY:
   O may I rev'rence more and more,
   And THEE in very deed adore;
     More and still more,
     Thee rev'rence and adore.

3 O Father-God, Creator art!
I but a creature, and my part
As lowly sinner low to bend,
And suppliant words to THEE up-send;
   That I may rev'rence more and more,
   And THEE in very deed adore;
     More and still more,
     Thee rev'rence and adore.

4 O Father-God, I keep my tryst
With THY ETERNAL SON, THE CHRIST,—
A man, but yet "God Manifest,"
"My Lord, my God," to be addressed:
   That I may rev'rence more and more,
   And THEE in very deed adore;
     More and still more,
     Thee rev'rence and adore.

5 O Father-God, Thy Spirit give,—
Not only now, or fugitive,—
That, hushed and awed, I never may
Presumption in THY sight betray:

That I may rev'rence more and more,
And THEE in very deed adore;
     More and still more,
     Thee rev'rence and adore.

6 O FATHER-God, to Thee I come;
In mercy rather hold me dumb,
Than that, unto Thee drawing near,
I think of mortal men that hear:
   O may I rev'rence more and more,
   And THEE in very deed adore;
     More and still more,
     Thee rev'rence and adore.

2. WORSHIP. *Isaiah vi. 3; Romans i. 19-21.*
7.7.7.5.

1 HOLY! Holy! Holy Lord!
God o'er all, by all adored;
Earth and Heav'n join'd in accord,
   Praise united bring.

2 The great cry in Heaven heard,
Holy! Holy! Holy Lord!
Let it our key-note afford;
   Sing, all mortals, sing.

3 *Repeat St. 1.*

4 By the guiltiest implored,
As the Gospel-leaves record;
Holy! Holy! Holy Lord!
   To the CROSS we cling.

5 *Repeat St. 1.*

6 Slaves of sin to sons restored;
Sin, by grace is now abh orred;
Holy! Holy! Holy Lord!
   Let thanks loudly ring.

7 *Repeat St. 1.*

8 O my heart! strike every chord!
All thy gratitude outpoured;
Holy! Holy! Holy Lord!
   Sound out voice and string.

THE GLORY OF GOD IN CREATION GOD'S FAIRNESS.

9   *Repeat St. 1.*
10 Draw us with Thy Love's strong cord,
    When Death's torrent we must ford;
    Holy! Holy! Holy Lord!
        Help, O heav'nly KING!
11 *Repeat St. 1.*
12 Grace and glory, in concord,
    Wait us, with all blessings stored;
    Holy! Holy! Holy Lord!
        Faith! rise on bright wing.

3. THE GLORY OF GOD IN CREATION.
                    7s.   *Psalm xix. 1.*
1 MORN unfolding gates of gold;
    Chariot of the DAY forth-roll'd;
        Still declares Thy glory Lord.
    And the Noon-day splendour's blaze—
    On which aw'd eyes upward gaze—
        Aye declares Thy glory Lord.
2 EVE as tranquilly she closes,
    Sprinkling the great WEST with roses;
        Still declares Thy glory Lord.
    Starry grandeurs of the NIGHT,
    Filling Heaven's infinite;
        Aye declare Thy glory Lord.
3 The great SEA in its far-booming,
    Thro' the fierce dark tempest looming;
        Still declares Thy glory Lord.
    Held there by Divine command;
    And no less the inviolate sand,
        Aye declares Thy glory Lord.
4 Broad-bas'd MOUNTAIN of all lands
    That like "GREAT WHITE Throne" up-
        Still declares Thy glory Lord [stands;
    STREAM and LAKE, in light and shadow;
    Rocks and Cornfields and green Meadow;
        Aye declare Thy glory Lord.
5 WOODS "clap hands," with jubilant voice
    As they many-ton'd, rejoice;
        And declare Thy glory Lord.
    SPRING'S rath freshness, SUMMER'S glow;
    AUTUMN'S red leaves, WINTER'S snow;
        Aye declare Thy glory Lord.

6 BIRDS of air and FLOWERS of field;
    Smallest things that tribute yield;
        Still declare Thy glory Lord
    From the lowest to the highest;
    From remotest unto nighest;
        Aye declare Thy glory Lord.
7 Thou, O MAN, dost thou refrain
    Now to swell th' ascending strain?
        Speak the glory of thy Lord.
    Sav'd by Him for thee died,
    Be not thy loud song denied—
        SHOUT *the glory of thy Lord.*

4.   GOD'S FAIRNESS. *Eccles. iii. 11.*
            8.4.4.8.4.4.8.8.

    Quae nemo alius potest facere, nisi tu une
  a *Quo est omnis modus, formosissime.*
            St. Augustine (Conf. i. vii.)

1 THY fairness, Lord, *to* all things fair
            Thou dost impart
                With subtle art;
    But chief, yea far beyond compare,
            In the "new heart,"
                Where THOU dost part
    Spirit and flesh, and "purge our dross,"
    Transforming us by Thy sad CROSS.

2 Thy fairness, Lord, *in* all things fair
            Thou dost reveal,
                As when man's seal
    Is plac'd on what is rich and rare:
            O more to feel
                Thy beauty steal—
    Like fragrance that the flower informs—
    That to THY image me conforms.

3 Thy fairness, Lord, *on* all things fair
            Thou dost bestow,
                And still dost show
    Amidst the WORLD'S mystery and care
            That e'en below,
                If THEE we know,   [white,
    Thou dost, Lord, clothe the meek with
    Them meet'ning for the LAND of LIGHT.

THE HIDING OF GOD'S POWER—GOD'S HAND

4 Thy fairness, Lord, *thro'* all things fair
    Thou causest rest :—
      Like peacock's crest
Or dove's neck turning in warm air ;
      So richly drest
    As does attest
THAT Heaven to our Earth comes down,
All hate and sin far from it flown.

5 *Repeat St. 1.*

5. THE HIDING O GOD'S POWER.
      8s.   *Habakuk iii. 3-4.*

1 Lo ! Gold on gold in furnace burning,
Or light in light to darkness turning
Where Paran's pinnacles up-tower ;
Yet 'twas "the hiding of THY power."

2 Majestic splendor and amazement ! —
To eyes of mortals the bedazement,
Seen in THY vast HAND'S flashing dower;
Yet 'twas "the hiding of THY power."

3 When Thou from Sinai's top tremendous,
Thy grand "ten words" in love did'st send
Lo ! Thine OWN Israel did cower ; [us ;
Yet 'twas "the hiding of THY power."

4 And when the strong sea is uprisen,
And its proud waves dash 'gainst their prison,
Whilst thro' the darkness tempests lour;
'Tis but "the hiding of THY power."

5 When forth the sunshine fiercely flameth,
The Lord our God HIS LAW so frameth,
That Night comes with its cooling shower ;
Ah, Lord ! "the hiding of THY power."

6 When THOU "plenteous rain" ordainest,
Thou THY control, Lord God, retainest
In "small drops"—unhurting flower,—
Gracious "hiding of THY power."

7 Laud, loving God, that thus THOU dealest,
And tenderly THYSELF revealest
To lowliest in saddest hour;
Laud, for "the hiding of THY power."

8 O Christ ! unseen on THY throne-altar,
Thy Church upon her knees doth falter ;
Knows Thou art near tho' foes devour,
But mourns "the hiding of THY power."

9 Heart-sick and lorn behold us praying,
For still to come Thou art delaying ;
O hear our cry 'midst strife and stour,
Flame on the World, "hide not THY power."

6. GOD'S HAND.   *2 Chronicles xx. 6.*
      7s.

1 *Power and might are in Thine Hand :*
None may venture to withstand
Thine inflexible command.

2 *Power and might are in Thine Hand :*
Ocean cannot break the band,
Fix'd, where THOU hast fix'd the strand.

3 *Power and might are in Thine Hand :*
Thrones by THEE, or fall, or stand ;
Who may dare to countermand ?

4 *Power and might are in Thine Hand :*
Thou dost save ev'n "burning brand ;"
Largely doth THY grace expand.

5 *Power and might are in Thine Hand :*
Gentle art THOU, Lord, and bland ;
Slow Thine Own to reprimand.

6 *Power and might are in Thine Hand :*
Thanks that we this understand ;
Bring us, Lord, to Thy " Good Land."

7 *Power and might are in Thine Hand :*
Make THY Church a holy band,
Telling out THY LOVE'S demand.

7. THE EVERLASTING ARMS UNDERNEATH.
      8s.   *Deut. xxxiii. 27.*

1 The child, that to his mother clings,
Lies not all safely on her breast,
Till she her arms around him flings,
    Sweetly caressing and caressed ;
E'en so, my God, THY mighty arms,
Not my poor FAITH, shield me from harms.

2 I bless Thy Name for every grace, [Own;
　Wherewith Thou dost enrich Thine
　Yea, I would seek each day to trace
　　Myself more like my Master grown;
　Yet, O my God, Thy mighty arms,
　Not my faint Love, shield me from harms.

3 I walk along this sin-scarr'd Earth,
　In brightness now and now in dole;
　Now all "cast down" and now in mirth;
　　Now griefs, now joys, possess my soul;
　But, O my God, Thy mighty arms,
　Not my dim Hope, shield me from harms.

4 Within, amidst the World's unrest, [given;
　Thou, Lord, the calming word hast
　Thy peace abides, howe'er I'm press'd;
　　And yields an antepast of Heaven:
　But, O my God, Thy mighty arms,
　Not my own Peace, shield me from harms.

5 My mouth Thou fillest with "sweet songs;"
　Makest my feet run in "the Way;"
　Giv'st me the joy to Thine belongs;
　　Nor scarcely ever sayest me nay:
　But, O my God, Thy mighty arms,
　Not my scant Joy, shield me from harms.

6 The child, that to his mother clings,
　Lies not all safely on her breast,
　Till she her arms around him flings,
　　Sweetly caressing and caressed:
　Ev'n so, my God, Thy mighty arms,
　Not aught of mine, shield me from harms.

8. Most Hidden and Most Manifest.
8s.

Secretissime et Præsentissime.—*St. August-*
ine (Conf. i. iv.) Amos iii. 7: Psalm xxxv.
14: cf. Ephes. i. 9, 18: St. John vii. 17.

1 *Most hidden and most manifest:*
　O Thou my worthless bosom's Guest,
　Tho' Thou dost fill the highest Heav'n,
　Thou, Lord, this grace to me hast giv'n;
　That I still know Thee in my breast—
　Most hidden and most manifest.

2 *Most hidden and most manifest:*
　Let carping Unbelief protest,
　Thou, lowliest believer, knowest,
　Thou, lowliest believer, showest,
　With him Thou still art pleased to rest—
　Most hidden and most manifest.

3 *Most hidden and most manifest:*
　Faith yet succeedeth in its quest;
　And lo! the peace all peace surpassing,—
　O sweetest peace of Jesus glassing;
　Thy Holy Spirit doth attest,—
　Most hidden and most manifest.

4 *Most hidden and most manifest:*
　Ye scorners in your wild unrest,
　O would that ye would turn to Him
　Thron'd far above the Seraphim;
　And of His mercy make request!
　Most hidden and most manifest.

5 *Most hidden and most manifest:*
　Let us the golden phrase arrest;
　By noble saint of old time spoken,
　It still to-day remains unbroken;
　Redeeming love His grand bequest—
　Most hidden and most manifest.

6 *Most hidden and most manifest:*
　Lo! Thou the mystery dost invest
　With Thy sweet human-ness, O Christ!
　Ay, sweetness, tenderness unpriced:
　O with this grace may we be blessed!
　Most hidden and most manifest.

9. Grandeur of Man's Soul. 2 Cor. vi. 15.
8s.

Quis mihi dabit adquiescere in Te? Quis
mihi dabit, ut venias in cor meum, et inebries
illud, ut obliviscar mala mea, et unum bonum
meum amplectar Te? S. Augustine (Conf.
i. v.)............aula ingenti memoriæ..........
infinita multiplicitas......Varia, multimoda
vita, et immensa vehementes.—(Ibid x. xii,
xvii).

1 Forgive, Lord, if 'fore THY great words
  Doubts pierce me as of piercing swords;
  For like him at the BURNING BUSH
  I hear, but cannot my fears hush:
  Great, O my God is Thy appeal!
  Wilt THOU my stopped ears unseal?

2 Wilt Thou my stopped ears unseal
  And fullness of Thy truth reveal?
  That it is true all that I hear—
  That THOU not only drawest near,
  But seekest entrance to my soul,
  And all its straitness to control.

3 And all its straitness to control;
  All its thick darkness off to roll;
  Breaking my will in its rebelling,
  Me glorifying for THY dwelling;
  "Walk" THOU in me that I may be
  Partaker of THY majesty.

4 Partaker of THY majesty
  Thou the Lord God, our God Most High;
  The spacious largeness for THY feet
  Where THOU didst with THY people meet
  In the great halls of Temple old,
  Fashion'd of cedar and of gold.

5 Fashion'd of cedar and of gold,
  As in the HOLY SCRIPTURES told;
  The fabric vast that there uprose
  In splendor of white Hermon's snows;
  O God! dost THOU indeed thus "dwell,"
  Yea, thus "walk"? 'Tis unspeakable.

6 Yea thus "walk"? 'Tis unspeakable,
  Yet abides it immutable;
  O thanks for these fore-glimpses giv'n
  By blessed light sent down from Heav'n
  Of the vast vastness of man's spirit,
  Enlarg'd so wide by Jesus' merit.

7 Enlarg'd so wide by Jesus' merit,
  That by the Gospel we inherit;
  Till Thou, O God, e'en here dost find
  In holy humble human mind
  Grander dwelling than above;
  Made grand by THY redeeming love.

8 Made grand by THY redeeming love,
  With mystic curtains all enwove;
  Reason's high throne and scepter'd state,
  With rank'd servants that on her wait:
  O many noble FACULTIES,
  With which power penetrative lies.

9 With which power penetrative lies,
  Touch'd with the splendors of the skies;
  Conscience—in purple-curtain'd shrine
  Making the heart semi-divine;
  Chambers nobler than palace-halls,
  Where MEMORY herself installs.

10 Where Memory herself installs,
   Girded with adamantine walls;
   Imagination's gorgeous rooms
   Near awful, with their lustrous glooms;
   The spirit's inner court, where WILL
   God's Holy Spirit doth fulfil.

11 God's Holy Spirit doth fulfil,
   With grace divine infused, until
   Imparting of divinest nature
   Creator crowneth HIS lov'd creature:
   O God! dost Thou indeed thus "dwell,"
   Yea thus "walk"? 'Tis unspeakable.

10. HOST AND GUEST. *Rev. iii. 20.*
8s.

1 I WALK within myself with awe,
  The HOUSE for me so spacious built;
  More stately than e'er Zion saw;
  The awful blood on its gates spilt;
  'Tis LOVE'S most gracious mystery
  That I, God's dwelling-place should be.

2 That I, God's dwelling-place should be,
  Not as of hewn and carven stone,
  Or beams of Leb'non's mighty tree,
  Or gold for wh ch men's hearts so groan;
  But wrought of BODY and of SOUL;
  God's Spirit ruling o'er the whole.

3 God's Spirit ruling o'er the whole,
  Yea ent'ring my heart's shrine aga'n,
  To minister in sweet control,
  Still seeking HOLINESS to gain;
  How stilly patient, lo! He waits,
  Nor of His tender love abates.

4 Nor of His tender love abates,
  But my poor straitness all enlarg'd,
  Fills with the grace that consecrates;
  Until all hush'd, amaz'd, surcharg'd,
  I cry out *glorious is this place,*
  As I behold His awful FACE.

5 As I behold His awful FACE,   [door;
  Who deigns to stoop 'neath my heart's
  A-trembling and bow'd down, I trace
  His constant PRESENCE, and adore;
  Supremest wonder! God in me;
  Yet is it no rapt ecstasy.

6 Yet is it no rapt ecstasy;
  Possessing and of HIM possesst;
  Walking in " glorious liberty "
  Thee blessing, Lord, and of THEE blest;
  'Tis Heav'n on Earth, EARTH summ'd of
  Fulfilment of His promise giv'n. [Heav'n;

7 Fulfilment of His promise giv'n,
  Foretaste of the great HOUSE above;
  O how with me my God has striven!
  And how magnanimous His love!
  I sing, I shout, I praise HIS NAME;
  O join all saints to spread His fame!

11. DARK THOUGHTS OF GOD.
  10s.

" *Wilt Thou be altogether unto me as a LIAR?* *Jer.* xv. 18 *and cf.* iv. 10.

1 I SAW the Great White Throne of sculptur'd light;
  A shadow mov'd across it, black as night,
  And fill'd all HEAV'N with horror and affright.

2 And whence that shadow? Lo! far off its birth:
  'God hath deceived him,' is with mock and mirth,   [Earth!—
  At saint, sarcastic flung. For, hear O

3 'God hath prov'd false,' he means in blank despair,   [hair,—
  With thin clench'd hands and grey dishevel'd
  The prayer of saint flung into empty air.

4 Across without a Christ—the heavens dumb;
  Oh who may dare the mystery to plumb!
  Or who to such a God, will longer come?

5 God's servant-seer, found out his dread mistake,
  That did his soul t' its inmost centre shake,
  And bow'd him 'fore his God, rash speech to make.   [Lord,

6 False prophets claim'd a message from the
  Persuading him they had a Heav'n-sent word;
  Which said "peace peace" when God had meant the sword.

7 O soul of mine, when thus assail'd with doubt,
  Flee to thy God and tell thy anguish out;
  He'll give the light and all thy tempter's rout.

12. GOD'S KEEPING SILENCE. *Habak.* i. 13.
  8s.

1 THIS SILENCE, O Lord God, is awful!
  Are thoughts of it by man " unlawful?"
  To see what all around I see;
  To hear what daily reaches me;
  To know how human lives are spent
  In sin and crime, or languishment;
  And God sees all and God all hears—
  It fills my eyes with burning tears:
  This SILENCE, O Lord God, is awful!
  Are thoughts of it by man 'unlawful'?

2 Hearts breaking near me right and left;
  Of light—of hope—of all bereft;
  Lives darken'd deeper than eclipse;
  Hoarse cries moaned out from pallid lips;
  Children born deom'd-seem at a glance—
  Heredity of circumstance;
  By breathing a malarial breath
  That hurries myriads to death:
  This SILENCE, O Lord God is awful!
  Are thoughts of it by man ' unlawful'?

3 Secret of all this misery
  In God's own keeping in the sky:
  A word! and lo! the spell should break,
  But ah, that word HE doth not speak;

Theheav'ns as brass, the Earth as iron;
Wrong and suffering souls environ;
"Lord, my God," art dead? or dumb?
That no least answers to us come?
This SILENCE, O Lord God is awful!
Are thoughts of it by man 'unlawful'?
4 I dare speak in integrity,
The doubts, the dreads that in me lie;
'What wilt Thou do to Thy Great Name,'
Thus hourly put to shame and blame?
O Father, wilt my spirit calm?
Put in my mouth some conqu'ring psalm;
Thou to the 'overcoming' givest
Assurance that THOU Lord God livest:
Wilt Thou this witness give to me
And Faith's 'walk' where I cannot see?

13. I KNOW THEIR SORROWS. *Exodus iii.7.*
8s.

1 'I KNOW their sorrows,' THOU saidst, Lord;
And still the great word standeth true;
The PAST and PRESENT in accord,
Bring an unchanging God to view.
2 My heart is heavy as a stone,
And yet I quiver in sharp pain;
O Lord, as on the grass new-mown,
Descend on me like sweet soft rain!
3 Wistful and sad, I look within,
But naught there do I find to heal;
Immitigable is this sin;
To THEE, O God, I make appeal.
4 I place me in the HANDS men nail'd;
I rest me on the HEART which bled;
My future, Lord, is thickly veil'd;
"I KNOW their sorrows,' Thou hast said.

5 *Repeat St.* 1

14. THE BROKEN HEART. *Ps. cxlvii. 4.*
8.6.

1 BROKEN in heart! broken in heart!
He bindeth up our wounds;
My God, how tender is THINE art!
Thy WORD, how soft it sounds.
2 I have a broken heart, O God!

Am smitten out and in;
The Tempter lays on me his rod;
Alas! is like to win.
3 O sin and sorrow weigh me down,
Until I scarce can see;
The billows swell as they would drown;
Now unto THEE I flee.
4 A broken heart! O trifle small
Beside the radiant skies!
Yet THOU, God, for my heart dost call,
When I myself despise.
5 Thou numberest the shining stars
As goldenly they roll;
The soul THOU healest that sin mars;
O come then, make me whole!

6 *Repeat St.* 1.

15. LOSING BY LEAVING GOD. *Heb. iii. 12.*
8.7.

Te nemo amittit, nisi qui dimittit. St
Augustine (Conf. iv. ix).

1 NONE God loseth but who leaveth,
None who leaveth but God grieveth,
God he grieveth, by forsaking;
Froward heart its own doom making:
O my God! I would THEE choose,
Thou wilt not my cry refuse.
2 Broken from all others trusting;
'Franchis'd from all "former lusting";
I THY freedman on THEE calling,
Thou dost guard me in my falling;
O my God! I would THEE choose,
Thou wilt not my cry refuse.
3 How uncertain my affection!
Cleaving follow'd by defection.
Ebb and flow, like tides of ocean,
In an ever-changeful motion:
O my God! I would THEE choose,
Thou wilt not my cry refuse.
4 Saviour God, well THOU me knowest,
Yea, me to myself THOU showest;
Save me, save, Christ, ever-living
Keep me by THY gracious giving:

DISTANCE FROM GOD. AWAKING WITH GOD.

O my God! I would THEE choose,
Thou wilt not my cry refuse.
5 Touch my eyes with THY OWN seeing,
Interpenetrate my being;
That by THEE "apprehended"
This lorn conflict may be ended:
O my God! I would THEE choose,
Thou wilt not my cry refuse.
6 If my feet, O Lord, be sliding
Lead me by THY gentle guiding;
Me redeeming by THY merit,
Keep me by THY mighty Spirit:
O my God! I would THEE choose,
Thou wilt not my cry refuse.
7 Repeat St. 1.

16. DISTANCE FROM GOD. *St. Luke xv. 13. 88.*

*Nam longe a vultu tuo in affectu tenebroso,
Non enim pedibus aut spatiis locorum itur abs
Te, aut reditur ad Te. S. Augustine (Conf. i. xviii.)*

1 Not change of place, but unchang'd heart,
Removes us, Lord, from where THOU art;
In weaken'd love the secret lies
Of men's far-sunder'd destinies.

2 Not change of place, but unchang'd heart,
Doth make the dear Lord Christ depart;
For distance measures not by feet
But as our hearts from HIM retreat.

3 Not change of place, but change of heart,
Doth win the sweet wounds of LOVE'S dart; —
Coming or leaving, THY power alone,
Shall reth or melteth heart of stone.

4 Not change of place, but change of heart,
(O precious change! O easeful smart!)
Will ever to the Cross us move,
And " closer walk" of saint approve.

5 Not change of place, but change of heart,—
Won by the Spirit's gracious art
God's temple is, to which HE comes,
With blessings nothing of Earth sums.

6 Not change of place, but unchang'd heart,
Removes us, Lord, from where Thou art;
Lo! darken'd love! Thrice-saddest wonder,
'Tis putteth God and man asunder.

17. AWAKING WITH GOD. *Ps. cxxxix. 18.*

1 THROUGH darkness and stillness THOU,
   watchest THINE, |shine;
When night cometh on, or the day doth
Thou touchest our eyelids that we may see,
Lo! *when I awake, I am still with Thee.*

2 All the toiling day, THOU art ever near,
All the restful night we have naught to fear;
For working or sleeping this aye the glad
   plea,
THAT *when I awake, I am still with Thee.*

3 Our hearts all unconscious keep beating on;
Our brain doth rest; and the night being
   gone,
Again THOU settest us for duties free;
Lo! *when I awake, I am still with Thee.*

4 We praise THEE, O God, that by day and
   night,
Thou keepest us safe " in the way" of
   right;
Adoring O Lord, I would bow the knee;
For *when I awake, I am still with Thee.*

18. EVER AT WORK AND EVER AT REST. *Romans viii. 28.*

Semper agens et semper quietus. -S. Augustine (Con. i. iv.)

1 EVER at work and ever at rest;
All things fulfilling THY high behest;
From the archangel and seraphim
To the wee child a-trilling its hymn;
Ever THINE blessing, ever most blest, —
Ever at work and ever at rest.

2 Ever at work and ever at rest;
Ever for guilty man in quest;
Still doth THY life-giving Word appeal;
Still doth THY Spirit His grace reveal;
Working so widely, from East to West,—
Ever at work and ever at rest.

3 Ever at work and ever at rest;
    Making Thyself a thrice-gracious guest;
  Dwelling in humblest, lowliest heart,
  With all the power of Love's subtle art;
  Knocking so gently at man's callous
  Ever at work and ever at rest. [breast,—
4 Ever at work and ever at rest:
    Catching up every pleaded request;
  Hearing man's cry and answering prayer;
  Sweetly regarding and lightening care;
  Daily THY love is made manifest,—
  Ever at work and ever at rest.
5 Ever at work and ever at rest;
    Never surceasing THINE interest;
  In the "far country" o'erwatching still,
  Striving the stoniest heart to thrill;
  Guarding the tiniest bird in its nest,—
  Ever at work and ever at rest.
6 Ever at work and ever at rest:
    By the whole Universe unopprest;
  Softening gently THY mighty HAND,
  Even to pluck out a "burning brand";
  As day by day THY mercies attest,—
  Ever at work and ever at rest.
7 Ever at work and ever at rest:
    Lo! 'tis a marvel still unexprest;
  Leading the vast world on and on
  Toward the Cross of Redemption;
  Ever THINE blessing, ever most blest,
  Ever at work and ever at rest.

19. OUR GOD A CONSUMING FIRE.
As. *Heb. xii. 29. Deut. iv. 22.*

1 O LORD my God, wilt Thou me bless
  With aw'd sense of THY holiness?
  Thy searching words my heart inspire,
  Our God is a consuming fire.
2 Shew me how pure, O GOD, THOU art,
  And THINE OWN purity impart;
  That, my poor life still hid in THINE,
  I may shew forth the life divine.
3 Give me to know Thou hatest sin,
  And "put"¹ like hatred me within;
  Forbid I should forget THY ire;
  Our God is a consuming fire.

4 But, though Thou hatest sin, we know,
  Not on the sinner falls the blow;
  For on the Cross of Calvary,
  Behold the sinner's SURETY die!
5 Now guilt removed is from all
  Who on THE CRUCIFIED shall call;
  Thus, thus alone, the words expire,
  Our God is a consuming fire.
6 Holy art THOU, O God, and Just,
  Thus the vast problem to adjust;
  Avenging sin, exalting LAW,
  Yet saving sinners without flaw.
7 Praise to THY NAME, O Holy One,
  Who the transcendent work hast done;
  Uplifting man e'en from the mire;
  In Christ, God no *consuming fire.*
8 O Lord, Thy Spirit to me give,
  To see and know how 'tis I live; [flame;
  That drops of blood have quench'd the
  The Blood of Him Who died in shame.

20. THE UNCHANGING GOD. *Mal. iii. 6.*
8.7.8.7.8.8.

1 Thanks that my God amid all change
    Unchanging still abideth;
  Broad-based stands the mountain-range
    The while the dark cloud glideth;
  Ev'n so, O Lord, by Thy sure word
  Nothing can blot, "Thou changest not."
2 Thou livest, though men come and go,
    Each age THEE still retaining;
  The tides perpetual ebb and flow,
    The sea always remaining;
  Ev'n so, O Lord, by Thy sure word
  Nothing can blot, "Thou changest not."
3 With open Hand, THY blessings free,
    Upon us THOU outpourest;
  In field and barn, in blade and tree,
    Rich gifts of Thine Thou storest;
  Ev'n so, O Lord, by Thy sure word
  Nothing can blot, "Thou changest not."
4 Erring and weak and prone to fall,
    Thee, Saviour, oft provoking;
  Still, Lord, upon us Thou dost call,

Never Thy grace revoking;
Ev'n so, O Lord, by Thy sure word
Nothing can blot, "Thou changest not."

21. GOD'S LOVING-KINDNESS. *Ps. li. 2.*
8s.

"My Song shall be ever of the loving-kindness of the Lord." Prayer-Book.

1 Thy "loving-kindness," 'tis the word
To sing the kindness of the Lord;
Not in mere kindness, but in love;
With tender feeling, hearts to move.

2 With us, in that for kindness meant,
Sharp word, chill look, is often blent;
Till, all the grace of kindness gone,
The heart is sore and still unwon.

3 Thy "loving-kindness," Lord, impart,
And give to us Thy gracious art, —
In kindness to be truly kind;
Nor wound the heart that we would bind.

4 Give us, O Lord, an eye to melt,
Revealing that we too have felt;
Give us the greeting word of cheer,
That tells our brotherhood sincere.

5 Yea, teach us, Lord, that there may be
No love ev'n in our "charity;"
Forbid our kindness should be alms
Dropt grudging into abject palms.

6 *Repeat St. 1.*

22. THE EARTH NOT GOD-FORSAKEN.
8.8.8.8.9.9.

"The Lord hath forsaken the Earth."— Ezekiel ix. 9.

1 Hath not the Lord forsaken Earth?
'Twas said of old in mocking mirth,
But read to-day with gleam of tears,
So deeply speaks it to our fears;
Alas! our FAITH by facts is shaken
And dreads our Earth has been 'forsaken.'

2 Hath not the Lord forsaken Earth?
Thought, at the first, of sinful birth;
But now, in shadow of events
Such, that to it e'en HOPE assents;
So utter is the mystery
Of things that all around us lie.

3 Hath not the Lord forsaken Earth?
I sit with darken'd heart and hearth;
Of all bereav'd, and not a spark
To lighten the appalling dark;
Unanswer'd prayer — peace from me taken,
If this be not, what *is* "forsaken"?

4 Hath not the Lord forsaken Earth?
O to o'ercross Death's narrow FIRTH!
To get to THEE, O Christ, and know
What is so thick-veil'd here below;
My early faith was not mistaken, —
And earth of God *is not* "forsaken."

5 Hath not the Lord forsaken Earth?
Nay, — light arises and shines forth;
I lay me down with mouth in dust;
Altho' HE slay me, I will trust;
O Christ, my Lord, hast THOU not died?
I'll cling to THEE THE CRUCIFIED.

23. MAN PROPOSES, GOD DISPOSES.
8.8.7.7. *Isaiah xlv. 5.*

1 *Man proposes, God disposes:*
FAITH on this great word reposes;
Leaves to Christ the yea or nay,
Whether bright or dim the way.

2 *Man proposes, God disposes:*
Hope, with the sweet maxim closes:
Anchors still within the vail,
E'en when heart and flesh do fail.

3 *Man proposes, God disposes:*
Guiding thro' our blind supposes;
Now holds up and now casts down,
Till, thro' Christ, we win the crown.

4 *Man proposes, God disposes:*
Whether thorns be ours or roses;
Silver light the clouds still line;
Stars in blackest darkness shine.

5 *Man proposes, God disposes:*
The event His end discloses;
Trials' fires no accident
But with gracious purpose blent.

6 *Man proposes, God disposes:*
This, each human life encloses;
With His great embracing love
Lifting to the peace above.

GOD TURNING THE BED. GENTLE GUIDANCE.

7 *Man proposes, God disposes:*
   Madly tho' our will opposes;
   O to have no will but His!
   Antepast of heavenly bliss.

24. God turning the bed. *Ps. xli. 3.*
                    8s.

1 As sick upon my bed I languish,
  My full heart knowing its own anguish,
  Softly there falls upon my ear
  Word that assures me God is near;
  Word like to rain on mown grass shed:
  When sick, the Lord will turn thy bed.
2 For e'en when heaviest lies Thy rod,
  Thus have I found it, O my God!
  All bruis'd and weak, I've cried to Thee,
  And, lo, in love, Thou strengthenedst me!
  Fulfilling all that Thou hast said:
  When sick, the Lord will turn thy bed.
3 Burden'd and pain'd, wistful and faint,
  I lifted unto Thee, my 'plaint;
  Nor ever found Thy promise fail
  That the tempter should not prevail;
  From night to morn, by Thy Hand led:
  When sick, the Lord did turn my bed.
4 Shadows fall deep, my eyes grow dim;
  I grasp a 'cup' filled to the brim;
  Deep and dark, it is like Thine Own
  Down-bent head, heart-shaking groan;
  One look to Thee, I'm strengthened:
  When sick, the Lord doth turn my bed.
5 *Will turn thy bed!* O tender word!
  Spoken by the mouth of the Lord;
  Still I will trust, still on it rest,
  Leaning, like child, upon Thy breast;
  Living, dying, I shall be sped:
  When sick, the Lord will turn my bed.

25. Judgment and Mercy.   8s.
      Lam. iii. 33. Is. xxviii. 21.

1 O God, of old Thy judgments came
  In war, in tumult, and in flame;
  Great earthquakes shook the solid Earth;
  Grim Pestilence stalk'd after Dearth;
  But, ah! how strange such work to Thee,
  Thy heart yearn'd o'er man's misery.
2 Thy Holy City, how it lies,
  In heaps on heaps 'neath parching skies;
  Thy glory gone, Jerusalem,
  Once Israel's lustrous diadem:
  But, Lord, Thy promises are sure,
  When Thy fix'd moment is mature.
3 Men of to-day, His judgments dread,
  Before Him bow your contrite head;
  Awake, awake! whilst yet 'tis day;
  Risk not the hazards of delay;
  His wrath 'gainst sin eternal burns,
  Yet Jesus saves whoever turns.
4 Now, even now, His Spirit strives,
  That sinners may shake off their gyves;
  Looking to Him Who on the cross
  Aton'd for man's infinite loss;
  His loud appeal, "Why will ye die?"
  Reverberating from the sky.
5 How long will ye forget your God!
  How long will ye invite the rod!
  How long neglect, and still neglect,—
  Yet, to repent, one day expect!
  Slow move His wheels but they do move;
  Then, listen to Incarnate Love.

26. Gentle Guidance. *Ps. xxxii. 8.*
                 7s.

1 Not like angel with drawn sword,
  Neither with rod threat'ningly;
  Leadst Thou, Lord, but giv'st Thy word;
  I will guide thee with Mine eye.
2 Thee we see not; Thou seest us;
  Where'er we be, Thou art nigh;
  Whisp'ring, timid, valorous:
  I will guide thee with Mine eye.
3 Dark days come—our path is dark;
  Know not or to go or fly;
  From sky falls, like trill of lark:
  I will guide thee with Mine eye.
4 Lord, we're wayward and we're weak;
  Gladness changing to sad sigh;
  Keep Thou us as Thou dost speak;
  Guide us ever *with Thine eye.*

5 So be it, through earthly life,
  Till in Thee, O Christ! we die;
Thy word strengthening in strife:
  I will guide thee with Mine eye.

6 *Repeat St. 1*

27. UPBRAIDETH NOT. *St. James i. 5.*
8s.

1 Thanks, O my God, Thou me receiv'd
  And all my misery reliev'd;
I came to Thee, my sins to blot;
Came late—came driv'n—with heart all hot;
Thou welcome gave, just as I was; [cause;
Bound up my wounds, nor ask'd their
Whisper'd with "still small voice" of cheer,
  "Thy sins are all forgiven" hear:
  Now comes back what I had forgot,—
  "*God giveth and upbraideth not.*"

2 I walk'd in darkness "in the way"—
  Ah, darkness in the blaze of day!
How ignorant I was, and weak,
But softly Thou to me didst speak;
Me teaching as Thy "little child"
Thou saw'st a weary and beguil'd;
Thou gav'st me wisdom, gav'st to me
Ev'n Thine Own "glorious liberty:"
  Now comes back what I had forgot,—
  "*God giveth and upbraideth not.*"

3 How diff'rent Thou, O my dear Lord,
From even those who know Thy Word!
With what reproaches, yea and taunt
And high looks, as of those who vaunt;
Men help their erring fellow men;
Mean to be kind, but then, but then—
Take all the grace from what they do
And all sin's stinging pain renew?
  Now comes back, what I had forgot,—
  "*God giveth and upbraideth not.*"

4 Gentle and patient, Lord, art Thou,
When wilder'd we before Thee bow;
Brought to a stand in doubt and fear,
Knowing alone that Thou art near;
But men—ah, how they will upbraid,
Until to speak we are afraid;
Almost provoking unto hate

As clos'd wounds they exacerbate;
  Now comes back, what I had forgot,—
  "*God giveth and upbraideth not.*"

28. THE WEAKER SIDE. 1 Cor. i. 27.
8s.

1 God standeth on the weaker side;
  The weaker oft is glorified;
Till mightier grows the spoken word
Than e'er the sceptre or the sword.

2 God standeth on the weaker side:
  Rebuking scorn—abasing pride;
The World's 'shame,' is no shame to Him;
Truth's martyr-names He will not dim.

3 God standeth on the weaker side:
  In His Hands it is "magnified;"
The "still small voice" breaks iron yokes
Far surer than by bloody strokes.

4 God standeth on the weaker side:
  Howe'er the base and false deride;
He taketh lowest by the hand;
Erect and strong makes humblest stand.

5 God standeth on the weaker side:
  If leaders ev'n be crucified;
The crown of thorns Christ's noblest crown
Cross-bearers He as great doth own.

6 God standeth on the weaker side:
  Lo! vict'ry comes as sure as t' tide;
When weakness lays hold of His strength
It conquest wins—right rules at length.

7 God standeth on the weaker side:
  As bridegroom standeth by the bride;
His benison He freely gives;
God-kept each man who for Truth strives.

29. THE EVER-LIVING GOD.
7s.

1 Man appears, to disappear:
  'God Lives'—hushes all our fear;
Each wave breaks upon the shore
But the sea rolls evermore.

2 Frail man's breath as flower of grass
  "*Over which the wind doth pass;*"
Indestructible the soul,
Ever in God's own control.

3 Sin its awful hold retains,
   As thro' marble run its veins:
   Blood of " God made manifest'
   Clears the stains and giveth rest.
4 Weary hearts in anguish toss,
   But to dim eyes beams the CROSS;
   Light of Glory bids rejoice;
   Softly speaks the "still small voice!"
5 Lonely spirits hide away;
   Dark amidst the blaze of day ;
   But Father, Thou draw'st nigh
   Giving Thy blest company.
6 Falleth now the great word " LIVE ;"
   Permanent not fugitive;
   Father, Son, and Spirit—God,
   Lifting from us SIN'S vast load.
7 *Repeat St. 1.*

30.   LEAN HARD.
                8s.
" *Thou wilt keep him in perfect peace whose mind is stayed [leans hard] on Thee; because he trusteth in Thee." (Isaiah xxvi. 3 and cf I. 10.*

1 COME thou to Me, afflicted one;
   Think not that thou art left alone;
   "I know thee," and keep watch and ward;
   Lean thou on ME, MY CHILD, *lean hard.*
2 Thy days are long—long, too, thy nights,
   By pain that stings—by fear that blights;
   See this—like daises on the sward,--
   Lean thou on ME, MY CHILD, *lean hard.*
3 Be to thy cross now reconcil'd,
   Nor of thy *trust* be thou beguil'd;
   All trial has its rich reward;
   Lean thou on ME, MY child, LEAN HARD.
4 Doth darkness gather round thy path?
   Doth e'en HOPE whisper 'child of wrath'?
   From all the tempter's darts I'll guard;
   Lean thou on ME, MY child, LEAN HARD.
5 Is FAITH sore-shaken? or LOVE chill'd?
   Thy heart with myst'ry of things fill'd?
   Does thy erst open WAY seem barr'd?
   Lean thou on ME, MY child, LEAN HARD.
6 Weary and tossing, lift thine eyes
   Up to the hills where thy strength lies;
7 Let nought thy coming steps retard;
   Lean thou on ME, My CHILD, *lean hard.*
   Repeat St. 1.

31. GOD NEAR AND FAR. 1 *Kings viii. 46.*
                8.6.8.6.8.8.

1 No one so far away as God,
   Yet none who is so near;
   Eternity is His abode ;
   But, lo! I find HIM here;
   Within my heart—that by HIS grace
   He chosen has for dwelling-place.

2 No one so far away as God,
   Yet none who is so near;
   O how it lighteneth our load
   And stilleth ev'ry fear !
   To look upon the Earth and sky,
   Assur'd that God is ever nigh.

3 No one so far away as God,
   Yet none who is so near;
   For HE who this Earth's acres trod,
   Wipes still the falling tear ;
   Altho' HIS THRONE is far ABOVE,
   He liveth yet INCARNATE LOVE.

4 No one so far away as God,
   Yet none who is so near;
   The UNIVERSE shakes at His nod,
   But guiltiest needs not fear;
   " My Lord, my God," doth see the Blood
   And HIS great COVENANT stands good.

5 No one so far away as God,
   Yet none who is so near;
   Far mightier than Moses' rod
   Is the great rod of prayer;
   Upheld within the hand of FAITH,
   Sure-fulfill'd is all " He saith."

6 No one so far away as God,
   Yet none who is so near ;
   For lo! 'twixt Heav'n and Earth the ROOD
   Uniteth sphere and sphere ;
   In light of light the great God dwells,
   But visiteth in lowliest cells.

7 *Repeat St. 1.*

My Heart.

A REMINISCENCE OF S. AUGUSTINE.

1. As in the stillness of the night
    I lie awake ;
  The hours—like birds wing-weary, flight
    T'wards HEAVEN take;
  And from the beating of my heart
    Untaught of Art,
  Quick FANCY from each pulse and pause,
    Quaint symbols draws.

2. A lifted axe it seems to me,
    With steady stroke
  Like woodman's that falls momently
    Against an oak ;
  Slow felling the proud tree of life :
    O fateful strife !
  I hush myself that I may hear,
    Yet do not fear.

3. The solemn sign I would receive—
    To Thy sweet will
  Yielding myself—its sense believe,
    Aye and until
  Thou, Lord ! shalt give the word to smite:
    It shall be right ;
  The tree may fall ; 'tis in THY Hand,
    I'll fearless stand.

2. God the Son.

I ... in Jesus Christ His [the Father's only Son] our Lord, Who was conceived by the Holy Ghost, born of the Virgin Mary, suffered under Pontius Pilate, was crucified, dead and buried. He descended into hell; the third day He rose again from the dead. He ascended into heaven; and sitteth on the right hand of God the Father Almighty; from thence He shall come to judge the quick and the dead.—The Creed.

32. THE MESSIAH EXPECTED.
8s.   Exodus iv. 10-13

1 'O Lord, send Him Whom Thou wilt send'!
 He shall the proudest Pharaoh bend;
 'SEND HIM,' the promis'd 'WOMAN'S SEED,'
 For Israel to intercede;
 Of slow speech and of a slow tongue
 I should like broken wave be flung
 Against the rock of so strong will:
 'Send HIM, O Lord!'—Thy word fulfil.

2 'O Lord, send Him Whom Thou wilt send'!
 The cry of God's most inner friend;
 A witness to the World's grand hope
 Of ONE omnipotent to cope
 With man's dire stress of utmost need;
 By shattering word and conqu'ring deed.

3 'O Lord, send HIM Whom Thou wilt send,'!
 And all this weary conflict end;
 Thy 'Second Coming' we believe:
 How long THY Church is left to grieve!
 The en'my comes in as a flood,
 Lord Christ, shall he not be withstood?

4 'O Lord, send Him Whom Thou wilt send,'!
 Awake! arise! Thy cause defend;
 Burst in Thy splendor from the skies
 And hear, O hear, our suppliant cries!
 Earth travails for Thee in sore pain:
 Are all our hopes to be in vain?

5 'O Lord, send Him Whom Thou wilt send'!
 These 's'gns' sure the 'last days' portend;
 Thy WORD belied Thy TRUTH tradue'd:
 Thy CHURCH to helplessness redue'd;[come;

Make bare Thine arm, "Thy Kingdom
Enfranchis'd Earth make Thy glad home.

33. BETHLEHEM.
Christ for all the World and all the World for Christ!.   8s.

1 FULL eighteen hundred years have flown,
 Since in the low skies burn'd a star
 More brilliant than in our skies are;
 And angels ministrant made known
  The BIRTH supreme, 'midst things ajar;

2 The BIRTH supreme, 'midst things ajar;
 O'er Bethlehem broke the gladdening song
  —That seers and saints should far prolong
 "Glory to God" and "peace" for war;
 A Saviour for our RACE "made strong."

3 A Saviour for our RACE "made strong:',
 O Christ to-day THY crimson CROSS
  —That wrought redemption of man's loss
 God's lever is—O God, how long!
  To move our Earth, no more to toss.

4 To move our Earth, no more to toss
  In anguish of a guilty sleep;
  To bring hope to sad eyes that weep;
  To sever pure ore from the dross;
  Back to the light the round globe sweep.

34. BIRTH OF CHRIST.
S. John iii. 19; S. Luke ii. 10, 15, 25;
S. Matthew ii. 2. 8.8.7.8.8.7.

1 O who are these with glist'ning pinions
Swift-crowding down from Heaven's
    dominions,
To our low Earth bright-winging?
Angels descending from ABOVE
With glad songs of INCARNATE LOVE,
To hearts expectant bringing.
2 Hark! the whole Heav'n and Earth rejoices,
As far proclaim celestial voices,
    Earth reconciled to Heaven;
Lo! In the fields of Bethlehem
Budded again KING David's stem
    The HOLY CHILD is given.
3 Their flocks and herds the shepherds
By sweet invasion of their sleeping [keeping,
    Do catch the mighty tidings;
Before HIM fall, with low adoring,
Full homage to "the BABE" outpouring;
    God, spite of lowly hidings.
4 O BIRTH most mighty of all time!
Heav'n, Earth, might well together chime
    And break forth into singing;
Well might the skies all radiant glow,
And op'ning heavens their splendor show,
    The fields with "glory" ringing.
5 For sages by His star led on,
Welcome the World's redemption;
    Their Kingly gifts rich-laying;
And in the Temple-courts there wait
Simeon and Anna consecrate,
    Their great hope them up-staying.
6 *Repeat St. 1.*

35. BETHLEHEM AND CALVARY.
S. Matthew ii. 1. and S. Luke xxiii. 33.
8s.

1 Lo! Bethlehem and Calvary—
A human CHILD! that God might die:
This the stupendous mystery
In Bethlehem and Calvary.
2 O Bethlehem and Calvary—
The crib, the cross turn'd to a throne,
That the whole round globe shall own:
This, Bethlehem and Calvary.
3 Lo! Bethlehem and Calvary—
Supremest Birth! supremest Death!
That the WORLD'S history doth sheath—
In Bethlehem and Calvary.
4 O Bethlehem and Calvary—
Did ever burst such splend'rous light?
Did ever darken Earth such night?
As Bethlehem and Calvary.
5 Lo! Bethlehem and Calvary—
Sweet picture of HUMILITY,
And Earth and Hell's hostility—
Are Bethlehem and Calvary.
6 O Bethlehem and Calvary—
The mystery of sin now solved,
Mercy with righteousness evolved—
By Bethlehem and Calvary.
7 Lo! Bethlehem and Calvary—
Shepherds and sages sought THE CHILD,
We seek a HIGH-PRIEST undefiled—
'Bove Bethlehem and Calvary.
8 O Bethlehem and Calvary—   [achiev'd
Now Death's dethron'd, man's life
Where'er the Gospel is believ'd—
Land, Bethlehem and Calvary.
9 *Repeat St. 1.*

36. THE BURNING BUSH. *Ex. ii. 1-6.*
7s.

1 Burning Bush—of thee I read
Aw'd as when on knees I plead;
This "great sight" I seek to greet
With unsandall'd rev'rent feet;
Hurtless is this leaping fire
Yet it flames as does a pyre.
2 Mystic is the burnish'd "sign,"
Lo! not mortal, but divine;
Horeb points to Bethlehem
And the "rod of Jesse's stem;"
God made manifest as CHILD,
Yet abiding undefil'd.
3 Tiny God-inform'd frame
Wonder far 'bove 'BUSH' of flame;
Mortal flesh of God illum'd

Yet like 'BUSH' still unconsum'd;
The appointed time is ripe,
Type pales 'fore the antitype.
4 GOD'S OWN HAND the 'BUSH' fire coo'ld
Law of burning over-rul'd,
That no touch of flame remain'd —
Leaping fires by HIM restrained,:
Even so at Bethlehem
Godhead burn'd not " Jesse's stem."
5 Give me grace, Lord, this to weigh,
That I ne'er shall say THEE 'nay;'
When THOU mak'st—in ruth, not ire —
My poor heart as " BUSH" of fire;
Let Thy fire within me burn
But naught into ashes turn.

37. IMMANUEL. *Isaiah vii. 14. S. Mat. i. 23.*
8s.

1 When the sky is as lead above,
 When all the Earth is black below;
When nothing—nothing— seems to move,
 Or all things backward still to go;
When TRUTH is fallen in the street —
 Street seeming near to neighbour Hell;
O God, I fall down at THY feet —
 Immanuel! Immanuel!
2 Lo! when the old WORLD's heart was sore;
 When "holy men" kept watch in vain ;
When God seem'd sworn to speak no more
 Tho' men were thirsting as for rain;
When few were left who waited still
 For the great hope of Israel;
Ah, then THOU didst that hope fulfil —
 Immanuel! Immanuel!
3 When the great hope once more had died,
 And dimness fell on the GREAT BIRTH;
When still dead rites were multiplied,
 But scarce faith found in all the Earth;
When godlessly men came and went,
 Controll'd as by some hideous spell;
Thou from THY Nazareth wast sent —
 Immanuel! Immanuel!
4 When by Thy mighty word and deed,
 Going about aye doing good;
Richly dispersèd was the seed,

And THY life in completeness stood;
When THY doom'd CHURCH in frantic hate
 Against the clear light did rebel;
Thou died'st for a world ingrate —
 Immanuel! Immanuel!
5 When the full triumph seem'd achieved;
 When THY cross was a name of scorn;
When e'en THINE OWN ELEVEN grieved
 All their sad hearts with terror torn;
When THOU, the King of men wast dead,
 Guards set at thy grave sentinel;
Thou lived'st! Death was captive led —
 Immanuel! Immanuel!
6 And so, O Christ, from age to age,
 Thou hast lived on and THOU hast seen;
What tho' Thine en'mies fiercely rage,
 Still art THOU silent and serene;
Still THY good cause THOU bearest on;
 'Tis THINE all enemies to quell;
No power that is can shake THY throne —
 Immanuel! Immanuel!
7 The waves of the WORLD's sea may surge,
 But the blue sky above is calm;
Tho' sometimes FEAR a doubt may urge,
 We still shall sing a conquering psalm.
Light spreads THY TRUTH its way doth wile;
 Clear 'midst the storm as wave-swung-bell
Comes THY great promise, " No more sin"—
 Immanuel! Immanuel!

38. GOD UNMANIFEST IN FLESH. 8s.
" *I will not meet thee as a man; I will take
vengeance.*"—*Isaiah xlvii. 3.*6

1 I will not meet thee as a man;
 O words of portent, words of ban!
Yet spoken, Lord, not to THINE OWN,
 But unto guilty Babylon.
2 I will not meet thee as a meta;
 O words of portent, words of ban!
Laud to Thy Name, O Lord my God,
 Thou all their terrors didst unload.
3 I will not meet thee as a man;
 O words of portent, words of ban!

Revers'd unto Thine Israel,
When Thou didst come Immanuel.

4 *I will not meet thee as a man;*
O words of portent, words of ban!
But ah! the crimson of THY blood
Did show THEE man, tho' also God.

5 *I will not meet thee as a man;*
O words of portent, words of ban!
Yea, Lord, but He THE CRUCIFIED
For man hath liv'd, for man hath died.

6 *I will not meet thee as a man;*
O words of portent, words of ban!
Wilt not meet us but we'll meet THEE
Clinging unto the bitter tree.

7 *I will not meet thee as a man;*
O words of portent, words of ban!
'Fore naked God we cannot stand:
O JESUS! reach THY nail-pierc'd HAND.

39. "HE COMES" "UNTIL HE COME."
St. Luke x. 23-24 and I Corinthians xi. 26.
8s.

1 "He comes"—in the dim ages old,
By sign and symbol greatly told;
Until "He come"—our watchword now
With upward look and wistful vow:
"He comes"—the elders were made wise
By priestly rite and sacrifice;
"Until HE come"—we joyful wait,
Expectant watching at the gate.

2 "He comes"—hearts hushed if that perhaps
They might catch echoings of HIS steps;
"Until HE come"—Lord, is it nigh,
When THOU shalt burst on ev'ry eye?
"He comes"—they had this mighty hope
Kindled by type, and sign and trope:
"Until HE come," Lord, at THY TABLE
We feel THY promises are stable.

3 "He comes"—the fathers falter'd not
Nor bated of their faith a jot:
"Until HE come"—we onward gaze
And notes of trust and hope still raise.

"He comes"—and so in faith they died
Still looking for THE CRUCIFIED:
"Until He come"—O Calvary
Thy sinless Victim sure is nigh!
"Until HE come"—our watchword now
With upward look and shining brow.

40. THE SCAPE-GOAT.   *Isaiah liii. 6.*
8s.

1 HIGH-PRIESTLY hands the lots have cast,
And forth into the desert vast,
Behold the doomed Scape-goat sent,
Life, death, in mystic union blent:
Thou, O my Saviour, for our sake
The anti-type THYSELF didst make;
Led forth into the wilderness
This fallen race of THINE to bless.

2 High-priestly hands the SCAPE-GOAT prest,
And thus by symbol caus'd to rest
Upon its fated head, the guilt
Figur'd by blood on altar spilt;
Thou, O my Saviour, not by sign
But very deed of Love divine,
Our sin upon the CROSS didst bear,
Nor for THYSELF one sorrow spare.

3 Voiceless, alone, and hunger-bitten,
Lo! where the Scape-goat stands smitten,
Or now amid sere sedges lying
Parched, and as by inches dying.
Jesus, my Saviour, there I see
Of THY dread DEATH, the epitome;
But ah! on THEE a mightier load
Thou God-forsaken Son of God!

4 High-priestly hands up-lifted were,
Sending the Scape-goat forth with prayer;
Seeking that Israel would now
Accept the rite and pay the vow:
O, THOU my Saviour-substitute!
Thy all-atoning death impute;
As to THY CROSS I dare to cling
Partaker of THY sorrowing.

41. The Divine Child.
Isaiah ix. 6; St. John iii. 16.
7.7.6.7.7.6.

1 O amazing, speechless wonder!
  To be sounded forth by thunder -
Mighty God on Earth a Child;
But as light and not as light'ning;
Drawing us, and not affright'ning;
  Earth and heaven now reconcil'd.

2 O infinitude of Grace!
  That our dreadest terrors chase -
Mighty God, on Earth a Child;
Mystery of mystery,
Coming not to live but die
  God's Belovèd "Undefil'd."

3 O unfathomable Sin,
  What a victory Thou did'st win!
But, O Christ! Thou "Woman's Seed"—
Thou didst then take up the gage,
Thou didst face Hell's fellest rage;
  And in Thy vast love didst bleed.

4 Joy, O Christ, for Thy work done!
  Joy, O Christ, for triumph won!
Great High-Priest for ever pleading!
Heart of human sympathy
As on earth, so in the sky,
  Ever for us interceding.

42. Twelve Years Old. *St. Luke ii. 42.*
108.

1 How sweet the story, Jesus, of Thy youth;
  When twelve years old to the great
    Temple taken;
  Hard must that heart be all untouched of
    ruth -
  In which that story doth not soft thoughts
    waken.

2 I see Thee—as I read—a bright-fac'd boy;
  Grave with a gravity beyond Thy years;
  I hear Thee breaking forth with a strange joy,
  All tremulous and aw'd and wet with
    tears.

3 I follow Thee as still I read—now going
  Amongst the white-hair'd Rabbis and
    priests stol'd;
  I catch Thy words from Thy pure mouth
    forth-flowing—
  Question and answers which deep truth
    unfold.

4 I join Thy mother with her wistful eyes,
  Seeking Thee, her lost son, with grief-
    fill'd heart;
  I mark her find Thee, in a meek surprise;
  'Midst doctors seated, filling doctor's
    part.

5 I list her ask as unto Thee she nears -
  "Son, car'st thou not that sorr'wing
    we sought Thee."
  I hear thee hush her questionings and fears;
  "I must about My Father's business be."

6 I read again, how back to Galilee,
  Still subject to Thy parents, Thou did'st
    go;
  Thrice holy, beautiful humility!
  O Sons of England, seek such grace to
    show!

43. Christ. *St. Luke ii. 11.*
8.7.8.7.

1 Many are Thy Names, O Saviour!
  All beyond what may be priced;
  None to rev'rent hearts goes deeper
  Than doth this, "The Christ! The Christ!"

2 For it tells how as "Anointed,"
  Thou shouldst come our Priest to be;
  Sacrifice and Sacrificer,
  By Love's all-supreme decree.

3 Seers and saints that hope proclaimed,
  Nor e'er from it were entic'd;
  Still they hush'd their hearts, and waited,
  Looking for "The Christ! The Christ!"

4 Wistfully they scann'd the heavens,
  For first dawning of His star;
  Listen'd for his coming footsteps
  Who should close Sin's weary war.

5 Age on age of expectation
  Vainly look'd for the great tryst;
  But at length the angels holy
  Sang aloud, "The Christ! The Christ!"

6. And the day is speeding onward,
   That shall all to judgment bring;
   When "The Christ" enthron'd shall summon
   The whole Earth before its King.

44. TEMPTATION. *Hebrews ii. 18.*
8s.

1 TEMPTED Thyself, Lord, Thou dost know
   How hard 'tis in THE WAY to go;
   How foes without and foes within
   Still hold us captive unto sin;
   How, even with THY full grace giv'n,
   THIS Earth too oft veils THY pure heav'n;
      O break our chain, Lord, set us free;
      Thou, tempted once, us tempted see.
2 These eyes of ours where'er they turn,
   Alas! see sights that make us burn;
   These ears of ours, how oft they list,
   And we are taken ere we wist;
   This heart of ours through vain desires
   Against THY grace, how it conspires!
      O break our chain, Lord, set us free;
      Thou, tempted once, us tempted see.
3 We would lift up our supplication:
   Lord, *lead us not into temptation*;
   Jesus, they're THINE OWN tender words,
   O let them touch hearts' deepest chords;
   When tempts the world, or flesh, or devil,
   Do THOU deliver from all evil;
      O break our chain, Lord, set us free;
      Thou, tempted once, us tempted see.
4 We mourn, Lord, that our wav'ring will
   So oft invites the tempter's skill;
   We must confess that still we find
   Old fleshly lusts war 'gainst the mind;
   Thou HOLY ONE, us purify,
   That unto all sin we may die!
      O break our chain, Lord, set us free;
      Thou, tempted once, us tempted see.
5 Lord, pour on us the SPIRIT of prayer,
   So that when tempted howsoe'er,
   We may, believing, to THEE cry,
   For THY help in our misery;
   Alas! Lord, 'tis our prayerlessness
   Gives to temptation its success;
      O break our chain, Lord, set us free;
      Thou, tempted once, us tempted see.

45. SUFFER THE LITTLE CHILDREN TO COME UNTO ME. *St. Matthew xix. 14.*
7s.

1 It was no mere accident,
   But with gracious purpose blent,
   That in our lov'd English tongue,
   E'en as tho' it had been sung,
   Read we in the Gospel story
   How the Saviour, Lord of Glory,
   Said of little children all,
   As He once to them did call:
   Suffer them to come to ME;
   Lord, Thou knewest it would be
   Very sore—our heart-strings riven—
   To resign them e'en for Heaven:
      Suffer—'tis a tender word;
      Strength and grace it doth afford.
2 LORD, Thou knowest with what pain
   I have heard the sad refrain;
   First-born, second, and a third
   Silenc'd, as a singing bird
   In the middle of its song;
   (O pathetic, cruel wrong!)
   Thou hast call'd to Thee away,
   Letting not our children stay
   In our mortal erring keeping—
   Now for years in cold grave sleeping.
   Our hearts ache, and verily
   Thy word *suffer*, feelingly;
      Suffer—'tis a tender word;
      Strength and grace it doth afford.

46. JESUS AND CHILDREN AT PLAY.
St. Mat. xi. 16-19; St. Luke vii. 31-35.
7s.

1 Crossing Naz'reth's market-place
   Jesus, with benignant face,
   Wont was willing steps to stay
   Near the children at their play.
2 Mimic marriage, mimic death,
   As they all together wreathe;
   He makes luminous with smiles
   That them from their sports beguiles.

3 Nor did He forget long after
  Their mimetic woes and laughter ;
  Wrought them into parable —
  Ringing warning like a bell.
4 Praise, in Heaven as on Earth,
  Christ still smiles on children's mirth ;
  Gladden'd as they are glad,
  Willing not they should be sad.
5 Praise, O Lord ! if we do know ;
  Praise, O Lord ! if we do show
  That RELIGION ne'er was meant,
  To be only hard restraint.
6   *Repeat St. 1.*

47. EPHPHATHA. *St. Mark vii. 34.*
7s.

1 O, the burden of that sigh
  When the Lord look'd up on High ;
  Speaking the Almighty word ;
  Gladdening, the blind restor'd —
      Ephphatha.
2 Laden 'twas with poignant grief,
  Thro' men's heart-hard unbelief ;
  Yet the miracle was wrought
  Even as the suppliant sought, —
      Ephphatha.
3 Ah ! Our 'sicknesses' He bore, —
  His great heart men oft made sore ;
  All our 'sorrows' on HIM met ;
  Mighty task for HIM was set : —
      Ephphatha.
4 Know, my soul, thou too art blind,
  After other deeper kind ;
  Has His quick'ning voice thee stirr'd ?
  Hast heard as the deaf man heard —
      Ephphatha?

48. TALITHA CUMI. *St. Mark v. 41.*
10s.

1 '*Talitha cumi*' sweet yet m'ghty word ;
  Once spoken to one DEAD by Christ the Lord;
  '*Talitha cumi*' the child's native tongue
  As o'er her cradle it had oft been sung.
2 '*Talitha cumi*' instant light for gloom ;
  Recall'd to life, not laid within the tomb ;
  'My little lamb, arise'— and she arose ;
  Strange conquest of Last En'my —with no
      blows.
3 '*Talitha cumi*' — and forthwith she walk'd,
  All filling with fresh wonder as she talk'd ;
  'My little lamb, arise' —what mighty power.
  The DEAD with a new life again to dower !
4 '*Talitha cumi*' —still the Lord thus speaks,
  As He, Good Shepherd, His own lambs
      still seeks ;
  'My little lamb, arise' is His Appeal ;
  Alas ! how slow into young hearts to steal !
5 '*Talitha cumi*' —Lord of Life and Death,
  Wilt Thou on us now breathe thy quick'ning
      breath ?
  'My little lamb, arise' —O may each child
  Take heed—and so the Tempter aye be
      foil'd.
6 '*Talitha cumi*' in the Gospels told,
  In million hearts now for all time enroll'd ;
  'My little lamb, arise' Thou GENTLE ONE,
  Bless ev'ry child with Thy REDEMPTION !

49. HE STOOD STILL. *St. Mat. xx. 29.*
7s.

1 '*He stood still.*' How like THE CHRIST !
  With His heart of love unpric'd ;
  Pausing, that BLIND BEGGAR may
  Sooner find to Him his way.
2 '*He stood still.*' Not walking on—
  O how sweetly it was done !
  For ami 1st that rushing crowd
  He had lagg'd cry ne'er so loud.
3 '*He stood still.*' So by-and-bye
  Bartimeus groping nigh ;
  Spite of hind'rance and harsh word,
  Tells his sore need to THE LORD.
4 '*He stood still.*' Nor grudg'd to stay
  To make blest to him that day ;
  Lo ! He speaks the word of might,
  As of old, "Let there be light."
5 '*He stood still.*' 'Twas even so
  By palm-circled Jericho ;
  And to-day He is the SAME
  When brave FAITH calls on His NAME.

6 'He stood still.' O sightless eyes,
    Have ye felt your miseries?
    O dark hearts, He will fulfil
    Softly, the words, 'He stood still.'

50. SEA OF GALILEE COMPOSED IN CASTLE OF TIBERIAS.
8s.

1 O thrice-fair Lake of Galilee!
    Thou art in truth a SEA to me;
    For unto Faith's anointed eye,
    Thy fairness turns to majesty.
2 Of Galilee, SEA "for all time";
    Than vastest ocean more sublime;
    Since thy low shores and thee were trod
    By Christ, incarnate Son of God.
3 Forsaken Sea of Galilee!
    More see we than the eyes do see;
    Two "little ships" from morn till eve
    Are all Thy bright expanse relieve.
4 Most sacred still, 'midst all thy harms,
    Wild-flowers here hold all their charms;
    As when THE MASTER by thee taught
    And with them truth of truths enwrought.
5 O hill-framed Sea of Galilee!
    Knee-bent I gaze and gaze on thee;
    Thy reeds are swaying to and fro,
    Red-luminous in after-glow.
6 O holy Sea of Galilee!
    Clad in their golden panoply
    The old stars shine as when He pray'd,
    Our sin for burden on Him laid.
7 How long, fair Sea of Galilee,
    Thy Israel lorn shall we see?
    O Christ may they their Land inherit,
    Redeemèd by the Saviour's merit!
8 O Sea of Galilee, farewell!
    For aye thou shalt in mem'ry dwell;
    Thy waters blue as bluest sky —
    A Sea of Immortality.

51. TEARS. *St. John xi. 35; Is. iii. 3; Ps. lvi. 8.*
8s.

1 SACRED are tears — for "Jesus wept,"
    When to His feet the shadow crept,
    Ah! soon to blacken into gloom,
    In lost Jerusalem's awful doom.
2 Sacred are tears — for "Jesus wept"
    At Bethany, when Laz'rus slept;
    He wept in human sympathy,
    Altho' deliverance was nigh.
3 Sacred are tears — for "Jesus wept;"
    As all our sorrows o'er HIM swept;
    A Man of Sorrows was His Name,
    Nor was it held of HIM for shame.
4 Sacred are tears — for "Jesus wept;"
    And He will not His saints except;
    But yet HE softens grief that shakes,
    And, lo! the burden lighter makes.
5 Sacred are tears — for "Jesus wept;"
    All that HE sends let us accept;
    He puts the "cup" into our hands,
    And all within it understands.
6 Sacred are tears — for "Jesus wept;"
    In trial we by HIM are kept;
    Then let us turn our weeping eyes
    To HIM enthron'd beyond the skies.

52. SEEKER WHO LACKETH NOTHING.
Is. xli. 10-14; Ezekiel xxxiv. 11, 12-16. Quaerens cum nihil desit tibi. — St. Augustine (Con. i. iv.)
10s.

1 JESUS nothing lacketh, yet HE asketh,
    Asketh me for my poor heart;
    Nothing lacketh, yet HIMSELF He tasketh,
    Tasketh to fulfil His part, —
    Part of SHEPHERD over dale and height,
    Seeking out each straying sheep;
    Asking, seeking, and with many a slight,
    Slight of love that makes HIM weep.
2 Jesus nothing lacketh, yet HE masketh,
    Masketh power as if weak;
    Nothing lacketh, yet our RACE, lo! basketh,
    Basketh 'neath His face so meek;
    Measuring not wrath to us, delaying,
    Long delaying, patient Christ,
    Nothing lacketh, yet our fond Hope staying,
    Sheweth us The CROSS unpric'd.
3 Jesus nothing lacketh, yet HE casqueth,
    Casqueth barèd brow with thorns;
    Nothing lacketh, yet with blood damasketh,

TEMPTED TO FORSAKE—FAITH NOT SIGHT.

Yea, damasketh, 'midst men's scorns;
With outstretchéd hands upon the ROOD;
Love all other love excelling!
Still before His Cross, our RACE has stood,
His transcendent love repelling.
4   *Repeat St. 1.*

53. TEMPTED TO FORSAKE. *St. John vi. 67,*
"*Would ye also go away?*"
7s.

1 PLAINTIVE comes THY word to-day,
Would ye also go away?
Lord, forgive the bursting tear,
As for our own selves we fear;
Lord, we tremble as we find,
We have from "the WAY" declin'd.
2 *Would ye also go away?*
Gently thus THOU sought'st to stay
When they stumbled at THY word,
As of THEE "the BREAD" they heard;
Ah! how many followers fled,
When they heard and wondered.
3 Mystic words THOU spakest then,
Words to shake the hearts of men;
Whilst alive THOU Lord, didst tell
Of a food unspeakable;
Only Heav'n-anointed eyes
See the meaning in them lies.
4 Peter's words rise like a chant,
Others proving recreant,
Lord, to whom then shall we go? —
O make THOU us it to know!
Thy words of eternal life,
Only Helper in Sin's strife.
5 *Repeat St. 1.*

54. THE HANDS OF JESUS. *St. Luke xxi. 40.*
8s.

1 THY HANDS I seek, my Saviour dear,
To toil, like THEE, in lowly sphere;
Thy dignity on labour shed
Makes noble earning "daily bread."
2 Thy Hands I seek, O Jesus, Friend;
Help me, like Thee, my time to spend
In seeking souls to win and guide,
And faithful be whate'er betide.

3 Thy Hands I seek, O mighty Healer,
Of true soul-health alone Revealer;
Sin-sick to heal—to comfort poor—
To help all in the'r trying hour.
4 Thy Hands I seek, O Gentle One,
That laid on child-heads benison;
O THOU Good-Shepherd, let me lead
To pastures green, THY Lambs to feed.
5 Thy Hands I seek, Messiah-Man,
Winnowing with THINE awful Fan;
That I may warn, yea, and affray,
And win back unto Thee "the WAY."
6 Thy Hands I seek, Thou Christ of God,
Nail-pierced to bear Sin's damning load;
That I may shew prints of the nails
And how Thy Blood for all avails.
7 Thy Hands I seek, O great High-priest,
Thy pleading office not surceas'd;
That I may by the might of prayer
Gain souls for THEE and Thee endear.
8 Thy hands I seek, THOU thronéd KING,
That to Thy cross men I may bring;
And trophies win my Lord for Thee,
Bold by Thy "glorious liberty."

55. FAITH NOT SIGHT. *Acts of Aps. ix. 31.*
13s.

1 EMPTY now THY Cross, O Christ! for Thou
   didst rise again;
Kept Thy sacred holy tryst, and faithful
   dost remain.
2 Now not on Thy Cross I look, but up to
   Thy WHITE Throne;
Nor my Faith nor PEACE is shook, that
   Thou from Earth art gone.
3 Thou, I know, art in the skies, the Living
   One o'er all;
Faint, I feel, my words and sighs; yet
   unto Thee I call.
4 Lord, I still would walk by Faith, and wait
   till I shall "see;"
By-and-by will come kind Death, and take
   me home to THEE.

56. Rest after Toil. *St. Mark vi. 30-1.*
10.8.

1 The Disciples were bow'd by stress of toil;
 The Master was touch'd, and with gracious
  smile,
 Said *"Come to the desert and rest awhile."*
2 When lamp-flame burns dim, there's need of
  fresh oil;
 With brightness and rapture comes sure
  recoil;
 Thou dost see and whisper *come rest awhile.*
3 Lord! Blest is the work Thou hast giv'n
  to me,
 To speak to my fellows, from sin to free;
 But Lord, my heart yearns to speak more
  to Thee.
4 A well always drawn on will cease its
  supplies;
 But springs on the hill-top flow when it dries.
 This lesson He taught, who never denies:
5 When battle is o'er men gather the spoil;
 And sweet 'tis to hear after strain and toil
 This *Come to the desert and rest awhile.*

57. The Two Sleeps Tabor and Gethsemane.
St. Luke ix. 32. and St. Mat. xxvi. 43.
10.4.

1 When Thou, Lord Jesus, stood'st on Tabor's
  height
            Transfigured;
 Thy vesture unto Heaven's own native
  light
            Configured;
 Thy Three Disciples then were with Thee
  there,
            The sight to share;
 Prophet and sage the dead on either
  hand
            Beside Thee stand;
 The wondrous theme of "talk" 'twixt Thee
  and them,
            Jerusalem;
 And Thy "decease" upon the awful tree
            Of Calvary;
 O wondrous scene! To see in that grand
  hour
            Thee, in Thy power;
 But as the splendor round about Thee shone,
            Self-humbled one;
 And the great sea of glory o'er Thee swept;
            Thine Own Three slept;
 Alas! alas! The cost of that sad Sleep,
            I needs must weep;
 For all ye "spake of"— who, Lord, would
  not moan?
            Remains unknown;
 O Three Disciples! That ye slept, ye slept,
            All Time has wept!
2 When, Lord, Thou mettest in Gethsemane
            Thine Agony;
 And once again Thy favoured Three were
            there,
            The sight to share;
 Thou soughtest that with Thee Thy Own
  should "watch"
            And, wistful, catch
 The mighty pleading of Thy prayers and
  tears
            In God's own ears;
 Alas! alas! e'en while their Master wept
            Again they Slept;
 Second and third time didst Thou come
  to ask
            In Thy dread task,
 And ask in vain. Alas! they did not weep;
            They were Asleep!
 O costliest, heaviest, saddest sleep of all
            Us could befall!
 Losing for us the prayer supreme and cry
            'Fore Calvary;
 Losing —and leaving but one broken phrase
            Us to amaze;
 O grievous Sleep! guilt most unspeakable
            Of them to tell;
 Yet, Gentlest One, Thy gracious pitying
  love
            Did it remove,

3 What are these SLEEPS to thee I ask, my
    soul?
            Do not they toll
E'en as it were a sadden midnight bell?
            Or cry from Hell?
Beware, beware, lest now thy Tabor be
            As to the Three;
Beware, lest even sad Gethsemane,
            Thou sleeping see
Awake! for now is the "accepted time,"
            The hour doth chime;
The Lord hath spoken, and the Lord still
    speaks ;
            The light now breaks;
Awake! awake! Lo! still the Spirit strives;
            Mercy forgives;
The preachéd Gospel still to thee appeals,
            And grace reveals;
Here in His House He doth expostulate
            Ere't be too late;
Awake! O soul! Why wilt thou longer
    sleep?
            The angels weep;
Awake! awake! Y'eld not to Slumber's
    sleight
            On Tabor's height;
Awake! and by Gethsemane's sad Three,
            Thy danger see!

4 Awake! awake! Church of the Living
    God!
            At home, abroad;
God's voice calls louder than the tempest
    loud
            From Sinai's cloud;
Awake! awake! Why will ye sleep? arouse!
            This is God's House;
Ye sleep; Why will ye sleep? O hear!
    O hear!
            The great Three fear;
Awake! awake! God in the world now
    speaks;
            The Earth He shakes;
He shakes and topples down the
    opposing host;
            The Holy Ghost
Still with His own magnanimous patience
    pleads,
Awake! awake! Time short is; life more
    short ;
            Loud I exhort!
Awake! awake! Ere Mercy hastes away;
            Lo! still 'tis day!
Awake! awake! 'Tis God's own voice
    that calls,
            On you it falls ;
Awake! Why will ye sleep? "Too late!
    Too late!"
            (O ye ingrate!)
May sudden peal from thunder-darken'd
    sky :
            Vain then your cry!

58. EMMAUS: FELLOWSHIP WITH JESUS.
    10s.   *St. Luke xxiv. 13-35.*
1 ABIDE *with us, for far spent is the day;*
To Christ, unknown the Two Disciples
    said :
O Jesus! known and lov'd, hear us we pray
While the old words again to Thee are
    pled ;
Hear us, dear Saviour, hear, as then,
Perplex'd and sadden'd sons of men.
2 *Abide with us,* when comes the ev'ning hour,
    And home we from Thy House and
    worship hie ;
Reveal Thyself, O Lord, in gentle power,
    Let not Thy preachéd Gospel in us die ;
But bless'd of Thee in sweet return,
Like theirs cause Thou our hearts to burn.
3 *Abide with us,* when dark'ning sorrows fall,
    And hope burns low and even faith is
    weak ;
Attend our cry, Lord, when on Thee we call,
    O let us not in vain Thy comfort seek ;
To our bruis'd hearts, and lonely, shew
Thou dost our lightest sorrow know.
4 *Abide with us,* when wilderéd and lost,
    We seem, O Christ, to have let go Thy
    Hand :

Draw near to us as we are tempest-tost,
  And bear us safely to the further strand;
When winds and waves beat threat'ningly,
  Come with Thy great " Fear not 'tis I."
5 *Abide with us*, when at THY SUPPER set,
  Rememb'ring Thee in Thy appointed
    sign ;
  Breathe Thou upon us with Thy People met,
  And feed us with Thy living bread and
    wine ,
  And whilst fulfilling Thy commands
  Shew us, as they, Thy nail-pierced Hands.
6 *Abide with us*, when our life's close draws
    nigh,
  And Jordan's swellings haunt the list'ning
    ear ;
  E'en then, O Christ, flash to our glazing
    eye,
  Visions of Thine Own self to conquer fear,
  O Saviour blest, thus let it be !
  Then go aye *to abide with Thee*.

59.   MORIAH AND CALVARY.
  8s.   *Gen. xxii. 12. Rom. viii. 32.*

1 GOD! Thou spared'st Abraham's son,
  But Thou spared'st not Thine Own ;
  Thou beheld'st the victim bound,
  But another, lo ! is found ;
  When the mighty faith is shewn ;
  When the knife was gleaming down.

2 God! Thou spared'st Abraham's son,
  But Thou spared'st not Thine Own ;
  Spared'st neither shame nor wrong ;
  Thorn-crown, spitting, smiting, thong ;
  Laid'st upon the Lamb of God
  All our sins in all their load.

3 God! Thou spared'st Abraham's son,
  But Thou spared'st not Thine Own ;
  Spared'st not the traitor-kiss,
  Nor the Twelve's unfaithfulness ;
  Anguish of Gethsemane ;
  Bitter cross of Calvary.

4 God ! Thou spared'st Abraham's son,
  But Thou spared'st not Thine Own ;
  Bruised'st Him with utter grief,
  Void of solace as relief ;
  While the darken'd earth and sky
  Shudder at His agony.

5 God ! Thou spared'st Abraham's son,
  But Thou spared'st not Thine Own ;
  Over His unspotted soul
  All Thy waves in thunder roll ;
  Till His heart with sorrow breaks ;
  Light His glazing eye forsakes.

6 God ! Thou spared'st Abraham's son,
  But Thou spared'st not Thine Own ;
  We adore that wondrous love,
  Which Thy matchless grace doth prove ;
  Him Thou spared'st not that we
  Might be spared and blest of Thee.

60.   BY HIS STRIPES WE ARE HEALED.
  6s.   *Is. liii. 5.*

1 *By His stripes we are healed :*
  This truth to us is sealed,
  Ev'n by the Holy Spirit,
  As witness to Christ's merit ;
  Sin-wounded, bleeding, sore,
  We catch "Go, sin no more,"
  As 'tis to us revealed
  By His stripes we are healed.

2 *By His stripes we are healed :*
  Long, long by trope concealed,
  We now, O Lord, perceive,
  Ev'n as heart-touched we grieve,
  This Thy one remedy,
  'For us the Lord did die' ;
  Love's law still unrepealed,
  By His stripes we are healed.

3 *By His stripes we are healed :*
  None vainly have appealed ;
  Thou, suffering Lamb of God,
  Bearing the World's dread load,
  How may we magnify
  So grand a clemency !
  To Thee, heart-changed, we yield
  By His stripes we are healed.

VICTIM VICTOR; VICTOR VICTIM — THE KING ON HIS CROSS-THRONE. 27

4 *By his stripes we are healed ;*
  Ah! tears must be congealed
  If this we will not own ;
  And heart as hard as stone ;
  If men weep not, nor feel
  Sweet anguish o'er them steal ;
  Let it aloud be pealed,
  By His stripes we are healed.

61. VICTIM-VICTOR: VICTOR-VICTIM. 8s.
      St. John I. 29.
"*Pro nobis tibi victor et victima, et ideo victor, quia victima; pro nobis tibi sacerdos et sacrificium, et ideo sacerdos, quia sacrificium. St. Augustine, (Conf. x, xliii.)*

1 VICTOR yet Victim manifest!
  Love to its mighty task address ;
  Victim yet Victor— Righteousness
  Suffering, our fallen race to bless.

2 Victim yet Victor— on the Cross
  Redeeming our stupendous loss ;
  Victim yet Victor— sacrifice
  By which eternally Death dies.

3 Victor yet Victim— lo! Lord Christ!
  Our sacrifice at once and Priest ;
  Victim, yet Victor over Hell,
  Atoning blood ineffable.

4 Victim yet Victor— O my soul!
  The waves of wrath see o'er Him roll ;
  Victor yet Victim— His work done,
  Finish'd a World's redemption.

62. THE ONCE MARRED FACE. *Is. lii. 14.*
      8,6,8,6,8,8.
1 OF human faces none so marred
  O Jesus, as was Thine ;
  But it is now no longer scarred ;
  Its lustre is divine :
  For crown of thorns, Thy "many crowns ;"
  And now all Heaven Thy conquest owns.

2 A soldier's cast-off robe they gave —
  Jest on Thy regal claim ;
  For sceptre a frail reed to wave,
  Thus putting Thee to shame ;
  But now Thy robe is woven light,
  Thy sceptre now the might of right.

3 All praise to Thee, THE CRUCIFIED!
  Thou did'st assume our blame ;
  All praise that when we must have died
  Thou barest all the shame ;
  Pierc'd hands and feet and red-mark'd brow
  The trophies of Love's victory now.

4 O Man of Sorrows, when on Earth,
  Thou us forgettest never ;
  Thou'rt kin to us by mortal birth,
  In sympathy for ever ;
  We Thee adore ; we Thee implore ;
  O haste the time Thee shall restore!

63. THE KING ON HIS CROSS-THRONE.
      7s.   *Gal. vi. 14.*
"*Dominus regnavit a Ligno;*" "*Throned upon the awful tree.*" —*John Ellerton.*

1 *Throned upon the awful tree :*
  Yea, Lord, this the sight we see ;
  Tho' men put Thee to all shame ;
  Cast despite upon Thy Name ;
  Yet Thou reignest, reignest now ;
  Crown of thorns upon Thy brow.

2 *Throned upon the awful tree :*
  Love's redeeming mystery ;
  Wondering, we watch Thee die ;
  Shuddering, we hear Thy cry ;
  Yet Thou reignest, reignest now ;
  Crown of thorns upon Thy brow.

3 *Throned upon the awful tree :*
  Releasing from captivity
  All, even all the sons of Time,
  Who by faith to Thee shall climb ;
  Yet Thou reignest, reignest now ;
  Crown of thorns upon Thy brow.

4 *Throned upon the awful tree :*
  Breaketh forth Thy majesty ;
  By Thy side "a burning brand"
  Pluck'd from Hell by Thy strong Hand ;
  Yes Thou reignest, reignest now ;
  Crown of thorns upon Thy brow.

5 *Throned upon the awful tree :*
  Thus Thou willed'st it to be ;
  Powers of darkness 'gainst Thee hurled ;
  So Thou didst redeem— a World ;

THE CROSS "BITTER TREE" STABAT MATER.

Yes Thou reignest, reignest now ;
Crown of thorns upon Thy brow.

64. THE CROSS ("BITTER TREE")
FORESHADOWED. 8s.

"*I have made the dry tree to flourish.*"—
Ezekiel xvii. 24.

1 *The 'dry tree' I have made to flourish:*
  Great words of wonder! words of grace!
  By them I seek my faith to nourish,
  Beneath the shining of THY FACE ;
  Thy Cross no 'high tree' but the '*dry tree*,'
  Uprais'd for lost World's misery.

2 *The 'dry tree' I have made to flourish:*
  O seer of God, Thy listn'ing ears
  The great truth caught, and it did cherish ;
  Before Him hushing all thy fears ;
  I see, Lord, in this vision folden,
  Thy crimson Cross and gospel golden.

3 *The 'dry tree' I have made to flourish:*
  'Twas so of old, and age to age ;
  Ah! Lord Christ, that men might not perish
  Thou didst endure their mad'ning rage;
  Thy Cross no 'high tree' but the '*dry tree*,'
  Whereon Thou wroughtst Thy clemency.

4 *The 'dry tree' I have made to flourish:*
  A light of glory on it glows ;
  So that all other, lo! is garish
  To him who Thy redemption knows ;
  I see, Lord, in this vision folden,
  Thy crimson Cross and gospel golden.

5 *The 'dry tree' I have made to flourish:*
  The Rose of Sharon it adorns ;
  The valley-lilies from lush 'marish' ;
  And wildings sharp with many thorns ;
  Thy Cross no 'high tree' but the '*dry tree*,'
  White DOVE upon it, lo! I see.

6 *The 'dry tree' I have made to flourish:*
  As trunk in Winter stark and gaunt—
  Yet clinging here, my faith I nourish,
  Nor Earth nor Hell shall e'er me daunt ;
  I see, Lord, in this vision folden,
  Thy crimson Cross and gospel golden.

65. STABAT MATER.   *St. John xix. 25.*
8s.

1 As pallid as the marble cold,
  Lo! near the stark Cross Mary stands
  With bowed head and claspèd hands ;
  While all the waves o'er Him are roll'd,
  Who naught of anguish countermands.

2 Again, and yet again His voice
  Proclaimeth to the shudd'ring skies,
  That on Him now a World's guilt lies,
  By no constraint but Love's great choice—
  Redemption by His agonies.

3 O mother-maid, within thy heart
  Bleed deeper wounds than by the nails ;
  And tho' we read not of Thy wails,
  We know how tragic was Thy part ;
  Each hurt to Him thy heart assails.

4 But what is this awaits her ear,
  St. John and she approaching nigh?
  No longer lamentable cry,
  But sweetest words of filial care
  A home provided tenderly.

5 Thanks to Thee, Saviour, for Thy Cross ;
  Thanks for the greatness of Thy love ;
  But thanks to Thee, all thanks above,
  That, in redeeming our dread loss,
  Thy breaking heart to HER did move.

6   *Repeat St. 1.*

In Latin
By Alexander Waugh Young, Esq. M.A.,
Head Master Tettenhall College, near
Wolverhampton.

DE MATRE DOMINI.

1. Ad crucem diram pallida
   Demisso vultu mater stat,
   Dum fluctus Illum devorat,
   Qui mala ferens omnia
   Levamen nullum sibi dat.

11. Eu, gemit Ille saepius,
    Peccata mundi sustinens :
    Coelumque tremit audiens!
    Sic Amor vincit caelicus,
    Nos luctu suo redimens.

III. O mater, virgo, gladius
 Transfixit alte tuum cor,
 Cruentis clavis durior.
 Dum cruciatur Filius,
 Ah, matri quantus est dolor!
IV. O, Sancta Jesu pietas!
 Quae rumpit vox silentium?
 Egloti domicilium
 Divina dat Humanitas,
 Orbaeque matri filium.
V. Ingentes, Christe, gratias
 Pro tua Cruce reddimus;
 Nec, Spiritus quod ultimus
 Ad matrem flavit, minimas
 Salvator suavis, agimus.
VI. Ceu marmor pallens Maria
 Afflicta juxta crucem stat,
 Palmisque pressio haesitat,
 Dum Illum mergunt aequora,
 Qui fugam Sibi denegat

66. It is Finished. *St. John xix. 30.*
7s.

1 Wreath'd His brow with crown of thorn;
 Frenzied Hate and bitter Scorn,
 Madly claim that He must die;
 Mockeries and insult heaping,
 Taunt and jeer from fierce lips leaping;
 Callous to His agony.
2 But what mean these dreadful signs?
 Are we on Hell's own confines?
 Thund'reth forth the Sea of Wrath?
 The great sun is black above,
 Shrouded as Incarnate Love
 Treads the dismal vale of Death.
3 Lo! the mighty work is done!
 Lo! Redemption is begun!
 Satan spoil'd and sin o'erthrown;
 Louder than the sev'n-fold thunder,
 Shaken Hell and Heaven wonder,
 As the Cross becomes a throne.
4 Upward soars the Son of God;
 Freed now from His awful load,
 Lo! He now re-enters Heaven;
 Hosts on hosts attend on Him

 Seraphim and Cherubim—
 All divinest homage giv'n.
5 Lift your heads, ye pearly gates;
 He who all things subjugates
 As a conqueror enters in;
 Man's redemption is achiev'd;
 Man from guilt is now reliev'd;
 By His blood purg'd is our sin.

67. Mystery of Sin Counterworked.
7s.
1 Corinthians xv. 24-28; Ephesians 1. 20-23.

1 Great disaster of the World,
 When man from his throne was hurl'd;
 When the tempter seem'd to win
 Through unfathomable sin;
 Ah! But it was only seeming;
 Lo! The Christ hath come redeeming.
2 Vast, unmeasur'd was the treason;
 Yet 'tis fundamental reason
 Of our Christianity,
 That enfolds humanity:
 See in blood-red flag unfurl'd,
 Jesus, Saviour of the World!
3 O Great reconciliation!
 O Supreme propitiation!
 Grace and Truth thro' Him resounding
 And redeeming love abounding:
 Lo! The hosts of hell are shatter'd
 By the Prince of Life far-scatter'd!
4 Grace *is* infinite and strong;
 Right *is* mightier than Wrong;
 Meagre are all Sin's resources,
 Against Love Eternal's forces:
 Christ! Gird on Thy conqu'ring robe;
 Hast Thou not redeem'd the globe?
5 O Church of the Living God!
 Lift up thine almighty rod;
 Far and wide the Gospel story
 Tell of Jesus thron'd in glory:
 Working in His love and might;
 Bringing back mankind to light.
6 Is it vain The Crucified
 For man liv'd and for man died?
 Can sin still be so tremendous

That His death no boon did send us?
Nay O Christ! Thou victor art
Thy Love yet shall Hatred thwart.

7 Hasten, Lord, the gladsome time;
Let the golden hour now chime;
When Thy Love destroying evil
Shall assur'd, dethrone the devil;
And the World's stupendous loss
Be regain'd by Thy great Cross.

68. SHAME CHANGED TO GLORY.
8s. Romans i. 16.

1 MEN thought all o'er when Thou hadst died
The Crucified! The Crucified!
Sunken beneath a load of shame
They dreamed they had befouled Thy name;
The crosses base of Calvary
Securing deathless' infamy.

2 But Thou on the supreme Third Day
Alive thro' grave didst take Thy way;
Forth stepping as a conqueror
From its stone-closed and sealed door;
Grasping in nail-pierc'd Hand the palm
With Thy Omnipotence's sure calm.

3 For forty days and forty nights
Thou shewdst Thyself to human sights;
To chosen witnesses appointed
Who knew Thee well the Lord's Anointed;
Fore-casting the far-onward strife
And telling not of death but life.

4 And now to-day in all the Earth
A thousand tongues tell of Thy worth;
The cross all luminous with glory
Blest sign of the old Gospel story;
And the World's heart will cease to ache
As men Thee for their Saviour take.

5 So, far and wide, the Gospel soundeth;
And whereso'er it goes astoundeth;
See faiths and worships of all ages
Sure toppling down 'midst priestly rages;
Nor shall pause be till, His work done,
The round globe for THE CHRIST be won.

69. THE SHED BLOOD.
7s.

"*Washed from our sins in His own blood.*"
--*Revelations i. 5.* "*I am Thine save me.*"
--*Psalm cxix. 94.*

1 Save me, Lord, for I am Thine!
Hear me, Lord, for Thou art mine!
Thou a sinner's only Way;
I grim Satan's wished-for prey;
Save me, Lord, for I am Thine!
Wash me in the blood divine!

2 Save me, Lord, for I am Thine!
Hear me, Lord, for Thou art mine!
Guilty, Lord, I am indeed;
But for me Thou once didst bleed;
Save me, Lord, for I am Thine
Wash me in the blood divine!

3 Save me, Lord, for I am Thine!
Hear me, Lord, for Thou art mine
I'm sin-stain'd, O wilt Thou cleanse?
Put away my deep offence?
Save me, Lord, for I am Thine!
Wash me in the blood divine!

4 Save me, Lord, for I am Thine!
Hear me, Lord, for Thou art mine!
Pity me, I am so weak!
Make me meek as Thou art meek!
Save me, Lord, for I am Thine!
Wash me in the blood divine!

5 Save me, Lord, for I am Thine!
Hear me, Lord, for Thou art mine!
When to that dark vale I come,
Where cold Jordan's waters foam;
Save me, Lord, for I am Thine!
Wash me in the blood divine!

6 Save me, Lord, for I am Thine!
Hear me, Lord, for Thou art mine!
Unto Thee I still shall cling,
And thro' Thee I still shall sing,
Save me, Lord, for I am Thine!
Wash me in the blood divine!

70. THE RISEN SAVIOUR.

6s.

"*The Lord is risen indeed.*" *St. Luke xxiv. 34.*

1 *The Lord is risen indeed :*
  We say it as a CREED ;
  But O to feel its power
  Each day thro' ev'ry hour.

2 *The Lord is risen indeed :*
  Glad, I the great word read ;
  For He for us hath died,
  Jesus, The Crucified.

3 *The Lord is risen indeed :*
  My heart would on this feed ;
  He is not dead ; He lives
  And every blessing gives.

4 *The Lord is risen indeed :*
  No more a bruised reed ;
  Most glorious of news!
  Who who shall it refuse ?

5 *The Lord is risen indeed :*
  Gone up to intercede ;
  On His Great Throne on High,
  No more, no more, to die.

6 *The Lord is risen indeed :*
  The Grand Fact we may plead ;
  O Christ ! Who liv'st above,
  Shew unto us Thy love.

7 *The Lord is risen indeed :*
  Grim Death himself did bleed ;
  The Last Foe conquered,
  And all in triumph led.

8 *The Lord is risen indeed :*
  O let the Gospel speed !
  Tell the "good news" all round
  To Earth's extremest bound.

9 *The Lord is risen indeed :*
  We say it as a CREED ;
  But O to feel its power,
  Each day thro' ev'ry hour.

71. THE ABIDING PRESENCE.

7s.

"*Lo! I am with you alway.*"—*St. Matthew xxviii. 20.*

1 BLESS, my soul, thy Saviour dear,
  As He still to Thee is near ;
  Still He is THE CRUCIFIED,
  Tho' in Heaven glorified ;
  From the sky He looketh down
  And the lowliest will own.

2 Bless, my soul, thy Saviour dear,
  As he still to thee is near ;
  With all human sympathy
  For all who lift pleading eye ;
  Near to humble and to poorest ;
  Friend of all friends, ah! the surest.

3 Bless, my soul, thy Saviour dear,
  As He still to thee is near ;
  Near to chief of sinners still
  That He may His words fulfil ;
  Lowly may thy "closet" be,
  Not at it he looks, but thee.

4 Bless, my soul, thy Saviour dear,
  As He still to thee is near ;
  Tell Him all that's in thy heart,
  Be it joy or be it smart ;
  He will breathe by Spirit mild,
  Witnessing thou art His Child.

5 Bless, my soul, thy Saviour dear,
  As he still to thee is near ;
  Him thou ne'er cans't weary, know
  With the longest tale of woe ;
  Tell it, tell it all, and He
  Will speak peace benignantly.

6 Bless, my soul, thy Saviour dear,
  As He still to Thee is near ;
  "Abba Father" be thy cry,
  Howe'er great Thy agony ;
  Plead, replead His promises,
  Richly, freely He will bless.

7 *Repeat St. 1.*

72. THE RESURRECTION. *St. Matt.xxviii. 8-10; St. Luke xxiv. 10.*
5s.

1 We have seen the Lord:
 O transcendent word!
 He is now alive
 Who with Death did strive,
 On "the bitter tree"
 Raised on Calvary;
 Yea, and in the tomb
 Made bright all its gloom;
 Light of Life THE LORD:
 O thrice-precious word!

2 We have seen the Lord:
 O hope-giving word!
 That the women brought
 When "THE TWELVE" they sought;
 We have seen the Lord:
 O joy-bringing word!
 Jesus' work all done,
 His great victory won;
 We have seen the Lord:
 O heart-calming word!

3 We have seen the Lord:
 O love-kindling word!
 All fulfilled HE said,
 Truth established;
 We have seen the Lord:
 Bearing no sharp sword;
 But sweet as before,
 Yea, more and still more;
 We have seen the Lord:
 O faith-working word!

4 We have seen the Lord:
 O amazing word!
 That all Hell confounds;
 Gospel that astounds;
 We have seen the Lord:
 We have Him ador'd;
 He the LIVING ONE,
 Goes back to His Throne;
 We have seen the Lord:
 Tell the mighty word.

5 We have seen the Lord:
 O fear-shatt'ring word!
 We have seen the Lord,
 From the grave restor'd;
 His omnipotence
 Clear to ev'ry sense;
 His abiding power,
 Our unchanging dower;
 We have seen the Lord:
 O transcendent word!

73. THE STONE ROLLED AWAY.
8s. *St. Mark xvi. 3.*

1 O WHY ye sad ones do ye moan,
 "Who'll roll away for us the stone?"
 As to His grave ye take your way,
 The darkness thick is turned to day;
 Behold He that was dead is risen,
 The seal'd door bursting of His prison!

2 "Who'll roll away for us the stone?"
 Why should your Faith thus, doubting,
 Forgotten have ye what He spake [groan?
 Foretelling how He Death should shake?
 For lo! the Great Third Day is come!
 No longer seek Him in the tomb.

3 Ye angels clad in flawless whiteness
 All radiant in heaven's brightness;
 Ye gracious bring your minist'ring word,
 Clear-heralding your risen Lord;
 The Lord of Death and Lord of Life,
 Victor unconquer'd in the strife.

4 O haste ye, sad hearts, haste to tell—
 Unless it be unspeakable!
 That He to Galilee is gone,
 As having "roll'd away the stone;"
 Lo! There He waits to re-proclaim
 His Gospel now free'd from all shame.

5 Ah! Heaven and Earth are now combin'd;
 Haste ye, haste ye, lo, ye shall find:—
 As Jacob's ladder spann'd the sky
 Above the spot where he did lie;
 So by bright angel-hosts attended
 The crowned Christ to Earth descended.

74. Ascension and Pentecost.
Acts of the Apos. i, ii. St. Luke xxiv. 50-51.
8,8,6,8,8,6.

1 Lo ! The Great Forty Days had sped
    When Jesus His disciples led
        As far as Bethany ;
    Earth three and thirty years He trod
    As the Incarnate Son of God ;
        Now He re-seeks the sky.

2 The Church's charter had been given
    That must be ministered from Heaven —
        Not footstool, but the Throne ;
    All fulness of the Holy Sp'rit,
    Bought for us by His flawless merit ;
        To our whole RACE made known.

3 Upward in Majesty he soars,   [pours
    Whilst on "THE TWELVE" He blessing
        With His outstretchèd Hands,
    Until the Cloud of Glory blazing,
    Conceals Him from their passionate gazing
        As each adoring stands.

4 Returning to Jerusalem,
    As their Lord had commanded them,
        Obediently they wait ;
    That in the three-fold Name forthgoing
    They all the gifts of His bestowing,
        To Him may consecrate.

5 Now dawns the Day of Pentecost ;
    Now comes in power the Holy Ghost,
        As He to them had said ;
    All glorious things of Zion spoken
    Fulfilled are — not one word broken
        Swiftly the great news spread.

6 O Christ ! Thou high-enthronèd One
    Thy conquest truly is begun ;
        Thousands prick'd to the heart ;
    Jerusalem sinners of all men
    First to be sav'd O whose the pen
        To tell the Gospel's start ?

75. Christ's Words. 10s.
"Never man spake like this man." — St. John vii. 46. "He taught them as one having authority." — St. Matthew vii. 29.

1 Amid the Babel of men's clam'rous speech,
    Lord Jesus, what a "still small voice"
        is Thine !
    And yet where are there words that men's
        hearts reach
    Like those of Thee the human and
        divine ?

2 Thy words rule men as statutes ne'er
        have rul'd,
    Not penalty but conscience gives them
        power ;
    Men find out soon or late themselves
        befool'd,
    And bruis'd, and broken, seek Thy
        Spirit's dower.

3 How have Thy words, Lord, quicken'd
        human thought !
    How have they penetrated human lives !
    How have they into grandest deeds been
        wrought !
    And how on their deep lines all Progress
        drives.

4 How have Thy words up-flamed as into
        swords !
    How have they gone straight to the
        world's great heart !
    How Freedom thence has fetched her
        battle-words !
    How Thy word-pictures glorified all
        Art !

5 How have Thy words passed on to end
        of Earth !
    Yea single words as 'come' and 'look'
        and 'lost'
    Caused wail of anguish break into glad
        mirth,
    And calmed the hearts a-weary, tired,
        and tost !

6 The thunder's loud reverberating roar
    Shakes not nor smites, but 'tis the

shatt'ring levin ;
And not men's words will slay proud
  Errors hoar
    But poignant words, like Thine, re-
      vealed from Heaven.
7 I seek retreat from all this empty noise,
  Mere human words in books that have
    no end ;
    In the one Book supreme I still rejoice :
      O Lord, more mighty fire-touch'd
        Preachers send !
8 Send Seers who know Thy voice and
    follow Thee !
    To height and depth, not sham'd of
      Jesus' blood ;
    O give us, Lord, these more and more
      to see ;
      Thy Words still their predestin'd
        heav'nly food.
9 Amid the Babel of men's clam'rous speech,
    Lord Jesus, what a "still small voice"
      is Thine !
    And yet where are there words that men's
      hearts reach
      Like those of Thee the human and
        divine ?

76.   JESUS REIGNS.

Psalm xcvi. i.; Isaiah lii. 7; Corinthians xv. 25; Revelations xi. 15.

8s.

1 I LOOK around and tumult see,
  Men toss'd about like tossing sea ;
  Hearts in unrest, and tired brains ;
  But God's Word speaketh—"Jesus reigns."
2 Blind Error's maze, Sin's downward road,
  The multitudes led far from God ;
  Lo ! as I gaze, ev'n Faith complains,
  But God's Word speaketh "Jesus reigns."
3 Ah ! treach'rous voices throng the air ;
  And false lights hang out ev'rywhere ;
  How wild the rush for Mammon's gains ;
  But God's Word speaketh "Jesus reigns."
4 Thick darkness broods where might be light;
  Truth falleth in the street—foes smite ;
  And all around are clanking chains ;
  But God's Word speaketh—"Jesus reigns."
5 Thy Cross, Lord, still a "stumbling-block";
  Thy Gospel, the World's wise men mock ;
  Thy Abels hated, slain by Cains ;
  But God's Word speaketh—"Jesus reigns."
6 Lord God, is not Thy set time come ?
  Aye wilt Thou to our cries be dumb ?
  Wilt Thou not end strife that profanes ?
  Yes, God's Word speaketh—"Jesus reigns."
7 Ah, Lord, Thou seest to the end ;
  All things to Thy Love's purpose tend ;
  Thou yet shalt cleanse Earth of its stains;
  For God's Word speaketh "Jesus reigns."
8 Praise to our God ! His Word is sure !
  Praise God the triumph is secure !
  Amidst all these discordant strains
  God's Word still speaketh "Jesus reigns."

77. LONGING FOR CHRIST'S SECOND COMING. *Hebrews ix. 28.*

7s.

1 EARTH still travaileth in pain
  That Thou, Lord, would'st come again !
  Waits and waits age after age,
  Searching still the holy page ;
  Still Thou comest not, nor yet
  Givest sign the time is set.

2 Emptied of Thy glory then,
  When Thou dwelled'st here 'mong men
  Thou art high-enthroned now
  "Many crowns" upon Thy brow ;
  Earth still travaileth in pain
  That Thou, Lord, would'st come again.

3 O Thou blessed Holy Ghost,
  Pleading, we dare Thee accost ;
  Hast Thou not from days of old
  Of His Second Coming told ?
  Hast Thou not by word and trope
  Giv'n Thy Church this mighty hope ?

4 Look, O Saviour, as we kneel ;
  Lord, Thou knowest all we feel ;
  Sinking heart and pulsing brain,
  That Thou comest not again :

CROSS-BEARING AFTER CHRIST   SAFETY AND COMFORT.

What Thy Spirit long has said
Give, O Christ; come to our aid!
5 O my God, how long, how long
   Thy return to Earth prolong?
   How long till Thou shalt appear
   All Thy foes to put to fear?
   How long till Thou Crucified,
   Take the world for which Thou'st died?

78. CROSS-BEARING AFTER CHRIST.
"*Take up thy cross.*" - *St. Matthew xvi. 24.*
8s.

1 *Take up thy cross*, My soul, *thy cross*!
  Take it, thou wilt not suffer loss;
  Thy Lord knows all its heaviness;
  Thou *sippest* but of His distress.
2 *Take up thy cross!* 'tis thine, my soul,
  But subject to thy Lord's control;
  Then take it up; to let it lie
  Will make it heavier by-and-bye.
3 *Take up thy cross!* nor fear to take
  Whate'er He sends, for His Name's sake;
  He is too loving to o'ertask;
  And He gives grace as we do ask.
4 *Take up thy cross!* still follow Him,
  Ay, even if thy eyes be dim;
  Take up thy cross, my soul, and know
  His eyes are on thee in thy woe.
5 *Take up thy cross! take up thy cross!*
  Take it, thou wilt not suffer loss;
  The Lord knows all its heaviness;
  Thou *sippest* but of His distress.

79.   UNSEEN YET LOVED.
1 St. Peter i. 8; St. John xx. 29.
8s.

1 *Unseen we love;* but hope to see
  When from this earthly body free,
  And pass'd to yonder world Above;
  But now, by grace, *unseen we love.*
2 *Unseen we love;* we know not how;
  Nor may we ever think to know,
  Till upward unto Thee we move,
  To find there how *unseen we love.*
3 *Unseen we love;* for Thou hast giv'n
  A thousand motives this side Heav'n,

To yield response, O Holy Dove!
To Thy alluring *unseen love.*
4 *Unseen we love;* as on Thy Rood,
  All crimson'd with Thy precious blood,
  We know Thee, Lord, our sins remove;
  This melts our hearts—*unseen we love.*
5 *Unseen we love;* O gracious Lord,
  Thou hast fulfill'd in us Thy Word;
  How long Thy patience with us strove!
  No marvel, that *unseen we love.*
6 *Unseen we love;* 'gainst guileful arts
  We yielded have to Thee our hearts;
  O keep Thou us that we ne'er rove;
  Still verify, *unseen we love.*
7 *Unseen we love;* rejoicing still
  To grow like Thee and do Thy will;
  Grant that our daily lives approve
  That Thee we know and *unseen love.*
8 *Unseen we love;* but hope to see,
  When from this earthly body free,
  And pass'd to yonder world Above;
  But now, by grace, *unseen we love.*

80. SAFETY AND COMFORT. *St. John x. 27-29*
7s.

1 I AM safe, for Christ holds me,
  Comforted, for I hold Him;
  Saviour, O thus let it be,
  When my dying eyes are dim;
   I hold of Thee, Thee holding;
   Thy strong love me enfolding.
2 Thou art strong and I am weak;
  Weakness clinging unto strength;
  Thus, dear Lord, Thou me dost seek;
  Taking home Thine own at length;
   Thy promises fulfilling,
   "Thy people making willing."
3 I am weak and Thou art strong;
  Thy strength girding me, so weak;
  Ah! my joy breaks forth in song,
  Lauding Thee in strength so meek;
   My sin by Thee forgiven
   Gives glimpse of op'ning Heaven.
4 When my sense of safety pales,
  Shew Thy nail-mark'd Hand in men;

When my sense of comfort fails,
 Place my trembling hand in Thine ;
  Lord, shew me Thy salvation !
  Lord, give Thy consolation !
5 I am safe, for Christ holds me ;
 Comforted, for I hold Him ;
Saviour, O thus let it be,
 When my dying eyes are dim ;
  I held of Thee, Thee holding ;
  Thy strong love me enfolding.

81. THE DIVINENESS OF THE CHRISTIAN. 7s.

"*Made partakers of divine nature.*" — 2 Peter i. 4; *Hebrews* iii. 10; 1 *Corinthians* ix. 10.

1 Lo ! The mighty act is done !
 Christ and I are now made one ;
 One in nature, yes, divine ;
 I am His, and He is mine.

2 Wondrous, Lord, that Thou should'st seek
 O'er me so great word to speak ;
 Word that does a sinner change
 And with God Almighty range.

3 God, the Holy Ghost divine,
 Making Jesus' merit mine ;
 Thou did'st quicken my dead soul,
 Thou did'st make me wholly whole.

4 Father-God, Thou call'dst me son,
 When this conquest high was won ;
 Grant that I be still Thy child,
 " Holy, harmless, undefiled."

5 My august name I will wear ;
 Claim my privilege as heir ;
 In each feature copy Thine ;
 My whole nature made divine.

6 Lo ! The mighty act is done !
 Christ and I are now made one ;
 One in nature, yes, divine ;
 I am His, and He is mine.

82. JESUS — SUN AND SHIELD. 7s.

"*The Lord God is a sun and shield.*" *Psalm* lxxxiv. 11.

"*Jesus! Sun and Shield art Thou,
 Sun and Shield for ever.*"
   — Dr. Horatius Bonar.

1 Jesus, Sun and Shield art Thou :
 Sun, art Thou for ever ;
But a Shield, Lord, only now,
 Yonder, never, never !
  There — no danger and no foe
  Nor e'er need to ward a blow.

2 Jesus, Sun and Shield art Thou :
 Sun, fails never, never ;
Shield too, whilst we walk below ;
 Guarding ever, ever ;
  Guard, O Lord, from fiery dart,
  That would seek to wound my heart.

3 Jesus, Sun and Shield art Thou :
 Sun, art Thou for ever ;
Make my path still brighter glow,
 Paling never, never ;
  And if tempted still to yield,
  O place over me Thy Shield.

4 Jesus, Sun and Shield art Thou :
 Like to Thee none ever ;
Rich and poor and high and low ;
 Blessing keeping never ;
  Our Sun — Heav'n's unsetting light ;
  Shield, but in Sin's earthly fight.

5 Jesus, Sun and Shield art Thou :
 Sun, art Thou for ever ;
But a Shield, Lord, only now ;
 Yonder, never, never ;
  Present armour all laid down ;
  Gain'd the robe, the palm, the crown.

83. LEADER AND GUIDE. 6s.

"*Shew me Thy ways, O Lord! teach me Thy paths.*" *Psalm* xxv. 4.

1 Shew me Thy ways, O Lord,
 Thy paths O do Thou teach ;
 I bring Thee Thine own word ;
 Hear me, I Thee beseech.

2 O take me by the hand,
   That I may feel Thee near;
   And when my foes withstand,
   I shall be kept from fear.
3 'Tis many "ways" there be,
   And "paths" that downward go;
   O grant that I may see
   Thine—Thine alone to know.
4 Calls me allure, left, right;
   Around—beneath—within;
   How they do me invite!
   Lord, arm me 'gainst all sin.
5 Each step, O Lord, me lead!
   I stumble in the way;
   Indwelling grace I need;
   Or I shall go astray.
6 Shew me Thy ways, O Lord!
   Thy paths O do Thou teach!
   I bring Thee Thine Own word,
   To Thee my hands I reach.

84. HEART-SURRENDER. 1 *Thessalonians* v. 23.   8. 7. 8. 7.

1 Lift us up in adoration,
   Seeing Thee upon Thy Throne;
   Save us Lord from mere prostration
   As to carven wood or stone.
2 Pour upon us Thine Own unction,
   That the Spirit witness may,
   By His sharp, yet sweet, compunction,
   Thou art leading in "the Way."
3 Calm in us that perturbation,
   Which instinctive thro' us darts;
   Take without one reservation.
   Full possession of our hearts.
4 Blend deep love with adoration,
   Adoration with our love;
   Set Thy seal of restoration,
   On each heart, O Heavenly Dove!
5 Burden'd, darken'd, in depression
   Lord, upon us flash Thy Face!
   Of us wholly take possession,
   Make us miracles of grace.
6 Thanks for hope of "heavenly mansion,"
   Thanks for all giv'n now and here;

For the soul's more wide expansion,
   Prelibation of more there.
7 More gifts, more of Thine Ascension,
   Through Thy holy grace and power;
   That in progress or declension
   We may share Thy blood-bought dower
8 Save us, Lord, from mere prostration,
   As to carven wood or stone;
   Lift us up in adoration,
   Seeing Thee upon Thy throne.

85.   ROSE OF SHARON.   7s.
   Song of Solomon ii. 1; *viii.* 5.

1 ROSE of Sharon! Mystic flower
   No man knoweth to this hour;
   Yet upon which sweetly lies
   Light more lustrous than of skies;
   Symbol of the supreme Birth
   Crown'd all beauty of the Earth.
2 Rose of Sharon! O how sweet!
   For the Gentle One most meet
   Falls the title, as Faith's ear
   To the Song of Songs draws near,
   List'ning for the voice of CHRIST,
   Keeping aye His holy tryst.
3 Rose of Sharon! What perfume
   As of incense fires consume:
   Floats around Thy gracious name
   Setting forth the Cross-mark'd shame
   Of that Holy Sacrifice
   Cleanses all our sin-stained cries.
4 Rose of Sharon! We are told
   No sharp thorns did thee enfold;
   Only royal crimson bloom
   Touch'd with spots of changeful gloom;
   Thus the King of kings forth-shewing
   In Thy sweet and hurtless blowing.
5 Rose of Sharon! May thy dower
   Rarest beauty on me shower!
   May the grace so typified
   Ever in my heart abide;
   Tender Saviour! wilt me bless
   With Thy spotless righteousness?

86. EVERLASTING LOVE. 8s.
"I have loved thee with an everlasting love."—Isaiah xxxi. 3.

1 ETERNAL Love! Eternal Love!
Give fervours, Lord, like those Above,
To tell how we from sin may part,
Holding from Thee the changéd heart;
Thy Spirit in us still must move;
Eternal Love! Eternal Love!

2 Eternal Love! Eternal Love!
To tell it all too vast doth prove;
In man's extremity of need,
Thou promised'st "the Woman's seed;"
E'en when Thy love from Eden drove:
Eternal Love! Eternal Love!

3 Eternal Love! Eternal Love!
In prophecy and gospel wove;
Thou did'st the mighty hope excite,
Nor ever fail'd to keep a-light;
O how can men still from Thee rove!
Eternal Love! Eternal Love!

4 Eternal Love! Eternal Love!
Man's primal sin Thy great heart clove;
As on the Cross 'twixt Earth and sky
For sinful man Thou deign'dst to die;
Whilst serried Hell against Thee strove:
Eternal Love! Eternal Love!

5 Eternal Love! Eternal Love!
O brood o'er me, Thou heav'nly Dove!
Make me to see Thy purpose stands,
Wrought out by Thy nail-piercéd hands;
Shew how strong faith doth me behove;
Eternal Love! Eternal Love!

87. LOVE OF GOD IN CHRIST. 10s.
"All things work together for good."—Romans viii. 28.

1 THY love, O God, flows round us tenderly,
As round and round the yellow sands,
the sea;
That breaks with musical lapse slenderly;
Telling how gentle Law is us'd by Thee.

2 And yet Thy love, like a bared sword can be;
Or, like the deep sea, hush'd and still,
and next—

Trod of the Tempest's feet—roused
them fringly.
Till ev'n the heart of Faith doth sink
perplex'.

3 Help us, whatever form Thy love may take,
To know and feel 'Tis Love 'neath ev'ry
form;
Or shine our face, or, Lord, our aw'd
hearts shake; [storm.
Still let Thine "It is I" come, calm or

4 Yea, O Lord God, give us to know Thy love
Mingleth the bitt'rest cup plac'd in our
hands;
Give us to rise the passing clouds above,
And, meekly willing, wait on Thy com-
mands.

5 Ah, Lord, for thus more grace, and more
we need,
Thou know'st it all; O on us more
bestow!
Thy love redeeming, all love doth exceed;
O give us its sweet restfulness to know!

6 Thy love, O God, flows round us tenderly,
As round and round the yellow sands,
the sea;
That breaks with musical lapse slenderly;
Telling how gentle Law is us'd by Thee.

88. BOUNDLESSNESS OF CHRIST'S LOVE.
7s. and 6s.
..."passeth knowledge." Ephesians iii. 19.

1 THY Love, O Christ, is boundless,
More boundless than the sky;
To deepest plummet soundless;
For Thou for me did'st die.

2 Thy Love is "Grace Abounding,"
With fulness like the sea;
Still—still is it forth-sounding,
"Glad tidings" unto me.

3 Thy Love no love can equal;
'Tis love without return;
Unchanging and perpetual;
Me, vilest, did not spurn.

4 Thy Love is meet for singing,
   With heart and string and voice ;
  I, sinner, to Thee clinging,
   How can I but rejoice?
5 Thy Love on Earth is treasure ;
   It tells of sin forgiven ;
  But who may seek to measure
   The perfect bliss of Heaven?
6 Thy Love, O Christ, is boundless,
   More boundless than the sky ;
  To deepest plummet soundless ;
   For Thou for me did'st die.

89. LOVE OF GOD – GOD OF LOVE. 8s.

"We read Thee best in Him Who came
To bear for us the cross of shame;
Sent by the Father from on High,
Our life to live, our death to die."
              Dr. Horatius Bonar.

"*For we are made partakers of Christ, if we hold the beginning of our confidence steadfast unto the end.*" *Hebrews iii.* 14. *(Cf.* 1 *Peter iv.* 13.*)*

1 OUR *life to live, our death to die :*
   Say, Singer, is thy note too high?
  Not sinful He, but sinless ever ;
  Aye, sinful we, and sinless never ;
  For ev'n in glory sinners saved,
  As in the crimson fountain laved ;
   Say, Singer, is thy note too high?
  Our life to live, our death to die.

2 *Our life to live, our death to die :*
  If so— whence that stupendous cry?
  Whence rocking Earth and livid skies?
  Immeasurable agonies? |broken?
  Whence cross of shame, and great heart
  Why no word by His Father spoken?
  Not thus, not thus, mere mortal dies;
  Or, His Own four-fold Gospel lies.

3 *Our life to live, our death to die :*
  Yea, Lord, by Thy fine alchemy
  'Tis even so—by Thy grace given
  Thou dost here meeten us for Heaven ;
  Thine Own strong life Thou dost impart
  With the great gift of the "new heart;"

And, breathing in us heav'nly breath,
Mak'st us partakers in Thy death.

4 *Our life to live, our death to die :*
  Incarnate Love, Thou did'st come nigh ;
  Thus Thou did'st live as we do live,
  By Thy divine prerogative ;
  Thus Thou did'st die as we do die,
  Sharer of our humanity ;
  Sweet paradox ! I see it now,
  Thro' grace, we live and die as Thou.

90. HEART-KEEPING BY JESUS. 8s.
Psalm cxxi. 5, *and Philippians iv.* 7.

1 WILT Thou, O Lord, me holier make !
   Wilt Thou, O Lord, me holier keep ;
  The power of sin within me break !
   Behold me as I troubled weep.

2 Behold me as I troubled weep ;
   Alas ! alas ! hard is the fight.
  What can I do but to Thee creep?
   Lord, I go dimly, give me light,

3 Lord, I go dimly, give me light,
   That I may not "unworthy" prove ;
  Shield me, O shield with gentle might,
   In the long patience of Thy love.

4 In the long patience of Thy love.
   That I may conquer lingering sin ;
  Yea, Lord, as dross from ore remove,
   Purge and repurge me all within.

5 Purge and repurge me all within,
   In thought and word, desire and deed;
  Fain would I final conquest win :
   Hear me as Thou for me did'st bleed.

6 Hear me as Thou for me did'st bleed ;
   Holy and lowly would I be ;
  I tell Thee, Lord, Thou know'st my need ;
   Help, help me of Thy clemency.

91. SERENITY. *St. John xiv. 27.* 6s.

Amas nec restuas. St. Augustine (Conf., lib. i. iv.).

"A God is! A Holy Will lives! however the human heart may stagger. High over the weavings of time and space lives the sublime purpose; and though all creatures groan in a circle of change, yet unchanging in the midst of change there is one Quiet Spirit." . . . —Schiller.

1 Thy love, Lord, is serene,
  No tumult marks its flow;
  Calm as that Sea was seen
  When forth Thy word did go;
  O that my love to Thee
  Shew'd Thy tranquillity.

2 Alas! Lord, I must own
  O'er all the love I feel
  Ev'n that unto Thee shewn
  Dim mists of passion steal;
  Lord! Pardon my offence,
  And from this taint me cleanse.

3 I mourn, Lord, that my love
  So poorly copies Thine;
  Unrest me still doth move
  With influence malign;
  Let Thy sweet quietness
  My whole soul re-possess.

4 Without I look to Thee,
  Within myself I look;
  O Thy strange constancy
  How it doth me rebuke!
  O hear me as I sigh,
  Shew me that Thou art nigh.

5 How changeful is our love;
  How mix'd of grief our joy!
  How short our raptures prove!
  How certain an alloy!
  Lord, Thy love in us burn;
  Restless to Thee we turn.

92. IMPUTED RIGHTEOUSNESS. 7s.

"The Lord our righteousness." Jeremiah xxiii. 16.
"Cover me with the robe of righteousness." Isaiah lxi. 10 (cf. xxviii. 10).

1 Lord, Thou gavest me for dress,
  Spotless robe of Righteousness;
  Woven in what loom, O Christ?
  On Thy Cross, by Love unpric'd.

2 Lord, Thou gavest me for dress,
  Spotless robe of Righteousness;
  It makes black or dew or rain;
  And an angel's tear would stain.

3 Lord, Thou gavest me for dress,
  Spotless robe of Righteousness;
  Who may set its praises forth?
  Who may tell its unmatch'd worth?

4 Lord, Thou gavest me for dress,
  Spotless robe of Righteousness;
  In my shame to Thee I went;
  Thy grace made me penitent.

5 Lord, Thou gavest me for dress,
  Spotless robe of Righteousness;
  Fully covering all my sin,
  Hiding all the guilt within.

6 Lord, Thou gavest me for dress,
  Spotless robe of Righteousness;
  Here now this fair robe I wear,
  Yonder shall in it appear.

7 Lord, Thou gavest me for dress,
  Spotless robe of Righteousness;
  Crimson sin 'neath Thy blood shed
  Is to white transfigured.

8 *Repeat Stanza* 1

93. NOT GRACES BUT CHRIST. 8s.
Galatians ii. 20-21.

1 I bless Thee, Lord, for all the graces
  That on Thine Own Thou dost bestow;
  By which we can lift up our faces
  In light that from Thy Face doth glow:
  But, Jesus, 'tis Thyself I seek;
  O hear me as I, pleading, speak!

2 I bless Thee, Lord, for Faith and Love,
  For Meekness Peace Humility ;
  For Patience sweet, like Thine above ;
  For Courage 'midst hostility ;
    But Jesus, 'tis Thyself I seek :
    O hear me as I, pleading, speak !
3 More grace and graces, Lord, impart,
  That to "full stature" I may grow ;
  Keep Thou all issues of the heart,
  Thou Who alone each heart dost know;
    But, Jesus, 'tis Thyself I seek :
    O hear me as I, pleading, speak !
4 For Thee Thyself, O Lord, I pine !
  Fulfil Thy word and in me dwell ;
  Myself am Thine, Thyself be mine ;
  Cast out all thoughts that do rebel,
    O Jesus, 'tis Thyself I seek !
    O hear me as I, pleading, speak !

94.   THE NAMES OF OUR BLESSED REDEEMER. *Ephesians* i. 20-23.   8s.

1 O JESUS ! Sweetest of Thy Names ;
  For "Jesus" saving grace proclaims ;
  O Jesus ! Saviour all men need,
  Laud for the Cross where Thou did'st bleed!
2 Christ ! Once by seer and sait expected;
  Christ ! Whom Thine Own of old rejected;
  Christ ! The Messiah true appointed ;
  Christ ! The one High-priest anointed.
3 Lord ! Mary-crowned King of men ;
  Lord ! Mighty still to-day as then ;
  Lord ! Who above all lords art Lord ;
  Lord ! Ruling all things by Thy word.
4 Lord Jesus Christ ! Our Three-in-One ;
  Lord Jesus Christ ! Thy will be done ;
  Lord Jesus Christ ! Adored be
  In the Most Holy Trinity.

95.   THE LIVING WAY.   8s.

"*I am the Way the Truth and the Life.*"
St. John xiv. 6 (*first*).

1 JESUS, we wake to see the light,
  For Thou hast kept us through the night ;
  Now may we hear Thee softly say,
  I am the true and living Way.

2 Jesus, we would this morning raise
  Upwards our hearts in votive praise ;
  We give ourselves anew this day
  To Thee, *the true and living Way.*
3 Jesus, protect our home-ones dear,
  Keep them and us within Thy fear ;
  In thought nor word to go astray
  From Thee, *the true and living Way.*
4 Jesus, when mingling with the crowd,
  Or silent, or 'mid clamours loud ;
  Be this our watchword while we pray,
  I am the true and living Way.
5 Jesus, help us Thy truth to keep,
  When we are glad, or when we weep
  The life within, grant that it may
  Shew forth, *the true and living Way.*
6 Jesus, may we Thy cause commend ;
  Receiving freely, freely spend ;
  The good attract, the base affray,
  In Thee, *the true and living Way.*
7 Jesus, from morning unto night,
  Sustain us in the paths of right;
  Make us to grow, as we obey,
  Like Thee, *the true and living Way.*
8 Jesus, we ask our "daily bread"
  From Thee, by Whom we all are fed;
  By more than earthly food us stay,
  Thyself bestow, *true living Way.*
9 Jesus, pour out on us Thy grace,
  To live as ever 'neath Thy face;
  Forbid that we should e'er betray,
  Or leave, *the true and living Way.*

96.   POWER FROM ON HIGH.   6s.

St. Luke xxiv. 49.

Da quod iubes, et iube quod vis.—*St. Augustine*
(*Con., lib. x. xxix.*)

1 COMMAND, Lord, what Thou wilt,
  But give what Thou commandest ;
  Thou knowest all my guilt,
  Me th'roughly understandest ;
  Whate'er be on me laid
  I shall stand unafraid

UNREST—FULL SUPPLY FOR UTMOST NEED.

2 Command, Lord, what Thou wilt ;
  All dangers I shall dare?
I flee to Thy Blood spilt,
  To Thy Word and to Prayer ;
Thus arm'd I'm clad in mail,
  When en'mies me assail.
3 Command, Lord, what Thou wilt,
  Thou all my wounds shalt cure ;
Howe'er fair they are gilt
  Sin's charms shall not me lure ;
O look on me and bring
  Me forth in joy to sing.
4 Command, Lord, what Thou wilt,
  My way be dark or bright ;
Upon the Rock I'm built,
  Thou shalt defend the right ;
I look to Thee O God !
  I bring to Thee my load.
5 Command, Lord, what Thou wilt,
  But give what Thou commandest ;
Thou knowest all my guilt,
  Me th'roughly understandest :
Whate'er be on me laid
  I shall stand unafraid.

97. UNREST. *St. Matthew vi. 28.* 6s.
1 I'M driven to and fro
  Unknowing where to go ;
As tho' a thing of chance
  Or of mere circumstance ;
O Lord ! I am hard-pressed.
Where—where shall I find rest ?
      "Come unto Me."
2 I hear, O Christ ! Thy voice ;
  I hear Thee and rejoice ;
I am no thing, I find,
  Nor do the Fates me bind :
O Lord ! I am opprest,
But Thou canst give me rest :
      "Come unto Me."
3 Again and yet again,
  Like to some sweet refrain ;
I catch Thy gladsome call
  As it doth on me fall ;

Thus bidding turmoil cease,
Imparting Thine Own peace :
      "Come unto Me."

98. FULL SUPPLY FOR UTMOST NEED. 10s.
Philippians iv. 9.
1 "My need, and all my need, Thou wilt
    supply" :
I take Thee at Thy word, and ask not why ;
Or, if I ask 'tis but Thy Name to bless,
Who art my "all in all," my righteousness.
2 "My need, and all my need, Thou wilt
    supply" :
O Lord, I place Thy words beneath Thine
    eye ;
See me as troubled to Thy Throne I'm led ;
Teach me to trust Thee for my "daily
    bread."
3 "My need, and all my need, Thou wilt
    supply" :
I praise Thee, Lord, for this sufficiency ;
For wants of me and mine, I look to Thee ;
From care, O living Saviour, keep me free.
4 "My need, and all my need, Thou wilt
    supply" :
O Lord my God, need is a constancy ;
Look on me from Thy dwelling-place in
    Heav'n,
And as Thou look'st, O let me be forgiv'n !
5 "My need, and all my need, Thou wilt
    supply" :
O blessed Jesus, hear my urgent cry ;
That I may grow in grace and lowliness,
Partaker of Thy blood-bought holiness.
6 "My need, and all my need, Thou wilt
    supply" :
O Saviour mine, give me Thy ecstasy ;
That day by day for Thee I witness may,
And others bring to walk along "The
    Way."
7 "My need, and all my need, Thou wilt
    supply" :
Thy word Thou dost fulfil right faithfully ;
O grant that all I am and have may be,
My Saviour, dedicated unto Thee.

99 CHRIST ALL IN ALL. *Col. iii. 1-3.* 11s.

1 ALL the World for Christ, and Christ for
  all the World;
   Hoist this watchword flag, and let it ne'er
    be furl'd;
   Wide as human need, yea wide as human
    sin;
   Full and free salvation, Christ has died
    to win.

2 Christ for all the World, and all the World
  for Christ;
   Tell, O tell it fully this great love
    unpric'd;
   Tell it bravely,— tell, whoever be the foes;
   Tell, O tell it out — one cure for human
    woes.

3 All the World for Christ, and Christ for
  all the World;
   Tell it proudly — sin from its high throne is
    hurl'd;
   Tell it plainly, tell that none may e'er
    despair;
   Tell it forth at all times — tell it everywhere.

4 Christ for all the World, and all the World
  for Christ;
   Tell it gailtiest — far from the Cross entic'd.
   Tell it to the lowest — whom none seem
    to heed;
   Tell it to the noblest — for the noblest need.

100. INDWELLING — DWELLING IN. 6s.
St. John vi. 56.

1 O DWELL in me, my Lord,
   That I in Thee may dwell;
  Fulfil Thy tender word,
   That Thy evange's tell;
  In me Thou, I in Thee,
   By Thy sweet courtesy.

2 But wilt Thou my guest be,
   In this poor heart of mine?
  Thy guest? Is this for me?
   In that pure heart of Thine?
  In me Thou, I in Thee,
   By Thy sweet courtesy.

3 Thy chamber, Lord, prepare,
   Whither Thou deignest come;
  I may not seek to share
   The making of Thy home:
  In me Thou, I in Thee,
   By Thy sweet courtesy.

4 Thy gracious gifts bestow,
   Humility and love;
  O cause my heart to glow
   By fire sent from above:
  In me Thou, I in Thee,
   By Thy sweet courtesy.

101. I, YET NOT I, BUT CHRIST.
Galatians ii. 20. 7.6.7.6.7.7.6.

1 LIKE to twin-stars that revolve
   Around the lorn wan moon,
  That the blackest clouds dissolve;
   Full of hope and high resolve,
    I found — ah God! how soon!
  That without Thy mightier might!
  I should soon stray from the light,
   Plunging in starless night;
    Thy grace, O Lord! my boon.

2 Vain all graces without grace,
   My heart to sanctify;
  Vain by any own strength to trace
   Noble plans, or to embrace
    Glad opportunity;
  Thou, my God, and Thou alone,
  Changing this hard heart of stone,
   Giving benediction,
    Dost lift and keep me high.

3 Loving Lord, to Thee I come!
   See me self-empti'd quite!
  Sin confessing in its sum,
   Brought in "guilty" I am dumb;
    Lord, see my heart contrite!
  I would feel when I am weak
  Then I'm strong; and now, Lord, speak
   That from Thee my strength I seek;
    Yea, more and more, give light.

4 Ah! my God, I still must sigh!
   As each day draws to close,
  Starting well, but by-and-by

THE DOOR—THE SAVIOUR NOT HIS CROSS.

  Self-convicted I descry
    That in my heart repose
  Evil thoughts and ill desires,
    Like to hidden smould'ring fires,
  Base self-pride that still aspires:
    A thorn beneath each rose.

102. THE DOOR. *Leviticus xvii. 3-4 ; St. John x. 3.*   7-7-7-7.

1 "At the door" the altar stood;
  "At the door"—was pour'd all blood;
  "At the door" the High-priest pled;
  "At the door" great words were said.
2 "At the door" Why was it thus?
  What doth all this mean to us?
  Be ye rich or be ye poor,
  This it means, "Christ is the door."
3 As first flowers foretoken Spring,
  So that "door" to us doth bring
  Shadows of Love's festival —
  Christ the "door" for each for all.
4 By the tent "door" pass'd but one,
  And but once a year 'twas done;
  Lo! "the many" Jesus seeks;
  On Faith's ear "if, any" breaks.
5 Joy, O man, if thou hast heard,
  And, by hearing, hast been stirred;
  Enter now—now whilst 'tis day;
  O mad folly to delay!
6 Saviour Christ, be Thou my "door,"
  That "outside" I stand no more;
  And my "Way" be Thou as well,
  That with Thee I aye may dwell.

103. DIRECT ACCESS. *St. John x. 3.*   10s.

1 O CHRIST! To Thee Thyself I take my way;
    O Christ! To Thee myself I dare to pray;
  To none, thro' none, shall I my sin confess;
    Thou only can'st with pard'ning cleansing bless.
2 Vain, vain, yea blasphemous he who arrests
    Access direct to Thee, the Priest of Priests;
  To none, thro' none, shall I my sin confess;
    Thou only can'st with pard'ning cleansing bless.
3 O not from Earth but Heav'n; or man, O Lord,
    Effective is a soul's penitent word;
  To none, thro' none, shall I my sin confess;
    Thou only can'st with pard'ning cleansing bless.
4 The way is open—rent the hind'ring vail;
    Whoever will may come, whatever ail;
  To none, thro' none, shall I my sin confess;
    Thou only can'st with pard'ning cleansing bless.
5 O gracious Saviour, Thou dost secrets keep;
    Nor dost bewray why sin sick souls sore weep;
  To none, thro' none, shall I my sin confess;
    Thou only can'st with pard'ning cleansing bless.
6 *Repeat St. 1.*

104. THE SAVIOUR NOT HIS CROSS.

1 I BEND not now, O Lord, before Thy Cross;
    That were to bow down to a crucifix;
  But to Thyself enthron'd—all else is dross;
    I dare not truth with deadly error mix.
2 Thy CROSS, O Lord, vacated, came the grave,   [Day;
    And RESURRECTION on the Great Third
  I will to Superstition be no slave;
    Thou, not Thy empty Cross, dost fears allay.
3 *Repeat St. 1*
4 The "First and Last, once dead and now alive";
    To Thee, to Thee I come, Thou LIVING ONE;
  No cross can e'er my guilt or sorrow shrive;
    Thou, the One Saviour the great "work" hast done.
5 *Repeat St. 1*

WORSHIP REFUSED TO MARY, MOTHER OF OUR LORD—TRIUMPH

6 I magnify Thee as Thy Church's Head;
　The cross a symbol of Thy love, no
　　more;
　I bow before Thyself THE CRUCIFIED;
　Thee, O my Christ, and not Thy cross
　　adore.
7 *Repeat St. 1.*
8 Thy Cross was fashioned by hands of
　　Hate;
　Who would bow down to such a thing
　　of shame?
　Nothing of FAITH or LOVE would I abate;
　But lo! Thy Cross, foul centre of all
　　blame.
9 *Repeat St. 1.*

105. WORSHIP REFUSED TO MARY, MOTHER OF OUR LORD.
St. Luke i. 26-28, 38 onward; i. 46-7; Psalm xxxv. 9.

1 EVEN to Mary, mother-maid,
　Of whom so mighty words are said;
　I dare not offer bended knee
　Withdrawing homage due to THEE,
　O Jesus, the Eternal Son,
　"God manifest in flesh" alone.
2 All honour for her meekness holy!
　All honour for her answer lowly!
　"Blessed art Thou" that gracious word
　Freely to her I would accord;
　But it were vain idolatry
　To lift to her or voice or eye.
3 Sweet handmaid of the Lord in Mary
　Lo, I see one who ne'er did vary;
　Modest and gentle, rev'rent, sweet,
　More and still more by grace made meet;
　Blessèd in her own SON divine;
　Forgiveness fetch'd whence I fetch mine.
4 O, living Christ, enthroned on High,
　Thou welcomest the guiltiest nigh;
　Thou hast all tenderness of love,
　Tho' God o'er all Thou be Above,
　No creature needs to interpose
　Betwixt Thee and my poor heart's woes.
5 *Repeat St. 1.*

106. TRIUMPH. *Revelations xi. 15.*
6s.

1 REJOICE! Rejoice! Rejoice!
　Come lift up heart and voice;
　Lo! nations at a birth
　　Of Him are making choice;
　Christ! King of all the Earth,
　　O 'tis a glorious noise!

　This universal mirth.
2 'Twas promised of old
　In vision of Thy Fold;
　Like thunder of sea-waves
　　From thousand shores 'tis rolled
　Behold the word that saves
　　Is being grandly told,
　And high His banner waves.

3 How long O Lord! how long!
　Till shall break forth the song?
　Old sage and seer foresaw
　　The dawning of this Day;
　And we with hush of awe
　　Behold it on its way;
　Lord! all hearts to Thee draw.

4 The valley of dry bones,
　Insensate as the stones,
　Beneath Thy quick'ning breath
　　Rose up a living host:
　O 'midst our sin and death
　　Come stir Thou Holy Ghost;
　We plead, we plead "He saith."

5 Rejoice! Rejoice! Rejoice!
　We will lift heart and voice;
　Lo! nations at a birth
　　Of Him are making choice;
　Christ! King of all the Earth,
　　O 'tis a glorious noise!
　This universal mirth!

107. Advance to Triumph.

1 Glory unto God on High!
  On the Earth and in the sky;
  Hallelujah! Jesus reigneth;
  Hallelujah! the light gaineth;
  Lo! the Lord's great Kingdom cometh:
  That all prophecy up-summeth;
      Let all "magnify" the Lord,
      Heart and voices in accord.
2 Far and wide the "good seed" sown
  That Thou mightily dost own;
  Hallelujah! Grace aboundeth;
  Hallelujah! Love astoundeth;
  Shout ye for the harvest waveth;
  Shout ye - Christ a lost world saveth:
      Let all "magnify" the Lord,
      Hearts and voices in accord.
3 Ages back the word was given
  That re-bound our Earth to Heaven;
  Hallelujah! Sin is smitten;
  Hallelujah! "It is written":
  Sing ye to the Cross hearts rally;
  Sound it forth o'er hill and valley;
      Let all "magnify" the Lord,
      Hearts and voices in accord.
4 Wistful eyes that swam with tears;
  Troubled souls o'ercome with fears;
  Hallelujah! all ye lowly;
  Hallelujah! by grace holy;
  The eternal Cov'nant standeth
  Whosoe'er against it bandeth;
      Let all "magnify" the Lord,
      Heart and voices in accord.

108. Vision of Glory. 20s.

1 On dream-wings lifted up I heard the
    stainless praise of the redeemed hosts
    above,
  Even as it was heard on Patmos isle, by
    the disciple whom the Lord did love;
  'Twas as the voice of many waters rolling
    clangrously towards a whitened shore;
  And as the voice of a great thunder,
    deep-booming, with Earth's and sky's
    commingled roar;
  And clear and high o'er all, as holy
    worshippers foregathered there with
    thronging feet,
  Harpers harping with their harps, that
    softened tenderly the awful with the
    sweet.
2 Then there flashed before my burdened
    eyes, like bickering flames, so vast a
    multitude
  That never mortal may essay to set it
    forth by any known similitude;
  And still in billowy swell forth from the
    myriad numbers of that vast un-
    numbered throng,
  There rose, like to the ring'd ascending
    smoke of incense, the melody of the
    "new song,"
  The song of His great love redeeming,
    Who, by cross of shame, had saved
    them on the Earth,
  And in His grace infinite transported them
    thither, though of sinful mortal birth.
3 I saw the Great White Throne to th'
    utmost verge, in purest splendor of
    Mount Hermon's whiteness,
  And in the midst THE LAMB, lo! as He
    had been slain, effulgent in His dreadful
    brightness;
  I saw too in the streets of shining gold
    that led up to the Lord Christ seated
    there,
  The glorious company of the redeemed
    from first of time, who the "new name"
    did bear;
  O it was such a beatific glimpse, that
    thus to me in my deep sleep was given,
  That now I walk this scarred, sin-
    shattered Earth, as tho' already I were
    there in Heaven.
4 And now beneath a lowly roof of God's
    Own House on Earth, I dare to offer
    praise,
  Ev'n though sin-stained, because from
    human lips, the highest notes mere
    mortal man may raise;

5 Ah! This sad globe of ours, so insignificant
amid the blaze of worlds supernal,
And marked yea branded with the brand
of human sin, by man's base fall,
through hate infernal,
In crimson vesture hangs before the
Throne, by Calvary's cross and Jesus'
blood redeemed,
So mightier grander far is this small Earth
of man's, than by proud Science it is
deemed;
We, therefore, God Almighty, Holy, Holy,
Holy One, would draw near with our
praise;
Accept of it, O Christ, and sanctify, as
with one heart we all adoring gaze.

6 Praise to God, Almighty Father! Praise
to the Son Eternal! Praise to the Holy
Ghost!
For hast not Thou, to chief of sinners'
Saviour, spoken from Thy Throne of
Grace on high,
Most gracious words of benediction:
"Whoso off'reth praise, the Lord doth
glorify"?
O Holy Intercessor, clarify with Thine
Own Spirit's breath, our poor frail
singing,
That not as music only but praise-prayer
it may reach Thee, like white doves
winging.

From all on Earth and in the heavens,
from a love-united and redeemèd host;
from child-lips praise, and praise from
dewy youth! from manhood praise, and
praise from hoar old age!
Praise from lowly huts and humble men!
from toilers praise, and praise from
broad-browed sage!
Praise from Faith, and Hope, and Love,
and Joy, and praise from Penitence, and
Grief's parched lips!
All who have being praise, until this
mortal life is lost in THE APOCALYPSE.

3. God the Holy Spirit.

Hymn to the Holy Ghost.—Tr. Ch. D.

110. God the Holy Spirit. *Romans xv. 30.*
8s.

1 O Holy Ghost! Come as the Dew,
　All soft and still this quiet eve;
　Our first love's joy do Thou renew,
　As to those who did first believe.
2 O Holy Ghost! Come as the Fire,
　In our cold hearts light up Thy flame;
　That, touch'd of Thee, we may aspire,
　And shrink not from His glorious shame.
3 O Holy Ghost! Come as the Wind
　To shake quick ev'ry barrier down;
　That, restfully on Him reclin'd,
　We Him, He us, may gracious own.
4 O Holy Ghost! Come as the Rain,
　That sweetly heals the new-mown grass;
　Refresh and strengthen, that again
　We on our upward way may pass.
5 O Holy Ghost! Come as the Light,
　Pure-breaking as doth break the Day;
　Work in us by Thy gentle might
　Such hopes as shall our fears affray.
6 O Holy Ghost! Be Thou our Life
　Our life that's hid with Christ in God;
　Make Thou us strong in the sore strife,
　Guarding us in the paths He trod.
7 O Dew! O Fire! O Wind! O Rain!
　O Light of Life! O Life of Light!
　We would the height of heights attain
　We would be strengthen'd by Thy Might

111. The Love of the Spirit.　7s.
Romans xv. 30 and Philippians ii. 1.

1 'Biding still on Earth with us,
　O Thou patient Holy Ghost!
　Had Thy grace magnanimous,
　Left us, we had all been lost.
2 Still Thy Presence is confessed;
　Still Thou flashest inward light;
　Still the strife continuest,
　Still the wayward dost invite.
3 Still stray'd feet Thou guid'est hence,
　From "far country" they have sought;
　Still dost shew Redemption come,
　On the Cross by Jesus wrought.
4 Heav'nly Dove, Thou might'st us shun,
　And spread wide Thy wings for flight;
　But till the Last Man is won,
　Thou shalt strive to reunite.
5 'Biding still on Earth with us,
　O Thou patient Holy Ghost!
　Had Thy grace magnanimous,
　Left us, we had all been lost.

112. The Holy Spirit our Strength.
8.7.7.　*St. John xiv. 16.*

1 O Comforter, The Holy Ghost!
　Before Thee mortal may not boast;
　Yet lowlily I would declare
　That I am strong as Thou art near;
　Thy Presence puts in me new strength,
　Until that now I can at length
　Take Thee for Helper—Advocate
　My Teacher, Guide, I were ingrate
　If I burst not into song,
　By Thy Presence still kept strong.
2 O Comforter, The Holy Ghost!
　Before Thee mortal may not boast;
　Yet not alone driest Thou my tears,
　Yet not alone stillest Thou my fears;
　But, when my blackest guilt I see,
　Thou showest me from sin set free;
　All accusations of The Law
　Are hushed, as near the Cross I draw;
　Therefore burst I into song,
　By Thy Presence still kept strong.
3 O Comforter, The Holy Ghost;
　Before Thee mortal may not boast;

SYMBOLS OF GOD THE HOLY SPIRIT:

I grasp Thy Name of Paraclete,
But find Thee strong as well as sweet;
Consoler Thou, as Thou giv'st peace
Still whisp'ring of the great release;
But more—Thy Presence felt so near
The eyes of Faith makes bright and clear;
My glad heart bursts forth into song;
By Thy near Presence still kept strong.

4 O Comforter, The Holy Ghost!
Before Thee mortal may not boast;
Lo! I, a sinner, now and ever,
A sinner safe, but sinless never;
And by Thy grace, O Thou most meek,
I cling to Thee or I am weak;
I draw from Thine Omnipotence
A strength divine, a precious sense
That Thou it is who giv'st me song,
Who by Thy Presence mak'st me strong.

113. SERENITY UNDER THE SPIRIT'S REPROOF.

St. John xvi. 8. 8s.

1 LORD, what is this that Thou hast sent?
My heart, like sea-wave turbulent,
Sways still with strange sweet agony!
O born not of the Earth but sky!
Of "*sin*" Thou seek'st me to *convince*
And 'neath Thy probing touch I wince.

2 Lord, what is this more Thou hast sent?
Lo! grace mix'd with Thy chastisement!
Accusing, yet Thou dost me bless:
Convincing me of Righteousness:
Behold I plumb the mystery;
I die not, for Thou, Christ, did'st die.

3 Lord, what is this? more blessing sent?
Thy righteousness with "*judgment*" blent:
But Saviour, in Thy boldness clad
I shall, by Thee, be no more sad;
Assured that on that fateful Day
Thou blessèd Christ will be my stay.

114. SYMBOLS OF GOD THE HOLY SPIRIT.

St. Matt. iii 16.; Acts of the Apostles ii. 2-3; xvi. 14; xvi. 23-24. 6.6.6.8.8.

1 THOU camest as the DOVE;
O Holy Spirit blest!
His heav'nly Father's love,
Thou fully did'st attest;
Grant that this witness to Him giv'n;
May seal me, too, a son of Heav'n.

2 Thou camest as the FIRE,
In the great "Upper Room";
In fervent love not ire,
With benison, not doom;
May this clear witness to them giv'n,
Seal me, too, Lord, a son of Heav'n!

3 Thou camest as the WIND;
Men heard it, in the street,
Jerusalem did find
Sound of invisible feet;
May this strong witness to it giv'n,
Seal me, too, Lord, a son of Heav'n.

4 Thou camest as the LIGHT,
Soft-op'ning Lydia's heart;
In gentleness of might,
To give "the better part";
May this sweet witness to her giv'n,
Seal me, too, Lord, a son of Heav'n!

5 Thou cam'st, with EARTHQUAKE SHOCK
To shake the prison-walls;
Jailor, as Earth doth rock,
For mercy on Thee calls;
May the witness to him giv'n
Seal me, too, Lord, a son of Heav'n!

6 O Dove! O Fire! O Wind!
O Light! O Earthquake dread!
By each, by all combined
Be my heart monishèd!
Grant that each witness of old giv'n
May seal me, too, a son of Heav'n.

115. THE HOLY SPIRIT INVOKED. 1 Thess. v. 23. 7s.

1 Holy Spirit in me move;
  Fill me with a deeper love;
  Take, O take from me away,
  What'er hind'reth Thy full sway.
2 Holy Spirit in me move;
  That from Thee I never rove;
  Still the "closer walk" be mine;
  Thy soft light upon me shine,
3 Holy Spirit in me move;
  Ah! against Thee long I strove;
  Thou forgive, and nearer draw,
  That I ever stand in awe.
4 Holy Spirit in me move;
  Powerful yet hush'd as Dove;
  The " new heart " in me create,
  That, as pain, I sin may hate.
5 Holy Spirit in me move;
  Thy o'ercoming grace still prove;
  Holiness be my strong law,
  Wakeful unto slightest flaw.
6 Repeat St. 1.

116. GRACE PERFECTING. 1 Corinthians vii. 9; 2 Corinthians vii. 1; Galatians iii. 3. 7s.

1 YEARS on years I went in dread,
  Gloom below and overhead;
  As " hard Master" Christ I served,
  Trembling when in aught I swerv'd;
  But "my chain" His sweet love broke,
  The Lord's ransom'd I awoke.
    Joy, O joy, to me is given
    Here to taste the bliss of Heav'n.
2 " God forbid" that I should boast,
  Knowing my redemption's cost;
  Pard'ning love I magnify,
  Nor His mercy may belie;
  Grace abounding is my song,
  Sinner, I to Christ belong.
    Joy, O joy, to me is given,
    Here to taste the bliss of Heav'n.

3 I have enter'd into rest;
  " Peace of God" doth calm my breast;
  " Perfect love" hast cast out fear,
  For the Lord is ever near;
  In me beateth " the new heart,"
  Wrought by gracious Spirit's art.
    Joy, O joy, to me is given,
    Here to taste the bliss of Heav'n.
4 Holier, I trust, I grow,
  Thro' " the seed" which Thou dost sow;
  Lowlier I fain would be,
  By Thy sweet humility;
  And the pureness of Thy Will
  Which I choose like light, doth fill;
    Joy, O joy, to me is given,
    Here to taste the bliss of Heaven !
5 Years on years I went in dread,
  Gloom below and overhead;
  Christ as austere Master served,
  Trembling when in aught I swerv'd;
  But "my chain" His sweet love broke,
  The Lord's ransom'd I awoke:
    Joy, O joy, to me is given,
    Here to taste the bliss of Heav'n.

117. FIRE OF THE SPIRIT. 8s. Stabat dum ferit. — Jer. xx. 9.

1 THY " fire," O God, let it be mine;
  Not in my bones but in my heart;
  I ache, Lord, to be wholly Thine;
  Thy " fire" bestow whate'er the smart;
  That Faith and Hope and Love may glow,
  Like theirs the " closer walk" who know.
2 Thy " fire" O God let it be mine;
  " Wood, hay, and stubble" to consume;
  Do Thou my whole heart, Lord incline
  To walk " the Way" Thou dost illume;
  He tring Thy call " Come higher Friend;"
  Foll'wing Thy steps to blessed end.
3 Thy " fire," O God, let it be mine;
  That burns to heal and heals in burning;
  As a Refiner me refine;
  Thy searching flame on me returning;

Speckless of dross, Lord, I would be;
Thy image in me I would see.

4 Thy "fire," O God, let it be mine;
  That I may know Thy prophet's rage;
  Yea, that with Thine Own wrath divine,
  I may a holy warfare wage;
  With Thy pure zeal, O Lord, me fill;
  In conscience, mind, and heart, and will.

113. THE TEMPLE RESTORED. *2 Cor. vi. 16.*
                                    8s.

1 A ruin'd temple is man's soul;
  Its ruins doth it "great" enroll;
  The fallen shaft—the shatter'd dome;
  The shrine, where 'doleful creatures' come;
  Its chambers bared to light of day;
  Shewing remediless decay;
  These all are symbols of man's FALL,
  And to heart-searching thought do call.

2 Who shall this ruin vast re-build?
  That with fresh glory it be fill'd?
  Thou, the Lord Christ, and Thou alone
  Prepar'st in us the mystic stone;
  Thou, the Lord Christ, by Holy Ghost,—
  Restors't the beauty man has lost;
  O wilt Thou now Thy work begin!
  Remake us, Lord, without, within.

3 The "new heart," O my God, bestow,
  That with Thine own deep love doth glow;
  The WILL, that gladly lost in Thine,
  Is strong and brave and half divine;
  The CONSCIENCE that with Thy peace
      fill'd,
  Sings as when Zion's songs are trill'd;
  Body and soul, all consecrate,
  By PURITY Thou dost create.

4 Lord even as in the days old
  All this by symbol was foretold;
  Do Thou to-day in love make good,
  Redeeming by Thy glorious blood;

Come in, O God, and in us dwell,
Possessing my heart's citadel;
Thy temple Thou in me restor'd,
Thou aye, O God, shalt be ador'd.

119. BREATHINGS. *Ps. li. 11-12.* 7s.

1 IN ashes the quick fire slumbers;
  Tho' dull smoke the flame encumbers;
  Ev'n so, Lord, within Thine sleeps
  That grace which Thy ruth still keeps.

2 Oft and oft, alas! O Lord!
  We forget Thy warning word;
  Suff'ring our Faith's light to pale,
  Letting DOUBT our HOPE assail.

3 But Thou leav'st us not alone;
  Thou dost take ev'n heart of stone;
  And in miracle of pow'r
  With our "first love" us redower.

4 Praise, O Lord, that it is so;
  But, more, cause my heart to glow;
  Yea, fill me with quick'ning fire
  That I may afresh aspire.

5 O to stand where once I stood,
  With clear vision of "the blood";
  Into Thine Own Kingdom born;
  Languid no more or sin-torn.

6 *Repeat St. 1.*

120.   MAN.   6s.

1 HOW GREAT art thou, O Man!
  More great, the more I scan;
  Most great, when by God's grace
  Thou tak'st thy rightful place;
  Deliver'd from this SIN
  That doth such triumph win;
  Redeem'd—restor'd—twice-made;
  Of thy God unafraid.

2 Thy BODY—fearful wonder
  Fit to be prais'd by thunder;
  Strong—yet how delicate!

One—yet how intricate!
'Tis small—but lo! a mansion
Of measureless expansion;
Yea, city of five gates—
A monarch there instates.

3 BROW—grander than a throne—
Lo! angels might it own!
The realm of naked thought—
Ideas thence are brought;
There CONSCIOUSNESS a-thrill
Fore God bows—aw'd and still;
Thro' mazes involute
Led to the ABSOLUTE.

4 EYES—that are as twin-stars
Fair as the Eve unbars;
Lips—sweeter than all sweet,
Made for "fine issues" meet;
How shall I laud the TONGUE!—
A weapon subtly strung;
Half Heaven, half of Hell—
A thing inscrutable.

5 Hand—fashion'd with keen art,
And deftly plays its part;
BRAIN—cunningly compact,
Seat of all thought, all act;
HEART—crimson-curtain'd shrine—
By grace made half divine;
Of "flesh and blood" enwrought;
Yet where Love's secret's taught.

6 Man's BODY—thing thrice rare,
Than fairness all more fair;
Or in bright childhood's hour—
Soft-op'ning as a flower;
Or as fresh youth, or maiden
With gifts and graces laden;
Or in full manhood's strength,
Or as white head at length.

7 *Repeat St. 1.*

II.—THE SOUL.

8 Man's SOUL—lo! how it stands
From its Creator's hands!
To walk with God made fit;
To God Himself close knit;
O tragedy of loss!
Admeasur'd by the CROSS;
When SIN of man laid hold,
His crown in Earth's mire roll'd.

9 But EVERLASTING LOVE
To rescue us did move;
Man summoned from his hiding,
And with RUTH'S own sweet chiding,
Told him of "Woman's Seed"
That yet for him should bleed;
Restoring greatness lost,
No more in anguish tost.

10 O COSTLY soul of man!
Seen in REDEMPTION'S PLAN;
O miracle of power,
Thus lost man to redower;
O mystery of SIN,
Such conquest dread to win!
O terror of all sleight,
To hurl from such a height!

11 In front stands INTELLECT—
That no knife can dissect;
WILL—no instinct of brute
But aye to choose acute;
No iron-like hard pressure,
To dictate or to measure;
But lissom as the air,
Free to go here or there.

12 IMAGINATION—high,
Conversing with the sky;
And—rainbow of the mind—
Rich FANCY—nought can bind;
God's warder CONSCIENCE—set,
Ne'er evil to abet;
DESIRES—like leaping flame,
Only God's grace can tame.

13 For higher good still aching,
Spite of dark passions' shaking;
Upwinging aspiration
By God's own inspiration;
Fire of all pureness burning
Next—to the swine-trough turning;

Fill'd now with "perfect peace,"
Then raging to God's face.

14 Of Earth, but for the skies
In final destinies;
Frail as a passing breath,
Yet conqueror of Death;
Erect, yet prone and weak —
Great secret where to seek?
By nature—naked, bare;
By grace—with Christ joint-heir.

15 *Repeat St. 1.*

....

121.   The Trinity.   7s.
At Thy Throne, O " Abba Father,"
We now reverently gather;
Jesus is to Thee "The Way,"
Therefore would we boldly pray:
Holy Spirit, our hearts move,
That, twice-born, we may approve.

2 Thou Eternal Father art,
And Thou hast reveal'd Thy heart;
Sparing not Thine only Son,
That redemption might be won;
Love incarnate on the Cross,
Purchases, redeems our loss.

3 God our Father, hear our cry,
As we low-adoring lie;
Help us by Thy Spirit's aid,
That we may be holy made;
We would worship God tri-une,
Father, Spirit, Son as one.

4 God the Father, Thou lov'st man;
From Thy heart came Love's great plan;
Thou, the Son, cried'st "Lo! I come,"
Freely paying man's debt-sum;
God the Holy Ghost abides,
True to all in Him confides.

4. The Holy Scriptures.

Holy Scripture containeth all things necessary to salvation; so that whatsoever is not read therein, nor may be proved thereby, is not to be required of any man, that it should be believed as an article of Faith, or be thought requisite or necessary to salvation. In the name of the Holy Scripture we do understand those canonical Books of the Old and New Testament, of whose authority was never any doubt in the Church.—Article of Religion.

122. THE BIBLE IN ALL LANGUAGES. 8s.

1 In full five hundred tongues to-day
   The Word of God holds saving sway;
   The Gospel of "The Crucified"
   Still more and more is magnified.

2 This He foretold; and, lo! 'tis done:
   How mighty, Lord, the triumph won!
   In Sin's immitigable loss
   Restored by Thy all-conqu'ring Cross.

3 From age to age increasing, till
   The name of Christ the Earth doth fill;
   Each year a fresh fulfilment brings—
   "He comes with healing on His wings."

4 We link us on, however few,
   With the vast multitude that sue
   To Thee, Whose Living Word alone
   Sweet peace doth bring to all that moan.

5 O grand and sweet the thought, to know
   That thus unitedly we bow:
   Diverse our language but one heart
   All choosing still "the better part."

6 How long, Lord, until Thou shalt pour
   Thy grace on all from shore to shore!
   And Thy Word sown o'er all the Earth,
   Shall bring the harvest-tide to birth.

7 *Repeat St. 1*

123. SYMBOLS OF HOLY SCRIPTURE. 8s.

Psalm cixx. 105 : St. John vii. 33 and 35 ; Hebrews iv. 12.

1 THY WORD, O God, is naméd LIGHT:
   It bends o'er us like starry night;
   Thou Book of God, all darkness flies
   When unto Thee I lift my eyes;
   My path grows more and still more bright;
   Great Book of God, 'tis well-nam'd LIGHT.

2 Thy Word, O God, is naméd LIFE:
   O precious name untouch'd of strife:
   It comes as with a mystic breath
   To wake the soul out of its death,
   With every gracious meaning rife;
   Great Book of God, 'tis well-nam'd—LIFE.

3 Thy Word, O God, is naméd —BREAD:
   By which our life is nurturéd :
   More sweet than angel's food that fell
   Upon Thine ancient Israel ;
   As day by day, Lord, I am fed ;
   Great Book of God, 'tis well-nam'd BREAD.

4 Thy Word, O God, is naméd— SWORD;
   A name of awe, yet in accord;
   For even as by flashing blade
   Way to life's citadel is made;
   So pierces me, O God, Thy Word:
   Great Book of God, 'tis well-nam'd —
      SWORD.

5 O Book of God ! O god of books !
   Whoe'er into thy pages looks,
   If brain and heart The Spirit touch,
   Will thy divineness sure avouch:
   O God, Thou in Thy Word hast spoken !
   Of Light, Life, Bread, and Sword, the
      token.

124. THE GUIDING LAMP. *Psalm cxix. 105.*
8s.

1 SOMETIMES I know not what to do,
   Or to give up, or to pursue;
   When darkness and when dangers meet,
   Thy Word, a lamp unto my feet.

2 I look around, and none is near,
   To whom I may confide my fear;
   Ah! then I see the Mercy-seat
   Thy Word, a lamp unto my feet.

3 When devil, flesh, or world would win
   My steps to tread the paths of sin;
   O God, to Thee I make retreat —
   Thy Word, a lamp unto my feet.

4 When I am languid, weary, slow,
   And my "first love" has lost its glow;
   Give grace, more grace, I Thee entreat —
   Thy Word, a lamp unto my feet.

5 Alas! dear Lord, how may I tell
   How vainly conscience clangs her bell;
   Warning against Sin's doom, Sin's cheat—
   Thy Word, a lamp unto my feet.

6 Yet praise, O God, Thou God of grace,
   That as I run the Christian race,
   Thou wilt all enemies defeat—
   Thy Word, a lamp unto my feet.

7 So shall I follow on and on,
   Until the promised Land be won;
   Where dwelling in the Light indeed
   My earthly lamp no more I need.

125. THE ENGLISH BIBLE. 7s.
1 ENGLISH Bible! Book supreme!
   For great Singers greatest theme;
   As my eye into thee looks
   Grandest I hold thee of books;
   Speech of noblest breed of Earth;
   Noblest speech of mortal birth.

2 English Bible! God's great dower
   To this Land of mighty power;
   Foremost she amongst the nations:
   Calm amidst all perturbations;
   Broadest freedom she has won;
   Most august work she has done.

3 English Bible! Charter great
   Of the Church and of the State;
   Tyndale, Coverdale of old
   Writ their names on leaves of gold;
   From the palace to the hut
   Book in place of honor put.

4 English Bible! Heritage
   Reverenc'd on from age to age;
   So long as we still shall be
   Land of brave men, land of free;
   None shall ever blot thy words,
   Guarded surer than by swords.

5 English Bible! Book supreme!
   For great Singers greatest theme;
   Greek and Hebrew — sacred source;
   But our English deeper force;
   Destin'd the one tongue to be
   Shore to shore and sea to sea.

126.
*The first Japanese Convert to Christianity
Through finding an English Bible floating
in Yeddo Bay in 1857. (See full note in
Notes and Illustrations at close.)* 8s.

1 A BIBLE fell into the sea
   Or meant, or accidentally;

THE ENGLISH BIBLE.

'Twas off a fiercely-heathen Land —
Where foam-maned surge roars on the strand.

2 If e'er thing might be held for lost,
Sure 'twas this Bible in sea tost;
A frail waif, and soft as a sponge,
What hope it should survive its plunge?

3 But He Whose is the great old Book,
Quick turn'd on it protecting look;
A heathen noble saw it float,
And to recover instant sought.

4 When told that 'twas GOD'S BOOK divine
Round which all weal or woe did twine;
He eager grew yet more to know;
Within his breast a strange warm glow.

5 Like flame of fire love in him burn'd,
As oft unto the BOOK he turned;
Until, O Jesus, found of Thee,
FAITH came in sweet simplicity.

6 Baptiz'd in the thrice-holy Name,
JAPAN'S first convert he became;
Thus by the sea-drift Bible led,
To Him Who for the World has bled.

7 O "Bread of Life" on waters cast,
Shielded from wave and whelming blast!
O BOOK OF GOD grown to great host
Art Thou upon that far-off coast.

8 Whose Bible 'twas is all unknown;
But to what "good seed" it has grown!
A living thing in His great hands;
O let us send it to all LANDS.

5. The Sabbath.

Remember the Sabbath-day, to keep it holy. Six days shalt thou labour, and do all thy work: but the seventh day is the Sabbath of the Lord thy God: in it thou shalt not do any work, thou, nor thy son, nor thy daughter, nor thy man-servant, nor thy maid-servant, nor thy cattle, nor the stranger that is within thy gates: for in six days the Lord made heaven and earth, the sea, and all that in them is, and rested the seventh day: wherefore the Lord blessed the Sabbath-day and hallowed it.—The Fourth Commandment (Exodus xx. 8-11, and if Gen. ii. 2-3).

The Son of Man is Lord even of the Sabbath day.— St. Matthew xii. 8.

127. THE RESURRECTION — SUNDAY MORNING. *Romans i. 4.* 8.6.

1 ARISE my soul, Faith's wings expand,
Soar upward to the Heav'nly Land;
Behold the great stone roll'd away!
Thy Saviour's Resurrection Day!
   A conqueror forth He came,
   Death and the Grave to shame.

2 Hark! hark! it is an angel's voice,
Who tidings brings that bid rejoice;
He stands by Death's wide-open'd door,
And cries, "Christ lives for evermore!"
   A conqueror forth He came,
   Death and the Grave to shame.

3 O hallow'd Day! O blessed Day!
That all Death's darkness did affray;
Far-flaming still o'er all the world,
Strong Satan from his vast throne hurl'd:
   A conqueror forth He came,
   Death and the Grave to shame.

4 Thou Prince of Life! Thou Saviour dear!
For us in Heav'n Thou dost appear;
Nor need most tim'rous tremble now
Since Faith beholds Thy crown-clasp'd [brow;
   A conqueror forth He came,
   Death and the Grave to shame.

5 O Lord, do Thou help us to watch
That we Thy mighty word may catch,
"Because I live ye too shall live;"
What could more strong assurance give?
   A conqueror forth He came,
   Death and the Grave to shame.

6 Arise my soul, Faith's wings expand,
Soar upward to the Heav'nly Land;
Behold Thy Saviour's grave unbarr'd!
White-wingèd angels for His guard:
   A conqueror forth He came,
   Death and the Grave to shame.

128. SUNDAY "MADE" OF GOD. 8s.
"This is the Day which the Lord hath made: we will rejoice and be glad in it."— Psalm cxviii. 24.

1 THIS is Thy House! This is Thy Day!
Lord, bless us on this hallow'd morn;
Thou art "the true and Living Way,"
Open'd for all of woman born.
No splendors of Apocalypse,
Burst on our Patmos us to fray;
Touch with Thine Own soft flame our lips,
Increase our faith, our fears allay.

SUNDAY FIRST DAY OF THE SEVEN.

2 We seek not terrors of Thy Face,
  Such as St. John this Day beheld;
  But here in Thine appointed place,
  Lord, let Thy Presence be reveal'd!
  "This is the Day which Thou hast made";
  Thy People are for worship met;
  "Be it to us as Thou hast said";
  Cast far and wide Thy Gospel net.

3 Those of Thine Own assembled here,
  Lord "stablish Thou in holy faith";
  Bestow on them "the hearing ear,"
  And sweetly, gently on them "breathe";
  Their hearts fill with Thy "perfect peace,"
  And make them know Thy restful rest;
  More and still more from sin release;
  To them the Day all through be blest.

4 Let not the World's dull cares intrude,
  Whilst "on the mount" we wait on Thee;
  O ne'er may conscience truth elude,
  Nor word for conscience fail to see;
  Thy Gospel in its gracious power
  Fill us with gratitude and joy;
  O give a Pentecostal shower,
  And Satan's realm this Day destroy.

5 Lord God, Thou seest from high Heav'n
  All who this Day are in Thy House;
  And whether they be drawn or driv'n,
  May they find Thee them all espouse;
  The strong and weak, the glad and sad,
  Those going on, those going back;
  The true and false, the good and bad,
  Thy love, each one, O Christ, will track.

6 This is Thy House! This is Thy Day!
  Lord, bless us on this hallow'd morn;
  Thou art "the true and Living Way,"
  Open'd for all of woman born;
  No splendors of Apocalypse,
  Burst o'er our Patmos us to fray!
  Touch with Thine own soft flame our lips;
  Increase our faith, our fears allay.

129. SUNDAY FIRST DAY OF THE SEVEN.
  Psalm cxviii. 24. 7s.

1 THE first Day of all the sev'n,
  Thy good gift, O God of Heav'n!
  Day, enclasping all the week!
  Day, when Thou dost bless the meek!
  Day, when Thou dost speak to us
  In Thy love magnanimous!

2 Now Creation's work was done,
  And o'er all beneath the sun
  Thou did'st utter "very good,"
  As all sinless forth it stood;
  Then Thou did'st on this Great Day
  Sabbath rest for man display.

3 When in the far-onward years
  Men by "shed-blood" hush'd their fears;
  And within the Temple bowed,
  Sinner all alone, or crowd;
  High-priest on this Day did plead,
  And His prayer, Lord, Thou did'st speed.

4 When, O Christ, upon the Cross
  Thou had'st paid a doom'd world's loss;
  When, Lord, as The Crucified,
  Thou for guilty man had'st died;
  Calm forth-stepping from Thy tomb
  Thou this Day did'st Conqueror come.

5 So, Lord, now as in the prime,
  Keeping promise thro' all time;
  Whosoe'er on this Day meet
  And, as brethren, brethren greet;
  Find Thy House is "holy ground,"
  And Heav'n's joys on Earth abound.

6 Be this Day such day to us!
  E'en to the most timorous;
  O may we by praise and prayer
  Our life's needs before Thee bear!
  May Thy preached Word unfold,
  Treasures far beyond Earth's gold.

7 The first Day of all the sev'n,
  Thy good gift, O God of Heav'n!
  Day, enclasping all the week!

THE LORD'S DAY—SABBATH PRAYER-SONG.

Day, when Thou dost bless the meek!
Day, when Thou dost speak to us
In Thy love magnanimous!

130. THE LORD'S DAY. *Rev. i.* 10. 8s.

1 Day, of glorious memories!
    Day, of Jesus risen again!
    Day, of grave, all powerless now!
    Pris'ners longer to retain!
    Day, for rescu'd saints of God!
    Day, to sons of men once giv'n!
    Day, of blessing and of grace!
    Light on Earth sent down from Heav'n!

2 Day, of mercy and of love!
    Day, of gladsome praise and pray'r!
    Day, of preaching of the Word!
    Day, when Jesus draweth near!
    Day, when with anointed eyes,
    We behold The Crucified!
    Day, on which the Holy Ghost,
    Witnesseth why Jesus died!

3 Day, when angels of the Lord,
    Hover, as on Bethel's height!
    Day, of "good news" Heavenwards borne,
    Fresh souls brought into the light!
    Day, of turnings unto God!
    Day, of gladness in the Lord!
    Day, of shaking of men's hearts!
    Day, of conquests by the Word!

4 Day, that girdles Earth with light,
    Grander far than Saturn's rings;
    Day, that still from East to West,
    Glory unto Jesus brings!
    Day, of His own promis'd peace,
    Calming the o'erdriven soul!
    Day of days, aye speeding on
    A redeem'd Earth to its goal!

131. SABBATH PRAYER-SONG. 7s.
Acts of the Apostles xiii. 32.

1 Bless, O Lord, Thy Word this Day!
    Speed it on its gracious way;
    Like the manna that did fall
    Give a portion unto all;
    Yea, Lord, may Thy truth now spoken
    Be as bread by Thy Hands broken.

2 Stablish, strenghthen, settle, keep,
    All O Christ, who are Thy sheep;
    Build them up in sanctity
    On this hither side the sky;
    Give them to be brave and strong,
    Each hour set to its own song.

3 Doubting, tempted, and afraid,
    Lord, with grace their weakness aid;
    Let them see Thou answerest prayer;
    Let them feel that Thou art THERE;
    Help them still to Thee to flee,
    Refuge, whosoe'er they be.

4 Burden'd, sadden'd, weary, lone;
    Wipe their tears and hush their moan;
    In their tremor and distress
    Think of Thine own "wilderness";
    By the Holy Spirit given,
    Fill Thou them with light from Heaven.

5 If into Thy House to-day
    Some poor prodigal should stray;
    Heart-sick, sin-sick, penitent,
    Shame and hope together blent;
    Loving Saviour, be Thou nigh,
    Save him in his misery.

6 O fill full the Heav'nly Home!
    In all Lands "Thy Kingdom come;"
    Toilers on dark shores uphold;
    Bring the glad Day long foretold;
    When, as by th' embracing sea,
    Love-clasp'd our whole Earth shall be.

6. The Church of Christ in its Work and Services.

I believe in the Holy Catholic Church: the Communion of Saints: the Forgiveness of Sins: the Resurrection of the Body, and the Life Everlasting.—The Creed.

132. THE HOUSE OF GOD.   8.6.8.6.
"Not forsaking the assembling of yourselves together, as the manner of some is."

1 "I JOY'D when to the House of God,
  Go up they said to me;"
 O Thou enthroned Son of God,
  This "joy" I ask from Thee.
2 My spirit THIRSTS for Thee, O God,
  My spirit THIRSTS for Thee";
 Wilt Thou, Lord, shed Thy love abroad?
  Wilt "put" this thought in me.
3 The "fellowship" of twice-born hearts,
  O God, grant me to know;
 That "not forsaking" by LOVE'S arts
  May my "first love" make glow.
4 That on the holy Sabbath, I
  May with Thy People meet;
 And with all tend'rest sympathy
  In Christ, my brethren greet.
5 Forbid that I should "dwell alone";
  Neglecting "House of Prayer";
 Bring me with Thine unto Thy Throne;
  Alike with joy and care.
6 God of the House ne'er from Thy House,
  May I be absent found;
 No ease or pleasure my soul chouse,
  No earthy harass wound.
7 *Repeat St.* 1

133. ONE IN CHRIST.   *Ephesians iv.* 2-3.
  6.5.6.5.6.5.

1 WE all are one in Christ,
   If in Christ we be;
  One God our Father is,
   All one family;
  Names differing we bear;
   Think in diff'rent ways;

  But each a sinner still
   Who on Jesus stays.
2 We all are one in Christ,
   If in Christ we be;
  All summon'd to His fold
   By His ministry;
  A grand cathedral here,
   Holds high festival;
  The lowly chapel there;
   God the same o'er all.
3 We all are one in Christ,
   If in Christ we be;
  In one dear Lord we trust,
   In Sin's misery;
  One Cross redeeming all;
   All by sin enslav'd;
  One Spirit giving life;
   One soul to be saved.
4 We all are one in Christ,
   If in Christ we be;
  One holy Book alone
   Whence we fetch our plea;
  But one the "life of faith"
   Any of us know;
  We sing the same sweet songs,
   Pilgrims here below.
5 We all are one in Christ,
   If in Christ we be;
  One anchor, one great hope
   In life's stormy sea;
  As we are all belov'd
   So we all must love;
  Our hearts united all
   To the Heart above.
6 We all are one in Christ,
   If in Christ we be;

Our one great task of love
Souls to bring to Thee;
Lord! forbid that we
"Fall out by the way";
O may a dying world
All things else outweigh.

134. THE CHURCH. 1 *Corinthians iii. 11.*
7.6.

1 Behold thy one Foundation
Church of the LIVING GOD!
'Midst all thy tribulation,
Know, thou art His abode.
2 Proclaim the one Salvation,
Wrought out upon the ROOD;
Proclaim the one Purgation,
By "Water and by Blood."
3 Behold the one Oblation,
On altar of the Cross!
Behold it ev'ry Nation,
Redemption of all loss.
4 Lo! Comes the "new creation,"
New heavens and new Earth;
That brings the consummation,
The blood-bought Church's birth.
5 Behold one Revelation,
Old Testament and New!
Tell it with exultation,
To many or to few.
6 Height of all adoration,
The Lamb amidst the Throne;
Let all lift supplication;
The vilest He will own.
7 Behold the attestation
From age to age secure;
Which bringeth jubilation;
Still doth His Word endure.
8 Hark! the reverberation
Throbbeth from earth and sky
Vain hell's exacerbation,
With Christ is victory.
9 *Repeat St.* 1.

135. WONDER. *Psalm cxiv. 18.* 9.8.9.8.8.8.
1 LORD, Nurture Thou my sense of wonder
O'er what the glorious Gospel tells;
Not crouching low in "place of thunder,"
But quiet as saints in holy cells;
The "old, old story," ever new,
However frequent the review.
2 Lord, Keep alive my sense of wonder,
Aye cent'ring in the living Christ;
Oft placing me His Great Throne under,
To hold with Him a gracious tryst;
The "old, old story," ever new,
And ever proving itself true.
3 Lord, Give me a fresh sense of wonder,
Thy Truth's rath beauty vivid still;
Love for THE BOOK aye growing fonder,
Lo! as it shapes and colours WILL.;
The "old, old story," ever new,
Whether my years be more or few.
4 My Lord, Forbid that sense of wonder,
E'er from my eyes should cease to shine;
Let not the World, or tempter plunder
Me of the joy that "THOU ART MINE";
The "old, old story," ever new, --
Ah! all my vows I would renew.
5 O Lord, I seek my sense of wonder,
May still remain, as when a child;
Let nothing ever my heart sunder,
From holy "first love" undefiled;
The "old, old story," ever new,
However frequent the review.

136. LONGINGS FOR A REVIVAL. 7s.
Acts of the Apostles, c. ii.

1 MET, O Lord, within "one place,"
We are suppliants of Thy grace;
Pentecostal fire bestow,
That our faith and love may glow;
Vision of Thine open'd Heaven
To each waiting heart be given.
2 Various the names we bear,
But how various soe'er,
O blest Jesus, make us one
In Thy Spirit's union!
Heart to heart, knit Thou in prayer,
Ev'ry one a worshipper.

3 We are met in Thy Great Name,
But look not for tongues of flame;
Nor " the mighty rushing wind"
Here, do we expect to find;
Pentecostal fire is Thine;
Grant it, Lord, without the sign.

4 O my God, we upward turn,
Not the "place" but souls make "burn",
Let the preaching of Thy Word;
Let our prayers in sweet accord;
Let our praise on joyful wing;
Days of blest REVIVAL bring.

5 God Almighty, hear our call;
Haste Redemption's Festival!
Gird Thy sword upon Thy thigh;
Forth to bloodless victory!
Save a world from death and sin,
Lead the grand Millennium in.

6 Christ enthroned! hear our cry,
Let not a redeem'd Earth die;
In the Gospel breathes Thy breath,
Life thro' Thy tremendous death;
O Salvation! at what cost!
Yet, oh! yet, shall souls be lost!

7 Conquering, gracious Holy Ghost,
Come as once at Pentecost!
Souls are sliding down to hell;
Daily the doom'd legions swell;
O put forth Thy mighty power,
Save them—thousands in an hour.

8 Met, O Lord, within " one place,"
We lift up entreating face;
Thine Own Church awake, awake,
Her dread languour do Thou shake;
'Twixt the living and the dead,
Stand, till Earth be conquered.

137. ON JOINING THE CHURCH ON A PUBLIC
PROFESSION OF FAITH.

(Agreeably to the Practice of Presbyterian Churches.)
St. Matthew x. 32.   8.8.7.7.

1 LOVE and Faith and Joy professing;
Thee, O Lord, by grace possessing;
See us here approach to Thee,
Keeping Thy " Remember Me."

2 Hear our mingling supplication,
In this hour of dedication;
That we may "perform our vows";
Nor e'er glow of " first love" lose.

3 Sav'd by grace, by grace abounding,
Rich and free, ourselves astounding;
Guide us, guard us in the Way,
Making progress day by day.

4 Grant, O Lord, Thyself unchanging,
Ne'er in us may be estranging;
Faithful, constant to the end;
All grace needed to us send.

5 May we each for Truth contending,
Daily Thee be still commending;
Walking in Thy footsteps here
With meek heart and conscience clear.

6 Thee, O Lord, by grace possessing;
Love and Faith and Joy professing;
See us as we stand 'fore Thee,
Keeping Thy " Remember Me."

138. PREPARATION FOR THE COMMUNION.
 " *A people prepared for the Lord.*"—
St Luke i. 17.   7s.

1 LO! O Lord, we gather here,
On our PREPARATION eve;
We would meet in " godly fear";
Grace we need, tho' we believe;
Looking, on Thy coming day,
Once again Thy death to "shew";
Shed on us The Spirit's ray,
That Thy Presence we may know.

2 Thou hast " kept" us in past years;
Faithful to Thy Holy Word;
Guarded us amid all fears:
Prov'd Thyself our cov'nant Lord;
Lo! To-night our song we raise,
Of Thy goodness and Thy love;
Lord, accept our sin-stained praise:
Worthier we will give Above.

3 Self-examiners us make,
   Lowly, willing to know all,
   And discover'd sin to take
   Unto Thee, as Thou dost call;
   O rekindle gratitude!
   As we see how much we owe,
   To Thy pard'ning plenitude,
   Which in grace Thou dost bestow.

4 Bring us to Thy Table pure,
   Filled with memories of Thee;
   Trusting in Thy Presence sure,
   As Thou say'st "Remember Me";
   Make our hearts within us burn,
   As with symbol "bread" and "wine";
   We in faith unto Thee turn,
   Seeking blessing on each sign.

5 Let Thy death upon the Cross,
   Rise before us in its power;
   Let us count all gains but loss,
   If we do but win Thy dower;
   And as onward gaze our eyes,
   Fain the mystery to plumb,
   Let not doubt or fear arise,
   Hold us with Thy "till I come."

139. The Lord's Supper. *1 Cor. xi. 23-26.*
7.7.8.8.

1 Lord, behold Thy Table spread,
   Wine outpoar'd and broken bread;
   Of Thy love the tender token,
   Symbol of Thy Body broken.

2 Hope accepts the simple rites,
   Walking still by faith, not sight;
   Restful, trusts Thee, the Unchanging,
   Never from Thy Red Cross ranging.

3 Bread of Thy pure flesh the sign;
   Shed blood, pictur'd in the wine;
   Grant thro' us, our love professing,
   May anew enjoy Thy blessing.

4 Lord, upon us breathe Thy breath,
   Witnessing of life thro' death;
   Touch us with Thy Spirit's flaming,
   As we Thine ourselves are naming.

5 Keep us lowly, holy, meek,
   Ready aye for Christ to speak;
   Wearing Thy gift-robe of whiteness,
   Meet'ning us for Heaven's brightness.

140. After the Lord's Supper. 8s.
1 Cor. xi. 23-26.

1 Vow'd yet anew as Thine, O Lord;
   Wilt Thou Thy grace to us afford,
   That we may never Thee betray,
   But walk with Thee "the living Way?"

2 Refreshed anew by bread and wine,
   Grant us to shew the life divine;
   For tho' we walk this sin-scarred Earth
   We're sons of God by heav'nly birth.

3 Lord, fill us with Thy "perfect peace,"—
   Thy pard'ning love gives sweet release;
   And, as thro' life we pass along,
   Do Thou our troubles set to song.

4 O guide us, guard us hour by hour
   And gird us by Thy gentle power,
   That trusting, praying, toiling still,
   We may a Christ-like part fulfil.

5 Vow'd yet anew as Thine, O Lord;
   Wilt Thou Thy grace to us afford,
   That we may never Thee betray,
   But walk with Thee "the living Way?"

141. At the Table of the Lord. 7s.

1 Jesus! Consecrate this place;
   Jesus! Crown us with Thy grace;
   Jesus! Lift on us Thy Face.

2 We are weak, but Thou art able;
   We are frail, but Thou art stable;
   Shield us at Thy blessed Table.

3 Use this Bread and use this Wine;
   Luminous, Lord, be each sign;
   Make Thee ours to shew us Thine.

4 Fear and doubt O Lord remove;
   Us surcharge with Thy sweet Love;
   Brood Thou in us Heav'nly Dove!

5 Lord, prepare us for all trial;
   Guard from flinching and denial,
   Nor dread any man's espial.

142. GETHSEMANE AND THE JUDGMENT-HALL.

"Did I not see thee in the garden with Him?"
St. John xviii. 26. 7s.

1 PETER, thee did I not see
Last night in Gethsemane?
O deniest thou thy Master
In the hour of His disaster?
 O those piercing questions put!
 Would that they his mouth had shut.

2 Ah! That still there thus should be
Grievous possibility
E'en in our own living day
Christ the Saviour to betray:
 Craven when we all should dare;
 And our very selves forswear.

3 At Thy Own Great Table now
Taking symbols, sealing vow, —
With all airs and looks devout —
Next day mix'd with evil rout;
 Greedy once more after gain
 As e'er thirsty soil for rain.

4 I accept the warning word;
I appeal to Thee, O Lord;
O, by Thy dear love so tender,
Be Thou still my sure Defender;
 Me protect from base denial,
 And all fear of man's espial.

5 Lord, forbid that I should be
Tainted with Gethsemane
Peter-like; Thy grace renew
That to Thee I may be true;
 That I never Thee betray
 Nor my Christianhood gainsay.

6 Week-day, Lord's day, to me give
By Thy love's prerogative,
That within, without, I still
May Thy Holy Word fulfil;
 Worthy of the Name I bear,
 Christ's always and everywhere.

143. UNWORTHY... UNWORTHILY.

1 Corinthians xi. 27, 29. 10s.

1 JESUS, alas! we feel our sinfulness;
And oft and oft — to tears — are in distress;
Yet at Thy Table, Lord, we take our place,
And praise Thee for Thy pard'ning words of grace;
 O Sinners' Saviour, hear our grateful cry,
 'Tis not "unworthy," but "unworthily."

2 Jesus, We still are full of fear, and weak;
Full many a fiery dart our peace doth break;
But at Thy Table, Lord, we take our place,
And praise Thee for Thy strong up-holding grace;
 O Sinners' Saviour, though we moan and sigh,
 'Tis not "unworthy," but "unworthily."

3 Jesus, We would now think alone of Thee,
Keeping in mind Thy word "Remember Me";
Thus at Thy Table, Lord, we take our place,
And praise Thee for the symbols of Thy grace;
 O Sinners' Saviour, mark each glist'ning eye;
 'Tis not "unworthy," but "unworthily."

4 Jesus, Smile Thou upon us at this hour;
Let no dark cloud upon our Love-feast lour;
While at Thy Table, Lord, we take our place,
And praise Thee for the brightness of Thy grace;
 O Sinners' Saviour, make us know Thee nigh;
 'Tis not "unworthy," but "unworthily."

5 Jesus, To Whom may such poor sinners go,
If not where Thou forgiving love dost shew?

EVANGELISATION—HOME-MISSIONS.

So at Thy Table, Lord, we take our place,
And praise Thee for the riches of Thy grace;
O Sinners' Saviour, now to Thee we fly,
'Tis not "unworthy," but "unworthily."

6 Jesus, O bless to us Thy bread and wine;
May we "discern" what they set forth to Thine;
Behold Thy Table, Lord! we take our place
And praise Thee for the mem'ries of Thy grace;
O Sinners' Saviour! we come hopefully,
'Tis not "unworthy," but "unworthily."

7 Jesus, Our doubt and fear we cast away,
Thy last appeal we dare not disobey;
Loving, we at Thy Table take our place,
Laying our sins on Thy great heart of grace;
O Sinners' Saviour, hear our grateful cry,
'Tis not "unworthy," but "unworthily."

144.   EVANGELISATION.   8s.

"They went forth and preached everywhere."
St. Mark xvi. 20.

1 WE bless Thee, Lord, that Thou didst preach
To all who came within Thy reach,
And bless Thee that where'er men came
Thou preachedst to them, without blame;
In synagogue and Temple-court;
But not there only was resort,
Thy full, free Gospel Thou didst tell
To one frail woman by a well;
And so in house, or mountain side,
Or where white Jordan swift did glide;
To "two or three," or unto many
Still preach'd, nor e'er refusèd any;
For EVERYWHERE Thy grace abounds,
Nor Earth nor Hell Thy love confounds.

2 And still, Lord, Thou wouldst have it so;
Still call'st Thy servants forth to go,
In Thy Great Name, and by Thy power,
Thro' Thy blood-purchas'd Spirit's dower;
Blessing Thy People in Thy House—
The hallow'd "place" which Thou dost choose;
Yet blessing, tho' place consecrate
Ope not for them its hallow'd gate:
Yea blessing 'neath the naked heaven,
If that no other place be given;
Or on the hill, or moor, or stream,
Or in the street—a place of shame;
Thou chargest servants of the Lord
To preach to each and all "the Word."

3 Lord, fill with Thy Own vehemence;
Save us from priestly arrogance,
And abject bondage to the Law
That still creates a pseudo-awe;
And still from Christ's work stands aloof,
Unless men gather 'neath Church roof;
Forgetting that by blood divine
The round Earth is incarnadine;
Forgetting that Thy charter'd "Go"
Secures fulfilment of Thy "Lo!";
The centre for all men Thy Cross;
Thy promise sure against all loss;
O break our fetters, Lord, that we
May preach in "glorious liberty."

145.   HOME-MISSIONS.   8s.

St. Luke xxiv. 47 ; Acts of the Apostles ii. 22-41.

1 BEGINNING at Jerusalem;
Lord, rich Thy mercy shewn to them!
Thousands on thousands penitent
By Thine almighty Spirit bent;
Thy love did point them to the Rood,
And sav'd them through Thine awful blood;
Hearing their cry of agony
And all their dark guilt passing by.

2 *Beginning at Jerusalem :*
'Midst sacred words, a priceless gem ;
For lo ! it telleth us to-day,
That as we Thy command obey,
To bear the Gospel forth, until
Knowledge of Thee, the whole Earth fill;
Thou bid'st us "seek" at our own door,
As well as on remotest shore.

3 *Beginning at Jerusalem:*
Give vision of Thy diadem
Lustrous with souls Thou hast redeemed,
Where'er Thy Gospel light hath gleamed;
And make us, Lord, to understand
That here in our own native Land,
Souls in deep darkness lie, and need
That swift we to their succour speed.

4 *Beginning at Jerusalem:*
Thanks, Lord, for Thou wilt not condemn,
If thro' all dens of vice we know,
Our hearts with earnest faith a-glow;
We bear the vilest of our kin
The good-news of free-pardoned sin:
Hoping 'gainst hope through Thee Above,
The worst to conquer by Thy love.

5 *Beginning at Jerusalem:*
O holy was the stratagem !
It sheweth how Thy cross stupendous
Did meet man's guilt the most tremendous;
We would believe, and dare to go
To utmost human want and woe;
Home-heathen, Lord, we fain would win,
Help Thou Thy Church to bring them in.

146. EVANGELIZING IN THE STREETS.
   6s.   *St. Luke xiv. 23.*

1 BENEATH the open sky
Lord, unto Thee we cry;
E'en in the public street,
We seek with Thee to meet.
Whilst we Thy truth declare,
Saviour, to whomsoe'er.

2 Thou Who Thyself of old
Thus Thy full Gospel told;
Upon us here and now
Thy saving power bestow;
O may Thy Spirit win
From lives of death and sin!

3 Thou did'st Thy servant's call
To "go forth" unto all;
To poor, maim'd, halt and blind,
Yea, to all humankind ;
To guilty and sore tried,
And every soul beside.

Repeat St. 1.

147. WEEDS WAILS. *1 Thess. iv. 8. 6s.*

1 O CALL it not a WEED,
God, our God, sowed the seed;
God, our God, tends the flower
Through sunshine and through shower :
Lo! look thou on the meanest,
Mean as in haste thou weenest;
Behold in it such tints!
Behold in it such glints!
See changes on their stems
As in dove's neck, or gems;
In sooth so delicate
That kings in all their State
Match not — call it not WEED,
God, our God, sowed the seed.

2 O call it not a WEED,
Rather of thanks give meed;
For the Great Gardener knoweth
The lowliest thing that bloweth;
Be it beneath the hedge;
Be it on steep crag's ledge,
Be it on cottage thatch
Of green a tiny patch;
By ord'ring of His Hand
Each in its place doth stand,
Bright'ning bare path of duty

With nicest touch of beauty;
He cares—call it not WEED,
God, our God, sowed the seed.

O call it not a WEED,
For each there is a need;
See how to it dews come!
See how o'er it bees hum!
See how the light it gilds!
See how the bird near builds!
See children at their play,
The commonest makes them gay;
See o'er all such sweet touches
As our God's care avouches!
That 'tis not of a chance
But order'd circumstance
They bloom—call it not WEED,
God, our God, sowed the seed.

O call it not a WEED,
God's own deep lesson read;
Ye supercilious eyes
Charge our God as unwise;
Shallow—know there's not child
Of slums, by sin defil'd;
Not poorest waif of street,
Trudging with naked feet,
But is beneath His eye
Who on the cross did die;
Know each one has a part
In the Great Father's heart;
O call no one a WEED;
The Christ for Him did bleed.

O call no one a WEED,
Or base must be your creed;
For as in humblest flower
God giveth gracious dower;
So to most wayward child,
From birth by sin beguil'd,
The broken heart Above
Gives tokens of His love;
In all are hidden springs;
They're men, not merely things;
Then speak to all unquailing—

All Satan's forts assailing;
Stand forth—call no one WEED,
Divine shall be your deed.

148. A DAY IN THE COUNTRY WITH (s. 'STREET ARABS.'

1 LORD! wilt Thou bless to-day
  The CHILDREN in their PLAY!
  Fetch'd from the lanes and slums
  As each wain laden comes;
  Do Thou upon them smile
  And all their griefs beguile;
  For one day heirs of beauty,
  O let it brighten duty.
    Lo! 'Tis "a day of Heaven"
    In love to poor waifs given.

2 The May is white as snow,
  For every spray doth blow;
  Like incense thro' the air,
  Steams fragrance rich and rare;
  The quaintly-drumming bees
  Are all in ecstacies;
  Down from a sapphire sky
  Fall larks' notes quiv'ringly;
    From greenwood to hill height,
    The landscape swims in light.

3 How great this gift of life,
  With all these blessings rife!
  How lips break into praise,
  Our gratitude to raise!
  How heart breathes votive prayer,
  God's goodness to declare!
  Like him by "Burning Bush"
  The whole soul bows a-hush;
    Lo! 'Tis "a day of Heaven"
    In love to poor waifs given.

4 How the glad children bound
  And gambol on the ground!
  'Twould stir most frigid heart,
  Yea, tears in hard eyes start;
  To mark their fearless mirth,
  Measuring the great tree's girth;

Or wading in the stream,
Or chasing a sunbeam;
"God bless them," one and all,
No shadow on them fall.

5 Kind hands and hearts are here,
And the GREAT HEART is near;
O Christ! do Thou inspire
More and more hearts with fire
Of Thy sweet sympathy;
That not a year pass by
Without a day like this,
Bringing to street-waifs bliss:
Lo! 'Tis "a day of Heaven"
In love to poor waifs given.

6 Alas! How few take thought
Of kindness cheaply bought!
Alas! What lavish waste,
By sin so oft defaced!
When out of mighty sums,
Sparing the meanest crumbs;
That yearly one bright day
May give the children PLAY:
Lord! hear Thou our appeal,
Fountains of love unseal.

149. WAIFS AT THE SEASIDE.
1 IT is a sight,
   Heav'n to delight,
To see street-waifs on sea-shore play;
   Once in the year,
   When Summer's here,
Comes to them, their one HOLIDAY.

2 What rounded eyes!
   What quaint surprise!
What clatter of quick-running feet!
   As joining hands
   On yellow sands
They frolicksome and eager meet.

3 Some shout some jest;
   Some run some rest;
All tingling with full life and glee;
   Some seek the shade;
   Some tim'rous wade;
'Tis their first day by the great sea.

4 The good Lord own,
   Yea, richly crown
The thoughtful hearts and willing hands!
   Who year by year
   Young lives to cheer,
Lead them thus forth in merry bands.

5 Much larger things —
   Of which FAME rings;
Methinks they will outweigh ONE DAY;
   For kindness done
   To "little one"
The Lord Christ marks and will repay.

150. THE SALVATION ARMY. *Ps. xxvii. 3.*
   11s.

1 ARMY OF SALVATION! forward to the fight!
Ye have dar'd and conquered, girded by
   God's might;
Still lift high Christ's banner, blazon'd with
   the Cross;   [loss.
Tell out the old Gospel, nor fear to suffer

2 ARMY OF SALVATION! the wide world is
   your field;
The round Earth predestin'd is unto Christ
   to yield;
Hurtless are your weapons, yet ye proclaim
   'THE BLOOD,'   [aloud!
Sin-atoning, man-redeeming, shout shout

3 ARMY OF SALVATION! many are your foes,
Terrible sin's thraldom, terrible men's woes;
Stout of heart be ye and strenuous of will,
The Lord God shall ye all with His Spirit fill.

4 ARMY OF SALVATION! let the world malign,
So it did your Captain, glory in the sign;
Love return for hate, as ye with pity glow,
That like unto The Master, ye may daily
   grow,   [patience strive,

5 ARMY OF SALVATION! with Christ's
Long-forgiving gentle to vilest soul alive;
Work, and Watch, and Pray, the end ye
   soon shall see
Jesus King of men, over Land and Sea!

151. EVANGELIZATION OF THE WORLD.
"Launch out into the deep." St. Luke v. 4.

6s.

1 LAUNCH out into the deep:
   I hear, O Christ, Thy call;
   Let tempests o'er me sweep,
   They shall not me appal.
2 Launch out into the deep:
   Before Thee, Lord, I stand;
   I know Thou wilt me keep,
   In hollow of Thy Hand.
3 Launch out into the deep:
   Thou rulest wind and wave;
   Thou wakest when men sleep,
   Thou wakest men to save.
4 Launch out into the deep:
   Yea, Lord, to farthest shore;
   Until all hearts that weep,
   Redeeming love restore.
5 Launch out into the deep:
   O Christ, 'tis Thy command;
   E'en if the billows leap
   In fury on the strand.
6 Launch out into the deep:
   Wherever souls may be;
   Launch out into the deep:
   Till there be "no more sea."

152. ULTIMATE CHRISTIANISATION OF THE WORLD.

St. Matthew xxviii. 19-20; xxiv. 14.

8.7.8.7.7.7.

1 COURAGE! Though the skies are clouded,
   Blackest clouds will pass away;
   Courage! Though the Future's shrouded,
   All is clear to Him as day;
   And His "purpose" shall endure,
   Ever faithful, ever sure.
2 Servants come and go successive,
   Doing each his little part;
   Slow the progress, and oppressive
   Sense of failure in their heart;
   But His "purpose" shall endure,
   Ever faithful, ever sure.
3 Courage! The crown'd Saviour liveth,
   And His promises abide;
   Courage! He His strong word giveth,
   That for our whole race He died;
   And His "purpose" shall endure,
   Ever faithful, ever sure.
4 We can't see where His truth goeth,
   Short at most our widest view!
   What, and where, and how He knoweth;
   Shields the many or the few;
   For His "purpose" shall endure,
   Ever faithful, ever sure.
5 Courage! Darkest lands are gleaming
   With th' advancing Gospel day;
   Courage! In far skies, light-streaming,
   Lo! The Cross makes conqu'ring way;
   And His "purpose" shall endure,
   Ever faithful, ever sure.
6 Forth then servants of The Master;
   Still His triumph claim for Christ;
   Long the way is, speed the faster;
   He will keep His Holy tryst;
   For His "purpose" shall endure,
   Ever faithful, ever sure.
7 Courage! Though the skies are clouded
   Blackest clouds will pass away;
   Courage! Though the Future's shrouded,
   All is clear to Him as day;
   And His "purpose" shall endure,
   Ever faithful, ever sure.

153. ALWAYS MORNING SOMEWHERE.

"'Tis always morning somewhere in the world."—Sun-dial legend on pier at Brighton. 10s.

1 'TIS always morning somewhere in the world:
   O not yet, not yet is the Christ's flag furl'd;
   Night darkens down, but yonder day has birth,
   And rounds and rounds—like Saturn's rings—the Earth.

TRIUMPH—"THY KINGDOM COME."

2 'Tis always morning somewhere in the
  world;   [hurl'd;
Thron'd Evil yet shall from its height be
The nail-pierc'd Hand holds still the
  "seven stars;"
Truth stronger nobler groweth by its scars.
3 'Tis always morning somewhere in the
  world;   [whirl'd;
The cause of Right ne'er into dark is
God lives, God reigns, God marshalls all
  events;   [laments.
Give o'er, give o'er, ye faithless, vain
4 'Tis always morning somewhere in the
  world;
For re-flow after ebb the waves are curl'd;
The Cross centre of all circumference;
Earth girded is by Love's omnipotence.
5 'Tis always morning somewhere in the
  world;   [purl'd;
Th' o'er-flooded stream anon has softly
Look up, look up, broad-breaking is God's
  light,
He yet will save our race in gentle might.
6 'Tis always morning somewhere in the
  world;   [furl'd;
O not yet, not yet is The Christ's flag
Night darkens down, but yonder Day has
  birth,   [rings the Earth.
And rounds and rounds like Saturn's

154.   TRIUMPH.   12s.

1 Ho! Ho! ye men of FAITH, ye that are
  faithless grown;
Hark, hark ye, to Christ's voice still
  sounding from the throne;
"Go ye to all the world, to all the Gospel
  preach;   [ye shall reach."
Lo! I am with you alway till Time's end
2 Up! Up! this is your CHARTER, Church of the
  Living God!   [task and load;
'Tis He, none else, sustaineth the mighty
The waves toss to and fro, but the blue
  sky is calm;   [grasp the palm.
O press ye ever onward, ye yet shall

3 How swiftly the light trav'leth, speeding
  on and on!   [not yet shone;
But there are worlds whose light on us has
"Behold I *quickly come*"—the great word
  standeth true—
As timeless as Eternity, He maketh all
  things new.   [birth;
4 Lo! nation after nation is travailing to
'Tis victory on victory over all the earth;
Behold, His knowledge spreadeth, even
  from pole to pole,   [roll.
And like a sea of glory far and wide shall
5 The en'my cometh in as an o'erwhelming
  flood,
But, as in Egypt old, our God doth see
  "THE BLOOD";
Work and pray pray and work the
  TRIUMPH marcheth on;
'Tis Christ's world, not a doom'd one; for
  Christ it shall be won.
6 Ye fainting faithless hearts, O why will ye
  despair?
Why will ye fail on Him to cast still all
  your care?
His covenant is seal'd, and every word
  He spake;
He cometh, yea, He cometh, the heavens
  and earth to shake.

155.   "THY KINGDOM COME."
St. Matthew vi. 10 (and cf. Numbers xiv. 21).

1   THANKS, O Lord Christ,
        For grace unpric'd,
    That tells us Thou dost not DESPAIR;
        Yea, Thanks, O Lord,
        For stable word
    Foreshadowing the great end clear;
Hadst Thou DESPAIR'ED of our world,
Thy flag of grace had long been furled.
2   O joy that still
         Events fulfil;
    Th' eternal purpose moving on;
        Man is froward;
        Things untoward;

ADVANCE. ORDINATION OF FOREIGN MISSIONARIES.

But still wrong after wrong o'erthrown;
Tho' men have deem'd Thy Truth imperill'd,
Thou hast despair'd not of our world.

3   Around I look
        And all unshook   [reigneth ;
    My faith that Thou the Lord Christ
        'Mid mazes lost,
        By errors tost
    Thou light for straying feet ordaineth ;
    However wildly, madly whirled,
    Thou hast despair'd not of our world.

4   Advance is slow ;
        Men seem to go   [sake ;
    As tho' Thee, Christ, they would for-
        But thy motion,
        Tided ocean,
    Shews ebb still wider flow doth take ;
    So, flood-tide comes, howe'er storm-curled;
    Thou hast despair'd not of our world.

5   O Lord Christ, chime
        The gladsome time   [Earth ;
    When Thy strong Hand shall rule the
        When Thy pure light
        Shall scatter night ;
    And fill all hearts with holy mirth ;
    The ancient throne of SIN down-hurled ;
    DESPAIR uplifted from our world.

6   Thanks, O Lord Christ,
        For grace unpric'd,
    That tells us Thou dost not DESPAIR ;
        Yea, thanks, O Lord,
        For stable word
    Foreshadowing the great end clear ;
    Hadst Thou DESPAIR'D of our world,
    Thy flag of grace had long been furled.

156. ADVANCE. *St. Matt. xxviii. 19-20, 7, 6.*

1 As star on star soft-gleameth
    With moonset in still eve ;
  So light on light forth-streameth
    Where'er we workers leave.

2 My heart, its vigil keeping,
    Sees thus Christ's word fulfill'd ;
  And knows His love unsleeping
    Shall conquer as He will'd.

3 The "sev'n stars" undecaying
    Still shine in His Right Hand ;
  And tho' it seems delaying
    His purpose fast doth stand.

4 Lo! Thus I catch a vision,
    Upon ten thousand shores ;
  Of mission after mission,
    And light of life down pours.

5 *Repeat St. 1.*

157. ORDINATION OF FOREIGN MISSIONARIES.

St. Matthew xxviii. 19-20 ; Psalms ii. 8. 8s.

1 SEE Thy servants, Lord, attending,
    Vow'd to pass to heathen Lands ;
  While their prayers Thy people blending,
    Place them in Thy mighty hands :
  Thou Who gav'st the great word "Go!"
    Dower it with Thine other "Lo!"

2 Lord, accept the dedication
    Of these lives, e'en as we pray ;
  And Thy Church's supplication,
    Answer, from this very day ;
  For fire of old sacrifice,
    Let Thy Spirit's light arise !

3 Through all toils and dangers guiding,
    Lord, on land and sea be near ;
  Day and night in Thee confiding,
    May our Faith Thy voice aye hear !
  Reaching their far goal at last,
    Find each promise has stood fast.

4 When midst heathen they have taken
    Posts of hazard and of care ;
  Never let their hearts be shaken !
    By Thy grace help them to dare ;
  Resting weakness on Thy strength,
    Assur'd that Thou wilt own at length.

5 For strange tongues that they must master,
  Lord, do Thou give patient skill ;
Nor let failure, or disaster,
  Ardour of their " first love " chill ;
Sow, and plant, may they work on,
'Neath Thy benediction.
6 *Repeat St. 1.*

158. THE MISSIONARIES AT SEA.
" We . . . do not cease to pray for you."
      Colossians i. 9. 8s.

1 LORD, teach Thy People still to pray,
For Thy dear servants on their way ;
Let their ships sailing o'er the sea,
From day to day remember'd be ;
  For Thine Almighty hand, directing ;
  For Thine Almighty heart, protecting.

2 When the good tidings have come home,
And they no longer onward roam ;
Grant still Thy People praying hearts,
And the strong faith, that nothing thwarts;
  That holding up Thy servants' hands,
  They may be bless'd in far-off Lands.

3 Lord, may Thy People ever feel,
How touching is the strong appeal
Of Thy brave servants out of sight,
Not to be left alone to fight ;
  But that, by thousand hearts sustain'd,
  They may go on from foot-holds gain'd.

4 Lord, may Thy People ever seek
To win for them all graces meek ;
Meek, but yet strong, that in their Eyes
Love may beam forth that never strives ;
  That they, like Thee, O Christ, may wait,
  Nor aught their patience alienate.

5 *Repeat St. 1.*

159.   MARTYRS OF OUR DAY.   7s.

1 Lo! The martyr-days return'd!
Men are tortur'd—mangled—burn'd ;
Heroes counting gain but loss
That they may lift high the CROSS —
Centre of all hope for men,
Mighty still in vilest den ;
As when on the Temple-steps
Peter preach'd—and none excepts;
Winning trophies wheresoe'er
FAITH and LOVE THE TRUTH declare ;
  Men and women still at ease,
  " Settle not upon your lees."

2 Far away 'mongst sunny seas —
Sunny as e'er Cyclades ;
On a mission of pure love,
One to win men's dark hearts strove :
PATTESON—the good and brave
Fills his Melanesian grave,
Lo! down-struck by treach'rous blow ;
Fallen, not for friend but foe ; —
Fell unarm'd and yet well-arm'd ;
Harmèd but ne'ertheless unharm'd :
  Saint of God, a nimbus thine,
  Thro' long years it bright shall shine.

3 Lo! The martyr-days return'd !
Men are tortur'd—mangled—burned;
In the vast " Dark Continent "
HANNINGTON, great-hearted, went ;
Girding on his thigh no sword
Save the bloodless-wounding WORD ;
Yet in midst of his strong prime
Wrought in him was such a crime
As Nyanza's waters stains
Redder than the blood of veins ;
  Mournful that so noble life
  Perish'd in ignoble strife!

4 Lo! The martyr-days return'd !
Men are tortur'd—mangled—burn'd ;
Not less noble, not less true
Of those who their Bishop slew ;
Converts by the sea-like Lake,
Who Christ's name on them did take—
In Masya and out-dar'd
His fate—as his faith they shar'd ;
Heroes, like in days of old ;
Long their story shall be told ;
  O the horrors of those pyres,
  Where each, mutilate, expires !

5 Lo! the martyr-days return'd!
Men are tortur'd—mangled—burn'd ;
What this lamentable cry

Loud re-sounding 'thwart the sky?
England mine, surcease thy mirth—
Is there God in all the Earth?
Not a cry from Atheist heart —
Scoffers of the baser sort;
But the sad moan at Christ's feet
While in PAUL's own Isle of Crete
   The immitigable Turk
   Now does his accursèd work

160.   THE JEWS.

Romans xi. 15-29 ; Colossians iii. 11.   6s.

1 How long, O Lord, how long,
  'Till Earth break forth in song!
  'Till Thine own Israel
  No longer shall rebel ;
  But contrite, and in shame,
  Call gladly on Thy Name.

2 Thou Who at Pentecost
  Sentest the Holy Ghost,
  And in Jerusalem
  Put in Thy diadem
  Of blood-stain'd souls the chief,
  Rebuke our unbelief.

3 Rend veil which hides the Lght,
  Help them to "read" aright ;
  O suff'ring Saviour shew,
  Yea, cause Thy Cross to glow ;
  Fulfilling their own Law,
  As seer and saint foresaw.

4 We plead Thy Covenant :
  Lord, our petition grant!
  We plead Thy promises ;
  Israel, Thine ancient, bless !
  Wake Abraham's seed; restore
  Thy " Chosen" yet once more.

5 Their Land long desolate
  Bring back to its old state;
  On holy Zion's hill
  Thy Gospel "dew" distil ;
  Making this mighty race
  Share Thy redeeming grace.

6 How glorious is their Past!
  Long have they been outcast ;
  O turn their hearts again !
  Revive as " latter rain " !
  The true Messiah Thou,
  Lead them to know Thee now.

7 Gentile and Jew unite,
  As Thou dost still invite ;
  That to the one Cross led,
  By Thy love conquered ;
  One holy Israel
  Own Thee Emmanuel.

161.   THE CHURCH AND SUNDAY SCHOOL.

Tune—The Queen's Anthem.

(Composed for the Jubilee of the Presbyterian Church of England, Blackburn, Lancashire, 18th June, 1878.) 6.6.4.6.6.6.4.

1 GOD keep our Church and School !
  Shed on them blessings full !
    Bless Church and School !
  Crown them from day to day ;
  All walking " In the way";
  All living as they pray ;
    Bless Church and School !

2 Fill with Thy Spirit's might,
  To know and do the right,
    And evil shun ;
  Here let each heart upraise,
  Sweet notes of prayer and praise,
  Bright'ning the Day of days :
    With Heav'n begun.

3 The PASTOR'S heart inspire
  God's Word to preach with fire—
    Loving and true ;
  ELDERS his hands up-bear
  Upon the Mount of Prayer ;
  And in the conflict share, —
    The crown in view.

4 MEMBERS ! Grant them to show
  That Christ indeed they know,
    And love their Lord ;

CHILDREN'S DEBT OF LOVE TO THEIR CHRISTIAN PARENTS.

  Let TEACHERS week by week,
  Truth from The Master seek,
  And with His patience speak —
   Scattering the Word.
5 CHILDREN of peace and light,
  Give each the robe of white,
   To wear for Thee!
  When each Lord's Day is done,
  May SCHOLARS, one by one,
  Be found to Jesus won
   This Jubilee!
6 Lord! Let Thy Gospel reign,
  And still fresh conquests gain,
   At home, abroad;
  Help us with heart and hand,
  To do Thy great command,
  Till souls in every Land,
   Welcome their God!
7 God keep our Church and School!
  Shed on them blessings full!
   Bless Church and School!
  To sow we will not cease;
  Give, Lord, the rich increase!
  Faith, holiness, and peace:
   Bless Church and School!

162. THE SUNDAY-SCHOOL TEACHER.
   Prov. xxii. 6.   8s.
1 AM I a teacher, O, my Lord,
  A teacher of Thy Holy Word?
  A teacher in the Sunday School?
  A teacher of the bright fresh soul?
   O may I then be taught of Thee,
   My Saviour, of Thy clemency.

2 Still in my class, O Lord, be found
  As Thy fair Sabbath Day comes round;
  And grant that, steeped in prayer, I may
  Each young heart still before Thee lay;
   Then teach as ever in Thy sight:
   Alluring them to truth and right.

3 Faith and "first love," dear Lord, impart;
  Yea, faith, that Thou dost change the
   In the first early-opening years; [heart;
  And scatter all my human fears.

  O Perfecter, as Author, Thou!
  Guard wilt the seed for Thee I sow?
4 The knowledge, Lord, that doth in-form
  Grant that it also may trans-form;
  Give Thou the light that brings a change,
  So that their hearts ne'er from Thee range,
  And, O my God, do Thou forbid
  My life be by my teaching chid.

163. SUNDAY SCHOOL TEACHER.   10s.
1 I WOULD not merely teach, I would
   inspire;   [hire!
  O Master, do Thou touch me with Thy
  Within my heart cause my fond love to
   glow,   [shew.
  Then all words of my lips Thy love shall
2 I would not merely teach, I would inspire;
  O for Thy early servants holy ire!
  Like unto Thine! my charge still to beseech,
  And hope — by grace — the "erring man"
   to reach.
3 I would not merely teach, I would inspire;
  Be mine to see, Lord, what Thou dost
   require;   [sin,
  Give me Thine Own deep insight into
  And all the tangling cobwebs it doth
   spin.
4 I would not merely teach, I would inspire;
  Set on "the Rock," when lifted from the
   mire;   [fill,
  O Christ! do Thou me with Thine ardour
  And grant that I it more and more instil.
5 I would not merely teach, I would inspire;
  Mine a great task of love and not of hire;
  Lord! stir me still to witness and to toil,
  Nor let e'en often thanklessness me foil.
6 *Repeat St. 1.*

164. CHILDREN'S DEBT OF LOVE TO
   THEIR CHRISTIAN PARENTS.
   (Autobiographical.)
"*Honour thy father and thy mother.*" —
   Exodus xx. 17.   7s.
1 FATHER! Greatest of great names,
  That our best affection claims;
  Mother! Sweetest of sweet words,

Touching our hearts' deepest chords ;
    Thanks, O Lord my God, that I
    Parents had, pass'd to the sky.
2 Praise still for a Christian home,
Into which Thou mad'st me come ;
Breathing atmosphere of prayer
That transfigured ev'ry care :
    Thanks, O Lord my God, that I
    Parents had, pass'd to the sky.
3 I remember all the way
That they "led" me day by day —
Guarding me in helpless years ;
Their love often mix'd with fears :
    Thanks, O Lord my God, that I
    Parents had, pass'd to the sky.
4 Wistful—watching mind's first dawn,
That my heart to Jesus drawn
By the Spirit from Above,
I might share their faith and love :
    Thanks, O Lord my God, that I
    Parents had, pass'd to the sky.
5 "Life of God" they did commend,
Yet they sweetly would unbend ;
Beauty of religion shewn—
Duty, not as law alone :
    Thanks, O Lord my God, that I
    Parents had, pass'd to the sky.
6 Grave—but pleasantly could smile ;
Stern—yet only unto guile ;
Kind—but not mere soft indulgence ;
Bright—fetch'd from His own effulgence :
    Thanks, O Lord my God that I
    Parents had, passed to the sky.
7 So they liv'd and so they died ;
More and more were sanctified ;
And to-day with sweet warm tears
Mem'ry still their voices hears :
    Thanks, O Lord my God, that I
    Parents had, passed to the sky.

165. Parents Debt of Love to Children.
2 Corinthians, xii. 14 ; Colossians iii. 21
7s.

1 Father ! reigning o'er the House !
Mother ! Queen ! yea, Christ's own spouse;
Firm, yet gentle, be your sway,
Seeking guidance when you pray;
Then the gifts you ask will come,
Yours shall be a Christian home.
2 Home ! "how dreadful is this place !"
Saving for God's guardian grace ;
Little ones, when He doth send,
Laying them on us to tend ;
But the covenant is sure,
And His benison secure.
3 Parents ! Well may you feel awe
'Fore the charge ye on you draw ;
Your own flesh and your own blood
To be train'd for ill or good ;
Plead "the promises," and call
Unto Him that knoweth all.
4 That full soon each tender heart
Free, may choose "the better part" ;
That full soon His Holy Word
Light may to young feet afford ;
That full soon the power they prove
That belongs to Faith and Love.
5 As the years shall onward sweep,
Parents, still self-vigil keep ;
That nor word, nor look, nor act,
Other be than shall attract,
To a Christ-like life, and holy,
Brave and strong and true, yet lowly.
Repeat St. 1.

166. Prayer Meeting "Two or Three." *St. Matt. xviii. 20.* 7s.

1 Lord, we bless Thee who dost greet
Thine Own People when they meet ;
Thy great word abiding true,
I am in the midst of you ;
Thou art faithful, Lord, we see,
Tho' 'tis but to "two or three."
2 We would meet, Lord, in Thy Name ;
Touch us with Thy Spirit's flame ;
That upon this quiet eve
Blessings full we may receive ;
Thou art faithful, Lord, we see,
Tho' 'tis but to "two or three."

76   THE MID-WEEK SERVICE—MARRIAGE "IN THE LORD."

3 Lord, we know our faith is weak ;
  Firmer, deeper faith, we seek ;
  And our hope too often pales ;
  Lord, give light when darkness veils ;
    Thou art faithful, Lord, we see,
    Tho' 't is but to "two or three."

4 Fill us with intense desire ;
  Largest askings, Lord, inspire ;
  Fill us with Thine Own vast love,
  That compassion in us move ;
    Thou art faithful, Lord, we see,
    Tho' 'tis but to "two or three."

5 Here in hour of mid-week prayer,
  We to Thee, Lord, would repair ;
  Be we many, be we few,
  Still Thou wilt Thy grace renew ;
    Thou art faithful, Lord, we see,
    Tho' 'tis but to "two or three."

167.   THE MID-WEEK SERVICE.
   Acts of the Apostles xvi. 13.   8.8.8.8.7.7.

1 LORD, at our mid-week service met,
  Do Thou in each of us beget
  The prayer of faith, the word of grace,
  That shall intrusive cares displace ;
    Look back upon the Sabbath past,
    And every coming one forecast.

2 We thank Thee, Lord, that thus we may
  Together meet to praise and pray,
  And from Thy blest Book speak and hear,
  With a sweet sense that Thou art near ;
    Look back upon the Sabbath past,
    And every coming one forecast.

3 Thus Thou hast own'd the "two or three,"
  Ev'n as Thou promised'st should be :
  Increase the numbers, Lord, who seek
  Sabbatic brightness all the week ;
    Look back upon the Sabbath past,
    And every coming one forecast.

4 Fill with a restful love our hearts,
  Born of the peace "the blood" imparts ;
  That of Thy Holy Spirit kept

  We may not from "the Way" be swept ;
    Look back upon the Sabbath past,
    And every coming one forecast.

168.   SUNDAY SCHOOL ANNIVERSARY.   7s.
   St. John xxi. 15.

1 "FEED My Lambs!" O golden word!
  That sweet warrant doth afford;
  Claiming all the good and wise,
  And all aid that in us lies;
  That with fire-touch'd heart and tongue,
  We may strive to win the young.

2 "Feed My Lambs!" Behold to-day,
  Jesus Lord, this fair array!
  Boys and girls their voices raise,
  And Thee as their Saviour praise;
  Their one hope The Crucified,
  Who in love for them has died.

3 "Feed My Lambs!" Another Year
  Lord, we close in holy fear;
  Grateful that us Thou hast spar'd;
  Grateful for all truth declar'd;
  Grateful for persuasive call;
  Grateful for our Festival.

4 "Feed My Lambs!" Lord, we have striv'n
  By Thy Word unto us giv'n;
  Day by day to guide their feet
  Where Good Shepherd Thou dost greet;
  Feeding them with "bread of life";
  Guarding them in Sin's sore strife.

5 "Feed My Lambs!" O Holy Ghost!
  We have nothing now to boast ;
  Yet we ask that Thou would'st own
  What in Christ's name we have done;
  Our whole School anoint this day,
  And all, bless'd, send on their way.

169.   MARRIAGE "IN THE LORD."   6s.

1 O LOVE that is a prayer!
  And O Prayer that is love !
  Strong 'gainst all foes soe'er,
  Lifting two hearts Above;
  Two hearts made one in Him

MARRIAGE.

    The Cross their dwelling-place;
    Light that no shadows dim;
    And all, the gifts of grace.

2 Praise to the grace of God!
    To God of grace all praise!
    Like to the prophet's rod,
      "Beauty" and "Bands" embrace;
    One cloud of incense sweet;
      One blending hymn, one flame;
    O Lord, lo, at Thy feet
      We magnify Thy Name.

3 Thro' years of wedded life
    Thou, Lord, hast kept us still;
    Behind the great world's strife,
      Thy 'peace' our hearts doth fill;
    For us and ours, dear Lord,
      Thy Word abideth true;
    With gratitude outpour'd,
      We would our vows renew.

4 O gracious unity!
    Two lives of God made one;
    Tender benignity
      Of holy fusion;
    Still, blessèd Jesus give,
      Our Home this 'peace' to shew;
    By Thy prerogative
      More and more love bestow.

170. MARRIAGE. *"Marriage is honourable in all."* Heb. xiii. 4.   8s.

1 Lo! Marriage came to Earth from Heaven,
    Before by sin the Earth was riven:
    O Father, 'twas by Thy love given.

2 Beholding man in loneliness,
    Thou, cov'nant-Lord, Thou fain would'st
    Eve bringing in her loveliness.   [bless;

3 The round Earth Thou didst give for dower,
    And didst on them rich blessings shower;
    Transfiguring their bridal bower.

4 Alas! They sinn'd! alas! they fell;
    Against Thy Law they did rebel;
    Their birthright for a trifle sell.

5 For them Thy heart of love did bleed;
    For them Thyself did'st intercede;
    Hope kindling by "the Woman's Seed."

6 The Law's curse falls on all men born,
    The race come into life forlorn;
    But Faith sees roses 'bove the thorn.

7 In fulness of the time appointed;
    When the world was all disjointed;
    Came our Saviour, "The Anointed."

8 He also holy Marriage blest;
    Went unto Cana as a guest;
    At once a Friend and minist'ring Priest.

9 He blessing gave upon the wine,
    Transmuting it to mystic sign
    By His beatitude divine.

10 And He by many a gracious word,
    Our hearts in every chord hath stirred;
    As Love's own whispers we have heard.

11 Is marriage hon'rable in all?
    He honours the sweet festival;
    And bids His blessing on it fall.

12 O gracious Saviour, from Thy Throne,
    Wilt Thou not now this marriage own?
    And with all purest blessings crown.

171. MARRIAGE. Heb. xiii. 4.   8.7.8.7.7.7.

1 BLESS, Lord, this new-wedded pair,
    With Thy purest, with Thy fairest;
    Hear our praise and hear our prayer,
      Give Thy sweetest, give Thy rarest;
    By Law of the Land made one,
    Seal Thou deeper union.

2 May the just-plac'd ring of gold,
    Symbol be of love unending;
    And the onward years unfold,
      Earthly life and heav'nly blending:
    Yea grant, Lord, that from this hour
    Thine may be the richer dower.

3 Forward into life they go;
    Clear to Thee— to them unknown;
    Come what will, may they still know,

MARRIAGE—BAPTISM OF CHILDREN.

That Thou ne'er forsak'st Thine Own;
Light and shadow sanctify;
Keep them living for the sky.

4 Let their plighted troth be true,
All in all the one to other;
On their home shed nurturing dew;
Early make them father, mother;
Thou the "Family" hast "set,"
Nor Thy promise dost forget.

5 Bless, Lord, this new-wedded pair,
With Thy purest, with Thy fairest;
Hear our praise and hear our prayer,
Give Thy sweetest, give Thy rarest;
By Law of the Land made one,
Seal Thou deeper union.

172. MARRIAGE. 6s.

1 Body and Soul make one,
Dissolv'd by God alone:
So MARRIAGE "in the Lord"
Is close as thought and word.
'Tis two lives interblending,
Nor ends till either's ending;
The Lord praise for this bliss,
Seal'd by first nuptial kiss.

2 O God, Thou by Love's art,
Heart bringeth near to heart,
Thou kindlest from Above,
The pure flame of first love;
Thou our web of life weavest,
With us joyest and grievest;
The Lord praise for this bliss,
Seal'd by first nuptial kiss.

3 Sacred the tie that binds;
That two hearts as one joins;
Deep symbol of Thy tryst
With Thy Church, O Lord Christ!
That Thy Bride is appointed,
With blessings full anointed.
The Lord praise for this bliss,
Seal'd by first nuptial kiss.

4 O Lord! wilt Thou now bless,
This pair, as their hands press!
May they from this bright hour
From Thee win gracious dower!
Joys double, and halve sorrows,
Till Age's snow each borrows:
The Lord praise for this bliss,
Seal'd by first nuptial kiss.

173. BAPTISM OF CHILDREN. 7s.

Acts of the Apostles iii. 25; St. Matthew xix. 14.

1 LORD, this child to Thee we bring:
Thine Own rite administ'ring;
Lift Thou now on us Thy Face;
Grant Thy purifying grace.

2 Lord, Thou seest Thy "little one":
Give Thou benediction!
Ah! Sin lieth in its soul;
Touch the child, and make it whole.

3 Lord, we look beyond the rite;
Walk by faith, and not by sight;
Thou alone giv'st the "new birth";
'Tis of Heaven, not of Earth.

4 But, Lord, Thou hast thro' the sign
Giv'n the blessing unto Thine;
O that it may be so now!
Answ'ring pray'r, accepting vow.

5 If it please Thee, spare the child,
Still to grow up undefil'd;
And on reaching years of sense
Grant divine intelligence.

6 That paternal vows made known,
He may make them all his own;
And may take Thee at Thy word,
And himself Thy son record.

Repeat St. 1.

BAPTISM.

174. BAPTISM. *"These little ones."*
  St. Matthew xviii. 10. 8s.

1 "THESE little ones": Ah! each Thou knewest;
  "These little ones": on each bestowest
  From the first dawning of their life
  Thy benediction, ere the strife.

2 "These little ones": O tender word!
  Falling like music from their Lord;
  We therefore bring them now to Thee,
  That of Thy Church they entered be.

3 "These little ones": ta'en from the crowd,
  Boasting no high descent, or proud;
  Them Thou received'st Lord, and Thou,
  Unchanging, dost receive these now.

4 "These little ones" Thou'lt not o'erlook;
  "These little ones"—all in Thy Book;
  Behold us, then, with heart of faith,
  Now seeking, Lord, Thy heav'nly breath.

5 "These little ones": in "narrow way"
  Keep them, O Jesus! day by day;
  And as they grow in years attest
  That in their BAPTISM they were blest.

175. THE FIRST CRADLE OF THE FIRST-BORN.
  7s.

1 SAFE-DEFENDED from all harms
  Lo! The babe in mother's arms!
  By God's own great hands there laid,
  LIVING CRADLE by God made;
  Innocent and sweet the rest,
  Taken in that fragrant nest!

2 Come to us 'mid hush of fears
  Gladness sprinkled o'er with tears;
  Life imperill'd by life giv'n,
  But o'erwatched of kind Heav'n;
  Lord! Thou didst Thy Word fulfil,
  Working tenderly Thy will.

3 Lo! upon that blissful morn
  Thou bestowedst our FIRST-BORN;
  Husband, wife, all to each other;

  Ah! but now 'twas father, mother;
  Making holy sacrament,
  By which our two lives were blent.

4 O deep mystery of being,
  Far beyond our human seeing;
  God's gift of a little child,
  Laid on bosom undefiled;
  Heavenly and earthly meet,—
  Than the meeting naught more sweet.

5 Soft Love's kiss: 'twas almost holy—
  As with stooped knee, and lowly,
  Our two hearts op'd pent-up flood,
  Whisp'ring of our gratitude;
  Gazing still upon OUR child,
  With a gravity that smil'd.

6 Safe-defended from all harms
  Lo! the babe in mother's arms!
  By God's own great hands there laid,
  LIVING CRADLE by God made;
  O how sweet the innocent rest
  Taken in that fragrant nest.

176. BAPTISM.
  Acts ii. 39; Romans iv. 13. 7s.

1 As this BABE unconscious lies
  Lord! we place him 'neath Thine eyes;
  By Thy Covenant of old
  As Thy 'seed' be he enroll'd;
  By great words of Pentecost
  Spoken to throngs anguish-tost;
  We, Lord Christ, make our appeal,
  That the ordinance Thou seal.

2 O Lord! Thou hast made the soul;
  All its springs Thou dost control;
  Wilt Thou look upon this child,
  Thou of all, THE UNDEFIL'D?
  Wilt Thou for Th'ne Own Name's sake,
  Him unto Thy keeping take?
  Touch him with Thy thrice-pure touch,
  And as Thy child him avouch.

3 What's to come to us is veil'd ;
   Safely kept, or if assail'd,
   Lord! Be Thou to him still near ;
   Then for him we will not fear ;
   Early win his heart to Thee,
   In Thy "glorious liberty";
   Build him up in Faith and Love,
   That he ne'er from Thee remove.

4 If Thou sparest him, O Lord !
   Hear us as we plead Thy word ;
   May he grow to be a MAN
   Men will bless and never ban!
   May he useful be, and kind,
   To all those who walk as blind !
   Still may he exemplify
   That he travels to the sky.

177. REMINISCENCES OF BAPTISM. 7s.
"*As a little child.*"—*St. Mark x. 15.*

1 WHEN I was a little child,
   Thou, O Lord, upon me smil'd;
   Giv'n to Thee with praise and prayer ;
   Entered of life, an heir;
   Water sprinkled on my brow
   Sealing true parental vow.

2 Ever since, Thou hast me kept
   As the years have onward swept;
   Bright'ning joys and hushing fears;
   Like a sunbeam drying tears;
   Leading me still on and on
   In sweet benediction.

3 Now grey hairs are on my head,—
   Age's snow-flakes on me shed ;
   But Thou spakest Thy " Except,'
   To grown men—and I accept;
   I am prone to be beguil'd,
   Make me as Thy "little child."

4 Let my heart, dear Lord, be young ;
   Thine Own joy upon my tongue ;
   Hold me in Thy sweet control,
   Granting childhood of the soul;
   As when child I went to sleep,
   Giving Thee my soul to keep.

5 And since my life's setting sun
   Has its westering course begun;
   At even-tide be it bright,
   White as Thine Own spotless white;
   Child-like as on mother's breast,
   Grant me Thine ETERNAL REST.

178. SHILOH. (*Composed under a large terebinth tree there.*) *Jer. vii. 12-14.*
(*cf. Joshua xviii. 1.* 6s.

1 'Tis even so, O Lord !
   Fulfill'd Thine awful word ;
   For as we come to see,
   Lo ! as in Thy decree,
   SHILOH—once holy shrine,
   Chief dwelling place of Thine,
   In foulest ruin lies—
   Like corpse that putrifies.

2 A broken arch and wall
   Slow-crumbling to its fall;
   Heaps upon heaps of stones,
   Ghastly as fleshless bones ;
   These all that now remain
   On this forsaken plain ;
   Thy glory, Shiloh, gone,
   The dread word of God done.

3 But e'er this ruin came
   Here thou hadst set THY NAME;
   Ne'er shall it be forgot ;
   Time ne'er the record blot ;
   Here Eli as God's priest,
   Fulfill'd his office blest ;
   And Hannah Samuel brought,
   Wearing his "little coat."

4 I look from plain to hill,
   All beautiful and still ;
   I look from earth to sky,
   Know Thou my God art nigh ;
   Yet, Lord, I awéd stand
   'Fore these strokes of Thy Hand.
   Speaks Shiloh to my heart
   From all sin to depart.

THE CHURCH ASLEEP—SAINTS.

179. THE CHURCH ASLEEP. 8s.

Isaiah lii. 1-2.

1 CHURCH of the LIVING CHRIST awake!
Thy slumb'ring languor from thee shake;
Thy crownèd Lord may soon be here;
Before Him how shalt Thou appear?
What hast thou with His CHARTER done?
His world, blood-ransom'd, still unwon.

2 Church of the LIVING CHRIST awake!
His promise vast on thy lips take;
His COVENANT, lo! still stands fast,
Faithful to-day as in far Past;
His Word has all its ancient power,
Made mighty by The Spirit's dower.

3 Church of the LIVING CHRIST awake!
Thy courage, let no foemen quake;
Plead and replead upon thy knees,
With the puissant faith that sees;
Put forth thy strength, and dare to win
Christ's victory over every sin.

4 Church of the LIVING CHRIST awake!
Earth's darkest places shining make;
Sound out the BROKEN HEART'S greatery—
"Turn ye, turn ye, why will ye die?"
Lengthen thy cords, strengthen thy stakes,
Till the one Gospel all hearts shakes.

5 Church of the LIVING CHRIST awake!
Hold fast thy plea "For His Name's sake";
Then rich art and increas'd in goods;
Not drops of blessing but full floods;
All that thou art, all that thou hast,
Be lowly at His pierc'd feet cast.

6 Church of the LIVING CHRIST awake!
Amidst no ancient "rubbish" rake;
Line apostolical to find
By which thee to "The Twelve" to bind;
Christ lives, Christ cries "Come unto Me,"
There lie thy life and pedigree.

180. ONE. *Deut. xv. 7; St. Luke, xv. 2-7; St. Matt. xviii. 10.* 7s.

1 As I read Thy Holy Word,
Saviour mine, in sweet accord
Comes the OLD and comes the NEW,
Bringing still in tender view,
How Thou dost o'er even "one"
Graciously speak Thy "Well done."

2 In the ancient wondrous story
That points out the way to glory,
Oft and oft we read of 'one'
In sweetest repetition;
Giving token that Thine eye
Least, lowliest doth desery.

3 Most of all in Gospel page,
Thou dost all our fears assuage;
There we see what Thou hast done
By Thy triumph on Cross won;
Ah! Thou tell'st of 'one' lost sheep;
Gladd'ning us e'en as we weep.

4 For Thou dost unveil the sky;
Showest what takes place on High;
How the finding 'one' lost sheep--
Lost on wild or mountain steep;
Adds to blessedness of Heav'n—
A great glad shout o'er it giv'n.

5 O my soul, bless Thou the Lord,
For the tender mighty word
Of a human heart relenting;
That 'one' sinner late repenting,
Moves to joy angels of God:
God Himself in His abode.

181. SAINTS. 8s.

(*After reading Newman's and Baring-Gould's "Lives of the Saints."*)

1 SAINTLY successors of the saints,
My heart fails and my spirit faints;
While pondering your Christ-like lives—
The LOVE that burns—the FAITH that strives;
Yet why should I, or faint or fail?
Or suffer doubt me to assail?

Why should I go with down-cast face,
When I may draw on the same grace?
"My Lord, my God," open my eyes
That I may know Thy full supplies.

2 Hast Thou not said—our fears to fray—
"Unchang'd am I from day to day";
Thy Cov'nant sure—Thy Promise fast,
In living PRESENT as in PAST;
Lord! Do Thou quicken me, that I
May "walk" with Thee confidingly;
Like to those saints of old abide
In joy near to Thy wounded side;
  Thy Spirit give that still I may [WAY,"
  Find Thee "the LIFE, the TRUTH, the

3 Saintly successors of the saints,
I envy ev'n your sighs and plaints;
Your broken prayers—your vigils sharp;
Your fastings—ay, tho' many carp;
Your fearless contact with the vile;
Your faith in the soft word and smile;
Lord Christ! Tho' cruel World doth rail
Give their invulnerable mail;
Yea give me Lord—like them—to glow
With the same love that Thou didst shew.

4 It may be these sad saints mistook
Their Church's dicta for Thy Book;
It may be that themselves they griev'd
When Thou of all cause hadst reliev'd;
It may be that they oft forgot
How Thy shed blood all sin doth blot;
It may be that they left unread
Thy great cry "It is Finished";
Yet Thou wast in them—they in Thee,
In gracious captivity.

5 *Repeat St.* 1.

182.   MORE SAINTS.   6s.

"*It is because we have so few high saints
among us that we have so many low sinners.*"
—*Hooker.*

1 O CHRIST, give us more saints!
Thy Church, yea the Earth, faints;
For more, still more true men
By whom blindest shall ken,

That ev'n in this late day
Thou dost lead "in the Way";
Expell'd all that taints,
Clear seen there still *are* saints.

2 Thanks Lord, for the strong brain
That highest heights doth gain;
Thanks Lord, for burning heart
Deed-doer beyond all art;
Thanks for all fullest learning,
Still richer guerdons earning;
But more—Christ, hear our plaints!—
Holy men—give us saints.

3 O Christ, give us more saints
That Earth with Heav'n acquaints;
Lowliest lowliness;
Beauty of holiness;
Serene and purified,
Like Thee THE CRUCIFIED;
Such as St. John's pen paints:
O Christ, give us more saints.

4 The many read not books,
Obtusest know saints' looks;
Controversy abstruse,
To few only of use;
But holy simple lives,
Strong by the strength LOVE gives;
These break thro' all restraints;
O Christ, give us more saints.

5 Aye faithful to the Cross;
Still counting gain but loss;
Still seeking brotherhood
By ever doing good;
By grace from Heav'n sent,
Spending and being spent;
O Christ, give us more saints!
The Church, yea the Earth faints.

183. THE HARVEST OF LIGHT. *Ps. xcvii. 11.*
      8.8.8.6.8.6.

1 SERVANTS, Lord, forth in faith we go,
With our hands full, Thy seed to sow;
Longing to hear Thy Spirit blow
  In a Revival NOW;
"*Light is sown*": O Christ Thou dost know,
  When will the Harvest show?

2 Hungry souls that for Thy Bread pine ;
Darkened souls that yearn Thou wouldst
  shine !
Weary souls that fain would recline ;
  Lord ! Thou seest them all ;
Lo ! Thy promises we combine ;
  Before Thy Throne we fall.

3 Long, long, alas ! doth EVIL last ;
Deathless souls in sin's bonds fast ;
And to Eternity they haste ;
  How long, how long, O Lord !
Shall we of "hope deferr'd" still taste ?
  O speak Thou the word!

4 O Christ ! To Thee we make appeal,
Thick clouds Thy kingdom now conceal ;
Send forth Thy light, Thy power reveal ;
  Lord ! Thy servants own !
Let Thy voice now like trumpet peal ;
  Raise the light long sown!

184. THE CROSS OF CHRIST. *Gal. vi. 14.*
8.7.8.7.7.7.

1 Lift it ! lift it ! lift it upward ;
Let the Cross assert its power ;
Lift it ! lift it ! lift it sunward—
'Tis the World's supremest dower,
And a thing of shame no more.

2 Lift it ! lift it ! lift it upward,   [spear;
Blood-drops, thorn-crown, nails, and
Lift it ! lift it ! lift it sunward –
Things of glory now they are,
Earth exults and Hell's in fear.

3 Lift it ! lift it ! lift it upward,
Out of darkness into light ;
Lift it ! lift it ! lift it sunward -
'Tis a banner in the fight,
Charge to triumph ; Satan smite.

4 Lift it ! lift it ! lift it upward ;
See THE CHRIST THE CRUCIFIED ;
Lift it ! lift it ! lift it sunward -
We shall live for He has died ;
No hope save the Cross beside.

5 Lift it ! lift it ! lift it upward ;
Angels to behold stoop down ;
Lift it ! lift it ! lift it sunward –
Let it win its grand renown ;
Jewels bringing to His crown.

6 Lift it ! lift it ! lift it upward ;
Shame is now by SHAME asham'd ;
Lift it ! lift it ! lift it sunward—
CURSE is now by CURSE defam'd ;
Life by death is now reclaim'd.

7 Lift it ! lift it ! lift it upward ;
Lo ! the Cross all foes confounds ;
Lift it ! lift it ! lift it sunward—
Grace to guilty man abounds,
"Good news" through the Earth
  resounds.

8 *Repeat St. 1.*

185. THE CROSS. *Col. i. 20 ; ii. 14.* 7s.

1 ONCE a thing of woe and shame,
Lo, the Cross now towers sublime !
Gath'ring lustre to its name,
  In the onward march of TIME ;
Rais'd 'twixt malefactors twain,
  "*In the place call'd Calvary*";
Who may gauge the deep disdain
  Of men's vengeful mockery ?

2 Thorns—but grapes upon them blush ;
Gall—yet sweeter far than honey ;
Thirst—and "living waters" gush ;
Poor—but rich beyond all money ;
Helpless, all, in hands and feet,
  Yet saves one the lion's prey ;
Terrible – but oh, how sweet !
  Darkness—and yet clearest DAY.

3 Branded - and thrice glorious ;
Naked—yet the " white robe " weaves ;
Conquered—and victorious ;
Weak—yet the vast world upheaves ;
Dead—and yet the source of life ;
Woe - but symbol of all bliss ;
Peace— and centre of all strife ;
Was e'er paradox like this ?

4 Sin's last trophy—and defeat ;
   Wrath—and heart of love reveals ;
   Law upheld—yet pardon meet ;
   JUSTICE, MERCY, it unseals ;
   Man condemned—and yet acquitted ;
   Fix'd—yet round it all revolves ;
   " Bitter tree "—where WHITE DOVE
      flitted ;
   Mystery—and all mystery solves.

5. Cross of Christ ! in thee I boast,
   Bearing high THE CRUCIFIED ;
   And my heart when anguish-tost
   Finds peace only by thy side ;
   Hold it up, ye men of God,
   Earth's heart aches for your good news ;
   Tell it out at home, abroad,
   Bid, accept it or refuse.

6. Mighty conquests of the past
   Shadow mightier to come ;
   The Lord's promise standeth fast,
   Drawing countless myriads home ;
   Once a thing of woe and shame,
   Lo ! the Cross now stands sublime ;
   Gath'ring lustre to its name,
   In the onward march of TIME.

186. THE UPLIFTED REDEEMER. *St. John, xii. 32.* 8s.

1 " If I from earth be lifted up,"
   I, all men unto me shall draw ;
   O Jesus ! thou did'st drink " the cup,"
   Mix'd deadlier than man e'er saw ;
   Betwixt the darkened earth and sky,
   Thy Cross on ghastly Calv'ry rose ;
   And there in complex agony
      Thou did'st endure our utmost woes ;
      Thou there, our SUBSTITUTE, did'st
         die,
         My soul, catch thence His thrilling
            cry.

2 Thou Cross of ever-glorious shame,
   I turn my wistful eyes to Thee ;
   Dark bearer of man's guiltiest blame,
   Thy mystery Thou mak'st me see ;
   To the great vision of my FAITH, [head;
   Bright light doth shine around Thy
   For in Thee ev'ry word He saith,
      Lo ! firmly is establishèd :
      The work is done—life given for
         death,
         Sing, my glad soul, the Cross
            beneath.

3 O Jesus ! Thy all-drawing power
   Wilt Thou to us here manifest ?
   Wilt us with Thy " free Spirit " dower ?
   Full filling us with Thy deep rest ;
   Forbid that even one should be
   Drawn to Thee only for his doom ;
   O give Thy " glorious liberty,"
   And pass us all to light from gloom ;
      Put Thou, Lord, on Thy strength,
         that we
         Rejoice in blest captivity.

4 O Saviour ! over all the world,   [men !
   How doth Thy love still " draw " all
   How long until from its throne hurl'd
   Shall SIN surcease its ruthless reign !
   Two mighty hosts are marching on,
   The Christ-redeem'd and the self-lost ;
   But all before Thy Great White Throne
   One day as Judge shall Thee accost :
      The great blood-purchas'd triumph
         won,
         Or " lost ! lost ! lost ! "—and all
            undone.

187. THE GOOD FIGHT OF FAITH. *1 Timothy iv. 12.* 8s.

1 Shout, ye believers, shout aloud,
   The en'my comes in like a flood ;
   But banner for the truth display ;
   Be brave—be strong—you'll win the day.

2 Ev'n as Jericho's walls fell down,
   Lo ! the Lord Christ, your faith will own ;
   Weak-seeming tho' your weapons be,
   Wield them in Him and wonders see.

3. *Repeat St. 1.*

4 The sky is dark, the earth is drear,
Beats in your hearts a pulse of fear ;
Above the earth, above the sky,
Jesus still lives and still is nigh.

5 *Repeat St. 1.*

4 " *He that sits in the Heav'ns doth laugh,*'
Foes plotting He scatt'reth as chaff ;
Fight on—advance—ye cannot fail,
Yours is invulnerable mail.

7. *Repeat St. 1.*

188.   ERROR.

They accuse me sometimes of treating with too much indulgence and gentlensss those who have not faith. When one has passed through the sufferings of doubt, one would feel it a crime to treat haughtily those unhappy ones to whom God has not yet granted the grace of believing.— Frederick Ozanam (" *Letters*" *by Coates, 1886). S. James v. 20. 8s.*

1 To ERROR, Lord, I would be just,
As I, in Thee, my Saviour trust ;
From terrorizing, Lord, me free,
Thy "gentleness" make me to see :
Terror—from Hell not Heaven sent,
Self-righteous bigot's instrument.

2 Teach me, my Lord, patient to wait,
Nor constant pity to abate ;
Speaking from wistful heart of love,
Words merciful from Thee above ;
Steeped in unceasing dews of prayer,
And never knowing to despair.

3 To Error, Lord, I would be just,
As I, in Thee, my Saviour trust ;
I would, O Lord, hope against hope,
Made strong by Thee with worst to cope ;
Still seeing in heart unrenew'd
What mine once was—humbly review'd.

4 Alas Lord ! pride of intellect
Thy truth with passion doth reject ;
Wilt Thou by Thy will-conqu'ring DOVE
Help me to conquer by Thy love ?
Still telling how Thou dost impart
The life-blood of Thy broken heart.

5 To Error, Lord, I would be just,
As I, in Thee, my Saviour trust ;
O give me yearning, souls to win
From thing so terrible as sin ;
Help me to trace blind ignorance
Full oft to evil circumstance.

189.   NOT PEACE, BUT TRUTH. *William Chillingworth. St. Matt. x. 34 ; St. Luke xii. 49. 6s.*

1 " Not peace, but truth," my soul,
As thy life-work is done ;
" Not peace, but truth," my soul,
If palm is to be won ;
Truth is of heav'nly birth,
And ring'd with foes on earth.

2 " Not peace, but truth," my soul,
Christ came to send a sword ;
" Not peace, but truth," my soul,
Search Thou His shining Word ;
Contend Thou for " the faith,"
All built upon, " He saith."

3 " Not peace, but truth," my soul ;
Buy truth and sell it not ;
" Not peace, but truth," my soul,
Ne'er let this be forgot ;
Christ, "Way and TRUTH and Life,
Leads in a noble strife.

4 " Not peace, but truth," my soul,
" Christ and Thee crucified ; "
" Not peace, but truth," my soul,
Where truth is still denied ;
Be Thou a child of light ;
Error with brave heart smite.

5 " Not peace, but truth," my soul ;
Peace gain'd thro' lies deceives ;
" Not peace, but truth," my soul ;

Vain all else that relieves ;
The cross the world's one "peace,"
There only is pure ease.

6 "Not peace, but truth," my soul ;
   Truth by the "shed blood" bought ;
   "Not peace, but truth," my soul ;
   By God the Spirit wrought ;
   Truth first that can't be shook,
   Then may'st thou for peace look.

7 "Not peace, but truth," my soul ;
   Tho' peace be as a pearl ;
   "Not peace, but truth," my soul,
   Truth fairer than fair girl ;
   Seek peace and still pursue it
   Thro' truth—or thou shalt rue it.

190.   CREEDS.   *St. Matt. x. 32.*   8s.

1 O God, widen our human CREEDS,
   To fit them for our present needs ;
   Lord ! give Thy Church anointed eyes
   To see Thee LIVING in the skies ;
   Whilst all things onward, upward move,
   Directed by INCARNATE LOVE.

2 Directed by Incarnate Love :
   Clear-witness'd by the Holy Dove ;
   That in the mighty nail-pierced HANDS
   The truth of God safe-guarded stands ;
   Nor needeth sword or symbol look
   Lest His redeemed Church be shook.

3 Lest His redeemed Church be shook,
   Or heresies, or enemies brook ;
   O Christ, 'tis as if Thou wast dead,
   Thy Word of Thee abandoned ;
   To mark men's blank despair and terror
   Before the vaunts of wilder'd Error.

4 Before the vaunts of wilder'd Error ;
   Of tir'd brains and hearts the mirror ;
   These mummied dogmas that distract,
   O God, wilt Thou not break the pact
   That binds the living to the dead
   Mistrustful, even with Thy Blood shed ?

5 Mistrustful, even with Thy Blood shed,
   That Heav'n and Hell astonied ;
   Narrowing Thy love earth-wide—
   For all, life by THE CRUCIFIED ;
   Height—depth—breadth of revelation
   Darken'd by men's limitation.

6 Darken'd by men's limitation ;
   Blind to the "so *great* salvation ;"
   The mystery of godliness,
   "God manifest in flesh," to bless ;
   The problem of Law and Love wrought,
   Redemption for the world blood-bought.

7 Redemption for the world blood-bought ;
   Redeem'd all who redemption sought,
   Not one lost but who chooses loss ;
   Safety for ALL at the one Cross ;
   The light that lighteth ev'ry man,
   Guiding still upward by Love's plan.

8 Guiding still upward by Love's plan :
   The one hope, or men bless or ban ;
   O Christ ! save the Spirit-taught soul
   From terror of the Bigot's scowl,
   Help each, help all, to turn to Thee,
   By thy "glorious liberty."

9 *Repeat St. 1.*

191.   ON LAYING THE FOUNDATION STONE
           OF A CHURCH.   8s.
   Ps. v. 7, lv. 14, Zech. iv. 9.

1 WE bless Thee Lord on this glad day
   As in Thy Name this STONE we lay ;
   A House of God we mean to build ;
   Lord ! With THY GLORY to be fill'd !

2 We ask Thee, Lord, that from this hour,
   Safe-guarded by Thy gracious power ;
   The walls from floor to roof may rise,
   To shine with light above the skies.

3 If the Lord will, may we be spar'd
   To see the Church complete prepar'd ;
   And joyous crowds upon Thee wait
   As, Lord, Thy House we dedicate.

4 Be our first entrance sanctified.
  By "lifting up" THE CRUCIFIED;
  With "certain sound" the trumpet blow,
  And "*none but Jesus*" ever know.

5 Glory to Father and to Son,
  And Holy Spirit—great Tri-une;
  Christ-Jesus, our chief corner-stone,
  And one alone FOUNDATION.

192. OPENING AND DEDICATION OF A CHURCH. 8s.

Ps. cxviii. 19, cxvii. 1.

1 IN FAITH and HOPE we plac'd the STONE
  Our House of God is built upon;
  And now beneath its roof we stand,
  Adoring Thy safe-guarding HAND.

2 Wide open be the doors to all,
  Who list to hear the Saviour's call;
  As with one heart unite us here
  On this first Sabbath we draw near.

3 Enthroned High-priest hear our prayer
  When unto Thee our needs we bear;
  Thy blood-bought gifts on us bestow,
  And cause our hearts within us glow.

4 May FAITH here lean upon its staff;
  HOPE, cup of consolation quaff;
  May LOVE here find the 'Broken Heart';
  And may PEACE sing by Heaven-taught art.

5 May JOY here break out into mirth;
  And GRACE know days of Heaven on Earth;
  May HOLINESS here antedate
  The pureness of the higher state.

6 May PENITENCE, here hush its fears;
  REMORSE, surcease its burning tears;
  HUMILITY, here learn to dare
  DEVOUTNESS, prove the might of prayer.

7 May CHILDHOOD, here rejoice to come,
  As to its heavenly Father's home;
  May YOUTH surrender here its strength;
  AGE, wistful wait its closing tenth.

8 May a full Gospel ever sound
  To farthest generations' bound;
  Redemption by the blood alone
  Offer'd on Calvary to atone.

9 May men of God from age to age
  With world, flesh, hell, stern warfare wage;
  But chief of all the conquest seek
  That turns the proud heart into meek.

10 May souls, Lord here be "born again"
   Shrinking not from the blessed pain;
   May multitudes, Christ's workers be,
   In consecrate alacrity.

11 By all Thine ordinances Lord,
   Wilt Thou fulfil Thy promise-word?
   Baptism—Marriage—wilt Thou bless?
   The "Supper" too in righteousness.

12 Glory to Father and to Son,
   And Holy Spirit, Three-in-One;
   Be this a House of God for aye;
   God of the House, here us we pray.

193. LOOKING UP. *St. Matt. xiv. 19.* 8s.

1 I OFT read in the Holy Book,
  My dear Lord, of Thy upward look;
  When Thou didst break the mystic bread
  By which the multitude was fed;
  To walk in Thy blest steps I yearn;
  Lord! give me grace that I may learn.

2 Lord! give me grace that I may learn,
  And Thy rich blessing daily earn;
  Help Thou me, Lord, each day to serve,
  Kept near Thee that I never swerve;
  Still looking up, and here below
  Some antepasts of Heaven know.

3 Some antepasts of Heaven know,
  However "running to and fro;"
  O Lord! give me Thy upward look,
  When Hope is dimm'd or Faith is shook;
  Or Love's glow pales, or zeal is chill'd;
  Thus be my heart with ardour fill'd.

4 Thus be my heart with ardour fill'd ;
  All murmuring and fretting still'd ;
  Lift me above Earth's wildering mists,
  Giving the courage that resists ;
  Lord! heav'nly thoughts with earthly blend,
  As upward look to Thee I send.

5 As upward look to Thee I send,
  Thy Spirit His rich unction lend ;
  Rememb'ring ever how I owe
  All that I am and have and know ;
  To Thy grace—ah ! Thy " Grace
      abounding,"
  Thy love excelling, yea astounding.

194. POWERS OF THE WORLD TO COME.
Heb. vi. 5.   5.5.6.5.5.6.

1 THE clouds are pinking,¹²
    The sun is sinking,
  A globe of quiv'ring fire ;
    The landscape glimmers ;
    The SEA far shimmers ;
  O heart of mine aspire !

2 Such splendour show'ring,
    The earth so dow'ring ;
  Think of Eternity,
    And its high being—
    The Lord Christ seeing
  At His RIGHT HAND MOST HIGH.

3 Thy love, Lord, shedding,
    Joy in me spreading ;
  Lo! even here and now ;
    Thro' grace abounding,
    All foes confounding,
  I catch Thy face's glow.

4 Soul ! upward winging,
    All Thy flight singing ;
  Let praise and prayer ascend ;
    At Heav'n's gate waiting,
    All consecrating,
  In worship 'fore Him bend.

5 Ev'ning skies flaming,
    All Earth's dyes shaming ;
  Ye hang a veil between ;
    But lo ! life ended,
    To Christ commended,
  We'll see the GREAT UNSEEN.

6 *Repeat St. 1.*

195. LIBERTY AND PEACE.

1 THE PEN is stronger than the SWORD,
  Howe'er that be of men ador'd ;
  The hour draws nigh when 'twill be crime
  To shed men's blood—O hour sublime !

2 Art not Thou, Jesus, " Prince of Peace?"
  O cause Thou then all wars to cease !
  No longer let the will of kings
  Launch fiats DESOLATION brings.

3 Thou gav'st a king for " curse " of old—
  As in Thy Holy Book is told ;
  Man's childhood past, Lord, let us see
  A CHRISTIANIZ'D DEMOCRACY.   [man

4 Choosing from 'mongst themselves the
  Of brain and heart to lead the van ;
  Strong, free, true, pure—Thy sov'reignty
  Held as their " glorious liberty."

5 Just laws, free speech, and righteousness,
  O God of nations with these bless !
  Our charters great, inviolate,
  With a FREE CHURCH in a FREE STATE.

196. SPOKEN TRUTH.   *Isaiah lv. 11.*   8s.

1 No true word spoken ever dies ;
  It passes sure into the skies ;
  And He Who is the Lord of Truth
  His ancient cov'nant keeps in sooth.

2 His ancient cov'nant keeps in sooth
  Unchanging in His tender ruth ;
  Speak, therefore, aye, the true great word
  Ye God-sent servants of the Lord.

3 Ye God-sent servants of the Lord,
  Fear not men's wrath or ev'n discord ;
  The Master oft did kindle fire,
  And evil things demand your ire.

MOCKING AGNOSTICS—THE LATTER DAYS.

4 And evil things demand your ire ;
  Speak bravely out, not as for hire ;
  Have faith in TRUTH, have faith in God,
  Remember Christ Who earth once trod,

5 Remember Christ Who earth once trod,
  That still He wields a sov'ran rod ;
  Ord'ring event and circumstance,
  To win full-orb'd deliverance.

6 To win full-orb'd deliverance,
  By Law of Love supreme o'er CHANCE ;
  No true word spoken ever dies,
  It passes sure into the skies.

197. EXTRA ECCLESIAM NULLA SALUS. 8s.

1 *Outside the Church there's no salvation*
  —Lord ! pardon Thou the obsecration ;
  Out of Christ, not outside the Church,
  Leaves a sinful man in the lurch.

2 O God, how straitened are we !
  Seeing but what we wish to see ;
  Misreading words of Holy Writ,
  Our own exclusive Church to fit.

3 Enlarge our souls, enlarge our hearts,
  Save us from sacerdotal arts ;
  Unchurching none, inchurching all,
  We upon the ONE SAVIOUR call.

4 *Outside the Church there's no salvation*,
  Of LOVE it is the desecration ;
  Where'er the SPIRIT witness gives,
  A soul is saved and in Christ lives.

5 We praise Thy Name that it is so,
  It kindleth in our hearts a glow ;
  CHRIST JESUS DIED FOR ALL THE WORLD,
  Still let this watchword be unfurl'd.

6 *Repeat St.* 1.

198.   MOCKING AGNOSTICS.   *Jude 18.*
8s.

1 SURCEASE your chants ! surcease your
    Ye mockers of this latter day ;   [taunts!
  Your blatant vaunts, Christ's Church not
        daunts;
  She knows His triumph speeds its way.

2 Your ignorance! your god of CHANCE!
  Poor praters ye, at second-hand;
  Advance! advance! Faith's shield and lance
  Blunt your fool-weapons where ye stand.

3 Pride's cup ye quaff—our God doth laugh,
  High-seated on His Great White Throne;
  Like vilest draff or empty chaff
  Before His power ye all are blown.

4 But whilst ye may— in your dismay
  Turn ye, O turn, why will ye die?
  Unto God pray—make no delay—
  No longer His vast love defy.

5 Now is the time—lo ! it doth chime!
  Ye still may on His mercy trust;
  Supremest crime—yet Cross sublime,
  Sin's awful problem doth adjust.

199.   THE LATTER DAYS.   6s.
                        Isaiah xlviii. 18.

1 Light spreads from East to West;
  From plain to mountain-crest;
  Light from our God enthron'd—
  The promise long postpon'd.

2 Slowly the light has gained,
  Yet thro' all Jesus reign'd;
  Long long " gross darkness " lay;
  Far off Christ saw His Day.

3 Onward from age to age,
  'Gainst Pagan's and Priest's rage;
  Christ gave free nations birth
  Lo! now, o'er all the Earth.

4 Countless the tongues that now
  The one sure Gospel know;
  For more than e'er to-day,
  The Christ o'er men holds sway.

5 Burden'd and toiling men
  Again turn and again;
  Cling to THE CRUCIFIED
  Who for them liv'd and died.

6 O wanderers in gloom,
  Hark to His mighty " Come"!
  The World's REDEMPTION stands ;
  Grasp ye His nail-pierc'd Hands.

200. Of the Increase of His Government there shall be no End. *Isaiah ix. 7.*

1 *King of kings and Lord of lords!*
Tho' without the pomp of swords;
On Thy Head are many crowns,
For the Universe Thee owns;
Toward Thee it still doth move,
Heart-drawn—not by Law but Love.

2 *King of kings and Lord of lords!*
Shout aloud the jub'lant words;
Send them over all the Earth,
And break forth in praiseful mirth;
Lauding Him in psalm and song
As unto His House we throng.

3 *King of kings and Lord of lords!*
O it holy joy affords!
Worthy "blessing" to receive;
"Honour," "power," none will aggrieve;
"Riches," "glory," "thanksgiving,"
Yea, Lord Christ, all we can bring.

4 *King of kings and Lord of lords!*
Heaven—Hell—Earth, this accords;
Far back in Eternity;
Onward till the Last Man die:
The Lord Christ He is the King—
This from sky to Earth let ring.

5 *King of kings and Lord of lords!*
Lift up voices, strike all chords;
Set it forth in Christ-like lives,
That supremest "witness" gives;
Set it forth in loving deeds,
Still unselfish 'midst world's greeds.

6 *King of kings and Lord of lords!*
This all sov'reignty concords;
Set it forth by look and word,
That we "walk" close to the Lord;
Set it forth with burning faith,
Resting on the great "He saith."

7 *King of kings and Lord of lords!*
O sweet note 'midst Sin's discords;
Set it forth in yearning prayer,
Laying on Him all our care;
Set it forth as watching till
"Lo I come," He doth fulfil.

7. Lights and Shadows of Spiritual Experience.

201. WATCHING BY A DEATH-BED.
"*God be merciful to me a sinner.*" – St. Luke xviii. 13. 10.6.

The dying. 1 "Weaker and frailer, day by day, I grow;
　　The lamp of life burns low—
　　　how low! how low!
　　Death is predestinate; yet hangs the blow."
Watcher.　　"O God, be merciful!"

The dying. 2 "The sleep of Thy belov'd, I seek in vain;
　　Through the long nights unresting in my pain;
　　O to be laid where lie the silent slain!"
Watcher.　　"O God, be merciful!"

The dying. 3 "How dark it is! how full of mystery!
　　That I as chained hound should useless lie;
　　Aching for death, but still I do not die."
Watcher.　　"O God, be merciful!"

The dying. 4 "Arrested in mid-life and laid aside,
　　Helpless and weary, Christ, to Thee I've cried;
　　But cries and tears alike unanswer'd bide."
Watcher.　　"O God, be merciful!"

The dying. 5 "God of my life! am I deaf? or dumb? or dead?
　　That I appeal to brazen skies o'erhead;
　　From which to Thine Own child no dews are shed."
Watcher.　　"O God, be merciful!"

The dying. 6 "It seems but yesterday that I was strong;
　　With life and health such as to youths belong;
　　Now I am like a child: O God! how long?"
Watcher.　　"O God, be merciful!"

The dying. 7 "I speak, O God, the thoughts that in me rise;
　　My doubts, my dreads, my anguish, my surprise;
　　Just as I am I come; aught else were lies."
Watcher.　　"O God, be merciful!"

The dying. 8 "Lord Christ! I cry to Thee from out the dark;
　　To my poor broken words, wilt Thou not hark?
　　And mid th' o'erwhelming flood, shew me the ark?"
Watcher.　　"O God, be merciful!"

The dying. 9 "Thou knowest all I am, Thou seest me lone,
　　Lord, lost: O Christ, interpret Thou my moan;

Watcher.
Hast Thou not died, O Lord,
for sin to atone?"
" O God, be merciful!"

These are the words of one who was my
FRIEND;
But light, and peace, and joy came in the
end,
And glory strange did to the dead face lend:
For God was merciful.

202. HE LEADS ROUND BUT HE LEADS RIGHT.[13]   7s.

" God led the people about by the way of the wilderness by the Red Sea."—*Exodus* xiii. 18. (*Cf. Deut.* ii. 7; viii. 2; xxxii. 10).

1 He leads round, but he leads right:
All the way is in His sight;
Be it rough, or be it long;
Void of joy, or set to song;
Bringing much, or mite by mite;
He leads round, but He leads right.

2 He leads round, but He leads right
He is with us in the fight;
Sin may lure or doubts assail,
Clad in Faith's celestial mail,
We are guarded by His might—
He leads round, but He leads right.

3 He leads round, but he leads right.
Let no danger then affright;
When to Him we lift our eyes,
Help doth like the morn arise;
Chasing clouds with conquering light;
He leads round, but He leads right.

4 He leads round, but He leads right:
Giveth song ev'n in the night;
O to listen to his voice
When in tears HE bids rejoice;
He our blackest can make white;
He leads round, but He leads right.

5 He leads round, but He leads right:
Heaviest burden groweth light;
Marah! Elim! Wilderness!

Each in turn the Lord doth bless;
Canaan shines, far-off yet bright;
He leads round, but He leads right.

6 He leads round, but He leads right:
Cloud by day and fire by night;
Morn by morn " Let God arise,
Scattering all our enemies";
And we'll sing with evening light;
He leads round, but He leads right.

203. "THE BLUE OF HEAVEN IS LARGER THAN THE CLOUD."
—*Mrs. E. B. Browning.*

" *Und so ist der blaue Himmel grösser als jedes Gewölk darin, und dauerhafter dazu*"
—*Jean Paul Richter* ("*the blue heaven is greater than any cloud that passeth over it.*")

Romans viii. 28.   10s.

1 Now with low voice and now in accents loud,
This truth, Lord, Thou would'st teach us still anew;
The blue of heaven is larger than the cloud:
Yet cloud, small as man's hand, will hide the blue.

2 I look around and see a surging crowd;
Their dark days 'gainst their bright days are but few;
The blue of heaven is larger than the cloud:
But ne'er the less they fret, and pine, and sue.

3 E'en Thine Own children, Lord, themselves enshroud;
Cause them look up Thy shining Face to view;
The blue of heaven is larger than the cloud:
O that all men could feel it to be true!

4 "All things" for us Thou say'st "co-work for good;"
Alas! alas! Thy words how men eschew!
The blue of heaven is larger than the cloud:
Howe'er perplex'd the maze, Love holds the clue.

THE FURNACE OF AFFLICTION—GROWTH IN GRACE.

5 No more, no more of mourning with head
     bow'd ;
   Thy note, deep Singer, falls like
     nurt'ring dew ;
   The blue of heaven is larger than the cloud:
   Our vows to love God's will we would
     renew.

6 Now with low voice and now in accents
     loud,
   This truth, Lord, Thou would'st teach
     us still anew ;
   The blue of heaven is larger than the cloud:
   With Thee Above Faith aye should see
     the blue.

204. THE FURNACE OF AFFLICTION.
*"I have chosen thee in the furnace of afflic-
tion." Isaiah xlviii. 10. (Cf. Daniel c. iii.)*
6s.

1 THY chosen ones, O Lord,
   Remember'd in Thy Word ;
   Cast into furnace-flame
   Because of Thy Great Name ;
   Thou shieldedst, that the fire
   Lit no funereal pyre ;
   But them transfigured,
   Thro' golden sunshine led ;
   And thus unharm'd they walked
   And all their enemies balked ;
   Stepp'd forth as from green sod ;
   Kept by the Son of God.

2 Ev'n thus, O Lord, I know
   Amid Affliction's glow,
   As of the furnace old ;
   Thou dost me close enfold ;
   That all unhurt I lie
   'Neath Thy benignant eye ;
   And feel that Thou dost stand
   Near, with Thy cooling hand ;
   To temper all my pain ;
   To turn my loss to gain ;
   O Lord, Thou art with me
   As with Thy chosen Three !

3 'Tis good to be thus tried ;
   It tells me I'm allied
   To those He loveth best,
   Throughout their heav'nly quest ;
   To Him, The Crucified,
   Who Man of Sorrows died ;
   O therefore, Lord, impart
   Such grace to my poor heart,
   As shall preserve me still
   Submissive to Thy will ;
   That I in furnace flame
   May glorify Thy Name.

205. THE LIGHT NOT SELF TO SHINE.
St. Matthew, v. 16. 8s.

1 My light, O Lord, which Thou hast sent
   Down from Thy most pure firmament ;
   My light, not me, Thou call'st to shine ;
   Not my poor self, but what is Thine.

2 My light, O Lord, which Thou did'st give,
   In Thy Love's great prerogative ;
   Not my poor self; for unto Thee
   All praise and glory aye must be.

3 My light, O Christ, Thou call'st to shine,
   That mine be Thine and Thine be mine ;
   Lord, keep me low and unrepining ;
   Let self be lost in Thy sweet shining.

4 My light, lit by Thy nail-marked hand,
   Shines only as in Thee I stand ;
   O may no thought of self intrude !
   My light let shine, and self exclude.

5 My light, O Lord, yet on me lift
   Thy Face's light, Thy Love's free gift ;
   My light, not me, Thou call'st to shine,
   Not my poor self, but what is Thine.

206. GROWTH IN GRACE. *"He giveth more grace." St. James iv. 6.* 10s.

1 GRACE, more and still more grace, O
     Saviour mine,
   That I may know that I am truly Thine ;

I bless Thee Thou hast eas'd me of Sin's
  smart,
But "more, still more"—I seek a holy
  heart.
2 Grace, more and still more grace ; Lord,
    I would be,
  —Since Thou hast promis'd it—made
    like to Thee ;
  Break my "remaining sin," in gentle
    might,
  That knowing, I may also do, the right.
3 Grace, more and still more grace, my
    God, as I
  Still bring Thee empty cups for fresh
    supply ;
  Fill me—still heavenward borne upon Thy
    wings—
  With Thine Own "perfect peace" that
    soars and sings.
4 Grace, more and still more grace, that I
    may run,
  Not merely walk ; and aye press daunt-
    less on ;
  Keeping Thee still, O Christ, before mine
    eye,
  Until my life reflect Thy life on high.

207. LOVE IS COLD. *St. Matthew xxiv.*
  12.   10s.
1 ALAS! O Lord, my love 'gainst Thine is
    cold,
  As tho' my heart were now aneath the
    mould ;
  I know, I see, how all to Thee I owe,
  But my thin flame is choked: O make it
    glow!
2 In momentary gleams I seem to burn,
  As on The Crucified my eyes I turn ;
  I cast myself in passion on my knees,
  But I must own it   soon my poor words
    freeze.
3 This " sin remaining," how it doth control
  The yearnings of my Spirit-touchèd soul!

O Thou Who knowest all, break now its
    spell;
  Possess Thee, Lord, of my heart's citadel!
4 The life of Thy life put Thou in my breast;
  Give me the restfulness of Thine own rest;
  Whatever chills, or chains, or drags me
    down,
  Remove, O Christ,—to all I guilty own.
5 Alas! O Lord, my love 'gainst Thine is
    cold,
  As tho' my heart were now aneath the
    mould ;
  I know, I see, how all to Thee I owe;
  But my thin flame is chok'd: O make it
    glow!

208. JOY IN SORROW.   "*Clear shining
  after rain.*"--*2 Samuel xxiii.* 4. *7s.*
1 TROUBLE comes; but trouble goes;
  This the blest Believer knows,
  Even on a bed of pain:
  There's clear shining after rain.
2 Whatsoe'er to us it send,
  Longest day comes to an end;
  Faith supports to bear the strain;
  There's clear shining after rain.
3 Cloud up-pil'd on cloud, Night mars,
  Yet thro' them doth gleam the stars,
  Prophesying Morn again;
  There's clear shining after rain.
4 Hope's bright rainbow spans our fears;
  His great Promise dries our tears;
  His sweet Mercy clears the stain:
  There's clear shining after rain.
5 Cag'd tho' bird be, yet it sings ;
  And the mown grass once more springs;
  Wounds will heal, though scar remain:
  There's clear shining after rain.
6 Losses oft are hard to bear,
  Filling hearts with carking care;
  But they sometimes turn to gain:
  There's clear shining after rain.

HEART SURRENDER —ANGELIC MINISTRY.

7 Friends prove false, but friends prove true;
    Who either of these ne'er knew?
  Heart, be brave! be steady brain!
    There's clear shining after rain.
8 Crosses, Lord, on us have prest;
    But this thought won us sweet rest;
  Ev'ry cross on Thee has lain;
    There's clear shining after rain.
9 Let us then still onward press!
    Through the dreariest wilderness;
  Singing for our sweet refrain:
    There's clear shining after rain.

209. HEART-SURRENDER. *Prov. xxiii. 26.*
6s.

1 "My son, give Me thine heart:"
    My God! how good Thou art
  To ask this heart of mine,
    That Thou may'st make it Thine.

2 Hard, cold, ill-yielding thing,
    My heart to Thee I bring;
  Thou hast the skill alone
    To change a heart of stone.

3 Lord, when I look within,
    I see scarce aught but sin;
  Through grace, I sin abjure;
    Lord, make and keep me pure!

4 Poor, weak and wavering,
    Help me to Thee to cling;
  That sharer of Thy strength
    Full height I gain at length.

5 Lord, still the World allures,
    Yea, oft my heart secures;
  Lord, wilt thou break its power?
    Guarding in evil hour.

6 The "life of God" bestow;
    In holiness to grow;
  Possessing and possessed,
    With Thine in Thee to rest.

7 "My son, give Me thine heart;"
    My God, how good Thou art
  To ask this heart of mine
    That Thou may'st make it Thine.

210. PLEADING. *Rom. v. 8; 1 Tim. i. 15.*
6.4.6.4.4.

1 Lord, others Thou hast sav'd,
    Save me! save me!
  Lord, others as enslav'd
    Thou hast set free;
    Free me! free me!

2 Lord, others by Thy grace
    Have "the new heart;"
  Lord, lift on me Thy face,
    This gift impart!
    Thou gracious art.

3 Lord, others daily grow
    Like unto Thee;
  Lord, grant me this to show;
    Thee ever see
    Near me! near me!

4 Lord, others know Thy rest
    Thy "perfect peace;"
  Lord, take this tossing breast,
    Cause fear to cease
    In sweet release.

5 Lord, others "walk by faith,"
    Thus would I walk;
  Command Thou that "He saith
    May all doubts baulk.
    So shall I be
    For aye with Thee.

211. ANGELIC MINISTRY. *Hebrews i. 14; and St. Luke xv. 7.*

1 Let God THE SPIRIT anoint my eyes,
  A-flame are seen the azure skies
  With seraphim and cherubim—
  Who noon day's utmost blaze bedim;
  On wings of whiteness, lo! they fly
  Twixt our dark world and fields on high;
  Heirs of salvation bringing home
  To gain the joyous welcome, "Come."

2 There is a glory on the grass
  As tho' angelic feet did pass;
  There is a splendour 'midst the trees
  As he sees who the unseen sees;

Amongst the hollows of the hills
A hush of awe as all else stills;
O God! Thy Spirit on me lies,
Lifting me up in ecstasies.

3 Ye holy angels ministrant,
Why is it now ye will not grant,
E'en unto Faith and Hope and Love,
Your seal of silence to remove?
Speaking as once ye used to speak
To weary hearts and like to break;
Glad tidings of glad souls set free
That e'en in glory fresh joy see.

4 Where'er I see a little child,
I know ye there, ye undefil'd;
To guide, to guard, to bless, to keep,
With love that knows not how to sleep;
And wheresoe'er a sinner turns
And for the sinners' Saviour burns:
But O to catch a whisper'd word
That not in vain I serve the Lord.

5 O idle yearning thus to grieve,
Our part, as servants to believe;
To labour and still labour on
Spreading the great Redemption;
In faith, that unto us *is* given
Abundantly to people Heav'n;
That souls by day, by night repent,
And angels still their names present.

212. THE ONE TALENT IMPROVED.

"*Unto one He gave five talents, to another two, and to another one.*"—*St. Matthew xxv. 15.* 4.4.8.4.4.8.4.4.8.

1 I MAY not preach;
    I cannot teach;
I dare not face the public gaze;
    But I rejoice
    I have a voice,
With which I can my Saviour praise:
    O this be mine,
    By grace divine,
To SING to some frail child of Thine.

2 The talents ten
    Are now, as then,
Entrusted but to very few:
    O may the one
    Be not as none —
To what I have may I be true.
    O this be mine,
    By grace divine,
To SING to some frail child of Thine.

3 Help me, dear Lord,
    To plead Thy word;
To visit 'mongst Thy sick and poor;
    And when to pray
    Barr'd is my way,
The grace of song upon me pour:
    O this be mine,
    By grace divine,
To SING to some frail child of Thine.

213. THE UNRENEWED HEART. *Jer xvii. 9.*

1 Ah! it is not mere conceitful
To pronounce the heart "deceitful;"
Nor may any wax irate
At the seer's word "desperate;"
All must own the poignant word
Given by Jehovah Lord!

2 Having, Lord, just such a heart,
Lo! Thy quick'ning gracious art,
It has changed from a hard stone,
Grinding still itself alone;
Into a soft heart of flesh;
Soft untying every mesh.

3 How this heart of mine deceiv'd!
How this heart of mine me griev'd!
Rocked to-day to "perfect peace"
By eve sad and ill at ease;
And to-morrow burning, panting,
Still all, all of evil wanting.

4 Never was there guile so deep!
Hard? Aye, such as made me weep;
Weak? As to the flint the tinder;
Cold? Yes as quenchéd cinder;

Native heart? Who can it know?
Native heart? Who can it shew?
5 "I the Lord, I search the heart;"
Thus Thou answ'rest, and Thy part,
O, how gentle, Lord, it is!
Leading on from bale to bliss;
Thou Thy word to me did'st bring,
And now, Lord, I joyous sing.
6 *Repeat St. 1.*

214.   AFTER A LONG ILLNESS.   8s.
Psalms ix. 13; xxiii. 4; and lxxxix. 48.
1 O LORD my God! by Thy good Hand
Once more within Thy House I stand;
Lord, Thou dost fill my mouth with praise,
For Thou art lengthening out my days.
2 Brought back by Thee from Death's dark
   I my reprieve would celebrate;   [gate
Spar'd, O my God, I here and now
Grateful, adoring, pay my vow.
3 Through the long day and longer night,
Sickness did lay on me its blight;
My heart grew weak, wilder'd my brain—
Ah! Languor edg'd with sharpest pain.
4 With the Eternal face to face,
Methought I saw Death's iron mace;
By Thy great love I felt no fear,
Why, Lord? I knew Thee to be near.
5 Thou spakest the still-sparing word,
Then felt by me, tho' all unheard;
And now in this Thy holy House,
Wilt Thou me, O my God, espouse?
6 *Repeat St. 1.*

215. LITTLE FAITH. *"O ye of little faith."—*
    St. Matthew viii. 26.   6.4.
1 O YE *of little faith;*
   This still THE MASTER saith;
Saith it to you and me
In His sweet clemency;
Seeking that we be strong
And break forth into song:
   Lord, we believe.

2 O ye *of little faith;*
   Lord, let us feel Thy breath!
That seed which Thou hast sown
May not abide alone,
But spring up, blade and ear,
As Harvest draweth near:
   Lord, we believe.
3 O ye *of little faith;*
   This Thou might'st say in wrath;
But 'tis a gentle word
Of Thine, our patient Lord;
That 'neath Thy Spirit's hand
In firmer faith we stand.
   Lord, we believe.
4 O ye *of little faith;*
   Ah "little!" Almost death;
Lord, for Thine Own Name's sake
Be pleas'd all souls to shake;
That leaning on Thy strength,
We strong shall be at length;
   Lord, we believe.
5 O ye *of little faith;*
   We hide Thy wings beneath;
Lord, help us, more to pray;
Lord help us, to obey;
Lord, help us, all to dare;
Thine own great faith to share:
   Lord, we believe.

216. WEARINESS. *St. John iv. 6, 31, 32.*
    7s.
1 TIR'D in brain and tir'd in limb,
Ah! I often think of Him
Who, as great St. John doth tell,
Sate a-weary on the Well.
2 Would his tiredness were mine,
Working at His work divine;
Walking over Galilee
One frail woman there to see.
3 Tir'd in brain and tir'd in limb,
Ah! I often think of Him;
I would seek His heav'nly "meat"—
Sweet as manna—on that seat.

4 Nor would I e'er fail to see
　How my Lord instructeth me,
　That well-ledge, or anywhere
　Pulpit be, truth to declare.

5 Wondrous words that there were spoken;
　Words that never shall be broken;
　Worship to no spot confin'd,
　Worship free to all mankind.

6 O my God, I Thee beseech
　That this lesson Thou me teach;
　To o'ercome all weariness;
　Toiling ev'n one soul to bless.

7 Let me take Thy larger view,
　Nor priest's sacred hold for true;
　But, in lowly parallel,
　Speak for Thee by wayside Well.

217. DIVINE CHOOSING. "*He shall choose our inheritance for us.*—Psalm xlvii. 4.
"*What I shall choose I wot not.*"—Phillippians 1.23. 10s.

1 CHOOSE Thou for me, Lord, leave not me
　　to choose!
　I know not what to ask, or to refuse;
　O God, my God, Thou art too wise to err!
　Choose Thou for me, I all to Thee refer.

2 Thou knowest poverty; Thou knowest
　　wealth;
　Languor of sickness; confidence of health;
　Choose Thou for me, I know not what is
　　best; [rest.
　Thou art too just to wrong—on Thee I

3 What work for Thee to do; where I
　　shall go;
　O my Lord order Thou! I do not know;
　I fear to choose self-pleasing scenes and
　　things; [it brings.
　Choose Thou for me, and give the peace

4 Or long, or short, or dark, or bright my
　　way,
　'Tis not, O gracious Lord, for me to say;
　Choose Thou for me, and make Thy
　　choosing mine,
　Whate'er Thy Love may unto me assign.

5 *Repeat St. 1.*

218. UNREST. "*O that I had wings like a dove; for then would I fly away and be at rest.*"—Psalm lv. 6. 10s.

1 Not wings of the eagle, great-feather'd
　　and wide
　That up on the tall cliff his eyrie doth hide;
　But O Thou, my Saviour, wilt in Thy great
　　love
　Bestow upon me as 'twere wings of a dove?

2 Timorous and weak, Lord, am I at the best;
　Soon flutters this tremulous heart in my
　　breast; [forgive;
　Ah! Then, gentle Saviour, my failings
　Like wing-weary dove, my lorn spirit revive.

3 All round me, O Lord, are sorrow and sin;
　Unfitted for striving, wilt Thou shut me in?
　All ruffled Faith's pinions as of rain-dabbled
　　dove, [I rove.
　To Thy heart take me home that no longer

4 O Home of the blessed! O mansions
　　prepar'd! [dar'd;
　For you I am panting; ah, for you I have
　Fain, fain would I fly as a dove to her nest'
　And enter, through grace, Lord, Thy haven
　　of rest.

5 Not wings of the eagle, great-feather'd
　　and wide
　That up on the tall cliff his eyrie doth hide;
　But O Thou my Saviour! wilt in Thy great
　　love
　Bestow upon me as 'twere wings of a dove?

219. REST. *St. Matt. xi. 28.* 10s.

1 We lay us down, O Lord, upon our
　　pillows,
　And, lo! Thou givest Thy beloved
　　sleep;

CASTAWAY—DESPONDENCY.

As came Thy great "peace" o'er the
   storm-tramp'd billows,
  Comes unto us Thy word that doth us
   "keep."

2 Or be it the "grey head," or fair young
   maiden,
  Who "lieth down" with care or toil
   opprest ;
  Thy voice sounds soft —"Come all ye
   heavy-laden,
  "Come unto ME, and I will give you
   rest."

3 Praise to Thy name, Lord, for those great
   words spoken,
  That still abide with their first force
   unspent ;
  How Thou dost graciously to Thine give
   token
  Of Thy deep love unchang'd by Thine
   ascent.

4 O Christ ! Amid all our life's grief and
   trials,
  Help us, or solitary or in throngs,
  To catch a vision of Thy "golden vials ;"
  Yea, on this hither side to hear Heav'n's
   songs.

5 So each day's cares with the day's close
   forgetting,
  We shall, Lord Jesus, enter on Thy
   PEACE ;
  And when our life's sun westers to its
   setting,
  Hear from Thy lips Thy " Come " that
   gives release.

6 *Repeat St.* 1.

220.   CASTAWAY. *Psalm lxxxix.* 49.
                    7.4.7.4.8.8.

1 O LORD, in uttermost distress
    Thou did'st me bless,
  As closely I to Thee did cling;
    Yea, mad'st me sing;
  Wherefore, my God, in present ill,
  I place me 'neath Thy gracious will.

2 Lo, dark and strong the tempest rose,
    With blows on blows;
  But by Faith's look I saw Thee nigh,
    And sent a cry   [not";
  That brought me Thy soft word " Fear
  And lo! all peril was forgot.

3 So in this time of stormful grief
    I seek relief;
  And will not my Hope-anchor lift,
    Nor from Thee drift;
  What Thou hast been, O Lord, Thou art,
  Still playing the true Keeper's part.

4 O God! my God! whate'er betide
    Be Thou my guide ;
  Nor suffer dark and cloudy day
    Me to affray;
  Thou hast me kept, Thou wilt me keep ;
  "Thou givest Thy beloved sleep."

221.   DESPONDENCY. *Ecc. ii.* 20. 8*s*

1 LORD CHRIST, I walk in blankest gloom,
  Shadows of death lade my dim eyes ;
  O wilt Thou cause light to arise ?
  O pity me, my path illume !
  Hear Thou my broken words and cries

2 Lord Christ, it was not thus of old ;
  My first love shone until it glowed ;
  Thy Cross revealed how much I owed;
  Thy Gospel wondrous things me told,
  And more and more me debtor showed.

3 Search me, O Lord, I Thee entreat ;
  Whate'er 'tis that this darkness brings
  And peoples it with ghostly things ;
  I cast me groping at Thy feet—
  I must lie low; I have no wings.

4 Lord Christ, Thy promises I plead ;
  In deepest gloom I still trust Thee ;
  I see not, but Thou, Lord, dost see ;
  O wilt Thou for me intercede ?
  Wilt Thou give light and set me free ?

REST GOD'S CHOOSING FOR US.

222. REST. *St. Matt. xi. 28.* 7s.

Requiescite in Eo, et quieti eritis.—St. Augustine
(Conf., lib. iv. xii.)

1 Rest in Christ and be at rest;
  Vain elsewhere will be your quest;
  Man as made for God alone
  Restless is as wave-washed stone,
  Till he welcomes Him for guest—
  Then he enters His Own rest.

2 Rest in Christ and be at rest;
  When by doubt or fear opprest,
  Telling to Him all Thy fears;
  Weeping at His feet Thy tears;
  By Himself Thou wilt be blest,
  From Him win His Own deep rest.

3 Rest in Christ and be at rest,
  Of our faith the sweetest test;
  If thy days be grey and dreary,
  If thy heart and feet be weary;
  Hie to Him, and, all confessed,
  He will give restoring rest.

4 Rest in Christ and be at rest,
  E'en if anguish wring thy breast;
  Lean on Him, whose heart was broken;
  He will give a secret token;
  With light, blackest cloud invest;
  "It is I," bring peace and rest.

5 Rest in Christ and be at rest,
  He is our "God manifest;"
  Sinners' Saviour, sinners' Friend,
  He all needed help doth send;
  Hears each word to Him addressed,
  Crowns all with heart-calming rest.

6 Rest in Christ and be at rest;
  Vain elsewhere will be your quest;
  The heart as made for God alone
  Restless is as wave-washed stone,
  Till it welcomes Him for guest—
  Then it enters His Own rest.

223. HEAVENLY USE OF EARTHLY THINGS.
  1 Corinthians vii. 31. 8s.

1 GIVE heav'nly use of earthly things;
  Use, O my God, that leaves no stings;
  Use, that to Jesus ever brings.

2 Give heav'nly use of earthly things;
  Use, that doth lift on sunny wings;
  Upsoaring to the King of Kings.

3 Give heav'nly use of earthly things;
  That sings at toil and toiling sings;
  Unto the harp of thousand strings.

4 Give heav'nly use of earthly things;
  Use, that still to the Cross firm-clings;
  And selfish idling from it flings.

5 Give heav'nly use of earthly things;
  Ev'n when sore doubt my spirit wrings;
  And nearer Hell than Heaven it swings.

6 Give heav'nly use of earthly things;
  From the great debt of Love that springs;
  Till Heaven with the music rings.

7 Give heav'nly use of earthly things;
  Use, O my God, that leaves no stings;
  Use, that to Jesus ever brings.

224. GOD'S CHOOSING FOR US.—*"Thy way, not mine, O Lord!"—Dr. Horatius Bonar.*
  Psalm cx. 3.

1 "My way, not Thine, O Lord!"
    This, my rebellious word;
  But Thou hast chang'd it quite,
    "Thy way, not mine," is right.

2 "My way, not Thine": my heart
    Loth was with this to part;
  "Thy way, not mine" by grace
    Now, Lord, has ta'en its place.

3 "My way, not Thine": alas!
    Still thro' my mind will pass;
  "Thy way, not mine," Lord, make
    Too strong for aught to shake.

4 "My way, not Thine": O Lord,
    It pierc'd me like a sword;

"Thy way, not mine," uplifts
And each temptation sifts.

5 "My way, not Thine," misleads
And brings forth all ill deeds ;
"Thy way, not mine," brings peace
And all its sweet release.

6 "My way, not Thine": I mourn
It ever should return;
"Thy way, not mine" ; all praise
I this refrain may raise.

225.   THE GOD OF PATIENCE.   8s.

Romans xv. 5   (Autobiographical.)

1 O God of Patience ! I extol
Thy long long patience with my soul :
Far back in childhood's sunny days
Thou guarded'st me in all my ways ;
Did'st give to me a Christian home,
Where oft I heard Thy sweet word
   " Come ; "
But still, alas ! delay'd, nor sought
To Thee, my Saviour, to be brought.

2 O God of Patience ! I extol
Thy long long patience with my soul :
As I grew up in days and years,
A father's and a mother's tears
I saw ; and heard them pray and speak
With silent drops upon their cheek ;
I promis'd ; but would not decide
And on and on my years did glide.

3 O God of Patience ! I extol
Thy long long patience with my soul :
When thought awoke within my brain,
And I all knowledge sought to gain ;
In pride of intellect I laugh'd,
The " higher learning " as I quaff'd,
Till, like unto a broken sword
I flung from me, O God, Thy Word.

4 O God of Patience ! I extol
Thy long long patience with my soul :
My mother's grave my Sinai was,
But light, not lightning, was the cause,
That won me from my unbelief,
And staunch'd an ageing father's grief ;
Softly my childhood's prayer return'd
And my old faith within me burn'd.

5 O God of Patience ! I extol
Thy long long patience with my soul ;
With wondrous love that never tires
Thou Lord, hast cleans'd me in Thy fires;
Hast held me, led me, taught me still,
And moulded me to Thy sweet will ;
And now Thy peace within my breast
Foretells " The Everlasting Rest."

226. THE DAISIES. *St. Matthew vi 30.* 7s.

1 DAN CHAUCER'S dulcet praises
Of grass scarce seen for daisies;
I'd been reading, till I sang
As the quaint-wrought phrasing rang ;
When, lo ! in sylvan meadow—
Dappled with light and shadow ;
Flash'd sudden before my eyne —
In silvery and golden shine
Of beauty, a very shower
Of the dear old English flower.

2 The vision of these daisies,
Tender thought in me raises ;
As by them I am borne back
On Memory's shimmering track,
To my child-days long ago,
When no sorrow I did know ;
And the lov'd ones —all now gone —
Radiantly upon me shone;
Mary ! Willie ! how we'd play
Whole length of a summer day !

3 'Midst " Upper Ten's" strange crazes,
I still cleave to the daisies;
Modest— simple— yet how fair !
(Tho' they be not marked ' rare');
Lying in a light of glory,
Shining from song and from story;
Dan Chaucer to Robert Burns —
Each unto the ' daisy' turns;
And in their immortal verse
Its simplicities rehearse.

4 Not where high Fashion blazes,
　Is fit place for sweet daisies;
　But in the green lane and field,
　Daisies their full beauty yield;
　Opening their speck of gold
　That red and white sweet enfold;
　To the music of the rain —
　Pure as dew, leaving no stain,
　Or folding their tiny cup,
　Not till the dawn to look up.

5 Lord! On Thee my soul gazes,
　Thou who makest the daisies;
　Joy, that heart on Thee may call,
　Thou who framest these flowers small,
　Joy, that the humble daisies
　Tell that nothing erases
　Humblest from Thy heart of love,
　Tho' upon Thy Throne above;
　The alluring world dazes,
　I keep with the sweet daisies.

6 And so 'midst all life's mazes,
　I'll think of the wild daisies;
　Look to Thee, Lord, that Thy Hand
　Still me guide as pos'd I stand
　Look to Thee, as my fair flower
　Looks up for the sunny shower;
　Look to Thee, nor ever doubt,
　Tho' Thou lead'st me round about,
　Thou wilt " keep " me to the end,
　And " Go higher " at last send.

227.　　Deadly Sweet.　　8s.

*Nam tu semper aderas misericorditer
saeviens, et amarissimis adspergens offen-
sionibus omnes illicitas iocunditates meas,
ut ita quaererem sine offensione iocundari.*
St. Augustine (Conf., lib. ii. ii.). *Morti-
fera suavitate . . . dulces laqueos (Ib., vi.
xii.)*

1 Besprinkle, Lord, with bitterness
　Whate'er of sweet Thou canst not bless;
　Let nothing pleasing be to me
　That is displeasing unto Thee:
　Do Thou me wholly sanctify,
　To love " with pure heart fervently."

2 Alas! The tempter doth prevail!
　Piercing with fiery darts my mail;
　Yea, pressing me in sorest straits,
　And snaring me with tempting baits:
　Do Thou me wholly sanctify,
　To love " with pure heart fervently."

3 Besprinkle, Lord, with bitterness
　Whate'er of sweet Thou canst not bless,
　Let nothing pleasing be to me
　That is displeasing unto Thee:
　Do Thou me wholly sanctify,
　To love " with pure heart fervently."

4 The red wine quivers in the cup,
　And I am urg'd to quaff it up;
　But ah! I've drunk the bitter dregs
　And so in vain now Pleasure begs:
　Do Thou me wholly sanctify,
　To love "with pure heart fervently."

5 Besprinkle, Lord, with bitterness
　Whate'er of sweet Thou canst not bless;
　Let nothing pleasing be to me
　That is displeasing unto Thee:
　Do Thou me wholly sanctify,
　To love " with pure heart fervently."

6 Lo, beauty comes with passionate breath;
　Thou hast me shewn " the way of death";
　Wounds deadlier than dagger's thrust
　Slow-sure avengers of past lust;
　Do Thou me wholly sanctify,
　To love "with pure heart fervently."

7 Besprinkle, Lord, with bitterness
　Whate'er of sweet Thou canst not bless;
　Let nothing pleasing be to me
　That is displeasing unto Thee:
　Do Thou me wholly sanctify,
　To love " with pure heart fervently."

8 Gain by lying! base success!
　Profanity, ungodliness;
　Thou hast torn the fair-seeming veil,
　That idly now they me assail:

Do Thou me WHOLLY sanctify
To love "with pure heart fervently."

9 Besprinkle, Lord, with bitterness
Whate'er of sweet Thou canst not bless;
Let nothing pleasing be to me
That is displeasing unto Thee;
Do Thou me WHOLLY sanctify
To love "with pure heart fervently."

10 O Saviour mine! upon the Cross
Thy blood restores my awful loss;
Now break my chain that I may be
Deliver'd from Sin's slavery;
Do Thou me WHOLLY sanctify
To love "with pure heart fervently."

228. DIVINE AND HUMAN LOVE.   6s.
Eph. iii. 10.

1 I PANT—I long—I pine,
I seek ONE to be mine;
Now in sweet ecstasy,
Anon I dread and sigh;
Tumultuous my love,—
How unlike Thine above!

2 E'en in best love to Thee
I lack tranquillity;
To-day walk in delight,
To-morrow in black night;
But stormy, changeful ever,
And calm as Thou art, never.

3 O for Thy "perfect peace"!
That never knows excess;
Thy stillness as sea-deeps;
Howe'er the tempest sweeps;
Thy silence so serene
Whatever intervene.

4 Thou lovest in pure love,
No passion doth Thee move;
Hush'd as that sea did show
When forth Thy word did go;
Give me this love of Thine,
So placid, pure, divine.

5 Alas! alas! O Lord!
I must bring lowly word;
Disorderly and toss'd
My love is at the most;
O for Thy holy love!
Born of the Heavenly Dove!

229. COMPENSATIONS. *Rom. viii. 28.*
7.8.7.8.7.7.

1 THERE are tears in many eyes,
There are also bright'ning smiles;
There are pleasures pain's disguise,
But there are joys that are not guiles;
Smiles or tears, or guiles or truth,
Keep us, Lord, in Thy sweet ruth.

2 There are hearts bow'd down in fear,
There are also hearts that bound;
There are friendless, with none near,
Friends too for the friendless found;
Glad or sad, friendless or friended,
Lord, let us be still defended

3 There are those who walk in gloom;
There are those who walk in light;
There are tempted overcome;
There are victors in the fight;
Shine or shade, vanquish'd or winning,
By Thy grace shield us from sinning.

4 There are those who sigh for Death,
Some to whom this life is great;
Some alas! count prayer but breath,
Others who on God do wait;
Death or life, prayerless or praying,
Keep us, Lord, from wrongly straying.

230. IMPATIENCE. "*I said in my haste,
all men are liars.*"—*Psalm cxvi. 2; St. Luke
xvi. 10; Romans v. 5; James i. 3; 2 Timothy
ii. 24.*   8s.

1 O LORD my God, I look to Thee;
Wilt Thou be pleas'd to look to me?
I mourn that I *impatient* am,
And dare Thy conqu'ring grace to claim;
O Lamb of God, how patient Thou!
Thy patience long, help me to show.

2 Like as the flint unto the tinder,
   Or smould'ring fire within the cinder;
   This stony heart of mine, O Lord,
   Is apt to flame up at a word;
   Forgive—forgive, and me constrain
   That I the vict'ry may obtain.

3 When passion Thou seest in me burn,
   Upon me, Lord, Thy meek Face turn;
   Such vision giving me of Faith;
   So touching me with Thy soft breath;
   That I shall not *impatient* be,
   But find myself conform'd to Thee.

4 How long Thou borest my neglect!
   Nor didst slow penitence reject;
   How oft forgave as oft I ask'd!
   How soon again Thy grace I task'd!
   O Lord, bestow self-mastery,
   That ruth not wrath on my lips lie.

5 I would not anger'd be but griev'd
   When I do find myself deceiv'd;
   I would be kind to ignorance,
   Rememb'ring Thy long-sufferance;
   I would Thy gentleness approach,
   On Thy name never bring reproach.

6 Like Thee I would hate only sin,
   But hating it, the sinner win,
   Not anger, Lord, but Thine Own grace
   Help me to show in voice and face;
   Impatient but with my own self;
   Impatience shunning as sunk shelf.

231. JOY BORN OF PAIN. *Acts of the Apostles cir. 22. 8s.*

"*Ubique majus quoddam modestia majori proceditur.*—St. Augustin. (Conf., lib. viii. iii.).

1 Joy is oft the white flower of Pain,
   Bursting from sere and rugged root;
   But comes the sunshine, comes the rain,
   And lo! at last hangs mellow fruit!

2 Joy is a red-tongu'd flame from fire,
   Leaping out of a sheath of smoke;
   Anon it quivers, spire on spire,
   And not without keen touch, yea stroke.

3 Joy is oft like to furnace gold,
   Shifted and sifted, seven times seven;
   Till gazing on it we behold
   All speckless by light of Heaven.

4 Joy oft times is like lightning flash,
   Life's sky left darker than before;
   But by-and-bye through thunder's crash
   Love's " still small voice " sounds midst the roar.

5 The greater pain the greater joy,
   The greater joy the greater pain;
   All earthly joys—how soon they cloy!
   Ah! Christ-sent loss is our best gain.

232. RETURNS. *Jer.* xviii. 20. 6.4.6.4.8.8.

1 I GIVE Thee hate for love,
     Thou love for hate;
   O sin all sins above,
     Heartless—ingrate;
   Reach hither, Lord, Thy crimson Hand,
   That I, heart-chang'd, before Thee stand.

2 I give Thee pride for grace,
     Thou grace for pride;
   I dare scarce lift my face,
     Yet would not hide;
   Reach hither, Lord, Thy crimson Hand,
   That I, heart-chang'd, before Thee stand.

3 I give Thee wrath for ruth,
     Thou ruth for wrath;
   Yea falsehood for Thy truth,
     E'en in "the path;"
   Reach hither, Lord, Thy crimson Hand,
   That I heart-chang'd, before Thee stand.

4 I give Thee dross for gold,
     Thou gold for dross;
   How may it all be told?
     Lo! Thy great cross!
   Reach hither, Lord, Thy crimson Hand,
   That I, heart-chang'd, before Thee stand.

5 I give at best my heart,
  Thou givest Thine ;
 O with Thy gracious art
  Thine mine combine ;
 Reach hither, Lord, Thy crimson Hand,
 That I, heart-chang'd, before Thee stand.

233. VICTORY BY DEFEAT. *2 Cor. 1. 7. 9. 14s.*

1 The battle lost to-day is oft a vict'ry later on ;
 Be true, be patient Brother, and it surely shall be won ;
 Sharp the discipline of defeat ; for weakness it reveals ;
 But weakness that lays hold of God, He with HIS OWN strength seals.

2 The whole stress of thy human need and burden lay on Him ;
 And let no mist becloud thy FAITH, or Hope's bright vision dim ;
 Our Earth shall yet sweep out from the shadow of death and sin ;
 Be strong—brave, Brother, the round world shall by-and-by be kin.

3 The clash of arms is heard still, and despots still have power
 The blood of noble men to spill ; but 'tis but for an hour ;
 The signs are in the heav'ns and Christ has given his sure word,
 The tongue and pen shall arbitrate and shiver War's red sword.

4 The mighty charters of free States abide beneath God's eye ;
 Tho' fallen is our race, the Earth is still bound to the sky ;
 No stroke for right against fell might, has e'er been struck in vain ;
 Lo! light spreads 'mong the people soon they shall burst their chains.

5 O Gospel of the Living Christ who died on Calvary's tree,
  Come in thy grace and masterdom that men Thy Face may see ;
 O Word of words for aching hearts, flash forth on our sad eyes,
 That soon Earth's grandest day upon Thy longing Church may rise.

6 *Repeat st. 1.*

234. IT IS WELL. *2 Kings iv. 26. 10. 3.*

1 DOST Thou take from us, Lord, what Thou hadst given ?
    " It is well."
 See'st Thou how sore beset we are, and driven ?
    " It is well."
 Come crowns or crosses, come or bright or dark,
    " It is well."
 For, Lord, we know Thou all our way dost mark.

2 Once our sweet home was brighten'd with child-faces ;
    It was well ;
 Thou them didst tear from our fond love's embraces ;
    " It is well."
 This, Lord, our joy, that all the lambs are safe ;
    " It is well."
 Thou keep'st them for us, and we do not chafe ;
    " It is well."

3 We had fair means from Thy aye bounteous Hand,
    It was well ;
 We trusted those who made us poor to stand ;
    " It is well."
 O God ! 'twas hard ; and yet we've come to see
    " It is well."
 The loss is but of lucre, not of Thee ;
    " It is well."

4 When strong and brave of heart we ne'er
  felt toil ;
          It was well.
Now Age snows on us, and low burns
  the oil :
          "It is well."
We sit upon Thy door-step, looking up,
          "It is well."
Whate'er Thou mixest we shall take Thy
  cup ;
          "It is well."

5 Once, O Lord God, our Faith and Hope
  were clear ;
          "It was well."
Now oft and oft there beats sharp pulse
  of fear ;
          "It is well."
Thy " little while " and Thou wilt end the
  n'ght ;
          "It is well."
And Faith and Hope be swallowed up in
  sight ;
          "It is well."

235. REMAINING SIN. *Rom.* vii. 24.

    3.3.8.3.3.8.6.6.

1   HE who doth send
        Will also end
  Whate'er of trouble comes to me ;
        Then I will rest,
        For He knows best
  When to hold bound and when to free :
        O my thrice-loving God,
        Shine Thou upon my road !

2   Ah, more and more
        My heart is sore
  Because of sin that still enchains ;
        But now I know
        'Midst all my woe,
  My Jesus loves and all ordains ;
        My Saviour, hear my cry,
        Behold my tear-drench'd eye !

3   Within, without,
        All evil rout;
  All ghostly tempters that assail ;
        O Lord, me take
        As now I quake ;
  And arm me with Thy heav'nly mail ;
        My Lord, let me not yield ;
        Protect me with Thy shield.

4   O Lord, I speak
        To Thee so meek ;
  Forgive forgive my wayward will ;
        O Christ, my Lord,
        By deed and word
  O tell me that Thou lovest still ;
        Yes, Lord, Thou'lt give me ease
        And from sin's gyves release.

236. MARY, SISTER OF LAZARUS.

St. John xi. 2, 70.

1 O to weep as Mary wept,
  And to keep where Mary kept !
  Blessed Jesus, at Thy feet
  Let me make my sweet retreat.

2 O to weep as Mary wept,
  And to keep where Mary kept !
  Sorrowing for all my sin,
  Yearning pard'ning love to win.

3 O to weep as Mary wept,
  And to keep where Mary kept ;
  Drinking in Thy mighty words
  E'en when they pierce as swords.

4 O to weep as Mary wept,
  And to keep where Mary kept !
  Hon'ring Thee with a full heart ;
  Gaining peace yet owning smart.

5 O to weep as Mary wept,
  And to keep as Mary kept !
  Ah ! Thou didst her softly bless ;
  Cleanse me in Thy tenderness.

6 O to weep as Mary wept,
  And to keep where Mary kept !
  I no record seek like hers
  Yet the name Thy grace confers.

7 O to weep as Mary wept,
And to keep where Mary kept!
Blessed Jesus, at Thy feet
Let me make my sweet retreat!

237. RUINS. *Acts of the Apostles xv. 16. 9s*

1 I SAW a dove, white-wing'd, close sitting
In broken altar of ruin grey;
That save for sunshine gold-bright flitting,
Seemed there to personify Decay;
Sweet dove! white-wing'd, thou life wast
    amidst dying
And broughtest brightness in thy level-
    flying.

2 O Holy Dove! in my heart dwelling;
Methinks 'tis to a ruin Thou hast come;
And yet the peace and hope within me
    swelling   [home;
Assure me Thou art making it Thy
Ah! Holy Ghost, 'tis broken hearts Thou
    hauntest,   [dauntest.
Nor the most desolate or foul Thee

238. "FAITH WITHOUT A PERHAPS."

—Count Agénor De Gasparin.
    1 Timothy ii. 8.   6s.

1 WHAT makes a man sincere,
Devout? *Soul* wilt thou hear!
A faith without 'perhaps':
If good or ill haps
Still on and on he goes,
Dauntless against all foes;
Weapons of proof his arms,
THE CHRIST shields in all harms.

2 What makes a man sincere,
Devout? *Heart* wilt thou hear!
A faith without 'perhaps':
His way THE SCRIPTURE maps;
Nor will he turn aside,
But still in Him abide;
And still with tranquil eye
Look up to Christ on High.

3 What makes a man sincere,
Devout? *Will* wilt thou hear!
A faith without 'perhaps',
That laughs at Death's lean chaps;
Fears not his sting or grave;
God's child and not a slave;
Knows well the Prince of Life
Is with him in the strife.

4 What makes a man sincere,
Devout? *Love* wilt thou hear!
A faith without 'perhaps':
God's Covenant has no gaps,
From childhood up to age
Thro' longest pilgrimage,
Still standeth firm and sure,
And shall to th' end endure.

239. THE BENDING BOUGH, OR SONG
AND WINGS. *Psalm lv. 6; lvi. 3.*

8, 7, 8, 7, 8, 8, 8, 7.

1 ON the tree top's topmost twig
    A nightingale clear-singing;
With passionate jug-jug and trig,
    The while the bough is swinging;
Bending—swaying; swaying—bending
Yet the song is still unending;
How is it so that thus it sings?
Ah! *It knows that it has wings.*

2 O heart of mine! the message take
    Straight home from th' Hand of God;
Let solid Earth beneath Thee shake,
    Tread thee where He has trod;
Duty aye with beauty blending,
Still a note of praise up-sending;
Singing as the sweet bird sings,
Feeling thy soul, too, has wings.

3 O charming bird of trustful breast,
    Singing on swaying bough,
Against the thorn thy brave heart prest;
    Thou teaching me art now;
Thy twig bending, downward tending,
But the root strong; and defending
Is God's gift of soaring wings;
So unfearing my soul sings.

MY CHOICE—LOVELINESS.

240. MY CHOICE. *Psalm ix. 14.* 8s.

1 LORD, By grace I've made my choice,
   In Thy salvation I rejoice;
   I as one of a fallen race
   Have grasp'd Thy universal grace.

2 Lord, By grace I've made my choice,
   In thy salvation I rejoice;
   No price I brought, no price I bring;
   Thy free salvation makes me sing.

3 Lord, By grace I've made my choice,
   In Thy salvation I rejoice;
   I empty was, I'm empty still,
   Thy full salvation doth me fill.

4 Lord, By grace I've made my choice,
   In Thy salvation I rejoice;
   I doubted sore, doubts yet assail,
   Thy strong salvation gives me mail.

5 Lord, By grace I've made my choice,
   In Thy salvation I rejoice;
   Ah! Transient are all things that move,
   But Thine is everlasting love.

241. LONGINGS. *Ps. cxix. 20.* 8s.

1 WITH ev'ry wild'ring mist dispersed,
   In great deeps of Thy love immersed;
   Thee holding as my heart's best treasure,
   By Thy Love's measure without measure;
   O God, keep me a child of light,
   Yea, ev'n with Thine Own brightness bright.

2 Not with my senses but with sense,
   Seek I to grow in excellence;   [heart
   Make Thou my mind, make Thou my
   To conquer all Thy Will would thwart;
   My cleansèd soul a temple be.
   Like Thine in speckless purity.

3 Alas! alas! the World hard tempts,
   Nor the most gracious heart exempts;
   Alas! how prone to turn "aside"
   Ev'n those who close to Thee abide:
   O for Thy thrice-controlling force,
   From sin, Lord Christ, me to divorce!

4 Thou seest, knowest me, my Saviour,
   O'erwatching daily my behaviour;
   Wilt Thou me of Thy grace, forgive?
   Wilt Thou to my dead heart say 'live'?
   I mourn, I weep, that I should be,
   So easily led to stray from Thee.

242. LOVELINESS.

Argument on such a subject is purely vexatious and barren, and wastes the time which should be spent in thankful hymns for the precious gift of loveliness.—WALTER BESANT ("Children of Gibeon," Bk. I. c. i.)
8s.

1 O I HAVE seen a face so fair!
   Form—features—colours, all so rare,
   That, charmed by its pure loveliness,
   I did for it the dear Lord bless.

2 It was the face of five-year'd child
   That all unconscious as she smil'd,
   Lo! made me look for flash of wings
   Such as to Earth a cherub brings.

3 O miracle of radiant eyes!
   Subtle as hues of sun-set skies:
   Rains, dews, and thunders, and the levin:
   Ah Half of darkness, half of heaven!

4 As tho' Eve's star o'er it did shine,
   There rose—mind full—a brow divine,
   With golden wealth of shimm'ring hair—
   That seem'd as sunbeams mingled there.

5 O wonderful are her small hands!—
   Like to the Queen of Fays she stands;
   Her dulcet voice in throat and tongue,
   Most cunning instrument of song.

6 May God thee bless, my little MAUD,
   Thy beauty fills my mind with laud;
   Lord, Thou hast made it, do Thou guard,
   That all harm be from her debarr'd.

6 *Repeat St. 1.*

243. A Jubilee Royal Saying.
... *deliciosas lassitudines.* —*St. Augustine*
(*Conf., lib. x. xxxiv*). *2 Cor. xi. 25-30.*

A pleasing little episode was recorded in the public prints of her Majesty on alighting from her carriage after the THANKSGIVING SERVICES in Westminster Abbey. The lord in waiting who was assisting the Queen in getting out of her carriage, asked whether her Majesty did not feel fatigued. "No," was the bright, grateful and graceful reply, "I am too happy to feel tired." This is only one of a thousand human touches that knit our Queen to her subjects far beyond her sovereign dignities. Nehemiah had found this out when he gave the counsel—"This day is holy unto the Lord; neither be ye sorry; for *the joy of the Lord* is *your strength.*" (Nehemiah iv. 10.)

78.

1 *I'm too happy to feel tired:*
   Words of our beloved Queen,
As her human heart was fired
   By the august sight just seen;
When, in grey Westminster bowed,
   Queen and subjects all re-vowed.

2 *I'm too happy to feel tired:*
   Words of our beloved Queen;
Merely to be read? admired?
   Nay; for "fine issues," I ween;
Taken for impulse to bring
   Glad service to our God and King.

3 *I'm too happy to feel tired:*
   Words of our beloved Queen;
Ye who serve God as if hired,
   See how 'tis your work's so mean;
All who, in love, The Master serve
Shall surely their first joy preserve.

4 *I'm too happy too feel tired:*
   Words of our beloved Queen;
May we all by them be inspired,
   Catching something of Heaven's sheen;
Combining work with heart-fill'd zeal
We never tiredness shall feel.

5 *Repeat St. 1.*

244. Cup Running Over. Ps. xxiii. 5.
108.

1 I HAVE a home with Heav'n's own lustre
   bright;
A wife and children, "walking in the
   light";
My means a happy mean, if 'tis not
   wealth,
And day by day strong in unbroken
   health;
  O Lord! my heart-thanks forth I pour;
  For truly "my cup runneth o'er."

2 I have a LIBRARY of many books—
   The spoil of long years searching i' hidden nooks;
Choice knowledge gained on rare and
   elect days
From men and books, in many lands, in
   sunny ways;
  O Lord! my heart-thanks forth I pour;
  For truly "my cup runneth o'er."

3 An inner circle of true friends I love,
Anchored not changeful,—ties are from
   Above;
Trusted and trustful or in grief or joy,
Aye drawing nearer, if has come annoy;
  O Lord! my heart-thanks forth I pour,
  For truly "my cup runneth o'er."

4 I have THE MASTER'S charter Him to
   serve
(From line Christolical ne'er let me
   swerve);
He uses me His great "good news" to
   preach,;
Land to His grace if I men's hearts do
   reach;
  O Lord! my heart-thanks forth I pour
  For truly "my cup runneth o'er."

5 I have received Thy chastening, dear
   Lord;
To me Thou hast fulfilled Thy tender
   word;

As son, not servant, Thou hast with me
    dealt ;
Musing o'er all Thy way, O Lord ! I melt;
Yea, Lord! my heart-thanks forth I pour,
In this too "my cup runneth o'er."

6 Full oft, O Lord ! has come to me and
    mine,
Abounding blessing, such as seem'd
    divine ;
Surcharged so that I could hold no more
Ah! —David's great word — "My cup
    runneth o'er" ;
    O Lord ! my heart-thanks now I bring,
    Like him I would adoring sing.

7 If later, Lord, Thy heavy rod has come,
I would not make complaint ; I would be
    dumb ;
All things laid on me have co-worked for
    good,
For sanctified have all been by "The
    Blood" ;
    O Lord ! my heart-thanks forth I pour
    Still—still my cup keeps "running o'er."

245.   THE BOW IN THE CLOUD.
            Genesis ix. 13.   7s.

1 DARK without, within I go ;
   Fearful, faintful, weary, slow ;
   Groping through the broad'ning dark ;
   Prithee, Lord, my way to mark :
       Look upon me in my woe,
       Bend o'er me Thy cov'nant Bow ;
       As the dawn across the wold
       Flash its brightness seven-fold.

2 Earth is black—I look above ;
   Man is hard—Thou, pitying Love !
   Creeping where I cannot see,
   Weeping, where words my lips flee ;
       Look up in me in my woe,
       Bend o'er me Thy cov'nant Bow ;
       As the dawn across the wold
       Flash its brightness seven-fold.

3 Thanks, O Lord, For Thou hast heard ;
   Praise, my God, for Thy true word ;
   Lo ! I see the yearned-for sign ;
   Lo ! I know that Thou art mine ;
       Thou hast bent Thy cov'nant Bow,
       Whence no vengeful arrows go ;
       As the dawn across the wold
       Bursts its brightness seven-fold.

243. WAKEFULNESS AND UNREST —"*Speak
Lord! for Thy servant heareth.*"—1 Samuel
iii. 9.   8.7.

1 "SPEAK, Lord, for Thy servant heareth."
   Let me catch Thy guiding word ;
   My heart waiting, watching, feareth ;
   Thou alone can'st peace afford.

2 "Speak, Lord, for Thy servant heareth,"
   Tossing—wistful—languid—weak ;
   O my God, the morning neareth,
   Wilt Thou not Thy silence break ?

3 "Speak, Lord, for Thy servant heareth,"
   Thou my aching heart dost know ;
   Thy blest Spirit's witness cheereth ;
   Lord, Thy witness now bestow.

4 "Speak, Lord, for Thy servant heareth,"
   Rough the sea and dark the night ;
   But I know, O Lord, who steereth ;
   Lift Thy face and all is light.

5 "Speak! Lord, for Thy servant heareth,"
   I am trembling like a reed ;
   Star ! That in our need appeareth ;
   Shine on me in this my need.

6 "Speak, Lord, for Thy servant heareth,"
   By Thy "still small voice" release ;
   Then howe'er my poor heart veereth,
   I shall enter into peace."

247.   THE CUP OF CONSOLATION.
           Jeremiah xvi. 7.
   "*The God of Consolation.*"—*Romans xv. 5.*
                                10s.

1 THOU gavest me the "Cup of Consolation,"
   When I was left in utter desolation ;
   Alone, upon the gaunt peak of Despair

THE ROD THAT BUDDED AND BLOSSOMED

I stood; but not alone, for Thou wast
  there.
2 Thou stooped'st o'er Thy bruisèd child,
    O Lord ;
  And 'mid the dark, did'st breathe the
    healing word ;
  My heart, grief-laden, all life's light gone
    out ,
  Thou wast not angry e'en with my wild
    doubt.

3 I strove like him by Jabbok—heart of
    evil
  Affirming that not God reign'd but the
    devil ;
  Thou knewest all, and with mild mighti-
    ness
  Granted'st a mother's kiss in my distress.
4 Thou gavest me the "Cup of Consolation,"
  When I was left in utter desolation ;
  Alone, upon the gaunt peak of Despair
  I stood; but not alone, for Thou wast there.

5 O Saviour! Praise for Thy magnanimous
    grace,
  That thus me follow'd to my hiding-place ;
  I had forsaken Thee, yet was Thy child,
  Nor would'st Thou of Thy lost one be
    beguil'd.

6 Wild words of anguish from my parched
    lips broke ;
  An atheist's heart invited vengeful stroke;
  Thou heardest all, and mightest me have
  Thou heardest all but only all to blot. [smote;

7 Thou sound'st the deeps of a bewilder'd soul
  When all Thy billows over it do roll ;
  And still rememb'rest Thy forsaken pang,
  When Thou 'neath blank skies on Thy
    Cross did'st hang.

8 Thou gavest me the "Cup of Consolation,"
  When I was left in utter desolation ;
  Alone, upon the gaunt peak of Despair
  I stood ; but not alone, for Thou wast there.

248. THE ROD THAT BUDDED AND
BLOSSOMED. *Numbers xvii.* 8s.

1 FAR back of God's own Israel,
   The Word of God doth to us tell
   How Aaron's rod, that was a wand,
   Budded and blossomed in his hand ;
     For God a great word had spoken,
     And seal'd its truth by this token.

2 O Lord my God, Thou changest not,
   Nor deed of kindness e'er doth blot ;
   I, too, through Thy so tender ruth
   Have come to know this precious truth ;
     Thy heaviest rod upon me laid,
     To bud and blossom Thou hast made.

3 '*Thy rod and staff they comfort me*' :
   'Tis David's sweetest melody ;
   O Lord, I would catch up his song !
   Affliction ne'er has done me wrong ;
     For still Thy rod like growing thing,
     Fragrance and fruit from Thee did bring.

4 I bless Thee, Lord, that I can say
   That light has come in darkest day ;
   Sickness and grief transfigured,
   Made me of my cross unafraid :
     Praise be to Thee, "my Lord, my God."
     Thou sanctifiest every rod.

249. ROOTED BY THE RIVER.
(Written by the Wells of Elim.)
Psalm i. 3o. *Jerem. xvii.* 8. 6s.

1 TREES rooted by a river
   Their fresh leaf fadeth never ;
   Tho' sere and parch'd the earth
   In long and rainless dearth ;
   They put forth " living green "
   Affording welcome screen.

2 Great Gardener ! look on me !
   I would be such a tree ;
   Rooted by gleaming river
   That flows, still floweth ever ;
   Nursed by Thy Spirit's breath ;
   Redeemèd by Thy Death.

3 Sometimes we see an oak
  Blasted by lightning's stroke;
  It stands a spectral thing,
  Tho' 'tis life-breathing Spring:
  Forbid such oak should be
  Symbol of mine, or me.

4 Thy gracious word fulfil!
  Work in me by Thy Will;
  Rooted in Thee, to grow
  Where " living waters " flow;
  And so with fruit abound
  Ev'n in Earth's sterile ground.

250. "WE ARE TIRED, MY HEART AND I."
Mrs. E. B. Browning.
Galatians vi. 9 and 2 Thessalonians iii. 13.
7s.

1 LONG the way by which I hie;
  Flags my spirit wearily;
  Let Thy gracious Hand me grasp;
  Let my trembling hand Thine clasp;
  We are tir'd, my heart and I:
  Ah! But Jesus Thou art nigh.

2 Faith, once full, has ebbed away;
  Hope, once bright, has turned to gray;
  Love, once warm, alas! is chilled;
  Heart of peace, with tremor filled;
  We are tir'd, my heart and I:
  Ah! But Jesus Thou art nigh.

3 Might, seems winning 'gainst the right;
  Darkness, gaining on the light;
  Falsehood, putting down the Truth;
  Heartlessness, loud mocking Ruth;
  We are tir'd, my heart and I:
  Ah! But Jesus Thou art nigh.

4 Fools, still heaping up their wealth;
  Toilers, not e'en given health;
  Wickedness, o'erpowering good;
  And all this spite of Thy Rood;
  We are tir'd, my heart and I:
  Ah! But Jesus Thou art nigh.

5 Dread, that God himself is dead,
  And by Evil conquerèd;
  Life, o'er-ruled by circumstance;
  Destiny, a thing of chance;
  We are tir'd, my heart and I:
  Ah! But Jesus Thou art nigh.

6 Living Christ, anoint mine eyes,
  Let not these things me surprise;
  All events Thou dost foreknow;
  Sure slow conquest Thou dost show;
  We are tir'd, my heart and I:
  Ah! But Jesus Thou art nigh.

7 Thy reign cometh, like the tide,
  Ebbing, flowing, yet still wide;
  As it widens o'er the world
  Sin shall from its seat be hurl'd;
  We are tir'd, my heart and I:
  Ah! But Jesus Thou art nigh.

251. SONS AND DAUGHTERS OF GOD.
"*Now are we the sons of God*". *1. John iii. 2.* (*Cf. 2 Corinthians iv. 17-18.*) 7s.

1 *Now are we the sons of God:*
    Spread the tidings far abroad;
  Sons of God in Jesus Christ;
  Sons of God, by love empric'd;
  Slaves of sin but now set free,
  Giv'n His " glorious liberty";
  Now are we the sons of God:
    Spread the tidings far abroad.

2 *Now are we the sons of Gods:*
    Spread the tidings far abroad;
  Sons and heirs,—joint-heirs with Him,
  Far far above ev'n seraphim;
  Blessed Saviour! grace impart
  That we yield up our whole heart;
  Now are we the sons of God:
    Let us sing along the road.

3 *Now are we the sons of God:*
    Spread the tidings far abroad;
  Here on Earth we may be poor,
  But our treasure yet is sure;
  Here we may contemnèd be,
  But are one in royalty;

Now are we the sons of God:
  Spread the tidings far abroad.

4 *Now are we the sons of God:*
  Spread the tidings far abroad;
  Christ in us and we in Christ,
  By His ever-holy tryst;
  Now it doth not yet appear;
  Yonder all shall be made clear:
  Now are we the sons of God:
  Heaven is our prepar'd abode.

5 *Now are we the sons of God:*
  Spread the tidings far abroad,
  "Abba Father"! be our song
  As we, joyous, move along;
  Liker to Him daily grow,
  Shewing what to Him we owe;
  Now are we the sons of God:
  Spread the tidings far abroad.

6 *Now are we the sons of God:*
  Spread the tidings far abroad;
  Help us, Lord, Thee still to serve,
  Never from Thy paths to swerve;
  Help by thought and word and deed,
  To commend Thy "holy seed";
  Now are we the sons of God:
  Soon to lay down Sin's sad load.

7 *Now are we the sons of God:*
  Spread the tidings far abroad;
  Face to face we shall abide,
  In Thy likness satisfied;
  Knowing e'en as we are known;
  Manifested as Thine Own:
  Now are we the sons of God:
  Spread the tidings far abroad.

252. IN THE FAR COUNTRY BY THE
  SWINE-TROUGHS.   7s.

". . able to save to the uttermost." *Heb. vii. 25.*

1 GOD, against Thee I have striven,
  Hanging as 'twixt hell and heav'n;
  Conscious of Sin's driving stress;
  Conscious of my wilfulness;
  Conscious that, though knowing good,
  I the paths of ill pursued:
    Sinners' Saviour, hear my cry,
    Look Thou on my misery.

2 Plung'd to-day in stinging grief,
  Morn brings frivolous relief;
  Climbing mountains of Despair,
  Breathing atheist's thinnest air;
  Then, a rush—I bear my load
  Unto Thee, Incarnate God:
    Sinners' Saviour, hear my cry,
    Look Thou on my misery.

3 Shudd'ring as temptation nears,
  Lusts of flesh, that conscience sears;
  Ne'ertheless again I'm bound,
  And by swine-troughs I am found,
  Gored by Mem'ry's awful tusks,
  Reft of even this World's husks:
    Sinner's Saviour, hear my cry,
    Look Thou on my misery.

4 Tainted in my very blood,
  I betake me to Thy Rood;
  God, Thou know'st my poignant fears!
  God, Thou see'st my seething tears!
  Now delaying, now repenting,
  Now heart-callous, now relenting:
    Sinners' Saviour, hear my cry,
    Look Thou on my misery.

5 God, behold me very weary,
  And my days forlorn and dreary;
  Wilt Thou hear as I still turn?
  Must Thy wrath for ever burn?
  God, O God, a castaway,
  May I dare to pray to Thee?
    Sinners' Saviour, hear my cry,
    Look Thou on my misery.

6 See my struggles! O how vain!
  Fast bound round as by a chain;
  See me set on fire of Hell;

THE UPLIFTED SERPENT—LITANY.

Conscience tolls her portent bell,
But Thy Blood the flames can quench,
And my soul from ruin wrench :
   Sinners' Saviour, hear my cry,
   Look Thou on my m'sery.

253. THE UPLIFTED SERPENT. *Numbers xxi. 4,9 ; St. John, iii., 14.* 8s.

1 "THE PEOPLE" all a-dying lay,
To fiery serpents a swift prey ;
But lo! the serpent on the pole
To all proclaims, " Look and be whole !"
   'Whoe'er," the all-embracing word,
   And Thou to it stoodst true, O Lord !

2 Here one might crouch at the pole's foot
Where as palm shaft tall it did shoot ;
The " look " straight up, or from far rim,
The pole and serpent small and dim ;
Or near or far, or young or old,
Life for a look, of all was told.

3 The poison'd blood now ebb'd no more,
But sure heal'd, flow'd strong as before;
Eye glazing, flash'd like ashen lamp;
Pallid brow lost its clammy damp ;
   "Whoe'er," the all-embracing word,
   And Thou to it stoodst true, O Lord !

4 Lo! dying mother, dying child,
Each other clasp'd in anguish wild ;
Up-looking trustful to the pole
Again the red life-stream doth roll :
And feeble Age by Faith's strong "look,"
No longer pain'd by weakness shook.

5 O joy to read the story true,
That no one look'd yet died in view;
But grander the uplifted Rood,
All crimson'd with the priceless blood :
   " Whoe'er,' the all-embracing word,
   And Thou to it standst true, O Lord.

6 Beyond the PLAIN and Israel,
A fuller Gospel we've to tell ;

Life for a look to EVERY ONE,
By the great work on Calv'ry done ;
Life for a look — denial never ;
Life for a look — assuréd ever.

7 Rejoice, rejoice, O all the Earth ;
And break forth now with holy mirth ;
The serpent old death-wounded now,
The Cross of Jesus struck the blow;
   " Whoe'er," the all-embracing word,
   And Thou to it standst true, O Lord !

254.   LITANY.   8s.
St. Matt. iii. 1.6.

1 O LORD, I hear the Baptist's cry,
" Repent ! The kingdom cometh nigh;'
I catch it up ; nor would I seek
To thrust it from me, or to wreak
On olden Scribe or Pharisee,
The symbol'd woes of axe and tree.

2 Before Thee, Lord, I bow my head;
Accept ev'n all the Baptist said;
His loudest call, " Repent ! Repent!"
I feel as unto me 'twas sent;
O the long patience of my God!
And doom still lingering on the road.

3 Alas! O Lord, my penitence
Still follow'd is by fresh offence ;
Unfruitful is my life of good,
Tho' crimson'd by Thy sacred blood;
O for a sharper sense of sin !
And high resolve the fight to win.

4 Thy Spirit, Lord, in me abide,
That I keep closer by Thy side ;
Or send me Thy sweet chastisement,
That lowlily I may " Repent";
I own, O God, my negligence,
I cast me on Thy love immense.

5 O, Lord, I hear the Baptist's cry
" Repent ! The kingdom cometh nigh!"

PENITENCE. THE PENITENT.

I catch it up, nor would I seek
To thrust it from me, or to wreak
On olden Scribe or Pharisee,
The symbol'd woes of axe and tree.

255.   PENITENCE.   9.9.8.8

"*Prick'd to the heart.*" *Acts of the Apostles,
ii. 37.*

"*Cut to the heart.*" *Acts of the Apostles vii. 54.*

1 *Prick'd to the heart:* Lord, I would borrow
These blessed words to tell my sorrow;
Responsive to Thy Spirit's touch,
I would to Thee my guilt avouch.

2 *Cut to the heart:* but savingly;
Melted—not madden'd—tremblingly;
Cut to the heart: like them of old,
But with a different meaning told.

3 *Prick'd to the heart:* as by an arrow
Shot through and through unto the mar-
O Lord my God, to Thee I turn;   [row;
Heal Thou, that I no longer mourn.

4 *Cut to the heart:* by Thy love's token,
Thy heart for me, on Calvary broken;
Forgiving mercy, healing grace,
I magnify with beaming face.

5 *Prick'd to the heart:* yet Lord, believing
Thou workest in my keenest grieving;
I place myself before Thee now,
Uplifting an unfearing brow.

6 *Cut to the heart:* but interblending
Strange happiness, from Thee descending;
O gracious Saviour, hear my cry,
I live in Thee, for Thou didst die.

7 *Prick'd to the heart:* O words of brightness!
Prelusive of the blood-wash'd whiteness;
Give, Lord, Thy Pentecostal dower,
Make me a trophy of Thy power.

8 *Cut to the heart:* Lord, I would borrow,
The changèd words to sing my sorrow;
My guilt I know, I mourn, I own,
Let Thy blood shed for me atone!

256.   THE PENITENT.   8s.

"*I will arise and go to my father.*"—*St.
St. Luke cxv. 18.*

1 O FATHER mine, I look to Thee,
Wilt Thou, forgiving, look to me?
In the "far country" which I sought
To utmost desolation brought;
Bereft by those who shar'd my all,
As was Thy storied Prodigal.

2 I catch Thy call of pity "Come,"
When well to me Thou might'st be dumb;
I feel Thy Spirit's mighty touch
As by the swine-troughs here I crouch;
Alas! to Thee I turned my back,
But Thou to follow wast not slack.

3 Sick, sick at heart, and sick in brain,
Remorse accentuates the pain;
For, O my God, I saw the light,
Yet plung'd in to the fouler night;
Thy Gospel heard, as child, and knew
From sainted mother's lips 'twas true.

4 Alas! How have I serv'd the devil!
Still lusting after all things evil;
Hard is the bondage, and exacting;
And all its pleasure, merest acting;
What am I, that thus Thou hast borne?
Immense the grace that bids return.

5 Bone-weary on my wretched quest,
An aching heart still longs for rest;
Dark memories my soul appal,
And "old sins" like to fire-sleet fall:
I lay me, Lord, at Thy cross down;
Hell-worthy, guilty—all I own.

6 Lo! at Thy feet I prostrate lie,
  Accepting Thy soft clemency;
  As now it quivers in my breast,
  "Come ye, come unto Me, and rest;"
  O Father mine, I look to Thee,
  Wilt Thou, forgiving, look to me?

257. Penitent Return. *Gen. xviii. 27.*
8s.

1 I grasp Thy hand, O God, in trust,
  Tho' I be but a child of dust;
  For when Thou wast with us below
  Children of dust to Thee did go;
    Nor ever one was bid depart,
    Bearing the same sin-laden heart.

2 I know my guilt, I own my shame;
  I take unto myself all blame;
  Askest Thou, did not I say "Come?"
  Before Thee, Lord, I must be dumb;
    For thro' long years alas! in vain
    Thou still hast sought my heart to gain.

3 Thanks, that I still am left alive; [strive;
  Thanks, that Thou still with me dost
  Thanks, that in long sweet patience Thou,
  Hast borne and borne with me till now;
    Thy Love griev'd by my evil ways,
    Yet Mercy giving me more days.

4 O Lord my God, send forth Thy light,
  Let it be lightning me to smite;
  O "make me willing," set me free;
  Help me surrender all to Thee:
    O Lord, forgive my late repenting!
    O pity my worn heart's lamenting!

5 I see, O Christ, "The Crucified,"[belied;
  How my "hard thoughts" have Thee
  My evil heart of unbelief
  Too proud to seek blood-bought relief;
    But Thou, my Saviour reconciled,
    Hast at long last made me Thy child.

258. Contrition. *Ps. xxxiv. 18; li. 17; Is. lvii. 15.* 7s.

1 O my God, my heart is sore!
  Wilt Thou heal me, I implore?
  Vain each remedy I seek;
  Thou the mighty word must speak;
    Hear me, Lord, O hear me yet!
    Pardon, pardon, and forget.

2 Even my dim eyes perceive
  Full enough Thee, Lord, to grieve;
  How much more by Thy keen glance
  Mightest Thou 'gainst me advance!
    Hear me, Lord, O hear me yet!
    Pardon, pardon, and forget.

3 Contrite make me, contrite keep,
  Look in ruth on Thy "lost" sheep;
  Ah! Good Shepherd of the Fold,
  See me wand'ring, tir'd, and cold;
    Hear me, Lord, O hear me yet!
    Pardon, pardon, and forget.

4 Patient, pitiful Thou art;
  Lord, Thou see'st my sin-pierc'd heart;
  Break its thraldom, and release,
  Speaking Thy great word of "peace;"
    Hear me, Lord, O hear me yet!
    Pardon, pardon, and forget.

5 Like pulse beating in the brain
  Lord, Thou knowest this sharp pain;
  For Thy Name's sake, let me rest,
  As a child on mother's breast;
    Hear me, Lord, O hear me yet!
    Pardon, pardon, and forget.

259. Each Day the Evening Comes at Last. *2 Cor. iv. 17, 18.* 12s.

1 Trials on trials come, but by-and-bye they go;
  Sorrows, but a soft hand o'er our wet eyes is pass'd;
  Darkness, but in the dark, stars more in brightness glow;
  It holdeth still, *Each day the ev'ning comes at last.*

2 Life is a voyage strange on a tempestuous
    sea ;
  Long, long have we to wait our anchor
    firm to cast ;
  But through the tempest fierce, Thou,
    gentle Lord, dost see ;
  And makest good, *Each day the ev'ning
    comes at last.*

3 Life is a journey vague, leading through
    Wilderness ;
  Weary the way, and long, and search'd
    by chilling blast;
  Pillar of cloud by day and fire by night
    still bless ;
  Fulfilling how *Each day the ev'ning
    comes at last.*

4 Christ's own do sometimes speak with
    weak and faltering lips ;
  Saviour! "My God! My God!" that
    cry made Heaven aghast !
  But "It is finished" flashed a grand
    apocalypse ;
  Still stablishing, *Each day the ev'ning
    comes at last.*

260.   GOD OF PEACE.   10s.
*"Now the God of peace be with you all."—
Romans xv. 33.*

1 O LORD my God, Look Thou into my
    breast,
  As troubled 'tis and toss'd in wild unrest ;
  O wilt Thou of Thy pard'ning grace
    impart
  To hush the tempest of a troubled heart?
  Thou, "God of Peace," calm my rebel-
    lious will,
  Yea, speak Thy word of old, say "Peace!
    be still !"

2 Alas ! alas ! O Lord, I must confess
  Returns of my first conflict's deep dis-
    tress ;
  When sin was felt with no sight of the
    Rood ;
  The Law accusing, but unseen "the
    Blood";
  O "God of Peace," hear Thou my des'late
    cry,
  That I may catch up Thy "Fear not,
    'tis I."

3 Sorrows and worries, Lord, like wave on
    wave,
  Bring me to Thee, O Thou the strong to
    save !
  Losses and crosses grieve and burden
    sore
  And seem to say "peace, thou shalt
    know no more ;"
  O "God of Peace," my old faith wilt
    Thou give?
  Then I shall see all these are fugitive.

4 O Lord my God, when trembling forth I
    look,
  I find my "first love" chill'd, my first
    faith shook ;
  Old fears and doubts glide back and me
    assail,
  Piercing with "fiery darts" my erewhile
    mail;
  O "God of Peace," reveal Thyself aga'n,
  Release me from this tumult and this pain.

261.   THE SHINING FACE.   8s.
"The skin of his face did shine.—Exodus
  xxiv. 29.

1 LORD, wilt Thou of Thy loving grace
  Bestow on me the shining face?
  O I would nearer and more near
  Get me to Thee—more sure and clear,
  Behold Thee as Thou art in Christ ;
  And, by Thy light be so rejoiced,
  That lustre of my hiding-place
  Will show its glow upon my face.

2 Of old Thy saint on Sinai's height
  No mortal food, or drank, or ate,
  Thou gav'st to him the heav'nly bread;
  Thy Spirit, soul and body fed;
  I may not seek such mighty grace,
  But I would have the shining face,
  That comes of closer holier walk
  While as a Friend with Thee I talk.

3 If Sinai's terrors on me fall,
  My God, upon Thee I will call;
  O let Thy " still small voice " uphold
  Whene'er Thy thunders loud are roll'd!
  Be thou to me sure hiding-place
  That still I shew the shining face;
  Then come the dark, or come the bright,
  I shall be seen a guiding light.

4 When I descend " the Mount " again
  Witnessing, walking on " the plain;"
  From Tabor's radiance brought back
  To grapple powers demoniac;
  O still, dear Lord, I seek That Thou
  Would'st give to me my first love's glow;
  Yea, in the fulness of Thy grace,
  Give and re-give the shining face.

5 Lord, wilt Thou of Thy loving grace
  Bestow on me the shining face?
  O I would nearer and more near
  Get me to Thee — more sure and clear;
  Behold Thee as Thou art in Christ;
  And, by Thy light be so rejoic'd,
  That lustre of my hiding-place
  Will shew its glow upon my face.

232.   LILY AND CEDAR.   8s.

Hosea xiv. 5,6.

1 FAIR as the LILY would I be,
  But all my fairness owe to Thee;
  Like CEDAR strong, strike out my roots,
  But only by Thy " dew " bear fruits:
  Fair, strong, and fruitful, Saviour mine,
  As Thou bestowest grace divine.

2 The LILY'S crimson at Eve's shades
  In bloom and leaf swift droops and fades;
  Not so, O Christ! my blood-bought dress.
  Thy crimson robe of righteousness;
  I wear it aye, and know no fears,
  Unstain'd, unchang'd thro' all the years.

3 As 'neath the CEDAR on its mountain,
  Deep-rooted by a cooling fountain;
  I would me shelter, Lord, for ever,
  Beside Thy Cross, and see "the River";
  Receiving still from Love's dear Hand
  New strength, new life, as there I stand.

4 CEDAR and LILY'S freshening green
  Catch up the sun's a-gold'ning sheen;
  So I — pass'd from Sin's darksome night —
  Would walk as Thine Own child of Light;
  Fair, strong, and fruitful, Saviour mine,
  As Thou bestowest grace divine.

263.   LAID ASIDE.   7s.

" *My stroke is heavier than my groaning.*"
Job xxiii. 2.

1 LORD, I cannot speak *to* Thee;
  Wilt Thou, gracious, speak to me?
  Thou see'st how with pain I'm wrung;
  How words falter on my tongue;
  O Thou mighty heart of Love,
  Send me succour from Above!

2 Lord, I cannot speak *for* Thee;
  Wilt Thou from this silence free?
  Souls are lying on my heart
  I would warn ere I depart;
  If it please Thee, break my chain
  That once more I speak again.

3 Lord, I cannot speak *with* Thee;
  For Thy Word is shut to me;
  As I languish on my bed,
  I nor read nor can have read;
  Burden'd are my sleepless eyes;
  Thy Hand heavy on me lies.

4 Lord, Regard me in my grief;
  Lord, Bestow Thy sweet relief;
  Cause me, as I anguish'd lie,
  Still to know that Thou art nigh;
  As to Thee my woe I bring,
  O heal Thou my sorrowing!

5 Blot out my defectiveness;
  With Thy perfectness me bless;
  And that strange disturbing power
  In the silent lonely hour
  When Thy voice, like breaking wave,
  Thunders on me—but to save.

6 Lord, I cannot speak to Thee;
  Wilt Thou, gracious, speak to me?
  Thou see'st how with pain I'm wrang;
  How words falter on my tongue;
  O Thou mighty heart of Love
  Send me succour from Above!

264. UNITY IN DIVERSITY. 7s.

"*There shall be one Flock and one Shepherd.*"—*St. John* x 16. *(Cf. St. John xxii. 20.23.)*

1 SHEPHERD-SAVIOUR! we behold
  Thy vast Flock that Thou dost fold,
  Gathering from age to age—
  Spite of man and Satan's rage;
  Hear, as on our knees we plead,
  Hear us! hear us! intercede!
    Thy word pass'd, Thy promise giv'n,
    O fulfil, Lord Christ from Heav'n;
    Thou one Shepherd of one Flock,
    One Church built on Thee "the Rock."

2 Shepherd-Saviour! Who dost keep
  Love's long vigil while we sleep;
  Thou dost see how o'er all lands
  Still contending Thy Church stands;
  Diverse sects, not friends but foes,
  Whilst conscience their schisms gloze.
    Thy word pass'd, Thy promise giv'n,
    O fulfil, Lord Christ, from heav'n;
    Thou one Shepherd of one Flock,
    One Church built on Thee, "the Rock."

3 Shepherd-Saviour! by Thy power,
  Give to us Thy Spirit's dower;
  All who bear Thy blessed name
  Do Thou teach their guilt and shame;
  Thy long-promis'd unity
  Unsolv'd problem still doth lie.
    Thy word pass'd, Thy promise giv'n,
    O fulfil, Lord Christ, from heav'n,
    Thou one Shepherd of one Flock,
    One Church built on Thee "the Rock."

4 Shepherd-Saviour! not one Fold
  May we hope to see enroll'd;
  Thine own chosen Israel
  Into twelve tribes banner'd fell;
  So, Lord, we; but with one heart
  Lov'd and loving, each take part.
    Thy word pass'd, Thy promise giv'n,
    O fulfil, Lord Christ, from heav'n;
    Thou one Shepherd of one Flock,
    One Church built on Thee, "the Rock."

5 Shepherd-Saviour! hear our cry;
  Yea, it turn to litany;
  None unchurching, churching all
  Would we, who on Jesus call;
  Diverse creeds, and modes, and names,
  Christ supreme above all claims.
    Thy word pass'd, Thy promise giv'n,
    O fulfil, Lord Christ, from heav'n,;
    Thou one Shepherd of one Flock,
    One Church built on Thee "the Rock."

6 Shepherd-Saviour, Thou know'st each
  Straying sheep Thy servants reach;
  Minist'rest Thy blood-bought gifts,
  To whoe'er Thy Cross uplifts;

Since 'tis thus, O, make us see
Oneness in diversity.
    Thy word pass'd, Thy promise giv'n
    O fulfil, Lord Christ, from heav'n ;
    Thou one Shepherd of one Flock,
    One Church built on Thee "the
       Rock."

265.   DIVINE TEACHING.   7s.
"Teach me Thy way, O Lord!"
Psalm cxxviii. 11.

1 TEACH me, O my God, Thy way,
    That I never more may stray ;
    Ah! How prone to "turn aside,"
    If Lord, Thou wilt not me guide :
    As a little child I cry,
    "Teach me, guide me, with Thine eye";
    Teach me, O my God, Thy way,
    That I never more may stray.

2 Teach me, O my God, Thy way,
    And let nothing from Thee fray ;
    Voices of the earth and air
    Need Thy warning word, "Beware";
    I would listen, and return
    As my cheeks with red shame burn ;
    Teach me, O my God, Thy way,
    That I never more may stray.

3 Teach me, O my God, Thy way,
    Never would I say Thee "Nay";
    Shew to me the path of duty,
    And of holiness the beauty ;
    Shew me, Lord, Thy gracious Face
    As each wrong step I retrace :
    Teach me, O my God, Thy way,
    That I never more may stray.

4 Teach me, O my God, Thy way,
    That I do not Thee betray ;
    Let Thy holy will be mine,
    Take my heart and make it Th'ne;
    That thus daily purified
    I shew forth The Crucified;
    Teach me, O my God, Thy way,
    That I never more may stray.

5 Teach me, O my God, Thy way,
    Pardon my long, cold delay ;
    Sinning now and now repenting ;
    Harden'd now and now relenting ;
    Make me see, and hear, and know
    Thou hast but one way to show ;
    Teach me, O my God, Thy way,
    That I never more may stray.

266.   "THY WILL BE DONE."   7s.
St. Matt. vi. 10.

1 CHANGEFUL is our earthly state,
    Now depress'd and now elate :
    Fainting now, now seeming strong,
    Silent now, now loud in song :
    Gracious Lord, *Thy will be done*,
    Walk we or in cloud or sun.

2 Thou led'st thro' the wilderness :
    Bread from Heav'n did them bless ;
    Thou Thy people led'st about,
    But '*the* Land' solved every doubt :
    Thus 'tis still : *Thy will be done*,
    Walk we or in cloud or sun.

3 Tabor's splendour Christ did see
    Ere came dark Gethsemane ;
    And when cup of wrath He held,
    Strength'ning angel help did yield :
    Thus to us : *Thy will be done*,
    Walk we or in cloud or sun.

4 Long the way and drear the road,
    Laden still with sin's great load ;
    Now we sink, and now we soar,
    One time rich, again we're poor ;
    Poor or rich, *Thy will be done*,
    Walk we or in cloud or sun.

5 Give us faith, Lord, give us strength
    Staying us thro' life's whole length ;
    In a "little while" we stand
    Safe, as sav'd, in that "Good Land,"
    Singing still, *Thy will be done*,
    Clouds no more and Thou the sun.

27. FADING LEAF. 7s.

"We all do fade as a leaf." Isaiah xliv. 6.

1 DAY-LIGHT shortens, night draws nigh,
 Shadows broaden in our sky ;
 At the longest life is brief —
 All do fade as doth a leaf.

 We grow poor and sad at heart ;
 One by one, dear ones depart,
 Gather'd like Autumnal sheaf :
 All do fade as doth a leaf.

3 Yet we would not faithless weep,
 For the lov'd and lost who sleep;
 He will one day end our grief,
 Tho' *all fade as doth a leaf.*

4 Leaves and blooms drop in the mould;
 Sleeping through the Winter's cold ;
 But the Spring brings sweet relief,
 Whilst *we all fade as a leaf.*

5 Light of Hope engrandeurs life ;
 Hope of light upbears in strife ;
 Death ! Thine is a cancell'd brief,
 Tho' *we all fade as a leaf.*

6 Touching are the signs around,
 But we know where we are bound ;
 The dread grave's no sunken reef ;
 Yet *we all fade as a leaf.*

7 Watchful would we be, O Lord,
 Staying us upon Thy Word ;
 That the end come not as thief,
 Whilst *we all fade as a leaf.*

8 Let us witness, work, and wait ;
 Never in our zeal abate ;
 As the longest life is brief ;
 We must *all fade as a leaf.*

268. THE BLESSINGS OF SADNESS. 6s.

" Blessed are they that mourn."
 St. Matt. v. 4.

1 Bless'd are they that mourn :
 Hard lesson, Lord, to learn ;
 Yet lesson we beseech
 Thou wouldest to us teach.

2 Blessèd are they that mourn :
 Our hearts, Lord, in us burn ;
 As Thou talk'st "by the way"
 Our anguish to allay.

3 Blessèd are they that mourn :
 E'en by the grave's sad bourn;
 There, Lord, Thou whisp'rest sweet,
 "All dead in Christ shall meet."

4 Blessèd are they that mourn :
 Yet, sharp, Lord, is the thorn ;
 As we go with bent head,
 And are not comforted.

5 Blessèd are they that mourn :
 Lord, unto Thee we turn,
 Whilst walking with sore heart,
 And naught will ease impart.

6 Blessèd are they that mourn :
 Thou hast, Lord, all grief borne ;
 Thy secret let us know ;
 Thy restfulness bestow.

7 Blessèd are they that mourn :
 Even when most forlorn ;
 Thou, Lord, mak'st light arise,
 With strange and sweet surprise.

8 Blessèd are they that mourn :
 Weak, weary-soul'd, and worn ;
 As it needs darkest night,
 To shew stars' golden light.

9 Blessèd are they that mourn :
 Thou wilt not humblest spurn ;
 To Thine hast thou not said,
 Ye shall be comforted.

269.   Dignity of the Body.   8s.

1 Corinthians iii. 16-17 ; Hebrews ii. 16.
"We leave our body behind ; that is done with. But we will not leave it behind without thanking God for the use of it. Touch it tender'y ; put it away carefully ; its work is done."— T. T. Lynch.

1 My Lord, this mortal flesh I see,
Thy vesture was, as 'tis to me ;
Thou, too, wast born a human child,
But "holy, harmless, undefiled";
Land for the record meets my eye,
Uplifting flesh to dignity ;
Yea, touching as with Heav'n's own light
And a splendour infinite.

2 Alas! O Jesus, I oft find
This 'flesh' o'ermastering my 'mind';
Alas! hard oft the fight I wage
Against its fierce tempestuous rage;
Thou sinless One, me sinful see :
Compassionate my misery.
Wilt Thine own purity impart ?
Wilt give to me the gracious heart ?

3 I dare not mortal flesh malign :
'Tis sacred e'er since it was Thine ;
But, Lord, I yearn to have expell'd
This sin by which I'm captive held ;
Take Thou my sin, O Christ, for me ;
My body consecrate to Thee ;
A temple by Thy grace made meet,
Traversed of Thy holy feet.

4 This body "wonderfully" made,
Still needs Thy gracious Spirit's aid ;
That following Thee, The Crucified,
I may be wholly sanctified :
Bind soul and body into one
In a most perfect union ;
That I may shew in mortal clay
The "glorious body" of that day !

270.   Compunction not Conversion.

Ezekiel xi. 19 ; Zech. vii. 12 ; Rom. vii. 9.
(Composed in the Quarry above Penmaenmawr, N. Wales.)

1 When I look upon this stone,
Tremors in my heart I own :
For though now the stone's so hard
As my heaviest blows to ward ;
Once in ages distant far,
Molten 'twas in fiery war :
   Bethink thee, soul,
   As bell did knoll.

2 Wrath of God may smite, amaze,
Kindling conscience to a blaze ;
Bowing in despairing fear,
Fetching moan and scalding tear ;
But the heart that has not died
Harder grows, unsanctified :
   Bethink thee, soul,
   As bell did knoll.

3 Heart of mine 'neath His great touch,
Faith in Christ thou did'st avouch ;
Thou did'st see His love, and melt,
His forgiving mercy felt ;
Is "first love" now on the wane ?
Art thou growing hard again ?
   Bethink thee, soul,
   As bell did knoll.

271.   Life is the Day of Grace.   6s.

"... and the door was shut."   *St. Matt. xxv. 10.*

1 *Life is the day of grace :*
Our lives they fleet apace !
O souls immortal wake :
Your all, your all's at stake ;
Christ standeth at your gate,
Not yet "too late ! too late !"

2 *Life is the day of grace:*
   O haste ye, haste your pace;
   Behold He calleth now,
   Long-lingering and slow;
   Still patient He, to win,
   You—you to enter in.

3 *Life is the day of grace:*
   Death comes with iron mace;
   While yet ye live, take heed;
   See, see THE VICTIM bleed!
   And hark! the Gospel call,
   Salvation free to all.

4 *Life is the day of grace:*
   Up! Strive to win the race!
   Lo! Grace and Truth have come;
   Turn, listen, be not dumb;
   Sweet is their voice and clear;
   Oh! e'er it passes hear!

5 *Life is the day of grace:*
   Your downward steps retrace;
   While yet the Word appeals;
   While yet the Spirit seals;
   Awake! awake! to-day,
   Oh! hazard not delay!

6 *Life is the day of grace:*
   Lift up a pleading face;
   Your Father sees you there,
   Sin-laden howsoe'er;
   Oh! cry a sinner's cry!
   WHY SOULS, WHY WILL YE DIE?

7 *Life is the day of grace:*
   Think not PAST to efface;
   While yet 'tis call'd to-day
   Up up to Him! away
   Eternity is near,
   Oh! hear the Saviour, hear!

8 *Life is the day of grace:*
   Our lives they fleet apace;
   O souls immortal wake!

   Your all, your all's at stake;
   Christ standeth at your gate,
   Not yet "too late! too late!"

272. THE SPENT BOTTLE AND THE WELL
      REVEALED.

    Genesis xxi. 14-19.   108.

1 HER bottle spent, the Well came into view;
   E'en so, O Lord, Thy People find it true;
   Cast out, sin-laden, in the Wilderness,
   Thou comest near and pitiest our distress.

2 O Saviour, see my bottle too is spent!
   Vain human help; be to my moan attent!
   My lonely wretchedness how can I tell?
   O Lord, ano'nt my eyes, shew me the
     Well!

3 Long, long alas! I've wandered far from
   And now lie helpless in my misery; |Thee,
   I have no strength; just as I am I come;
   Do what Thou wilt, before Thee I am
     dumb.

4 O Saviour, haste to answer my faint
     prayer! |spare;
   Grace hast Thou e'en for me enough to
   Weary and worn beneath Sin's luring
     spell, |Well!
   I turn, return: O Christ, shew me the

5 Praise to Thy grace, Lord, Thou my cry
     hast heard; |word;
   Praise for free mercy, Thou hast sent the
   Hast drawn me back, hast touch'd me by
     Thy Spirit; |merit.
   And now in Him, I plead my Saviour's

6 Alas! I dread I still may "turn aside;"
   O keep me, Jesus, that I ne'er backslide!
   Grant that I may near Thee for ever
     dwell; |Well.
   And when my bottle's spent, shew me the

273. There's a Bright Side to
Darkest Things.

" Now men see not the bright light that is in the clouds ; but. . ."—Job xxvii. 21.
10s.

1 O TROUBLED soul ! Take thou whate'er is sent ;
'Tis by thy Heav'nly Father kindly meant ;
    A bright side thou may'st see in darkest things.
O look Thou through the mists that veil the sky ;
The light *is* there to break forth by-and-bye ;
    Mount up, my soul, upon Faith's shining wings.

2 O'erladen heart ! One heart still knoweth thine ;
Think not " He careth not ;" fret not nor pine ;
    A bright side thou may'st see in darkest times.
Tell thou to Him confidingly thy care ;
Have no concealments ; to reveal ALL, dare ;
    He strongest is who the most closely clings.

3 O lonely spirit ! All thou lov'd'st now gone ;
No more than He was, art thou left alone ;
    A bright side thou may'st see in darkest things.
The Christ knows all about thee, and will give
His company, by sweet prerogative ;
    O try thou this ! the most sure peace it brings.

4 Conscience accusing lifts its burning eye ;
Ah ! But His precious blood will pacify ;
    A bright side thou may'st see in darkest things.
Place thy old sins and new thy God before
And thou shalt hear His "Go ! and sin no more !"
    Tho' grass be mown see how it quickly springs.

274. The Future. *Deut. xxix. 29.*

7·7·7·7·7·7·7·

1 I have wept, yet would not rail
That thou FUTURE wear'st a veil ;
That thou silent art, nor e'er
Answer gives to wildest prayer
E'en of FAITH driven to despair ;
Finger plac'd on thy shut lips,
That refuse Apocalypse.

2 Near to us as Yesterday,
Still thou holdest us at bay,
Lifting up thy veiled face,
That no feature we can trace ;
Dumb even to Love's embrace ;
TO-MORROW still dost delay,
Till it bounds on us TO-DAY.

3 Lord of life and Lord of Time,
In thy onward march sublime,
Thou the Past and Future holdest ;
Or Thou hidest or unfoldest,
Action and event all mouldest ;
Secrets clear disrob'd to Thee
Better, Lord, than unto me.

4 Grant to me the " walk of Faith,"
Ever trustful of " He saith " ;
Still thro' all Thy voice to hear,
Feeling Thee to be aye near,
Ready, lo ! to hush our fear ;
Let no doubts o'er me prevail :
FUTURE ! Ever wear thy veil.

275. AIMLESSNESS. *Phil. iii. 14.* 6s.

1 Ah, Lord, how aimlessly
Day after day goes by!
And yet Thou call'st for thought
And service finely wrought;
Dost bid us each awake
And for Thee some post take;
Shewing thro' op'nings rife,
Work is the salt of life.

2 Ah, Lord, how aimlessly
Day after day goes by,
O quicken me to serve!
O grant me will and nerve!
That by Thy grace e'en "driven"
Some task of love be given;
Finding 'midst petty strife
Work is the salt of life.

3 Ah, Lord, how aimlessly
Day after day goes by,
And yet Thou call'st for thought
And service finely wrought;
Dost bid us each awake,
And for Thee some post take;
Shewing thro' op'nings rife,
Work is the salt of life.

4 Ah, Lord, how aimlessly
Day after day goes by,
Tho' by Thy love embrac'd,
Tho' by Thy Spirit graced;
Alas! I show no shoot!
Alas! I bear no fruit!
Forth with Thy pruning knife!
Work is the salt of life.

5 Ah, Lord, how aimlessly
Day after day goes by!
The air is full of calls,
But ah! how vainly falls
The summons on my ear.
O rouse me, Lord, to hear!
Melt me with Thine Own grief:
Work is the salt of life.

6 Ah, Lord, how aimlessly
Day after day goes by!
And yet Thou call'st for thought
And service finely wrought;
Dost bid us each awake
And find some post to take;
Shewing thro' op'nings rife,
Work is the salt of life.

276. LONGING. *2 Peter iii. 14-15.* 6s.

1 How long, O Lord, how long
Until shall burst the song
That holy men of old
With burning lips foretold!--
Earth fill'd with Thy glory
Won by "the old, old story":
How long, O Lord, how long
Until shall burst the song!

2 How long, O Lord, how long
Until shall burst the song,
Of man no more beguil'd,
By Thy love reconcil'd;
The crimson cross supreme,
Prov'd mighty to redeem:
How long, O Lord, how long,
Until shall burst the song!

3 How long, O Lord, how long
Until shall burst the song!
The throne of Evil shattered,
The hosts of hell all scattered,
Heav'n on Earth begun,
Thy will by all men done:
How long, O Lord, how long
Until shall burst the song!

4 How long, O Lord, how long,
Until shall burst the song?
That all who love the Lord
Are walking in accord;
No jealousy, no hate,
All in love consecrate;
How long, O Lord, how long
Until shall burst the song!

5 How long, O Lord, how long
Until shall burst the song!
Hear our united cry!
Hear, hear our plaintive sigh!
Fulfil Thy promise spoken;
Let not Thy word be broken;
Redeem'd, make good Thy claim;
Take Earth in Thy Great Name:
How long, O Lord, how long
Until shall burst the song!

277. FRETTING. 8s.

"Fret not in any wise." Psalm xxxvii 8.

1 Save me, O my God, from Fretting:
Sin of sins the most besetting;
Make me know Thou livest still;
To Thine Own ne'er meanest ill.

2 Save me, O my God, from Fretting,
Sin all other sins begetting;
Grant that I may understand
All is 'neath Thy ruling hand.

3 Save me, O my God, from Fretting;
From all thankless, vain regretting;
By Thy grace help me to see
That Thou ord'rest life for me.

4 Save me, O my God, from Fretting;
Subtle weaver of Sin's netting;
Others may be great, I low,
Grace give to Thy Will to bow.

5 Save me, O my God, from Fretting:
Ne'er to World myself indebting;
Others may be rich, I poor,
Riches true I would prize more.

6 Save me, O my God, from Fretting,
Murmuring and envy whetting;
Others may be strong, I weak,
Thy strength, Lord, I humbly seek.

7 Save me, O my God, from Fretting,
Still ungracious thoughts abetting;
Others bright perchance, I dark,
To Thy sweet voice let me hark.

8 Save me, O my God, from Fretting,
On Earth's gifts false virtues setting;
Unto Thee I lift my eye,
Ever know Thee, Lord, me nigh.

278. FEAR CAST OUT BY LOVE. 6s.

1 John iv. 18; 2 Cor. vii. 1.

1 Freed from all FEAR by LOVE,
Lord! still within me move;
That I may ever know
The flame that now doth glow;
But, Lord, more grace impart
To fill my narrow heart;
This JOY unto me giv'n
Too much on this side Heav'n.

2 I walk'd in doubt and dread,
As thro' vast terrors led;
Above—beneath—around
Nothing but darkness found;
But, lo! upon my eyes
Burst in a strange surprise—
Thy Cross, uplifted high
On dark-bright Calvary!

3 O Lord, I do not boast,
Taught of the Holy Ghost;
All—all to Thee I owe
That I enfranchis'd go;
That I, as little child,
No more by foes beguil'd,
Laid me upon Thy breast,
And there found rest—found rest.

4 Before Thee, Lord, I fall;
Upon Thee, Lord, I call;
I knew not why that I
Enjoy this ecstacy;
Worthless—mere worthless none,
Out of my heart of stone;
Lo! Thou in me dost show
Thy Grace's overflow.

5 O who need longer fear?
Who, not to Thee draw near?
When such-an-one as I
Thy power exemplify;

And trophy of Thy love
Unto the World approve;
O Lord! I sing—I shout,
Let none of Thy grace doubt.

279. PROGRESS AND FIDELITY. 8.7.
Philippians iii. 12.

1 "*In*" the Way, Lord, Thy grace guiding,
Onward, upward, would we go;
Day by day Thy love providing
Armour 'gainst our ev'ry foe.

2 Let us not be found, Lord, standing
Idle in the market-place;
With Thine Own redeem'd ones banding
We would "*run*" the Christian race.

3 Looking unto Thee, Lord, pleading,
Where Thou art upon Thy throne;
From no service e'er receding,
Ev'ry day a something done.

4 Heeding not the World's mad scorning;
Seeking more Thy "*will*" to know;
And, "the way of life" adorning,
As Thy pilgrims forward go.

5 Voices right and left assailing,
Tempt us still to "turn aside";
But Thy mighty grace prevailing,
Keeps us near Thy spear-cleft side.

6 Thy great love our hearts enfolding,
"*In*" the Way may we be led;
Thy sweet Spirit us upholding;
Patience, dew-like, on us shed.

7 We would "watch and pray," expecting
Rich fulfilment of Thy Word;
Trusting to Thy great protecting,
And distrusting earthly sword.

8 "*In*" the Way, Lord, Thy grace guiding,
Onward, upward would we go;
Day by day Thy Love providing
Armour 'gainst our ev'ry foe.

280. "OH, NOT THIS, ANYTHING BUT THIS," OR CHOOSING OUR OWN CROSS.

1 "O, not this, not this, dear Lord:"
Ev'n if Thou make bare Thy Sword,
Piercing through and through my breast;
Yea, if from me Thou dost wrest
All I have—yet at the blow
I'll not murmur, nor say "No;"
"*Anything but this—but this,*"
Thou dost threaten 'midst my bliss.

2 "O, not this, not this, dear Lord:"
Plead I Thine Own quiv'ring word—
"Pass, if possible, this cup;"
O, my Saviour, I look up;
That dire rod Thou hold'st I know
Thou can'st make to bud and blow;
Hear my plaint, Lord, and remove
This great terror. Thou art LOVE.

3 "Oh, not this, not this, dear Lord;"
O forgive my soul's discord!
Thou dost know all my keen anguish
As my only child doth languish;
See how my poor heart doth break;
How I in the shadow shake;
Spare my Boy, Lord—good Lord, spare;
Drive Thou me not to despair.

4 "*Anything but this—but this;*"
Saviour, Thy stretched hand I kiss;
Lord, hear, answer and forgive
If half-madly thus I strive;
O my Boy, my life, my all,
Let not this stroke on me fall.
—Silent, Lord? "Thy will be done;"
Did'st Thou spare Thine only Son?

281. CRADLE-SONGS. 7s.
2 Timothy i. 5 and iii. 15.

1 PRAISE God, for my cradle-songs;
That I'M CHRIST'S, to them belongs;
Praise for a dear mother's speech;

Look of love that did beseech ;
  For the atmosphere of prayer
  Unto which I was born heir.

2 Praise God for my cradle-songs ;
  That CHRIST'S MINE, to them belongs ;
  Praise for sweet untroubled faith,
  All she taught me with "He saith";
  Praise for words of Holy Child,
  Still held fast and undefil'd.

3 Praise God, for my cradle songs ;
  That I'VE FAITH, to them belongs :
  Praise for " Our Father" I pray'd,
  Then softly slept, all unafraid ;
    Praise that with the waking morn,
    My first words to Christ were borne.

4 Praise God, for my cradle-songs ;
  That I'VE HOPE, to them belongs ;
  Praise for child-faith still abiding ;
  Praise for child-love still confiding ;
    For child-peace still deep as ever ;
    For a Saviour fails me never.

5 Praise God for my cradle songs ;
  That I'VE LOVE to them belongs ;
  Praise for child-heart me within,
  Sensitive to touch of sin ;
    Praise for rest on holy truth ;
    Praise that I know His soft ruth.

6 Praise God for my cradle-songs ;
  That I'VE JOY to them belongs;
  Praise that in my whit'ning age
  I still turn to the same page ;
    Praise that truth of morning days
    Fills my even-tide with praise.

7 Praise God for my cradle songs ;
  That I'VE PEACE to them belongs ;
  Praise that He still lights my way
  Leading to Eternal Day ;
    Praise, if I as little child,
    Love and serve Him unbeguiled.

232. THE GARMENT OF PRAISE.   8s.
Isaiah lxvi. 2, 3.

1 I SEE around me sadden'd faces,
  With bow'd down heads, heart-weary paces ;
  I've felt it all, yet songs I'll raise :
  The garment I'll put on of praise.

2 Lo, burdens, griefs, and troubles come,
  Yea, trials seem to strike us dumb ;
  I've felt it all, yet songs I'll raise ;
  The garment I'll put on of praise.

3 Oft toiling, moiling, sparsely fed,
  And out into the desert led ;
  I've felt it all, yet songs I'll raise ;
  The garment I'll put on of praise.

4 My pray'rs not answer'd, or with "No;"
  Or losses, crosses, blow on blow ;
  I've felt it all, yet songs I'll raise ;
  The garment I'll put on of praise.

5 O! fiery darts against me hurl'd,
  By the devil, flesh and world ;
  I've felt it all, yet songs I'll praise ;
  The garment I'll put on of praise.

6 Wave upon wave, the heart appalling,
  And with no "Fear not" to us calling ;
  I've felt it all, yet songs I'll raise ;
  The garment I'll put on of praise.

7 Thou, O my Christ, our way hast known;
  When alone we are not alone ;
  I've felt it all, and songs I'll raise ;
  The garment I'll put on of praise.

8 Help Thou, Lord, help to hold the fort ;
  Tho' sharp the fight, it will be short;
  I've felt it all, so songs I'll raise ;
  The garment I'll put on of praise.

283. Praise. 7.6.
"Whoso offereth praise glorifieth Me."
Psalm l. 23.

1 O LORD our God, we trust Thee,
  And we will sing Thy praise;
  Sin-stained at best it must be
    Each note our voices raise;
  But Thou hast us invited
    When to Thy courts we throng;
  With lips and hearts united,
    To break forth into song.

2 We know Heav'n's praise excelleth;
    For pure alone are there;
  We know the "new song" telleth
    Redeem'd no longer err;
  Yet, Lord, the songs of Glory
    Forbid not songs of Earth;
  For still "the old old story"
    Doth fill our mouths with m'rth.

3 O hear our invocation!
    That holier we may be;
  O give us consecration
    Of ev'ry faculty;
  That body, soul, and spirit,
    All vocal by Thy grace;
  We may, by Jesus' merit,
    Be made Thy dwelling-place.

4 Thus, thus as Pilgrims lowly,
    We'll go from strength to strength;
  Till in Thy City holy,
    We each appear at length;
  Full well it us becometh
    To sing thro' all the way;
  For blessings each life summeth,
    And for Eternal Day.

284. Morning Hymn of Praise. 8s.
"On Thee do I wait all the day."
Psalm xxv. 5.

1 O LORD my God, Thou dost me keep,
  I wake again from tranquil sleep;
  Refresh'd and brighten'd for the day,
  Beneath Thine eyes I go my way;
  Less than the least, grant Thou that I
  May ne'er the Name I bear belie;
  O God, to Thee mine eyes I raise;
  Accept, for Jesus' sake, my praise.

2 I think of those in pain last night,
  Toss'd to and fro in weary fight;
  I think of those who rise from bed
  In hunger, with no "daily bread";
  I think of those who godless live
  Despising their prerogative;
  O God, to Thee mine eyes I raise;
  Accept, for Jesus' sake, my praise.

3 I know not what this day may bring:
  It may be honey, may be sting;
  But sweet, or sharp, or joy or woe,
  Thy Love and Wisdom will it so;
  The cup Thou mixest, I will drink
  Nor from Thy bitterest potion shrink;
  O God, to Thee mine eyes I raise;
  Accept, for Jesus' sake, my praise.

4 Tempted my God, to Thee I'll turn;
  O let not fiery darts me burn!
  And if the World's allurements press
  Ensnaringly, and with keen stress;
  Break Thou their power, anoint mine eyes
  To see the world above the skies;
  O GOD, to Thee mine eyes I raise;
  Accept, for Jesus' sake, my praise.

5 And Lord, grant opportunity
  To speak for Thee, nor e'er deny;
  As each day runs, O let it shine
  With Thy benignty divine;
  So that some small debt I may pay;
  Or feel that I have lost a day;
  O GOD, to Thee mine eyes I raise;
  Accept, for Jesus' sake, my praise.

6 O keep me gentle, make me wise,
  And let no passion me surprise;
  Give me to live persuasively,

Both how to live and how to die ;
Forgiving as myself forgiven ;
Alluring men to Thy bright Heaven ;
O God, to Thee mine eyes I raise ;
Accept, for Jesus' sake, my praise.

285.   WITHIN AND WITHOUT.   8s.

"*Looking unto Jesus, the author and perfecter of our faith.*" *Hebrews xii. 2.*

1 O LORD, long long I look'd within,
  And strove, myself, to conquer sin ;
  But ah! too strong was SIN for me,
  Until I look'd away to Thee.

2 Thy finish'd "work" upon the Rood
  The purple covering of Thy blood ;
  Oh! How the vision of it calms [psalms,
  And fills weak hands with conqu'ring

3 Then, O my Saviour, I beheld,
  As sin's dark current in me swell'd,
  That Thou alone can'st speak the word
  That doth deliverance afford.

4 And speak the word Thou dost, and, lo !
  Sweet peace and joy together flow !
  O heart of mine, beyond the vail
  He lives, Whose power will never fail.

5 My part, Lord, is to look without
  When urg'd by sin, or toss'd with doubt ;
  Thine, Thine alone, to look within
  And "put away" my deepest sin.

6 Give me, Thou Holy One, to know
  Thy holiness—its peace and glow ;
  My spirit by Thy Spirit seal,
  In all I think, and say, and feel.

7 O Lord, long long I look'd within
  And strove myself to conquer sin ;
  But ah! Sin was too strong for me
  Until I look'd away to Thee.

286.   EXPERIENCE SANCTIFIED.   8.6.

"*Perfect through suffering.*"—*Hebrews ii. 10.*

1 I HAD not known, O "Man of Sorrows,"
  What sorrows Thou did'st bear ;
  Had I not borne a grief that borrows
  An accent from Despair.

2 I had not known the richest words
  Of Thy Word, O my God ;
  If treacheries, that pierce like swords,
  Had not increased my load.

3 I had not known to sympathise
  With others in their woe ;
  Had burning tears not filled my eyes,
  And made me quivering go.

4 I had not known how to speak peace,
  To hearts by anguish riven ;
  Had I not, hopeless, sought release
  From Thee, O Christ, in Heaven.

5 I had not known, O "Man of Sorrows,"
  What sorrows Thou did'st bear ;
  Had I not borne a grief that borrows
  An accent from Despair.

287.   DARKNESS.   *Isaiah l. 10.*

"*Wherefore should I fear in the days of evil?*" *Psalm xlix. 5.* 10s.

1 My "first love's" hopes all fade like
    flowers 'neath hail;
  And e'en the "Bright and Morning Star"
    grows pale ;
  O Lord my God, compassionate my wail!

2 I though' Thou had'st giv'n me Thy
    sweet release ;
  I thought I held, by grace, Thy "perfect
    peace" ;   [cease ?
  Must I my name of Christian now sur-

3 Or are these doubtings born of baseless
    fears
  Forgetful of Thy sympathy, Thy tears ?
  And that Thou art He Who knows all
    and cheers.

4 Alas! alas! I walk in darkness now;
  Alas! alas! my love has lost its glow;
  The peace and joy I knew, I do not know.
5 The groaning, the faint sigh Thou
      hearest, Lord:
  So is it written in Thy Holy Word;
  Fulfil it, Lord, to me, and light afford.
6 O God! I hold up pleading hands to Thee;
  Will Thou, O wilt Thou guide and suc-
      cour me?
  Remember, Saviour mine, Gethsemane!

288.   SLEEP—GOD'S GIFT.   8s.

Psalm cxxvii. 2

1 OUR thanks we give to Thee, O Lord,
  For the sweet phrase found in Thy Word;
  That telleth how Thou givest sleep
  To Thy belovèd; them dost keep:
      Still faithful, O our God, art Thou,
      As night by night we softly know.

2 Most mighty power, yet in Thy Hand
  It droppeth on our eyelids bland;
  Girds us with Thine omnipotence,
  Yet with no pressure felt by sense;
      Still faithful, O our God, art Thou,
      As night by night we softly know.

3 Through the dark night Thou watch dost
      set,
  Nor lowliest toiler dost forget;
  And when the morn illumes the skies
  Thou tranquilly dost ope our eyes:
      Still faithful, O our God, art Thou
      As night by night we softly know.

4 O Thou Good Shepherd, grant that we,
  Thus still refresh'd, may wake with Thee;
  Remembering that we are Thy sheep;
  That Thou giv'st Thy belovèd sleep;
      Still faithful, O our God, art Thou,
      As night by night we softly know.

5 And if, O Lord, I sleepless lie;
  O raise my thoughts from earth to sky;
  Yea give me, Lord, "songs in the night"
  To mitigate Time's laggard flight;
      Still faithful, O our God, art Thou,
      As night by night we softly know.

289.   A BRIGHT CHRISTIAN.   7s.

"*Whatsoever things are lovely . . . and of
good report.*"—*Philippians iv. 8.*

1 A BRIGHT Christian I would be;
  So to shine, all men shall see;
  Free from care by His release;
  Fill'd with joy thro' His Own peace.

2 A bright Christian I would be;
  Through his "glorious liberty;"
  Gentle, tender, not austere;
  Winning love, not starting fear.

3 A bright Christian I would be
  From all gloom by grace set free;
  My path like "the shining light"
  By His gracious oversight.

4 A bright Christian I would be;
  Singing with unsinning glee;
  Winsome deed and winsome word,
  Creed and life both in accord.

5 A bright Christian I would be;
  Made strong by the bended knee;
  Going forth from morn to eve,
  Drawing others to believe.

6 A bright Christian I would be;
  Shewing clear my pedigree;
  Heir of Heav'n; soon to be there,
  Grand inheritance to share.

7 A bright Christian I would be;
  Not afraid of pleasantry;
  Sweet of temper, affable;
  Thus upon the world to tell.

8 A bright Christian I would be,
  So to shine, all men shall see ;
  Free from care by His release ;
  Fill'd with joy thro' His Own peace.

290.   SUNSET LONGINGS.   8s.
  Ps. lv. 6.

1 WHILE gazing on the setting sun,
  The evening clouds in splendor spun,
  With glorious crimson seam'd with gold
  Like curtains of God's tent of old;
  I seem to catch a glimpse of Heaven,
  Such as to seer of Patmos given ;
  There comes a stirring in my breast
  To fly away and be at rest.

2 If mortal skies have beauty rare,
  That but the outer hangings are ;
  If all these golden stars of light
  Are candles of our earthly night ;
  What must "the many mansions" be,
  Domed by vast eternity !
  There comes a stirring in my breast
  To fly away and be at rest.

3 Lo ! one by one earth's ties are broken ;
  Of my own end the sure foretoken ;
  And one by one to Heav'n above
  Pass up those of our deepest love ;
  Thus life grows poorer — Heav'n richer ;
  My Lord, Thou art a tender teacher !
  There comes a stirring in my breast
  To fly away and be at rest.

4 And Thou, O Jesus, Thou art there,
  Drawing me upward howsoe'er
  The stress and strain of this Earth's life
  Engross thought and compel keen strife ;
  O lift me up, Lord, more and more,
  At last Thyself and mine restore :
  There comes a stirring in my breast
  To fly away and be at rest.

291.   BARRENNESS.   8s.
  2 Peter i. 8.

1 O GRACIOUS Lord, when Thou did'st give
  By Thy Divine prerogative,
  Warning that men bear fruit for Thee,
  I bless Thee it was thro' a tree ;
  Thou mightest choice, O Lord, have made
  Of ag'd Rabbi, and him dead laid ;
  But in compassion most benign,
  Thou gav'st a portent and a sign.

2 Give me, O Lord, to read and mark,
  And to Thy tender warning hark ;
  Forbid that I in Thy Church be,
  As barren as that doom'd fig-tree ;
  FOR EVER USELESS ! What a doom !
  Lord, let it not upon me come !
  But graff'd in Thee, the living Vine,
  To bear "more fruit" each day be mine.

3 O gracious Lord, when Thou did'st give
  By Thy divine prerogative,
  Warning that men bear fruit for Thee,
  I bless Thee it was thro' a tree ;
  Thou mightest choice, O Lord, have made
  Of ag'd Rabbi, and him dead laid ;
  But in compassion most benign,
  Thou gav'st a portent and a sign.

4 Praise, O Lord, for grace bestow'd,
  If graces fair in me have shew'd ;
  For growth as of fair leaf and flower,
  By Thy good Spirit's quick'ning power ;
  But fruit, "much fru't," O Lord, I ask,
  As I 'neath Thy sweet shining bask ;
  Enrich me as I urge my suit,
  With nothing less than plenteous fruit.

292.   MIZPAH.   8,7,8,8.
  Genesis xxxi. 44-45.

1 The Lord will watch 'twixt me and thee :
  He seeth tho' we do not see ;
  MIZPAH the word, the cov'nant-word;
  May it be ours, O gracious Lord !

2 The Lord will watch 'twixt me and thee;
    As we bow down on bended knee;
    When parted, there's one meeting-place;
    Lord, 'tis Thy mighty throne of grace.

3 The Lord will watch 'twixt me and thee;
    He seeth tho' we do not see;
    MIZPAH—the word, the cov'nant-word;
    May it be ours, O gracious Lord!

4 The Lord will watch 'twixt me and thee;
    He loves to mark us thus agree,
    Still to be true, and still to love;
    Still fellow-heirs of Heav'n above.

5 The Lord will watch 'twixt me and thee;
    He seeth tho' we do not see;
    MIZPAH—the word, the cov'nant-word;
    May it be ours, O gracious Lord!

6 The Lord will watch 'twixt me and thee;
    The "living God" our watchword be;
    That each in thought, and word, and deed,
    May copy Him for us did bleed.

7 The Lord will watch 'twixt me and thee;
    He seeth tho' we do not see;
    MIZPAH—the word, the cov'nant-word;
    May it be ours, O gracious Lord!

293.   TREMBLING.   7s.

Isaiah lxvi. 2 ; Ezra ix. 4 ; v. 3.

1 I BEHOLD the trembling string
As the player forth doth bring
Very passion of sweet sounds—
Such as deepest speech confounds.
And I mark the trembling most
When the player's hands are crossed,
Up and down in cunning skill,
Moving listeners at will:
    Even so, O gracious Lord,
    Would I tremble at Thy Word.

2 Shrinking from its purity,
Low-abas'd, I trembling lie;
But Thou tak'st me by the hand
And o'er me in love dost stand;
Touching "harp of thousand strings,"
Giving me the Faith that sings,
E'en while trembling lowlily;
Thinking of Thee holily:
    Ah! 'Tis so, O gracious Lord;
    Thus I tremble at Thy Word.

3 O my Saviour! when I tremble
(Thy frail child need not dissemble)
Feeling that retreat I must;
I, a simple worm of dust,
"Tremble," and am ill at ease;
"Tremble," ay, when on my knees;
"Tremble," e'en in praise and prayer;
"Tremble," Lord, for Thou art there:
    Ah! But Thou regardest, Lord,
    Him who trembles at Thy Word.

294.   DISCIPLINE.   *2 Cor. v. 17, 18.*   8s.

1 O MY Lord Christ, I needs must own—
As tho' mine still were heart of stone—
Sore is the strife, without, within,
Thy GRACE entrapp'd, coerc'd by Sin:
Insidious, subtle, wearing masks
That all my utmost effort tasks.

2 Vain-glory, honours, and earth's treasures,
Unsatisfying painted pleasures,
I have o'ercome; but, like a flood,
Lo! bursting banks, comes SEEMING GOOD,
Most deftly winning my consent
As tho' 'twere by the Lord Christ sent.

3 Then follows, Lord, sharp discipline
From Thee, O Christ, as I am Thine;
Sweet chastisements me to abase,
Ah! even proud heart to amaze;
But humbling, not humiliating:
O sweet rest born of perturbating.

4 Help me, O Lord! that I may seek
Thy gracious word unto "the meek;"
Help me to choose "the lower place,"
If only I may see Thy Face;
Yea, teach me, Lord, to know my nature,
And show me lowness of my stature.

5 To know myself and Thou unknown,
  Ah! Lord, should cause me only moan;
  But howe'er sinful, Christ I be,
  Myself full safe in Thee I see;
  Thus I am kept from blank despair,
  For I on Thee cast all my care.

6 My God, all guilt and stains remove
  In plentitude of pard'ning love;
  O fill my mouth with wond'ring praise,
  That hallelujahs I may raise;
  Yea unto Thee with glad heart bring
  Such songs as Thy redeem'd ones sing.

7 Thou askest the impossible,
  Not that my failure Thou may'st tell,
  Nay, but to keep me very lowly
  That I to grace be debtor wholly;
  Sav'd not by my own righteousness,
  But as in mercy Thou dost bless.

8 I'll welcome then "my Lord, my God,"
  Thy heaviest, sharpest, sorest rod;
  Tender refusals, sweet delays,
  Enriching, brightening my days;
  Warning regards in gentlest ruth
  Lest I aside turn from THE TRUTH.

295.   IT IS TOWARD EVENING   THE
           DAY IS FAR SPENT.   10s.

St. Luke xxiv. 29.

"In a little while the dying Saint turned round, and pressing the hand of a loving attendant, muttered, 'Advespera-rit, et inclinata est jam dies.' They were the last words he spake, save that the Name of Jesus hung awhile upon the lips that had so often lovingly named IT, and which would next be opened to take part in the Song of the Lamb."—Lear's "Life of S. Francis de Sales," c. viii. p. 265 (1871).

1 "*It is toward ev'ning, the day far spent*":
  O, soft and sweet words from the Gospel sent;
  They drew Thee, Lord Jesus, to be their guest,
  Who spoke them to Thee, and on Thee did rest.

2 "*It is toward evening, the day far spent*":
  We plead it to-day—our Faith with Hope blent;
  Come Thou in, and with us, dear Lord, abide;
  Thou still lov'st us though Thou be glorified.

3 "*It is toward evening, the day far spent*;"
  Plac'd in God's Word and for our learning meant;
  May it be ours nightly e'er we fall asleep
  To place us in Thy Hands—all safe to keep.

4 "*It is toward evening, the day far spent*;"
  Saint Francis of Sales on the sweet words leant;
  Praising, praying as down the vale he sped;
  Light of Heav'n, not of Earth, about him shed.

5 "*It is toward evening, the day far spent*;"
  To the monition we would be attent;
  O give us grace to catch the "still small voice"
  That ev'n 'midst death-shadows we may rejoice.

6 "*It is toward evening, the day far spent*;"
  We would list now e'er too late we lament;
  Living or dying may we be the Lord's;
  Girded and "kept" by His life-giving words.

296.   STROKES.   8s.

"*My stroke is heavier than my groaning.*"

Job xxiii. 2.

1 Father! Thy strokes upon me fall;
  For grace to bear I on Thee call;
  O God! Order the *when* and *where*,
  But guard Thou me against despair.

2 A weary day brings wearier night;
  How laggard, Lord, their tardy flight;
  Sharp pain within, darkness without,
  My soul toss'd on a sea of doubt.

3 As at a stroke, gone was my wealth;
  Another—and gone was my health;
  A third, and childless I was left;
  Of Thee Christ only not bereft.

4 Wistful and weaken'd here I lie,
  Yet turn upward my burning eye;
  To succour me, O God, make speed;
  Thou seest how my wounds all bleed.

5 Alas! my God! I scarce can pray;
  My wonted praises terrors fray;
  Parch'd are my lips and parch'd my tongue;
  Body and soul with anguish wrung.

6 O God, my God, Thou knowest my fears; [tears;
  With Thy pierc'd Hand wipe Thou my
  Vain are all comforters but Thee;
  Compassionate my misery.

7 Waves of impatience o'er me come,
  And I "offend" tho' I be dumb;
  O God! Wilt Thou me of sin cleanse,
  Forgiving me my deep offence?

297. QUI SE PLAINTE PÈCHE. FRANCIS
     DE SALES.   6s.

1 Whoso complaineth, sins,
  And condemnation wins;
  Lord! I would not complain,
  Let me not strive in vain.

2 Whoso complaineth, sins,
  And net of evil spins;
  Lord! wilt Thou me help send?
  Against all foes defend?

3 Whoso complaineth, sins,
  And lays for himself gins;
  Lord! shew Sin's snares that I
  May all complaining fly.

4 Whoso complaineth, sins,
  However it begins;
  Christ! I would look to Thee
  In Thy dumb misery.

5 Whoso complaineth, sins,
  Ah! are they not born twins?
  In Thy sweet grace prevent;
  Be to my cry attent.

6 Whoso complaineth, sins,
  Begun, it hardly lins;
  O Thou, my Saviour dear,
  Be ever to me near.

298   FRIENDS.   7s.

1 *We aye need true friends in sorrow*,
  Their fond sympathy to borrow;
  When our FAITH and HOPE are shook
  We draw strength from tender look;
  But then, O Lord Christ, 'bove all
  Thou our friend art, when we call;
  For to Thee we all may speak
  When our hearts are like to break.

2 *We aye need true friends in gladness*,
  Ev'n as much as e'er in sadness;
  Freely all Thy gifts to share,
  Brightening each other's care;
  And together lifting up
  Praises for a love-fill'd cup;
  Singing as we onward go,
  Grateful all to Thee to owe.

3 *We aye need true friends in weakness*,
  When deep-yearning for Thy meekness,
  We lo! find ourselves backsliding—
  Vain, most vain to think of hiding;
  Healing word and quiet tear,
  Whisper low of love not fear;
  Then to go as first we went,
  Ah, heart-bruis'd and penitent.

4 *We aye need true friends in serving*,
  Still THE MASTER's word observing,
  Of the prayer-agreeing "two"
  For His grace and strength to sue;
  Pleading promises together
  Each close-leaning on the other;
  Both united in the Lord,
  Ever guided by His Word.

5 We aye need true friends when pained,
And our cares are scarce restrained;
The soft hand upon our brow
And the helpful word breath'd low;
The heart speaking in the eye,
Brave and strong—yet tenderly;
Laud, O Lord, Thy love me sends
Still thro' all, ABUNDANT FRIENDS.

299. HEAVENLY AND EARTHLY LIFE IN ONE.
(*Composed at Geneva*). 9.9.8.8.7.7.

1 Lo! Rhone and Arve, twins, flow together,
Yet mingle not one with the other;
Lord! Be not thus my two-fold life;
But BLUE and BROWN mix without strife;
 Life below and life ABOVE,
 Grace-united onward move.

2 Thanks, O my God, for love-born being;
For walk of FAITH and walk of SEEING;
My duty done, but more and more
FAITH'S eyes set on the golden shore:
 Life below and life ABOVE,
 Grace-united onward move.

3 Laud, that 'tis Thee, my God, I'm serving,
Yet from no earthly duty swerving;
Aye grateful for all Thou hast giv'n,
Whilst on my pilgrimage to Heav'n:
 Life below and life above,
 Grace-united onward move.

4 My Saviour, teach me Thee to follow;
Still "doing good," and each day hallow;
Thy 'steps' discerning in my way,
In brightest and in darkest day;
 Life below and life ABOVE,
 Grace-united onward move.

5 *Repeat St.* 1.

300. DAYS OF HEAVEN UPON THE EARTH.
Deut. xi. 21.   8s.

1 Lo! *Days of Heav'n upon the Earth:*
The promise fills our mouths with mirth;
Lord! Wilt Thou it to us fulfil,
Moulding us to Thy gracious will?
By Thy good Spirit's ministration,
Be ours the "*joy* of salvation."

2 Lo! *Days of Heav'n upon the Earth:*
Immortal, not of mortal birth;
As lifting up to holy heights
By Love's penitent, gracious sleights;
Beyond great Bethel's ladder-vision
Or aught e'er known by the Concision.

3 Lo! *Days of Heav'n upon the Earth:*
Ah! Heav'nly manna for our dearth!
Openings of God's windows high,
Our low earth dimming the sky;
The Spirit striving—souls awaking
The Church of Thy full gifts partaking.

4 Lo! *Days of Heav'n upon the Earth:*
From praise and prayers aye going forth;
Girded with words out of THE WORD,
That light, and peace, and strength afford;
Walking by faith, to Heav'n ascending,
Our HOPE and LOVE together blending.

5 Lo! *Days of Heav'n upon the Earth:*
O how extol their priceless worth!
Each day begin with heav'nly thought;
Thro' each day heav'nly deeds be wrought;
So thus and thus to us is given
To antedate the "days of Heav'n."

301. ANGUISH OF SPIRIT. *Ex.* vi. 9.   8.4

1 O Lord! Thou seest how I'm bow'd
 Beneath my load;
Yea how by tempters I am cow'd,
 My God, My God!
Thou knowest the anguish of my soul—
 Like waves that roll;
Forgive, O Lord, forgive, that I
 Feel THEE not nigh.

2 Thy promises I read in vain,
 They only pain;
Far off they sound and leave me sad
 Nay, well-nigh mad;

CORDS OF A MAN—GRAFFED.

The world is out of joint—and yet
    Thou dost forget;
Thou "keepest silence" 'midst it all;
    Thou dost appal.

3 O Christ! Wilt me compassionate,
    Not wax irate?
I am encompassed of EVIL
    In man and devil;
I'm overwhelmed, heart-sore and crush'd,
    Ev'n conscience hush'd;
Look on me in my misery,
    O Lord, keep me!

4 And help me, Lord, still more to feel
    For sore bested,
When making passionate appeal,
    'Tis hindered;
By stony eyes of wordless care
    And blank despair;
Keep me in touch, Lord, with sad hearts
    From whom FAITH parts.

302. CORDS OF A MAN. *Hosea xi. 1.* 8s.

1. How Thee, my God, shall I extol!
   As the sea-waves with clangor roll
So, O my God, I look around,
   And rage 'gainst Thee is ever found;
Yet SILENT Thou dost still remain—
   As the calm sky above the main.

2 Full of all tend'rest pity, Thou
   All in vastest city dost know,
And in least and lowliest hut;
   And patiently in each doth put [makes,
That grace of Thine which conquest
   And ev'n uttermost hatred shakes.

3 Laud, O, my God, for Thy rich love
   That thus toward our RACE doth move;
How tender and forgiving still,
   "*Convincing*" and "*converting*" till
Thou pluckest very brands that "burn;"
   Chiefest of sinners to Thee turn.

4 Ah! my Saviour, dissembling's vain
   Trembling I come—Thou'lt not disdain;
Guilty—I must myself confess,
   But lay hold of Thy righteousness;
Me still, in love, Thou hast pursu'd;
   My sinful heart in peace renew'd.

5 *Repeat St. 1.*

303. TODMUDT.—PRINCE BISMARCK. 8s.

1 ABOVE me all is grey and drear;
Around all fill'd with shapes of fear;
Within me all like a heath tir'd—
Todmudt—O, Christ, I am *dead-tir'd*.

2 The World has been too much with me
Sharp-tooth'd is my misery;
Still round and round—ah, as if gyr'd—
Todmudt—O, Christ, I am *dead-tir'd*.

3 The "flesh" me captive still hath ta'en
My heart hard'ning—stings in my brain;
Yet "half my days" are unexpir'd
Todmudt—O, Christ, I am *dead-tir'd*.

4 The devil claims me for his own,
And so *he* letteth me alone;
Against myself I have conspir'd—
Todmudt—O, Christ, I am *dead-tir'd*.

5 But what is this that thrills me so?
Is it Thy touch that makes me know
Thy loving patience ne'er retir'd,
But still has followed me—*dead-tir'd*.

6 I "magnify" Thy grace, O, Christ!
Thy love redeeming, all unpric'd;
Me, "castaway," Thou hast inspir'd;
No more—no more—am I *dead-tir'd*.

304. GRAFFED. 8.6.8.6.8.8.
St. John xv., 1-8.

1 The flower of the inner life
   Sprung from a heav'nly root;
Still blossoming 'mid cold and strife
   It rounds to mellow fruit;
I praise the Lord if so that I
The palest blossom can descry.

2 Thanks, O, my God, for Thy grace giv'n
   To know Thee my true Vine;
   Thanks too, for all the airs of Heaven
   That bathe this heart of mine;
   Deep-graff'd in Thee, Lord, I would shew
   The life of God on Earth below.

3 What dew is to the tiny seed;
   The "small rain" to mown grass;
   Thou who for man didst on Cross bleed,
   In me wilt bring to pass;
   In Thee I ever would abide;
   To Thee I would my all confide.

4 Thy Holiness I seek, O Lord!
   My life conform'd to Thine;
   I humbly plead Thy gracious word,
   Thy promises divine;
   Let Thy rich grace in me appear,
   Like flowers blooming all the year.

305. JOHN BUNYAN AND HIS OWN HEART.
(Grace Abounding, § 296.)

1 "God let me down into my heart:"
   He shew'd me sights that made me start;
   'Twas as a dungeon dark and foul,
   Clanking with chains— Bethink thee soul!
   Spirit of God, aid me to tell
   All the blest anguish me befell.

2 "God let me down into my heart:"
   O that I had the Painter's art
   That I might limn— yet not despair—
   The hidden chambers there laid bare;
   Crypts that for the first time I saw;
   Bowing me on my face in awe.

3 "God let me down into my heart:"
   Ah, thro' and thro' me still would dart
   Stinging sense of His purity
   And my own bitter enmity;
   'Till stripp'd of all cunning dissembling
   There came to me His gracious trembling.

4 "God let me down into my heart:"
   Alas! It was a thronged mart
   Of evil buying, of evil selling,
   My conscience loudest warnings quelling;
   What my Lord Christ for temple made
   Turn'd into market for Sin's trade.

5 "God let me down into my heart:"
   The light burn'd fierce with lightning's smart;
   I quiver'd in my agony;
   Words would not come, I could but cry,
   Shew mercy, Lord, 'fore Thee I weep;
   Shew mercy, Lord, and cleansing deep.

6 "God let me down into my heart:"
   He sought that with it I would part;
   Thrice gracious words to me were spoken,
   And, lo! the pierc'd Hand reach'd Love's token;
   "Behold how I make all things new!
   The "new heart" I will give to you."

7 "God let me down into my heart:"
   My Saviour dear, how good Thou art!
   Thou foundest naught in me but ill;
   I needed, Lord, thy utmost skill;
   But lo! by Thee my heart was sought,
   And Grace's miracle is wrought.

306. CHIEF OF SINNERS. 8s.

1 A FORTRESS face, four-square and massive,
   And to all sentiment impassive;
   Eyes that swift veil themselves, yet give
   Glances furtive and fugitive;
   Mouth, sensual and negro-lipp'd;
   Tongue, as in fetid poison dipp'd;
   Locks, leonine and iron grey;
   Hands, restless as in gambling play;
   A strong, bad man, but grandly gifted—
   Brain's wondrous matter finel'est sifted.

2 Such was the man— now dead— I knew
   Far back when my own years were few;
   I shunn'd him— as a pest'lence shunn'd—
   By his foul speech I had been stunn'd;
   If e'er there was a "burning brand"
   'Twas he. But lo! the nail-pierc'd hand
   Reach'd e'en to him, touch'd him, and
   sav'd

In crimson fountain he was lav'd ;
'Twas done by a low-whisper'd word—
A child's—that smote like a drawn sword.

3 O wonder-working power and love !
Such a mire-implung'd heart to move;
A trophy of Christ's grace, to take
Soul darkest, foulest, and remake ;
O cleansing mercy and vast word
By all on Earth and Heav'n ador'd !
O conqu'ring and redeeming hand,
To make e'en him a SAINT to stand ;
Never shall I of man despair,
With " chief of sinners " made Christ's
   heir.

4 Day after day, for years, I watch'd
This soul thus from the burning "snatch'd;"
Precious to see how he grew " meek "
As grace, still more grace he would seek;
Humble and gentle, patient, still
Eager to do THE MASTER'S will ;
To hallow every " talent " given
And draw souls after him to heaven :
Laud, unto Thee, O Christ my Lord,
Fulfill'd—fill'd full—Thine utmost word.

307. THROUGH MUCH TRIBULATION. 7s.
Acts of the Apostles xiv. 22.

1 PAIN doth sting, but Christ is nigh,
Why then change for ease, my pain ?
Clouds that fleck the Summer sky,
  Bring the Summer's silver rain ;
    Pleasant things are not the best ;
    Always blest would be unblest.

2 FEAR doth crush, but Christ is LOVE !
Why exchange for mirth my fears ?
Roses blow their thorns above,
  Turning them to guarding spears ;
    Pleasant things are not the best ;
    Heav'n not Earth our house of REST.

3 LOSS doth try, but Christ my Lord,
Shall I yield for gain my loss ?
Trembles, sweetest-sounding chord;

Deepest joy is 'neath the Cross ;
    Pleasant things are not the best ;
    Always blest would be unblest.

4 HOPE doth pale, but Christ is yonder,
Why give up for light my Hope ?
The Bow belts the throne of thunder ;
  Trust I shall e'en while I grope ;
    Pleasant things are not the best ;
    Heav'n not Earth our house of REST.

5 FAITH doth fail, but Christ, I cling :
Why seek walk of sight for faith ?
Birds are best seen on the wing ;
  Sight comes with benignant Death ;
    Pleasant things are not the best ;
    Always blest would be unblest.

308. SECOND COMING. 6s.
Romans viii. 22.

1 *Earth shall not always groan
In wordless monotone ;*
Redemption draweth nigh ;
His " signs " are in the sky ;
FAITH hears His coming feet ;
HOPE hastens forth to meet.

2 *Earth shall not always groan
In wordless monotone ;*
Lo ! the " Last Days " are come ;
E'en godless are struck dumb,
To see the things foretold
In far back days of old.

3 *Earth shall not always groan
In wordless monotone ;*
Thy Word to the World's end
The light of life doth send ;
The Spirit " witness " gives,
Wherever man now lives.

4 *Earth shall not always groan
In wordless monotone ;*
Behold Thine Israel
Throng in their Land to dwell ;
Behold far heathen lands
Lift up their pleading hands.

5 *Earth shall not always groan
In wordless monotone ;*
Christ hath not died in vain ;
Broken Sin's galling chain .
God's mighty word is pass'd,
Evil shall down at last.

6 *Earth shall not always groan
In wordless monotone ;*
Christ Who these skies did climb,
Cometh the second time,
Without a sacrifice,
The round world to surprise.

7 *Earth shall not always groan
In wordless monotone ;*
Truth than a Lie more strong,
Till it shall win— how long?
Right shall o'ercome mere might,
And Love all men unite.

8 *Earth shall not always groan
In wordless monotone ;*
The Lord cometh again,
And coming comes to reign ;
O God, the Great Day speed !
Help us Thy " signs " to read.

309   Heaven on Earth.   8s.

Ephesians ii., 6 (cf. Colossians ii., 12).

1 The red West's great clerestory
Flames high with clouds of many a dye ;
Whilst shoots of brightness come and go,
As tho' God's Heaven on Earth to shew;
A hush of awe upon me steals,
And the Lord Christ Himself reveals.

2 And the Lord Christ Himself reveals,
Until my fluttering spirit feels
Its own great being's majesty,
Thus while on Earth link'd to the sky :
Ecstatic moments that me send
With deeper love 'fore Him to bend.

3 With deeper love 'fore Him to bend
Who His great Presence thus doth lend;
Till "caught up" beyond words to tell —
I enter bliss ineffable ;

Ideal yet most realiz'd ;
Most real yet idealiz'd.

4 Most real yet idealiz'd !
Of " my Lord, my God " aggrandiz'd ;
So all luminous grows life's road,
God's own glory all " shed abroad ;"
A hush of awe upon me steals,
And the Lord Christ Himself reveals.

310.   Overflowing Grace.   8s.

Isaiah lx., 5.   Psalms, cxix., 32.

*Domine, contine undas gentior Tuas, Domine,
recede a me, quia non possum sustinere Tuæ
dulcedinis magnitudinem, unde prosternere me
cogor.*   Francis de Sales.

1 Thy floods of grace, O God restrain !
Rush not thus on my soul amain ;
Spare me this swooning ecstacy ;
Withhold ! Withhold ! or I shall die.

2 Thy sweetness, O God, inundates
As wave on wave rolls thro' sea-gates ;
Hold back Thy Hand compassionate ;
Or slay me quite, and change my state.

3 But lo ! O God, Thou floodest still !
Hear then my sigh Thy word fulfil ;
Enlarge my soul that I may hold
Thy gifts of grace so manifold.

4 Ah ! weak and shallow is my heart !
O God, my God, with Thy bless'd art
Wilt Thou, by grace, make strong its walls
That I stand true whate'er befalls ?

5 Too dazzling is this light that shines ;
'Tis as the fierce fire that calcines ;
O Son of God now intervene ;
Be Thou my shelter and my screen.

6 Still, O my God, Thy grace Thou pourest,
And still each ebb by flood restorest ;
Behold ! I place me in Thy hands ;
Me qualify for Thy demands.

311.   MISTRUST THYSELF, BUT THY GOD
              TRUST.   8s.

*"Mistrust of self is a very good thing pro-
vided it be accompanied by trust in God, and the
more we have of the last the deeper will be the
first. But discouragement is a false humility."*
S. FRANCIS DE SALES.

1 MISTRUST thyself, but thy God trust,
  Ev'n when He lays thee in the dust ;
  Self-pleasing shun, but please thy God,
  As thou would'st not invite His rod.

2 Mistrust thyself, but thy God trust,
  Who is all-holy and all-just ;
  A sinner thou, He sinner's friend,
  He thee all needed grace will send.

3 Mistrust thyself, but thy God trust,
  Despair far from thy soul He'll thrust ;
  Where sin abounds more grace abounds :
  O Love ! that Heav'n and Earth astounds.

4 Mistrust thyself, but thy God trust,
  He safe will steer thro' Passion's gust ;
  Just as thou art, before Him plead
  As knowing who doth intercede.

5 Mistrust thyself, but thy God trust,
  In His strength conquer thou each lust ;
  Have no concealments unto Him,
  Tell all, tho' tears thy eyes may dim.

6 *Repeat St. 1.*

312.   THE CHOICE.   7s.
            I. Corinthians xv., 31.

1 *Love or Death, yea, Death or Love :*
  These me onward, upward move ;
  No love to Thee, O my God !
  Ah ! Far better life disload !
  Love to Thee, then welcome Death,
  That but stops our mortal breath.

2 *Love or Death, yea, Death or Love :*
  The grand old Saints' words reprove,
  That I still have so cold a heart
  And that I fill so poor a part,
  O my dear Saviour for Thee,
  Amidst a World's misery.

3 *Love or Death, yea, Death or Love :*
  O send Thou down from above
  Thy thrice-gracious Spirit, Lord,
  My will with Thine to accord ;
  Thee possessing and possest ;
  O antepast of the blest !

4 *Love or Death, yea, Death or Love :*
  Brood within me Heav'nly Dove !
  My " harp of a thousand strings "
  Touch Thou until each cord sings ;
  Be my love aye strong as Death
  Sustained by Thy holy breath.

313.   WONDER AND NO WONDER.
        Isaiah lv. 8.   10.8.10.8.12.4.4 4.12.

1 I wonder not, when 'mong the fresh glad
      leaves
    I hear the early Spring-birds sing ;
  I wonder not, that 'neath the sunny eaves
    The swallow flits with glancing wing,
  But I do wonder, O Thou snow-plumed
      HOLY DOVE,
        In my dark breast
        To find Thee rest
        And make Thy nest—
  For what am I   so vile ! —to win this
      grace, this love ?

2 I wonder not, when in the meadows green
    I see the flocks—white-fleeced   repose ;
  I wonder not, that thro' the Winter keen
    They have soft shelter from the snows ;
  But I do wonder, that seeking o'er hill
      and wold
        Me—far off straying,
        Me—long delaying,
        Poor pleasures weighing ;
  My gracious Shepherd, guides me safe
      into His fold.

3 I wonder not, when on the graffèd branch
    I find fair leaf and dainty bloom ;
  'Tis life in life ; God's hand the wound
      doth staunch,
    And rich fruits in their seasons come ;

But I do wonder, Lord, that I, a "burning
  brand,"
    Tied for the fire,
    Snatch'd from the pyre—
    In ruth not ire,
By the Great Gardener's skill bearing good
  fruit do stand.

4 I wonder not, when in the beetling rock,
  Which sternly fronts the clamorous sea,
  I mark the wild fowl 'scape the tempest's
    shock,
  Secure thro' its slow agony;
  But I do wonder, Lord, to find THE ROCK
    eternal
      Has clefts for me,
      Where I may see
      From terror free,
  The surges of Thy wrath crash on the
    shores infernal.

314.   LOVE'S ENIGMA.   8s.

Romans v., 1–9.

1 The centre small—a lowly mound,
  Horizon vast as e'er was found;
  A cross, and on it a man dead,
  But that man God, and His blood shed:
    O Myst'ry fathomless of things,
    That life unto our RACE thus brings.

2 I gaze on the great sight stupendous;
  Dead—than all man's deeds most tremen-
    dous;
  God dying that lost man might live—
  Love now pleading "Father forgive:"
    Immensity of grace divine,
    Thee making mine, Lord, and I Thine.

3 The LAW abides inviolate;
  And JUSTICE reign is consecrate,
  As with a "still small voice" she speaks:
  And this poor heart of mine God seeks;
    Extremity of human guilt, [spilt.
    Cleans'd by the blood on gaunt ROOD

4 O Thou great BROKEN HEART of Love!
  Draw me beneath the HEAVENLY DOVE:
  I would a broken heart possess;
  Do Thou all suff'ring to me bless;
    Yea, let not Thy white flag be furl'd
    Till rallies to the Cross—the WORLD.

315.   KEPT.   *2 Co. xii., 9.*   6s.

1 Command, Lord, what thou wilt;
  But give what Thou commandest;
  Thou knowest all my guilt;
  Me throughly un'erstand'st;
  Whate'er be on me laid,
  I shall stand unafraid.

2 Command, Lord, what Thou wilt;
  All dangers I shall dare;
  I flee to Thy blood spilt;
  To Thy Word and to Prayer;
  Thus arm'd, I'm clad in mail;
  No en'my shall prevail.

3 Command, Lord, what Thou wilt;
  Thou all my wounds shalt cure;
  However fair they're gilt
  Sin's pleasures shall not lure:
  O look to me and bring
  Me forth conq'ring to sing.

4 Command, Lord, what Thou wilt;
  Be my way dark or bright;
  Upon THE ROCK I'm built,
  Thou shalt defend the right;
  I look to Thee, O God,
  I lay 'fore Thee my load.

5 *Repeat St. 1 in full.*

316.   "IF IT BE POSSIBLE."—*St. Matt. xxvi. 39.*   8,8,7,8,8,7.

1 I may not tread Gethsemane,
  I may not share Thy agony;
    O Jesus Christ, my Saviour!
  Yet hear me, Lord, Thy prayer I pray,
  As I am fainting on my way,
    O Jesus Christ, my Saviour!

317. PERFECTION ON EARTH.

1 Trembled I to see my child
  Day by day so PERFECT growing;
  By no breath of sin defil'd;
  Purer than rose purely blowing:
  For on earth PERFECTION given,
  Ah! 'tis ominous of heaven.

2 Strangest dread did fill my breast,
  As I watch'd his sweet unfolding;
  More and more I was opprest,
  So much beauty there beholding;
  For on earth PERFECTION given,
  Ah! 'tis ominous of heaven.

3 Mystic light dwelt in his eyes,
  Soft yet keen as altar's flaming;
  What of earth or what of skies,
  Far beyond our mortal naming;
  Thus on earth PERFECTION given,
  Ah! 'tis ominous of heaven.

4 Thoughtful—wistful—quaintly grave,
  Blithe as bird on branchlet swinging;
  Bearing pain, silent and brave,
  Guileless prayer to Jesus bringing
  But on earth PERFECTION given,
  Ah! 'tis ominous of heaven.

5 Meek and gentle in his face,
  MIND his ev'ry look informing;
  A fine nature touch'd of grace;
  Aye submissive, never storming;
  But on earth PERFECTION given,
  Ah! 'tis ominous of heav'n.

6 So I wrote and so I felt
  Of my child the Lord has taken;
  In me, ah, my heart doth melt;
  Yet Lord, FAITH abides unshaken;
  Laud for him PERFECTION giv'n,
  Less of earth and more of heav'n.

318. LULLABY.

1 SLEEP, my sweet child, sleep;
  Let thy mother weep;
    Lullaby my son;
  Lo! thy father dead,
  Light of home all fled;
    Lullaby my son.

2 Sleep, my sweet child, sleep,
  Jesus Christ thee keep;
    Lullaby my son;
  Thou, the widow's God,
  Knowest well my load;
    Lullaby my son.

LULLABY (cont. / prior hymn verses)

2 Darkness around me thick enfolds
  A "cup of trembling" my hand holds,
    O Jesus Christ, my Saviour!
  Forgive me, O forgive my cry,
  "If it be possible" pass it by,"
    O Jesus Christ, my Saviour!

3 My "little one" Thou lovest is sick,
  And hour by hour he grows more weak,
    O Jesus Christ, my Saviour!
  I mark the thinning of his face,
  And awful lines upon him trace,
    O Jesus Christ, my Saviour!

4 This is the cup to me Thou'rt reaching,
  Lord, hear me in my poor beseeching,
    O Jesus Christ, my Saviour!
  "If it be possible," spare him, Lord;
  Speak Thou ev'n now the healing word,
    O Jesus Christ, my Saviour!

5 We gave him to Thee in our vow,
  Thy Name was nam'd upon his brow,
    O Jesus Christ, my Saviour;
  Life is a great gift; I would fain
  Have him a MAN, for Thee to train,
    O Jesus Christ, my Saviour.

6 "Yet not my will but Thine be done,"
  Alas! alas! my little son,
    O Jesus Christ, my Saviour!
  My heart is sore; I can but sigh
  "If it be possible," hear my cry,
    O Jesus Christ, my Saviour.

3 Sleep, my sweet child, sleep ;
  To the Cross I creep ;
    Lullaby my son ;
  God of fatherless,
  Spare my child, and bless ;
    Lullaby my son.

4 Sleep, my sweet child, sleep ;
  Let thy mother weep ;
    Lullaby my son.
  Lov'd and loving gone,
  All but Thee, sweet one ;
    Lullaby my son.

319. IN THE WOODS.

"Lo, we heard of it at Ephratah; we found it in the fields of the wood." — Psalm cxxxii. 6.

1 How I love green solitudes !
  They beget my happiest moods :
  And like barren Bethel's height,
  Where the angels did alight ;
  But with such strange beauty fill'd,
  As the Psalmist with awe still'd.

2 God is with me in this place
  Op'ning unto me His grace :
  And His Presence is so near,
  Half I joy and half I fear ;
  Hush my fears, O Holy Ghost !
  Let not my first joy be lost.

3 Humblest bush appears a-blaze,
  Kindl'd by celestial rays ;
  Each tree as an altar stands
  Where I may lift pleading hands ;
  Lo ! I catch the rush of wings,
  Angels in their ministrings.

4 O my God in days of old
  Sight of Thee was manifold ;
  Nor hast Thou e'er left our Earth
  Scene of Thine Own mortal birth ;
  Without witness of Thy Being,
  To Faith's anointed seeing.

5 So to the green woods I go,
  That the Lord I nearer know ;
  In their quietness and peace
  Seek from a mad world release ;
  Touched by Thy Spirit Holy,
  With a gracious melancholy.

320. STAYING POWER. 6s.

Isaiah x. 20.

1 O GRANT me help "to stay ;"
  Still keep me "in the way"
  Which I, Lord, quick forsake ;
  And yet my heart doth ache
  For more, and more, still more
  Nearness — Thee to adore.

2 I mourn my wayward will ;
  O Christ, Thy Word fulfil ;
  And so possess me quite
  That I be child of light ;
  Nor ever "turn aside,"
  But still in Thy Hand hide.

3 O this reviving sin !
  Let it not vict'ry win ;
  O God, break Thou its power!
  Be near in evil hour,
  That the o'ercoming life
  May save me in the strife.

4 If trials come on me,
  Lord, keep me near to Thee ;
  Make glorious Thy great name
  Thro' me when in the flame ;
  That "witness" I may be
  To Faith's sweet constancy.

5 I am but fragile "Besh,"
  I cannot bear the rush
  Of Thy "glory's" greatness ;
  O pity Lord, my straitness ;
  Do Thou my soul enlarge
  E'er Thou me thus surcharge.

6 Come from their lightless regions
Satan's assailing legions;
I shall not fear at all;
On Thee, O Christ, I'll call;
And holding up my shield
I shall refuse to yield.

321. "Strong Crying." 7s.
Heb. v. 7.

1 Not tears only—silent tears,
Will disburthen grief or fears;
If there in keen anguish lie
Send up, my soul, the "strong cry."

2 Self-contain'd is self-depending,
Not before the Saviour bending:
Sorrow that sits all alone
Hardeneth the heart to stone.

3 Awful in Gethsemane
Lord Christ was Thine agony;
There "strong crying" from Thy lips
Sought from God apocalypse.

4 Mine be it in all my weeping
Thy example to be keeping;
Broken words, with moan and sigh;
Even, Lord, Thine own "strong cry."

5 Prayer of Faith 'tis maketh strong;
Prayer of Hope bursts into song;
Ah, Lord, if I live or die,
Grant unto me Thy "strong cry."

6 Worn and weary oft I'm dumb,
Words to me refuse to come;
But Lord, Thou dost ne'er deny;
Still bestow Thine Own "strong cry."

322. The Burning Heart. 8s.
Exodus iii. 1-6.

1 Lord! work Thy miracle of old
Sweetly in Holy Scripture told;
O make my heart by grace illum'd
A "Burning Bush" and unconsum'd;
Stalk, leaf, and bloom of fire untouch'd,
Thy strong protecting power avouch'd.

2 Thy strong protecting power avouch'd,
Of Earth and hell all unencroach'd;
Broken, and fir'd, yet held in calm,
Jehovah-Rophi pouring balm;
I seek a burning heart of love,
But still kept scathless from Above.

3 But still kept scathless from Above,
Neath brooding of Thy Holy Dove:
My weakness on Thy strength lays hold,
And pleads Thy promises of old;
Ardent but flameless I would burn
And ever to Thee, Jesus, turn.

4 And ever to Thee, Jesus, turn;
Or fill'd with joy, or when I mourn;
Like rings of incense my prayer rise,
Faith seeing Him beyond the skies;
All Thy graces that do not falter,
Hurtless blazing on my heart's altar.

5 Hurtless blazing on my heart's altar:—
Triumph without the pain of martyr;
Lo! Lord, Thy softly-soothing breath
Rich-nurtures Thy great gift of faith;
That I still 'walk,' yea even run,
Trophy of redemption won.

6 Trophy of redemption won;
From world of sin by Thy 'work' done;
My opposition all disarming
Tenderly, and me still unharming;
The burning heart Thou hast bestow'd
As Thy full grace to me o'erflow'd.

7 As Thy full grace to me o'erflow'd,
And Thee unchanging to me shew'd;
My stains all cleans'd, my guilt remov'd,
Redeeming love thro' peace approv'd;
Thus, thus a heart by grace illum'd
Is "Burning Bush" and unconsum'd.

323. Conversion: *1 Peter. i. 23.* 7s.

1 Mystic flame that burneth not,
Of no earth-born fire begot;
Can its wonders e'er be told?—
Worthy to be grav'd on gold;

Human and divine are blent
In this gift from High Heav'n sent;
God meets man and man meets God,
By THE SPIRIT " shed abroad."

2 Miracle of love and grace,
Virgin's womb, God's dwelling-place;
Miracle of grace display'd,
Holy Child in manger laid;
Scarce less miracle of love
Lord! That Thou dost in me move!
That in me a sinner great,
Thou dost the " new heart " create.

3 Conscience wounded—conscience heal'd,
By the Blood of Christ reveal'd;
Will address'd and quick-persuaded,
Yet my choosing uninvaded;
Life of life within me put,
All Love's marvels in it shut;
Lord, I would extol THY NAME,
Such as I thus to reclaim.

4 Light of life upon me shine
Father, Son, and Spirit Trine;
Lift me up and keep me high,
That I commerce with the sky;
In the World, not of it, Lord,
Nurtur'd by Thy Holy Word;
Showing even on the Earth
Marks of my great HEAV'NLY BIRTH.

324. NEW BIRTH. *St. John iii. 7.* 68.

1 'Born again'—twice-made man,
Such is LOVE's mighty plan;
Born into mortal flesh,
That the soul doth enmesh;
'Born again' from ABOVE,
By life from HOLY DOVE.

2 'Born again' wondrous gift
That to God doth uplift!
'Born again'—O blest dower
Thro' my God's soft'ned power;
'Born again' O the glow
When 'new birth' mortals know.

3 Thee I bless, O my God!
That Thy love 'shed abroad'
Gives to me a sweet sense
Yea grace-felt confidence,
That in me is begun
What shall win Thy " Well done."

4 'Born again'—bluest blood
Brings noblest no such good;
'Born again'—heav'nly touch
Not rite doth this avouch;
'Born again' Christ alone
Turns to flesh heart of stone.

" NEGLECT THE ROOT TO TRIM THE
FLOWER."—*George Meredith.* 88.
Proverbs xxxi. 30.

1 *Neglect the root to trim the flower:*
Lo! Thou wilt find in evil hour,
That not the seen but the unseen
Lies nearest to bright Heav'n's sheen.

2 Lies nearest to bright Heav'n's sheen —
Soft as the light but as flame keen;
That stem and leaf, bud, bloom and fruit,
Their CHARACTER take from the root.

3 Their CHARACTER take from the root —
The Gardener or glad or mute;
Lo! The outward is fugitive
" Inward adorning," that doth live.

4 " Inward adorning," that doth live:
O Lord! do THOU to us grace give
That this we see, and feel, and know,
Till mind and heart with ardour glow.

5 Till mind and heart with ardour glow,
Whilst still more grace Thou dost bestow;
Made temples of the Holy Ghost
Ne'er of mere beauty shall we boast;

6 Ne'er of mere beauty shall we boast,
But grasping firm Redemption's cost,
Walk holily, and Thy strength seek,
To live as those Thou keepest, meek.

7 To live as those Thou keepest, meek:
Whether we act or whether speak;
Turn Thou to warning and to power
' *Neglect the root to trim the flower.*'

326. CROWN OF THORNS AND 'THORN
IN THE FLESH.' *2 Corinthians xii* 7. 8s.

1 O King of Sorrows! my heart turns
  To Thee crown'd with THY crown of thorns;
  To me a 'thorn' lo! Thou hast given
  By which my "heart and flesh" are riven;
  Wilt THOU in Thy great pity deign
  By THINE, to mitigate my pain?

2 Thy cruel-platted crown of thorns
  Was plac'd on THEE amidst men's scorns;
  Unwitting all, that they fulfill'd
  The full curse-bearing THOU hadst will'd.
  My 'thorn' THOU placest in my flesh:
  Lord! Is't that I may 'scape PRIDE's mesh?

3 My heart, O Christ! within me burns:
  Sad, I gaze on Thy crown of Thorns;
  For Thou Who didst endure all anguish
  Dost soften mine as here I languish;
  Yet, Lord, wilt Thou my 'thorn' remove;
  Or sanctify it in Thy love?

4 Alas, O Lord, proud Nature spurns
  The message of Thy crown of Thorns;
  My 'thorn' stings and my PATIENCE tries
  Conceal'd from me Thy 'purpose' lies;
  Be pleas'd, Thorn-crown'd, to show it me,
  That I may softly walk with THEE.

327. "LORD A THORN FROM THY
  CROWN." 6s.
  "*When one is happy, praised, borne along
  on the breath of the public favour, one must
  make one's constant prayer, of the words,
  "Lord, a thorn from Thy crown."*
  Philippians i. 29.   ALEXANDER VINET.

1 " A thorn, Lord, from Thy crown "
  Grant if Thou dost me own:
  Lord! Suffer me to bring
  Tears even while I sing.

2 " A thorn, Lord, from Thy crown "
  Grant if Thou dost me own:
  Thy cross alone atones
  But I would know Thy groans.

3 " A thorn, Lord, from Thy crown "
  Grant if Thou dost me own;
  That I heart-feltly know
  The pathos of Thy woe.

4 " A thorn, Lord, from Thy crown "
  Grant if Thou dost me own;
  Made sharer of Thy grief
  But given sweet relief.

5 " A thorn, Lord, from Thy crown "
  Grant if Thou dost me own;
  That I unmurmuring
  May TASTE Thy suffering.

328.   THE CRUCIFIED.   7s.
  Gen. iii. 18. Matt. xxvii. 29.

1 O the taunt! and O the vaunt!
  From these coarse lips dissonant;
  Kingly names and bended knee
  Blasphemous the mockery.

2 Ah! what blame! and ah! what shame!
  In this mock'ry of Thy Name:
  And 'twas SIN that did it all
  As all sin on THEE did fall.

3 I draw near; but O to hear
  With Faith's open list'ning ear!
  That Thou, Jesus, for us died
  Grandest as THE CRUCIFIED.

4 How may I trace, all the grace
  Lord, of Thy most marred Face!
  Crown'd with thorns, Earth's curse to bear,
  Lifting man from his despair.

5 Lo! I sing as O my King
  To Thy Cross I lowly cling;
  My guilt borne, by Thy flesh torn,
  " Man of Sorrows " crown'd with thorn.

329. MY BODY IS MY CROSS. *1 Cor. ix. 27.*
                                    6s.
"*A man's body is often the cross on which
his soul is crucified.*" —*Thomas Toke Lynch.*

1   My body is my Cross
      On which I'm crucified;
    In pain I writhing toss,
      Anguish to anguish tied;

I fain would rest on Thee,
 In faith and hope and peace;
Alas! my misery,
 No moment find I ease.

2 Sleepless from night to morn,
  I know not what to do;
 By hairsbreadths rack'd and torn
  In vain I to Thee sue;
 O Christ! Thou know'st me all,
  Seest me as here I lie;
 I faintly on THEE call;
  Relieve—or let me die.

3 " Harp of a thousand strings,"
  Ah! Pain strikes ev'ry note;
 I sigh for Thy Dove's wings,
  To fly to place remote;
 My Body is my cross,
  On which I'm crucified;
 In pain I writhing toss,
  Anguish to anguish tied.

4 Forgive if I complain;
  Forgive my restlessness;
 Forgive that subtle pain
  Hides e'en when Thou dost bless;
 I plead Thy Cross, O Christ!
  And all Thou suffered'st there;
 Come with Thy Love unpric'd,
  Deliver from Despair.

330. THE ABANDONED. *St. Matt. xi. 28.*
6, 5, 6, 5.

1 'Fallen fallen fallen'!
   Whither can I go?
  Tempted master'd "taken"!
   I am very low;
  O my heart is sick'ning!
   Man to man's a foe;
  O my heart is breaking!
   Whither can I go?

2 'Fallen—fallen—fallen'!
   Piercing words of scorn,
  Leave me mad, forsaken,
   Talk'd of, crush'd, and torn:
  O the cruel talking!
   Accusation, wrath!
  All my efforts baulking,
   Closing up my path.

3 'Fallen fallen fallen'!
   I am very low;
  Wounded trampled driven;
   Whither can I go?
  In sore thrall who goeth,
   Bend must to His will;
  He Who all things knoweth,
   Knows and loveth still.

331.   HEART-SEARCHING.   8s.
Ps. cxxxix. 3: St. John ii. 25.

1 The gossamer swings in the air,
  With threads so deftly spun, and rare,
  That not until like to pearls strung
  The dew-drops are upon it hung;
  Can you follow it with your eye
  Or that matter it is, descry.

2 Is it not e'en thus with our thought,
  Cunningly in the mind's loom wrought?
  More swiftly flitting to and fro
  Than shuttle that skill'd hand doth throw;
  You know not what 'tis till your tears
  Gleam like dew on a rose's spears.

3 Ah! But the Lord pierces behind
  Face and look to innermost mind;
  Needeth not that man testify
  Or hidden secrets notify;
  He—O how gently!—always knows
  How our stream of thought ever flows.

4 Be it ours so to live and die
  That never need we fear His eye;
  Be it ours so to Him to come
  With our thought and desire in sum;
  That cleans'd without and cleans'd within
  Even He shall see no speck of sin.

332. Mergere nos patitur, sed non submergere Christus.—*Mediæval Saying.*
2 Cor. iv. 9. 6s.

1 Christ suffereth His Own
  To sink—but not to drown;
  If fiercest tempest come,
  Whit'ning the sea to foam;
  Or, blows wave-tramping wind
  No human force can bind;
  Or, thund'rous lightnings flash
  As tho' the sky would crash;
  Lo! His outstretched Hand
  As we in safety stand:
  Christ suffereth His Own
  To sink—but not to drown.

2 Lord, unto Thee I creep,
  Look on me as I weep;
  Lord, unto Thee I look,
  See how my faith is shook;
  Lord, unto Thee I cling,
  Heal Thou Sin's deadly sting;
  Lord, unto Thee I cry,
  Look on my misery;
  I know not what to think,
  Alas! alas! I sink:
  Ah! Christ suff'reth His Own
  To sink—but not to drown.

3 Comes oft temptation sore,
  Ah! pressing more and more;
  Reviving native sin,
  That still lurks me within;
  Comes, too, temptation sly
  As Pleasure's mimicry;
  Yea, cometh ev'n in prayer,
  In praise, in all soe'er;
  And comes temptation still
  In God's own "holy hill";
  Ah! Christ suff'reth His Own,
  To sink—but not to drown.

4 A touch of His own Hand
  As we near to Him stand;
  A light not fetch'd from skies,
  Or aught in our Earth lies;
  Strength not of limbs or thews
  That "daily bread" renews;
  The overcoming life
  Still victor in the strife;
  The "closer walk" with God,
  These all to Jesus ow'd;
  Christ suffereth His Own,
  To sink—but not to drown.

333. In la sua voluntade 'e nostra pace.—*Dante.* 'Thy will be done': *St. Matt.* vi. 10. 6s.

1 *In His Will is our peace*
  Its source and its increase:
  Lo! From the ghastly Room —
  Red with His awful blood;
  Death, which all death exceeds,
  And terror in us breeds,
  Our 'peace' comes. —
         Wondrous giving,
  Life dying and Death living.

2 *In His Will is our peace* —
  O ne'er such sweet release!
  From God's all-holy Law,
  That frights the soul with awe;
  From conflict stern of sin,
  The burthen'd heart within;
  From flesh and spirit's strife,
  That wounds more deep than knife.

3 *In His Will is our peace* —
  O joy that ne'er can cease!
  Like to full-tided sea
  That floods an estuary;
  Behold this shallow heart
  Remade by Thy Love's art,
  By life of God surcharg'd,
  Is still by grace enlarg'd.

4 *In His Will is our peace* —
  The peace that bringeth ease;
  Peace with "my Lord, my God,"
  Peace, by uplifted load;
  Peace, flowing like a river;

Peace, multiplying ever ;
Peace, waxing strong thro' weakness,
Reflecting His own meekness.

5 *In His Will is our peace* –
O Christ ! all turmoil chase !
By Thy soft strength upheld,
Daily to us reveal'd ;
By Thee still sanctified,
My fears all scatter'd wide ;
Mine be this peace to know ;
E'en vale of shadows glow.

6 *In His Will is our peace* —
The great truth I embrace ;
I draw my mortal breath,
Sustain'd His breath beneath ;
My soul's more subtle being,
Kept safe by His o'erseeing ;
In ALL, my Lord Divine,
My life be hid in Thine.

334. LOVE WITHOUT MEASURE. *After St. Bernard. Romans iv. 4-5   7s.*

1 All I have, I have receiv'd ;
All hold, as I have believ'd ;
Trusting, by Christ's gracious art,
That gave to me the "new heart."
Ah ! the "new heart" that He takes
And for His Own temple makes.

2 All I do, He does in me,
In "glorious liberty,"
Freedom that marks me the Lord's
By the grace which He affords ;
Making that I loud rejoice
With my heart and with my voice.

3 Praise, Lord, for intelligence,
Intellect made excellence ;
Excellence produc'd by Love,
Quicken'd by the Holy Dove ;
That in me hath sweetly wrought,
As I by His blood am bought.

4 Vain all glory but in Him,
His all glory else doth dim,
Save, as we're by grace, THE CHRIST'S.

Ah ! He keepeth His sweet trysts !
Keepeth, and still shows the Way,
Leading to Eternal Day.

5 What the measure of our love,
That aye toward Him doth move ?
Toward Him our richest treasure,
Treasure for transcending measure ;
Measure yea, that knows no bound,
Only in the boundless found.

335. SANCTIFIED ILLS. *1 Peter iii. 15.   7s.*

1 As the sunshine in the clouds ;
As the foam-bells on the floods ;
As the fragrance in the flower ;
As the new-mown grass's dower ;
  Thou dost, Lord, in love assuage
  Troubles' sorest, keenest rage.

2 Clouds distil the "tender rain,"
Foam-bells beautify the main ;
Fragrance glorifieth shape ;
Rain from hurt gives sweet escape:
  Thou dost, Lord, in love assuage
  Troubles' sorest, keenest rage.

3 Flood doth come on ebb anon ;
Tempests bring not harms alone ;
Lightnings do not merely smite ;
Stars enrich the darker night :
  Thou dost, Lord, in love assuage
  Troubles' sorest, keenest rage.

4 Sickness is not always loss ;
Oft it brings us to the Cross ;
Nor is weakness, if at length
It send us to Christ for strength :
  Thou dost, Lord, in love assuage
  Troubles' sorest, keenest rage.

5 Loss of riches may enrich
If our thoughts we upward pitch ;
Sorrow may be discipline
That shall make us nigh divine :
  Thou dost, Lord, in love assuage
  Troubles' sorest, keenest rage.

6 As the sunshine in the clouds ;
   As the foam-bells on the floods ;
   As the fragrance in the flower;
   As the new-mown grass's dower ;
   Thou dost, Lord, in love assuage
   Troubles' sorest, keenest rage.

336. THANKFULNESS.
"Be ye thankful." —*Colossians iii. 15.*

1 WERE I more thankful, Lord,
   Methinks more joy I'd find ;
   Wilt Thou fulfil Thy Word,
   And thus to Thee me bind ?
   Lo ! Thankfulness and Joy are twins ;
   Who seeks to separate them, sins.

2 Were I more thankful, Lord,
   More bright my life should be ;
   No day but doth afford
   Proofs of Thy grace to me ;
   Lo ! Thankfulness and Joy are twins ;
   Who seeks to separate them, sins.

3 Were I more thankful, Lord,
   I should discern Thy love,
   And Thou be still adorn'd
   Tho' 'neath dark clouds I move.
   Lo ! Thankfulness and Joy are twins ;
   Who seeks to separate them, sins.

4 Were I more thankful, Lord,
   "Walk" should I nearer Thee ;
   Thus "walking," ev'ry chord
   Yield grateful melody ;
   Lo ! Thankfulness and Joy are twins ;
   Who seeks to separate them, sins.

337. DESPAIR AND GOD. 7s.
Ps. cxxxix. 8 ; Is. l. 10.

1 IN the blackness of DESPAIR —
   Starless darkness ev'rywhere ;
   Over all my lonely path
   Portents of Thy holy wrath ;
   There doth come voice soft and low
   'Midst light as of after-glow;
   Whisp'ring me that as is told

   In lorn David's psalm of old,
   The Lord husheth our despair—
   "Make thy bed in hell, I'm there."

2 Laud, my God, that thus it is ;
   It to know is sweetest bliss ;
   When o'er me Thy billows burst,
   And alas ! I lose my trust ;
   When my way is as steep slope,
   And alas ! I lose my hope ;
   When I blindly, darkly move,
   And alas ! I lose my love ;
   Comes to brighten my despair—
   "Make thy bed in hell, I'm there."

3 Strange that I, a Child of Light,
   Should still walk thus in affright ;
   Ah ! The mystery of things,
   And deep shadows that it flings !
   My Lord Christ, to Thee I cry,
   Pity my sore misery ;
   For despite Thy patient love
   I Thee grieve, O HEAVENLY DOVE !
   O forgive ! Say to *Despair*—
   "Make thy bed in hell, I'm there."

4 Blessèd Saviour, see my sin
   Palpitating me within ;
   Tho' Thy grace in me is strong,
   Notes of anguish mar my song ;
   E'en on knees, Thy Face is hid ;
   From "the Rock" alas ! I've slid ;
   Sword is dinted, loosen'd mail,
   As the Tempter doth assail ;
   Lord ! Thy mighty word declare —
   "Make thy bed in hell, I'm there."

338. DESPONDENCY. 8s.
Isaiah xlv. 4.

1 NONE can redeem but He Who paid,
   None can remake but He Who made ;
   Redeem me, Lord ! Re-make me, Lord !
   Hear as I plead Thy gracious word.

2 Justly, O Lord, Thou mightest burn,
  And my late pleading from Thee spurn;
  But ah! Thou patient art and sweet
  To whosoe'er bows at Thy feet.
3 *Repeat St. 1.*
4 Forgive, that I so long delay'd;
  Forgive, that I still disobey'd;
  Forgive, that vainly conscience stung;
  Forgive, that to the world I clung.
5 *Repeat St. 1.*
6 My deepest guilt to Thee I bring,
  Deal with me as to Thee I cling;
  O sheath thy "furbish'd glitt'ring sword;"
  Thy word fulfil—Thy tender word,
7 *Repeat St. 1.*
8 Thy Holy Spirit me doth touch,
  As in keen anguish, Lord, I crouch;
  I lift unto Thy Cross my eyes,
  And, lo! my guilt-born terror dies.
9 *Repeat St. 1.*
10 I know not that I've found THE WAY,
  From whence I had gone far astray;
  But I know, Lord, Thou hast me found,
  And that my "chain" Thou hast unbound.

339. THE RICH YOUNG MAN. 8s.
". . . . . *And he went away sorrowful.*"
St. Matt. xix. 22.

He "*went* away," not "*sent* away;"
  Lord! I would lay this word to heart.
He "*went* away" not "*sent* away;"
  Lord! give me grace to see my part.
He "*went* away" not "*sent* away,"
  The "young man" chose himself to go.
He "*went* away" not "*sent* away,"
  The Lord's great heart to him did glow.
He "*went* away" not "*sent* away,"
  His "great possessions" hindering;
He "*went* away" not "*sent* away;"
  Ah! Had he faced the sundering!

He "*went* away" not "*sent* away,"
  His riches came 'twixt Him and Christ.
He "*went* away" not "*sent* away,"
  Alas! the Lord was under-priced!
He "*went* away" not "*sent* away,"
  The Lord had meant him "gain" for "loss!"
He "*went* away" not "*sent* away,"
  How blest had he but ta'en the Cross!
He "*went* away" not "*sent* away,"
  Making himself a castaway.
O heart of mine! this "one thing do,"
  At all costs to THE CHRIST be true!

340. GENUINENESS. *St. Mark vii. 13.*
8.4.8.4.8.8.

1 I WOULD be genuine, O Lord!
    With Thine Own rank'd;
  Instructed of Thy Holy Word,
    Not sacro-sanct;
  I would not from the World retreat,
  But follow still Thy tireless feet.

2 My Body I will not malign,
    As tho' 'twere vile;
  Neither my dignity resign,
    Nor honour soil;
  Thou, Lord, didst make me and remake;
  All praise and glory to Thee take.

3 Commandments by man only giv'n
    I value not;
  The pure light shining from high Heav'n,
    They dim, yea, blot;
  Thy mind to know, Thy will to do,
  Lord help me aye keep these in view.

4 After Thy likeness, O Lord Christ,
    Be I renew'd;
  Then keeping with Thee hallow'd tryst
    Evil eschew'd;
  I shall up to "full stature" grow,
  Reflective of Thy life below.

5 Forbid that I mistake a mask
    For living face;
  Forbid I should my life mis-task
    With pseudo-grace;

WEARYING FOR THE SECOND COMING OF THE LORD.

False virtues and false vices shun,
That I may yet win Thy " well done."

6 O Lord, I come in very weakness ;
    Save me from CANT ;
Graces bestow'd I'd hold in meekness,
    Fuller or scant ;
I would be genuine, O Lord,
Instructed of Thy Holy Word.

341. NECESSITY AND FREEDOM. 8s.

1 Cor ix. 16 ; Romans vii. 18.

1 As the leaf springs out of the bough;
    As the flower bursts forth from the bud ;
As the song from the bird doth flow ;
    And as comes and goes the quick blood;
So necessity is laid on me,
To grow liker and liker Thee.

2 For hast Thou, Lord, not won my heart,
    Made willing captive unto Love ?
Even life of life beyond art,
    Like beating pulse in me doth move;
So necessity is laid on me,
To grow liker and liker Thee.

3 But alas ! this mystery of sin,
    It rebels so to set me free ;
So oft it doth victory win
    That I moan in misery ;
Yet necessity is laid on me,
To grow liker and liker Thee.

4 O the conflict ! the joy! the grief !
    Thrall inwrought with liberty ;
O Spirit of God send relief,
    And assert Thy supremacy ;
For necessity is laid on me,
To grow liker and liker Thee.

5 I walk this sin-scarr'd Earth,
    In hope, not as bondman held ;
But me Thou hast thrill'd to new birth;
    And 'gainst this sin I have rebell'd ;
So necessity is laid on me,
To grow liker and liker Thee.

5 O paradox, strangest e'er seen !
    Two natures in arms before Heav'n ;
To-day as of old it hath been,
    Now success and now failure giv'n ;
Still, necessity is laid on me,
To grow liker and liker Thee.

342. WEARYING FOR THE SECOND COMING OF THE LORD. 8s.

1 How long, Lord, till Thou shalt appear,
    Thy broken Church's heart to cheer !
How long till " all things " be put under
    Amidst the Earth's and Heaven's wonder;
O Christ forth-burst upon the world,
Let SIN from its vast throne be hurl'd.

2 A weary sameness, shorn of Hope ;
    Faith's way all dark, with slope on slope;
Men's hearts still failing them for fear,
    As still, O Christ, Thou draw'st not near;
When, flaming to the farthest heaven
Like lightning—shall Thy "sign be giv'n?"

3 Thou spakedst, Lord, Thy burning word,
    (Dread as the flash of furbish'd sword);
To Pilate saidst a DAY should come
    That all the days of TIME shall sum :
When Thou with clouds of angels seen,
Shalt make Earth splendid with heav'n's sheen.

4 Alas, O Christ ! weary and worn,
    We look to Thee with eyes forlorn ;
Thy Church enringed with mortal foes,
    Calleth on Thee to interpose ;
Arise ! arise ! assert Thy power,
Let this be Thine accepted hour.

5 How long, O Christ, Thy Church has pray'd,
    And still Thy COMING is delay'd !
How long has th' Enemy prevail'd !
    Art Thou not in Thy Church assail'd ?
Lord Christ, hear Thou our wistful cry,
Deliver from our agony !

343. REVIVAL. *Ezra ix. 8-9.*
9.9.8,8,8,8.

1. ALAS! O God, Thy Church doth languish;
But half-awake 'midst a world's anguish;
Enthroned Christ, we turn to Thee;
Thou wilt us hear—Thou dost us see;
Lord, us REVIVE! Thy 'work' revive;
All our past apathy forgive.

2. Alas! O God, Thy Church doth languish:
Wilt Thou all our lukewarmness vanquish?
To us, Lord, Thou Thy grace hast given,
But still we mourn a deathly leaven;
Fulfil to us Thy mighty word;
Come, if Thou comest with a sword.

3. Alas! O God, Thy Church doth languish:
But half-awake, 'midst a world's anguish;
'Tis stark and still as desert stones;
Lord! We should welcome even moans;
But Thou by a word quickened;
A living host stood panoplied.

4. Alas! O God, Thy Church doth languish;
And fervour from her work doth banish;
Come then as with Thy strong "four winds";
Come smite what hardens—lift what blinds;
Strong brains and wills, O consecrate?
Thy 'gentleness' true hearts make 'great.'

5. Alas O God, Thy Church doth languish;
But half-awake, 'midst a world's anguish;
All hearts baptize with reverence;
Deep-root our CREEDS in common-sense;
Thou Christ our Great Exemplar be,
In Faith and Hope and Charity.

6. Alas! O God, Thy Church doth languish;
Tho' the wide world its sword doth brandish;
Great riches with Thine own abounds,
Yet the poor aggregate astounds;
O Thou Who hast bestowed all,
Cause millions to Thy treas'ry fall!

7. Alas! O God, Thy Church doth languish;
But half-awake, 'midst a world's anguish;
Lo! Thou Thy Gospel hast us sent;
And Thou Thy Spirit hast us lent;
Thy heart of love yearns o'er the world,
Why should Thy banner e'er be furl'd?

8. Alas! O God, Thy Church doth languish;
Souls are starving as they who famish;
Give "Bread of Life," O Holy Ghost!
Flame of compassion for the lost;
To care for all as Jesus car'd;
To dare even as Jesus dar'd.

344. GOD FORGOT ME AND I FELL.—

Lady Mildred, in Browning's " Blot on the Scutcheon." St. Luke xix. 10. 7s.

1. " God forgot me, and I fell"—
Cry of anguish! wail from Hell!
Lady, list to no such plea,
God hath not forgotten thee.

2. " God forgot me and I fell,"
Nay, the truth thou dost not tell;
Long God strove to make Thee His,
Flash'd upon Thee bliss of bliss.

3. " God forgot me and I fell "—
Vain thus conscience seek to quell;
Vain thy God thus to accuse,
When thou mercy didst refuse.

4. " God forgot me and I fell "—
Do such proud words in Thee swell?
Let Thy cheek with blushes burn;
" Guilty " to Thy God return.

5. God forgot me and I fell"—
On the PAST no longer dwell;
As Thou art, to Jesus flee;
Let Him show His power in thee.

6. " God forgot me and I fell "—
Rings the Cross, Despair's death-knell;
Jesus never has forgot;
All thy guilt He waits to blot.

345. Conscience; or, Short Work with Unbelief.

"This is John the Baptist; he is risen from the dead."—Herod the Sadducee (St. Matt. xiv. 2 and St. Mark xii.; and Acts of the Apostles xxiii.) 98.

1 What—what is this that me startles so?
   I thought old beliefs I had let go;
   Lifting anchor and sailing far off [scoff!
   Where I might more freely think—and
   But lo! a strange terror on me lies
   As tho' a ghost stood before my eyes;
   My sin of old I find is not gone
   Or buried as dead beneath a stone:
   There it flames! ha! I feel as if haunted,
   Nay, I must e'en own it. I am daunted;
   In spite of myself pierc'd is my mail
   And an awful something doth me ail:
   What—what is this that me startles so?
   I thought old beliefs I had let go.

2 So long as 'tis only intellect
   That the great truths of God doth reject,
   There may be a quiet—call it ease
   There may be a kind of pseudo-peace;
   But when the deep moral nature rises
   It stirs the soul—ah! with dread surprises;
   Conscience clanging like a wave-swung bell,
   Low-ton'd, yet searchingly audible;
   Calling up the long-forgotten Past
   So that the man is bowed aghast
   Before himself; and beneath the stress
   Wakes up and affirms his humanness:
   What—what is this that me startles so?
   I thought old beliefs I had let go.

3 Thus was it with base Herod of old [cold
   Who, while the murder'd John still lay-a-
   In his lowly Samaritan grave;
   Cower'd like a hound or a beaten slave;
   When tidings ran thro' his public hall
   That the Lord Christ held high festival;
   Proclaiming His kingdom from Above
   And working His miracles of love;
   Mutter'd as between his clenched teeth—
   As sabre bright-flashing from its sheath—
   "'Tis beheaded John! ha! I put in prison,
   The murder'd John again up-risen!"
   What—what is this that me startles so?
   I thought old beliefs I had let go.

4 Ev'n as with the erewhile Sadducee [see;
   Who conscience-conquer'd, the truth did
   His disbeliefs fell off like spray
   And not a beast but a man stood at bay.
   So in the present far-on time
   There throbbeth within us, clear, sublime,
   That life of life which no creed can bind,
   That something deeper than even mind;
   The moral, firm-asserting itself
   Unbribable by logic as pelf;
   Ah! the soul in presence of a sin
   Breaks all nets Unbelief can spin!
   What—what is this that me startles so?
   I thought old beliefs I had let go.

5 I've seen it oft—with a sweet relief
   What short work is made of unbelief,
   When conscience awakens, and with a cry
   Penitentially owns its agony;
   By the grave of the lov'd I've seen it wake
   And atheist to his centre shake;
   Until with whisper'd, "It may be true,"
   He has been led his creed to review;
   I've heard as the tempest swept the sea
   Your atheist sob "God have mercy on me!"
   And thus 'tis ever. Conscience will live,
   Ruling by deathless prerogative;
   What—what is this that me startles so?
   I thought old beliefs I had let go.

346. Purity. *St. John viii. 10-11.*

1 The purity of fire not snow,
   That chills not but as flame doth glow;
   The purity that takes no stain
   Tho' it at Danger's post remain;
   O this be mine Thou "Holy One"
   By Thy sweet benediction.

2 Tho' in the World not of it Lord,
  May I no more forget Thy Word;
  However "tempted," my watchword be,
  "Pure by the Lord's Own purity;"
    O this be mine Thou "Holy One"
    By Thy sweet benediction.

3 I would not from the vilest turn,
  Rather with Thy compassion burn;
  Wherever by Thy Spirit "led,"
  Go would I, Lord, all unafraid;
    O this be mine Thou "Holy One"
    By Thy sweet benediction.

4 Forbid that I should seek to shirk
  The doing of ne'er so trying work.
  With Thy "call," lift on me Thy Face,
  That for all DUTY I find grace;
    O this me mine, Thou "Holy One,"
    By Thy sweet benediction.

5 *Repeat St. 1.*

347.   HOLY MADNESS.   6s.
Acts of the Apostles c. xxvi. 25.

1 THE WORLD may count me "mad"
    Because I sing and shout;
  But how should I be sad,
    Free'd from an evil rout?
  I'll sing and sing again;
  JESUS, my glad refrain.

2 Hell-worthy long I was;
    Captive and slave of sin;
  Hasting without a pause,
    Base eminence to win;
  But JESUS broke my chain
  E'en as I rush'd amain.

3 Christ-conscious now, I know
    He all my guilt has borne;
  I find my heart to glow,
    As still to Him I turn;
  So sing and sing again;
  JESUS, my glad refrain.

4 Like lame man heal'd me see;
    What wonder if I dance!

  How can I silent be,
    With light for ignorance?
  Lo! Jesus broke my chain
  E'en as I rush'd amain.

5 Poor am I here on earth;
    Unknown of rich and great;
  But giv'n the great "new birth,"
    I know my high estate,
  And sing and sing again;
  JESUS, my glad refrain.

6 I sing, I shout, I leap,
    To tell my boundless joy;
  I am so glad I weep,
    None shall my song destroy;
  I'll sing and sing again;
  JESUS, my glad refrain.

343.   ECSTASY.   *2 Cor. xii. 2.*   6s.

1 LAUD, Lord, for ECSTASY
    That lifts from Earth to sky;
  That, by THE SPIRIT shaken
  I Lord to thee am taken;
  "Caught up," like Paul of old,
  To see things manifold.

2 I seem to touch the stars;
  I've plac'd my hand on Mars;
  My soul expands its wings
  Shown inmost life of things;
  I "walk" with Thee, O God!
  Freed from my body's load.

3 Call it not mysticism —
  Term base as ever — SCHISM;
  For 'tis the "mind of Christ,"
  In His love all unpric'd;
  "I and the Father One,"
  Ye One in Me alone."

4 I rise above terrene;
  I see the else unseen;
  Gaze on the INFINITE,
  The source of life and light;
  Rise unto the Eternal
  In His great House supernal.

5 Behold! I traverse SPACE;
   I heed not TIME to trace;
   Leave Earth and Sin behind,
   Swift-speeding as the wind;
   Still toward God high soaring,
   The triune God adoring.

6 My being's apparition
   I see by intuition;
   Nets subtly interlac'd;
   Light by vast shadow chas'd;
   The unseen clear, as seen
   Without a hind'ring screen.

7 "Powers of the world to come"
   So awe me I am dumb;
   I worship God a-hush,
   O'er me there seems to rush
   Angelic wings full wondrous
   With blended praises thund'rous.

8 Lord! Blessing, honour, thanks,
   For grace me, sinner, ranks
   With high-adoring hosts
   Arriv'd on Heaven's coasts:
   Laud for Eternity
   Flash'd me in ECSTASY.

9 My soul, like tongues of fire
   Leaping from altar-pyre;
   Hands-breadth of incense smoke
   O'er which strange brightness broke;
   Beneath a burning heart
   Empierc'd with many a dart.

10 Above a pleading eye
   Turn'd Christ-ward steadfastly;
   All hieroglyphs, I ween,
   Yet deep truths in them seen;
   Thereby are bodied forth
   Things all unseen on Earth.

11 Things subtle 'bove our touch
   That in the unknown couch,
   Fine-spun as gossamer
   Or rainbow in dark air;
   Threads woven in a loom
   Whose finish'd web is doom.

12 Laud, Lord, for ECSTASY
   That lifts from Earth to sky;
   I leave my body's tent
   And climb the firmament;
   Laud! I can ante-date
   The great words ultimate.
   Laud Father, Son, and Holy Ghost!
   Who 'fore the Three-One God may boast?

349. LIFE A MYSTERY. 78.
Col. i. 19.

1 O HOW life swarms in the grass!—
   Shewn as sunbeams thro' it pass;
   How upon each tiny leaf
   Yea, in cut grain and in sheaf;
   Pulsates, quivereth and gleams;
   And in each drop of the streams,
   And rank pool and wayside pond,
   Ev'n by naked eye is found
   Ever-palpitating life,
   Interlink'd with a strange strife:
      O the mystery of things!
      Dark the shadow that it flings.

2 Still it comes, and still it goes,
   And perpetual change it shews;
   Hidden life is universal,
   This mimetic sad rehearsal
   Of our very human being—
   Lord God! all beneath Thy seeing;
   Gives me pause and on bow'd knee
   I implore a-wonderingly
   If this dread strife came of SIN
   Or what was its origin?
      O the mystery of things!
      Dark the shadow that it flings.

3 Thus is it where'er I turn,
   Nor will questionings inurn;
   Fruitless all and fugitive,
   One of thousand blooms will live;
   Form'd nurtur'd then defac'd:
   Prodigality of waste;
   Insect-life: how short the date!
   So rich-hued no Art can mate,

DESPONDENCY   PENITENCE.

Yet from birth to death, one day:
'Tis like labour flung away;
   O the mystery of things!
    Dark the shadow that it flings.

4 I look deeper—still 'tis thus,
Law of least life holds of us;
Lo! each beating of our pulse
May well even FAITH convulse :
Mother's travail kindling joy
In fair infant—the alloy
Follows—swift and suddenly—
Scarcely born until they die;
Homes all darken'd, heart-hopes quench'd,
Lfe not taen but rather wrench'd ;
   O the mystery of things!
    Dark the shadow that it flings.

5 O have patience, my sad soul :
On THE CHRIST thy burden roll ;
He is Lord supreme of life,
He is PEACE through all this strife ;
His the secret—'tis not thine ;
PURPOSE He works is divine ;
What thou know'st not, cannot know,
Whilst Thou walkest here below,
By and bye on other side
Thou shalt know—and more beside :
   O the mystery of things!
    But the Cross light to us brings.

350.   DESPONDENCY.   9.5.9.5.
Isaiah xl. 31.

1 O LORD, I come before Thee kneeling,
But I bring no praise ;
Thy joy I do not know ; no feeling
My sunk heart doth raise.

2 O Lord, I come before Thee kneeling,
But I cannot fly ;
To Thee, my inner thoughts unsealing ;
Laggard, dull am I.

3 O Lord, I come before Thee kneeling,
But I do not run ;
To do Thy will—'twere but concealing
The sad truth to shun.

4 O Lord, I come before Thee kneeling,
But I only creep ;
Come wasted-conscience bell-like pealing
As from some high steep.

5 O Lord, I come before Thee kneeling,
But my faith is gone ;
Forgive my sorrowful appealing,
From a heart of stone.

6 O Lord, I come before Thee kneeling,
But I dare not pray ;
Blank, blinding darkness o'er me stealing
Takes my words away.

351.   PENITENCE.   7s.
St. Luke xviii. 13.

1 SINNER'S Saviour ! Wilt impart
To my heavy-laden heart
HOLY SHAME of PENITENCE ?—
Glorifying even sense ;
Tinging the pale cheek with blush
Pure as red rose on its bush.

2 Sinner's Saviour ! Thou know'st all ;
In dismay, 'fore Thee I fall ;
Knowest how Prosperity
Chill'd " first love " till it did die ;
Pardon, Lord, and me restore ;
Let me hear " Go, sin no more."

3 Sinner's Saviour ! Wilt refuse ?
Hold at arm's length and accuse?
Nay, in mercy dost declare
Welcome sure to whomsoe'er ;
Blot out all my sin and shame,
As I call upon Thy Name.

4 Sinner's Saviour ! lo ! I turn
To Thy Blood—O do not spurn ;
Save me, Lord, from " second death,"
Quicken by life-giving breath ;
Penitence into love change,
That from Thee I ne'er may range.

352. Self-Emptiness: "The Precious Blood."

1 Peter, i. 19. 7s.

1 Not in me, Lord, not in me,
Is there "good" that Thou can'st see ;
If there's "good" to meet Thine eye,
It Thy grace doth magnify ;
   All of fair, or bright, or good,
   I owe to "the precious blood."

2 Not in me, Lord, not in me,
Is there power from sin to free ;
If there's freedom—Pride dismiss ;
To Thee be ascrib'd the bliss ;
   All of fair, or bright, or good,
   I owe to "the precious blood."

3 Not in me, Lord, not in me,
Is it from my sin to flee ;
Ah ! To flee I am so slow !
Yea, I need Thy scourge, Thy blow ;
   All of fair, or bright, or good,
   I owe to "the precious blood."

4 Not in me, Lord, not in me,
Found is Thy saints' holy glee ;
Faint and fitful is my voice,
Rare the moments I rejoice ;
   All of fair, or bright, or good,
   I owe to "the precious blood."

5 Not in me, Lord, not in me,
Is there argument or plea ;
Save that I a sinner am,
Thou, the all-atoning Lamb ;
   All of fair, or bright, or good,
   I owe to "the precious blood."

6 Not in me, Lord, not in me—
This my plaint on bended knee ;
Aught of "worthy," is of grace,
Lord lift Thou on me Thy Face :
   All of fair, or bright, or good,
   I owe to "the precious blood."

353. Noblest Things find Vilest Using."—John Keble. *Jude* 4. 7s.

1 "*Noblest things find vilest using,*"
Man his God's best gifts abusing ;
Lo ! the broad fields of the corn
Of benignant sunshine born ;
Turn'd into deadliest bale,
Hell's own dreadful lord might hail.

2 "*Noblest things find vilest using,*"
The clear light of Heav'n refusing ;
The sweet warblers of the Wood
Fashion sheds their inn'cent blood ;
Rank and Beauty's heartless pride
Wear their plumes whate'er betide.

3 "*Noblest things find vilest using,*"
Highest-seated lo ! accusing ;
Riches giv'n for others weal
Held fast as with bands of steel ;
Self the centre, and God's poor,
Scour'd—to heap up more and more.

4 "*Noblest things find vilest using,*"
Vain all shallow, false accusing ;
Art pandering unto Sense
With audacious insolence ;
Meant to awe and purify
Reworking myth of "the sty."

5 "*Noblest things find vilest using,*"
Hidden poison deft infusing ;
Genius writes the evil book,
Faith in God and man is shook ;
Turning light to darkness deep ;
Hopeless, leaving men to weep.

6 "*Noblest things find vilest using,*"
Nor is the sharp charge traducing ;
Lo ! the holy thing call'd Love
Oft does it degraded prove ;
Fit the soul to lift to God,
Alas ! It turns to Passion's rod.

7 "Noblest things find vilest using"
How proof rises to our musing!
Ev'n the very Church of Christ
Bought by Jesus' love unpric'd;
Fails his Charter to make good;
Tramples on "the precious blood."

354. "Lord! I believe, help mine unbelief." —St. Matt. ix. 24.   10s.

1 Why this fear mingling with thy faith, my soul
As trembling points the needle to the pole?
Thy care, and all thy care, upon Him lay,
He asks it of thee: Wilt thou say Him nay?

2 Why this fear mingling with thy faith, my soul?
Why sinks thy heart 'cause waves around thee roll?
Come dreadest tempest, He is ever nigh;
Catch thou His great word "Fear not, it is I."

3 Why this fear mingling with thy faith, my soul,
Thy Hope beclouded whilst thou dost extol?
Rest thou on Him—who trusts in Him is blest;
He will not leave thee or see thee opprest.

4 Why this fear mingling with thy faith, my soul?
The Lord preserves His own, from start to goal;
Whom the Lord loves He loves unto the end;
Nor ever fails, all needed help to send.

5 Why this fear mingling with thy faith, my soul?
Ring out the joy-bells, do not doleful toll;
He thy glad mouth will fill with conqu'ring mirth;
Thy Saviour sure, tho' God of all the Earth.

6 Why this fear mingling with thy faith, my soul?
Fill thee up, page by page, thy life's full scroll;
Or clear, or dim, or fair, or blurr'd, His eye.
Reads all, knows all, in sweet benignity.

355. CHI FA COSE DI CRISTO, CON CRISTO DEVE STAR SEMPRE.—*Vasari*.
"I have set the Lord always before me."—Psalm xvi. 8.

1 Who does the things of Christ with Christ must always be:
O ever-present Saviour, open my eyes to see!
That I may know and feel that Thou art to me near
My upward looks to mark —most broken prayer to hear;
Thy sainted servant's words, Lord, I bring unto Thee:
Who does the things of Christ with Christ must always be.

2 Who does the things of Christ with Christ must always be:
Can privilege so wondrous be given unto me?
Yea, Lord, for Thou hast spoken Thy least ones to sustain,
That he who seeks Thy presence shall never seek in vain;
Lord! Fit me for Thy presence and for Thy ministry:
Who does the things of Christ with Christ must always be.

3 Who does the things of Christ with Christ must always be:
Saviour divine yet MAN, Thou comest tenderly;
With "still small voice" Thou whisp'rest to the list'ning heart,
"Lo! I am with you alway;" nor e'er shalt Thou depart:

Rejoice, rejoice my soul in thy sweet
  liberty ;
*Who does the things of Christ with Christ
  must always be.*

Who does the things of Christ with Christ
  must always be :
I'd read the poignant words in all
  humility ;
From Thee, in Thee, with Thee, fulfil
  would I each task,
The grace I need bestow'd, not what I
  dimly ask ;
Yet ask I ever would, and this my lowly
  plea ;
*Who does the things of Christ with Christ
  must always be.*

*Who does the things of Christ with Christ
  must always be :*
My life's sweet music, Lord, wilt Thou
  set to this key?
That on this hither side I aye may walk,
  in whiteness
Myself, my work, my all, transfigur'd by
  Thy brightness ;
So all that hurts or hinders, shall I, grace-
  held, still flee ;
*Who does the things of Christ with Christ
  must always be.*

356   HALTING. *Gen. xxxii. 31.* 8s.

O GOD, my God, I seek to know
How is it I thus "halting" go?
I have not prov'd of pray'r the might
By wrestling thro' the long lone night ;
I have not felt Thy awful touch
Lest I should boast me over-much :
Alas ! I've naught at all to boast,
A sinner sav'd at best and most :
O God, my God, I seek to know,
How is it I thus "halting" go?

2 Reveal, O God, in love reveal,
If secret sin my strength doth steal ;
If unsuspected in me lie
That which to Thee is treachery,
Let Thy light flash a poignant flame,
That I may see in red-cheek'd shame ;
At all costs, my course would I run
As I would hear Thy great "Well done ;"
O God, my God, I seek to know
How is it I thus "halting" go?

3 Not Jacob's "halting" but his "power"
I cry for, of Thy blood-bought dower ;
Bestow on me Thy holy strength
That I may overcome at length :
Yea, find within my heart such life
As makes conqueror in all strife :
Thy grace within, no foes without
Shall fill me or with fear or doubt ;
O God, my God, I seek to know
How is it I thus "halting" go?

4 O God I am in sorest need,
But " smoking flax " or " bruised reed ;"
Kindle my flame, my bruises heal,
Thy full Name unto me reveal ;
No longer "halting" may I go,
But with my first love's fervour glow ;
Constrain, restrain, by Thy sweet will,
That my full stature I fulfil ;
O God, my God, I seek to know
How is it I thus "halting" go?

357. BUBBLE. *James iv. 14.* 8s.

1 THOU BUBBLE swimming thro' the air
With changing tints to Art's despair ;
Sapphire — emerald — dazzling gold,
Onyx and crimson, fold on fold ;
What a sharp message Thou dost give
By Thy strange beauty fugitive !
Radiant as ever Beauty's daughter,—
Anon, a drop of turbid water.

2 Even so all that our Earth proffers
In its madly-alluring offers ;
Ah ! Deftest masks will slip awry
And we the Temptress' face descry ;

Tendering in her fleshless hand
Pleasures that no scrutiny stand;
Sweet i' the mouth but bitter soon,
And ah! no sooner gain'd than gone.

3 My soul, wilt Thou the lesson 'tend?
Swift let it to thy knees thee send;
Real pleasures are permanent,
Ev'n tho' with bitter they be blent;
Walk thou the Earth 'franchis'd of Him,
This will all transient glory dim;
" Kept " of the Lord, still look Above,
Thou shalt in joy and peace on move.

4 *Repeat St. 1.*

358   MYSTERY OF BEING.   6ft.
Acts of Apostles xvii. 28.

1 I hear the rush of the sap, within the veins
    of the trees,
  Above the deep-breathing wind, and the
    birds' sweet melodies;
  The mystery of life! Yet "dead" o'er it
    we dare to write;
  Lo! It is all around me—far, near, and left
    and right.

2 And does not God its Maker, the Universe
    sustain?
  Is not CREATION'S travail the lengthening
    of Christ's pain?
  I see THE CROSS all round me, on green
    earth and blue sky;
  How long, Lord Christ, till Thou lift this
    shadow scatt'ringly?

3 Growth—life in death—decay—where'er
    my eyes I turn,
  Reigning 'midst flower-starr'd grass, and
    up where the planets burn;
  My God, wilt Thou break silence and our
    aching hearts assure
  That not for aye and aye these enigmas
    shall endure?

4 As re-l leaves fall in the forest and flowers
    fade on the lea,
  So cycles of men pass still into vast
    Eternity;
  Aye sinning, striving, falling—the struggle
    old abides;
  But Thou o'errulest all things as Thou
    dost rule the tides.

5 Fill us with Faith, Lord Jesus, in Thy
    great Word and Thee,
  That come the deepest darkness, we still
    Thy Face may see;
  O help us on Thy Promise still more and
    more to rest;
  That all things work together to Thy
    chosen for the best.

359. DAS UNBEWUSSTE (THE UNCONSCIOUS).
Acts of the Apostles xvii. 28.   6s.

" I cannot help observing the remarkable force with
which the Unconscious—das Unbewusste—vindicated
its power. The weight of this element in human affairs
is so much taken hold of that whole theologies have been
founded upon the observation of the working of this
single power e.g. Calvinism and Mahomedanism. By
whatever name you call it, the Unconscious is found
onward in each man's destiny without, or in defiance
of his will."—MARK PATTISON (Memoirs c. vii. p.p.
32-3).

1 Creator of my soul
  Thou dost its tides control;
  Thou dost on me bestow
  All grace for ebb and flow;
  Yea, dost me still upstay,
  That I walk " in the WAY."

2 For the UNCONSCIOUS, Lord,—
  Tho' speaking rebel word;
  A note of thanks I raise,
  That thro' my darkest days
  Upon it I can rest,
  Nor longer be opprest.

3 " My Lord, my God," I feel
  " The wheel within a wheel;"
  Thy Spirit holds me up,
  And sweetly fills my cup;
  That I do know THY Being
  Far far beyond mere seeing.

4 I ever find THEE nigh,
  Whether I sing or sigh;
  Closer than ambient air;
  Nearer than nearest near;
  Piercing me through and through,
  Whatever I may do.

5 Thy PRESENCE me invests,
  Thrice-proven thro' all tests;
  Lo! Thy fix'd purpose stands—
  As Sea within its strands;
  Yet 'tis no rigid FATE,
  Man is inviolate.

6 Laud! For the Holy Breath
  That brings life out of death;
  That raises Sin's vast load;
  That makes me son of God;
  That lifts all fears above;
  That melts my heart in love.

7 Ah! THE UNCONSCIOUS, Lord,
  Lies like a sheathèd sword;
  Keeping still watch and ward,
  From evil to retard;
  Silent, but strong its power,
  Enclasping ev'ry hour.

8 Lord! As heart's diastole
  Thou secrets of the soul
  Holdest in THINE Own Hand;
  Rulest without command;
  Persuading the free will;
  Safe-guarding us from ill.

9 'Tis not as we were things
  Devoid of moral springs;
  Thou leavest us to choose,
  But savest from abuse;
  Thy grace more strong than sin,
  That we may vic'try win.

10 As David his harp smote,
  I strike a grateful note;
  For instincts Thou hast seal'd,
  Be my loud thanks still peal'd;
  THE UNCONSCIOUS, in me
  Shapeth my destiny.

360. A BACKSLIDER AWAKENED AT KESWICK CONVENTION, 1890. *(Under an address by the Rev. H. C. G. Moule, M.A. Principal of Ridley Hall, Cambridge).*

8, 7, 8, 7, 8, 7.

1 I heard THY words of love and grace—
  Tears in my eyes glistening;
  I lifted up to THEE my face,
  In enchanted listening;
  I knew not then or time or space;
  It was concious christening.

2 Thy "still small voice," Lord, in those years
  Ran thro' all thought—all action;[fears;
  Bracing FAITH's strength—stilling HOPE's
  Drawing with gentlest traction;
  Alas! alas! how disappears
  FIRST LOVE's glow—save mere fraction.

3 I come to THEE in penitence;
  To THEE, and to no other;
  O soften THINE omnipotence,
  Thou my Great Elder Brother!
  Conquer this cold indifference;
  This world-love grace doth smother.

4 All my transgressions, Lord, I own;
  "*My sin is aye before me;*"
  O never—never can be known,
  How oft THOU didst restore me!
  Still rescue, Lord! THY grace be shown;
  As here, I, shamed, implore THEE.

5 Be this, O Lord! THY day of power;
  As my soul Thou art thrilling;
  Thou mightst have limited my hour,
  Thy holy wrath fulfilling;
  But ah! not yet, my doom doth lour;
  Now—now "make THOU me willing."

361. THE SECRET OF THE LORD. 6s.
Ps. xxv. 14.

1 " *The Secret of the Lord* "
 O sweet phrase of the Word ;
 Yet pierces as a sword.

2 Alas ! O Lord, I feel,
 Ev'n as 'fore Thee I kneel,
 Thou still hast to ' reveal.'

3 " *The Secret of the Lord* "
 With richest blessings stor'd ;
 How it doth all accord !

4 I mourn, when Thou wast nigh,
 I rais'd no heart-born cry,
 Yea, lifted not my eye.

5 " *The Secret of the Lord* "
 Of Heav'n and Earth ador'd ;
 'Tis like sweet ointment pour'd.

6 Lord ! I to Thee draw near;
 Give me the list'ning ear;
 Thy " still small voice " to hear.

7 " *The Secret of the Lord*,"
 His peace and joy restor'd ;
 What strength it doth afford.

8 My Saviour, hear my sigh;
 As at Thy feet I lie;
 Pass O pass me not by !

362. WORTH OF HUMAN LIFE. 8s.
Job x. 8-12; Ps. xci. 11; 1 Peter iv. 4; Romans vi. 23.

1 O the stupendous worth of life !
 As witness'd by the complex strife
 To win men or for Heav'n or Hell
 God to obey, or to rebel.

2 What possibilities of good,
 Roll in upon us, like a flood !
 What possibilities of ill,
 Inflame desire and capture will !

3 O human life is splendid dower
 If known is secret of its power !

The Christ of God for Saviour taken,
And FAITH and HOPE and LOVE unshaken.

4 " *The suff'rings of this present time* "
 As mists fade, when, Faith-wing'd, we climb
 To Him Who sits upon the Throne,
 God over all, and God alone.

5 Forbid, O Lord, that I should fail,
 Clad in invulnerable mail ;
 Still may I fight for TRUTH and RIGHT,
 The world's woes lessen, in Thy might.

6 Alas ! for SIN importunate !
 Alas ! for selfishness and hate !
 Alas ! That with God's love reveal'd
 Men's hearts should still abide so steel'd.

7 O the stupendous worth of life !
 As witness'd by the complex strife
 To win men or for Heav'n or Hell —
 God to obey, or to rebel.

363. CHRIST'S FREEDMAN. — *Ephesians iv. 22-24 ; 1 Cor. viii. 5.* 8s.

1 The holy bondage of Thy love
 Lord ! Wilt Thou unto me impart ?
 More and still more within me move ;
 Take full possession of my heart,
 Possession full — whate'er the smart.

2 " The holy bondage of Thy love ; "
 Thy bondsman, Lord, but not a slave ;
 May my obedience still approve
 How conquering Thou art to save ;
 Soft-hushing Passion's strongest wave.

3 " The holy bondage of Thy love ;"
 O'ercoming life in Thee " made strong,"
 The gifts of grace all gifts above
 That sets all discords unto song ;
 Placing the " heavenlies " among.

4 " The holy bondage of Thy love ;"[grace ;
 Blood-bought, blood-seal'd, and all of
 Thy white wings flash, O Holy Dove !
 My heart be aye Thy dwelling-place ;
 And Jesus ! lift on me Thy Face.

8. Christian Graces.

364. HOLINESS. 8s.
"Ye know not what ye ask." —St. Matt. xx. 22 (Cf. St. Augustine: "De Civitate Dei," lib. xix., cxxvii. for st. 5.)

1 O Lord, I bear an aching heart;
 Ease me of sin, whate'er the smart;
 Within, without, I would be pure;
 Lord, hear my cry! Lord, work my cure!
  I know not all I ask in this,
  But give, O give me holiness.

2 Wild is the tumult in my breast;
 Oh! how I long for Thy deep rest;
 Behind thick clouds is hid Thy Face;
 Thy Face reveal of Thy great grace;
  I know not all I ask in this,
  But give, O give me holiness.

3 O Lord, to dust my faint soul cleaves;
 Rich is Thy sowing, few my sheaves;
 I own Thy bounteous gifts, but mourn
 My scanty and perverse return;
  I know not all I ask in this,
  But give, O give me holiness.

4 O Lord, accept my stammering pray'r;
 Work in me by what means soe'er
 The change I need; to sin I'd die
 That I may live with Thee on high;
  I know not all I ask in this,
  But give, O give me holiness!

5 Break ev'ry earthly tie that binds;
 Disperse each wildering mist that blinds;
 Search me, and try, and clean remove
 Whatever shares with Thee, my love;
  I know not all I ask in this,
  But give, O give me holiness!

6 O Lord, I bear an aching heart,
 All pierc'd with sin's empoison'd dart;
 Thou, Good Physician, work the cure,
 Me purify as Thou art pure;
  I know not all I ask in this,
  But give, O give me holiness!

365. HATRED OF SIN. *Ps. xcvii. 10; cxxxix. 22.* 7s.

1 O for God's Own hate of sin!
 As it stings and taints within;
 Seen of no one's eyes but mine,
 Search'd all thro', O Christ, of Thine;
 Bow me, Lord, in lowliness,
 That I all may full confess.

2 Thy pure hate of sin impart,
 Mostly, Lord, in my own heart;
 That I guilt feel more than woe,
 Seek Sin's sinfulness to know;
 Not as damning, but as stain,
 Nor Thy pard'ning grace disdain.

3 Thine Own hate of sin, O Lord,
 Wilt Thou in gracious love afford!
 That whilst it elsewhere I see
 I may see it pityingly
 Sinner sev'ring from his sin —
 Eager, erring men to win.

4 Thy pure hate of sin, that grieves,
 Whilst against hope it believes;
 Give me this, Lord, as I cry,
 Deeper human sympathy;
 With no supercilious glance
 On excusing circumstance.

5 Thine Own hate of sin, with sense
 Of self-needed penitence,
 All untouch'd of injury;
 Folly holding it to be,
 To hate sin but as we find
 It some duty on us bind.

6 Thy pure hate of sin, that moves
 In Incarnate Love's great grooves;
 Not in anger, striving still
 To enfranchise shackled will;
 By the Gospel's tender art
 Draw to choose Mary's "good part."

7 *Repeat St. 1.*

GOD OF HOPE. FAITH.

366. GOD OF HOPE. *Romans* xv. 13.
7.6.

1 "God of Hope!" O golden word!
  But with gleam as of a sword
Unto those, who unbelieving
  Still walk faint and ever grieving;
Still go in perplexity
Tho' the lamp of Love be nigh;
Not a star in all heav'n's cope,
Yet Thou, God, art "God of Hope."

2 "God of Hope!" O winsome name!
  Fitted to put us to shame;
Who e'en with the light clear-shining
  Still go wayward and repining;
By Despair in darkness led,
Lorn and all uncomforted;
Deeming it not fact but trope,
That Thou art the "God of Hope."

3 "God of Hope!" O dulcet note!
  Sweet as that from Heav'n did float,
When to shepherds erst appointed
  Came the song of "The Anointed:"
Why, O why will men not hear?
Why still live in doubt and fear?
Why not see but dimly grope?
When Thou art the "God of Hope."

4 "God of Hope!" O quick'ning phrase!
  Worthy of adoring praise;
Finding our hearts pierc'd by sin
  That still victory doth win;
Throbbing, aching, restless, sad
How are we once more made glad!
As to drowning comes a rope
This me rescues, "God of Hope."

5 "God of Hope!" for Jesus died;
  Was He not The Crucified?
"God of Hope!" for Christ is risen,
  Now the grave no more a prison;
"God of Hope!" Behold He stands
Holding up High-priestly hands;
Rise my soul, no longer mope,
God is still thy "God of Hope."

367. PEACE. *St. John* xiv. 8.6.8.6.

1 O JESUS, Fill us with Thy Peace
  The Peace that knows no change;
The peace that guarded by Thy strength,
  Counts trials nothing strange.

2 O Jesus, Fill us with Thy Peace
  The peace that looks without,
And sees a heav'nly Father's smile,
  Nor ever knows a doubt.

3 O Jesus, Fill us with Thy Peace
  The peace that lives Above;
And running in the Christian path,
  Wins the great prize of love.

4 O Jesus, Fill us with Thy Peace—
  The peace that turns to rest;
The peace that with a John-like trust,
  Leans on Thy beating breast.

5 O Jesus, Fill us with Thy Peace—
  The peace that changeth never;
The peace that sanctified of Thee,
  Still floweth as a river.

368. FAITH. *Ephesians* vi. 10.18.
7.6.7.6.6.7.7.6.

1 O FAITH, which Christ bestoweth
  On the heart-changèd breast!
O Faith, which inly gloweth
  To reach the heav'nly rest!
Lord, make it still more strong;
  All hindrances subduing;
The "narrow way" pursuing:
  At most, not very long.

2 O Faith—a shield quick-shifted,
  'Gainst ev'ry fiery dart!
O Faith, that bold, uplifted,
  Fencest the tempted heart!
Lord, Thou dost give this shield,
  And be it struck or dinted
  By weapons in hell minted,
God's children do not yield.

3 O Faith, thou sword that smitest,
   With more than mortal blow!
   O Faith, that naught affrightest
   Howsoe'er deadly foe!
   Lord, this Thy sword who takes,
   The grimmest fight advancing,
   He feareth no mischancing ;
   Hell's fortress, lo! He shakes.

4 O Faith a lamp that shinest
   On pathway lone and dark ;
   O Faith, that ne'er repinest,
   But sing'st like soaring lark :
   Lord, Thou wilt guard our light,
   When dim, " fresh oil" inpouring,
   Attent to our imploring ;
   And guide thro' darkest night.

5 O Faith, to end still daring,
   E'en in the vale of Death !
   May I, Thy courage sharing,
   Yield to my God my breath !
   'Mid deep'ning broad'ning gloom
   May I, still forward going,
   Whither I go, well knowing,
   Find Thee, Christ, not the tomb.

369. PATIENT WAITING. 8s.

" *Rest in the Lord, and wait patiently for Him.*"—*Psalm xxxvii. 7.*

1 LORD, wilt Thou Thine Own pat'ence give,
   Since thus Thou askest us to live ?
   That wrong'd, or fainting 'neath our cross
   We still bear on, nor " suffer loss :"
   Rest in the Lord ; wait patiently.

2 Still Thou dost whisper, to restrain
   On bed of languor or of pain ;
   When weary, or when low and weak,
   And half-complainingly we speak ;
   Rest in the Lord ; wait patiently.

3 Alas ! alas ! 'tis hard to bide
   When toss'd and sleepless and sore tried ;
   Look on us, Lord, in our unrest ;
   Calm with one word our troubled breast :
   Rest in the Lord ; wait patiently.

4 Long, silent, sweet, Thy patience is ;
   When Thou might'st smite, bestowing bliss,
   Lord, may we still in Thee abide
   Aye looking to THE CRUCIFIED :
   Rest in the Lord ; wait patiently.

370. FORGIVINGNESS. 8s.

" *Forgive us our trespasses as we forgive those who have trespassed against us.*"—*St. Matt. vi. 12.*

1 ALL thanks, O God of Earth and Heaven,
   For Thy thrice-gracious word Forgiven ;
   All thanks and praise, Thy " still small
   In early years made me rejoice ; [voice "
   Softly it came, like breathing wind, [find.
   When me Thy " lost sheep " Thou did'st

2 All thanks, O God of Earth and Heaven,
   For Thy pitiful word— Forgiven ;
   And do Thou make me so to live
   Through all the years Thou mayest give ;
   That I shew forth from day to day,
   Thy rich forgivingness alway.

3 All thanks, O God of Earth and Heaven,
   For Thy transforming word Forgiven ;
   This this I ever, Lord, would keep
   In heart of hearts, ev'n when I weep ;
   Wrong'd and belied betray'd forsaken ;
   Their sting from all, Thy grace has taken.

4 All thanks, O God of Earth and Heaven,
   For Thy most loving word Forgiven ;
   And when at times my heart has swell'd
   And 'gainst hard usage has rebell'd ;
   Myself I've conquer'd through Thee
   Forgiving as Thou forgivest me.

5 All thanks, O God of Earth and Heaven ;
   For Thy great, holy word Forgiven ;
   Alas ! O God, I must confess
   But for Thy grace, my helplessness ;
   Ingratitude it stings me sore ;
   Thy clemency give more and more.

6 *Repeat St. 1.*

371. THE MEEK. *St. Matt. v. 5.* 7s.

1 Blessed Jesus, we would seek
To be made, and still kept "meek;"
Wilt Thou take our sin-thrall'd will
And us with Thy meekness fill?

2 Slow to anger we would be ;
Ever Thine example see ;
Smitten, turn the other cheek
By Thy tender grace held "meek."

3 Never loud and harshly speak,
Softly, as becomes the "meek ;"
Patient as Thou patient wast,
Ev'n with insult on us cast.

4 Kindness, met with base return,
Let not passion in us burn ;
Never vengeance try to wreak ;
Knowing "blessed are the meek."

5 Lord, alas! We are but weak,
Apt to shrink from being "meek;"
Hold it manly to be strong ;
Never deign to suffer wrong.

6 Change, O Lord, our thought and
    feeling,
Thine Own meekness still revealing ;
Blessed Jesus, we would seek
To be made, and still kept, " meek."

372. SONG OF JOY. 8s.
Philippians iii. 3: 1 Thess. v. 16.

1 Lord, we would not only seek Thee,
When our souls are dark and sad ;
We would come and sing before Thee,
For the light that makes us glad.

2 Lord, we would not ever grieve Thee,
With our anguish and annoy ;
We would bound and sing before Thee,
For the fulness of our joy.

3 Lord, We would not always bring Thee,
Plaints, and wails, and sobs, and sighs ;
We would eager sing before Thee,
Of our Cross-drawn ecstasies.

4 Lord, We would not ever lift Thee
Eyes all swimming with hot tears ;
We would thankful sing before Thee,
For the hushing of our fears.

5 Lord, We would not wait upon Thee,
As in some confessional;
Thou art ours, we sing before Thee,
We no longer are in thrall.

6 Lord, We would not only seek Thee,
In our dull and lonely days;
We would joyous sing before Thee ;
We would fill our mouths with praise.

373. PURITY. *St. Matt. v. 8.* 10s.

1 Thou tell'st us, Lord, "blest are the pure
    in heart ;"
We would be blest : Wilt Thou Thy grace
    impart ?
Alas, thick falls on us as falls the dust,
The thought that stains, desire that taints
    our trust ;
O! undertake Thou, Lord for us, and cure ;
Whate'er it cost, make us and keep us pure.

2 Thou tell'st us, Lord, "blest are the pure
    in heart ;"
To purify ourselves, we have no art ;
The secret, Lord, is Thine : Wilt whisper
    low
That by Thy "still small voice" we may it
    know ;
O Christ, unworthy we this to procure ;
Yet, gracious Lord, we would, we would
    be pure.

3 Thou tell'st us, Lord, "blest are the pure
    in heart ;"
But when we long for it, sin will us thwart;
Again and yet again we quiv'ring feel
How that we would not do will on us steal;
O Lord, how can Thy patience thus endure !
Forgive, forgive, and Thyself make us pure.

OBEDIENCE, OR "THE NEW CART," v. "THE NEW HEART."

4 Thou tell'st us, Lord, " blest are the pure
    in heart ,"
But hard it is our grace and sin to part ;
Thou know'st the tumult and the conflict
    sore ;
Thou seest how passions like chain'd lions
    roar ;

O Lord, stand by, as we all sin abjure ;
By Thy grace conquering, we shall be pure
5 Thou tell'st us, Lord, " blest are the pure
    in heart ;"
Behold us in the home and in the mart:
Where'er we go, whate'er we do, this sin
Still us besets and victory seems to win ;
But Thou O Lord, the conquest dost assure;
That we may see, O do Thou keep us pure.

374. OBEDIENCE, OR "THE NEW CART,' v. "THE NEW HEART."

1 Chron. xiv. 7-14.   6s.

1 Lord ! teach me to obey !
  Lord ! lead me in Thy way !
    Exactly to fulfil
    Thy clear-revealed Will ;
  Nor fail, nor go beyond
  With my own fancies fond.

2 Searching Thy Holy Word
  It flames to me like sword,
    To read of " *The New Cart*"
    That did divine law thwart ;
  The ark as on high throne
  Priests were to bear alone.

3 — So when the ark was taken
  In " new cart," and was shaken
    As on the road it went,
    But not of God thus sent ;
  Uzzah stretching his hand,
  Fell dead at God's command.

4 My soul, beware, beware,
  Doth not this still declare
    That none may God's words change
    Or from them dare to range ?
  Lord ! fill me with all awe
  That I may keep Thy Law.

5 Ah Lord ! I must confess
  Apt am I to transgress ;
    And bring Thee "*The New Cart*"
    Instead of " *The New Heart*,"
  Lord ! hear me, I beseech,
  And by Thy Spirit teach.

6 Obey, not sacrifice ;
  Old keep, not new devise ;
    Lord! this I seek to learn
    Thy blessing still to earn ;
  And bring Thee no " *new cart*"
  But choose the "better part."

375. TO-DAY AND NOT TO-MORROW.

James iv. 15. 11s.

"*I have not had a to-morrow for very
many years.*" *James Robertson, of Newington, Edinburgh.*

1 *I've not had a to-morrow for many years ;*
  I am trusting and living from day to
    day ;
  I'm often in weakness and often in fears,
  But I know my dear Jesus knows all my
    way.

2 *I've not had a to-morrow for many years ;*
  Why should I be anxious? To-morrow is
    His ;
  Through all my life's voyage I sail as He
    steers ;
  For He's at the helm and safe guides me
    to bliss.

3 *I've not had a to-morrow for many years ;*
  No choosing, no willing, save only His
    will ;
  Be it loss, be it gain, be it joy or tears,
  Lo! He leads me, and feeds me, and
    helps me still.

4 I've not had a to-morrow for many years:
  Dark at times my road, but light gleams by-and-by;
  Temptation and trouble come, yet as each nears
  He is still nearer with "Fear not, it is I!"
5 I've not had a to-morrow for many years:
  His loving-est answer has sometimes been "No;"
  I've seen it and felt it, aye spite of men's sneers:
  He ordereth all well, where my feet shall go.
6 I've not had a to-morrow for many years:
  O my Saviour! grant it may always be;
  While my Faith still close clings and Hope perseveres,
  And in Thine Own good time, I shall be with Thee.

376. CONTENT. 7s.

"*I have learned in whatsoever state I am, therewith to be content.*—Philippians iv. 11."

1 I have learn'd to be content;
  But, my Lord, 'twas He that taught;
  Rebel was my temperament:
  O! the conquest in me wrought!
2 I have learn'd to be content;
  Pacing in me Thy dear will;
  Holding all I have as lent;
  Trusting Thee not mine own skill.
3 I have learn'd to be content;
  But, my Lord, 'twas He that taught;
  What soe'er to me is sent,
  I accept it, much or naught.
4 I have learn'd to be content;
  Working as and where I may;
  Spending now and being spent;
  Singing thro' the longest day.
5 I have learn'd to be content;
  But, my Lord, 'twas He that taught;
  Joyous or in languishment:
  Yet no choice have I in aught.
6 I have learn'd to be content;
  E'en when walking without light;
  Groping, troubled, diffident,
  Stars have risen in the night.
7 I have learn'd to be content;
  But, my Lord, 'twas He that taught;
  Gentle yet omnipotent,
  In His net of grace me caught.
8 I have learn'd to be content;
  But, my Lord, 'twas He that taught,
  Rebel was my temperament:
  O! the conquest in me wrought!

377. PLEASING. 10s.

"*Let every one of us please his neighbour for his good to edification.*—Romans xv. 2.

"*Give none offence . . . even as I please all men in all things.*"—1 Corinthians x. 32-33.

"*Walk worthy of the Lord unto all pleasing.*" Colossians i. 10.

"*Adorn the doctrine.*"—Titus ii. 10.

1 SEEK to be pleasant, seek to be winning:
  Rudeness and sourness are kin to sinning;
  Seek to bring sunshine wherever you go;
  Trust in a bright word far more than a blow.
2 Seek to be gladsome as 'mongst men ye move;
  Frigid integrity quencheth all love;
  Seek to be hopeful, and patient, and sweet;
  Sombreness falls upon sore hearts like sleet.
3 Seek to be human to tempted and driven,
  Grasp the Lord's words "to seventy times seven;"
  Seek to be gentle with vice ev'n and woe;
  One look of love will cause tears to flow.
4 Seek to be "care full" for nothing at all,
  Cheerful and thankful whatever befal;

Seek still to show that He healeth your
  scars ;
Trials bring joy as the Night bringeth
  stars.

5 Seek to know more how much you yourself
  need
Pardoning mercy of Him Who did bleed ;
Claim no false perfection—old Pharisees'
  art—
Loveable weaknesses knit heart to heart.

6 *Repeat St.* 1.

373. BE COURTEOUS. 1 *Peter iii.* 8. 8s.

1 "Be courteous"—such, Lord, is Thy will,
  And with Thy gentleness Thou'lt fill
  In Thy benignity divine,
  The heart that seeks to copy Thine.

2 " Be courteous"—or to rich or poor,
  To either, neither less nor more ;
  Soft answer anger turns away
  More than when passion holdeth sway.

3 " Be courteous ;" even to the rude,
  And evil overcome with good ;
  While some will bless thee, some will ban,
  Through all, be thou Christ's gentleman

4 " Be courteous " too, when fighting sin ;
  'Tis thus most sure wilt vict'ry win ;
  Ne'er smite as lightning ; shine as light ;
  For truth be strong, and brave for right.

379. UNFEARING. 8s.

" *I will trust and not be afraid.*"— Isaiah
xii. 2.

1 *I'll trust and will not be afraid :*
  Be it in light, be it in shade ;
  The enemy visible and strong
  Or creeping stealthily along ;
  O ! by Thy grace I shall be bold,
  If that Thy grace doth me enfold.

2 *I'll trust and will not be afraid :*
  With Thy great Hand upon me laid ;
  And my poor hand enclasping Thine,
  And holding it in truth for mine ;
  Dangers may threaten me and lour,
  I'm in no enemy's hand of power.

3 *I'll trust and will not be afraid :*
  By Thine up-holding Sp'rit stay'd ;
  Beside Thee, Lord, I cannot fail ;
  Thou girdest me with Thine Own mail ;
  Dost give to me for conqu'ring sword,
  The strength and power of Thy great
    Word.

4 *I'll trust and will not be afraid :*
  Thou my whole life-path hast survey'd ;
  Aye, ordering all my steps aright,
  Enclosing me with Thy strong might ;
  O grant, my God, that in Thy strength
  I may attain my home at length.

5 *I'll trust and will not be afraid :*
  But, ah ! I need Thy grace to aid ;
  Still show to me, Lord, Thy salvation
  From all my sin's erst degradation ;
  And fill my mouth with that glad song
  Which I in Heav'n shall prolong.

380. SYMPATHY. *St. Matt. xii.* 17-12.
10s.

1 O LORD, how hard and harsh we are ! too
  oft
  The sharp word speaking rather than the
  soft ;
  How well may we in Holy Scripture read,
  Of "smoking flax" of Thine, and "bruisèd
  reed !"

2 The timorous heart that kindness only
  lacks
  To rise in flame of faith, like "smoking
  flax,"
  Breath'd on but gently ; we too often
  quench,
  And where we ought to fan we only drench.

3 The weary soul that toils along the way,
We chafe not soothe, exasperate not allay;
Ah! Lord, how different Thou, to human need!
How true, Thou "breakest not the bruised reed."

4 O give Thy patience, Lord, Thy gentleness,
And with Thy lowliness our spirits bless;
That we in wounded hearts may drop Thy balm,
Till e'en in midnight dark they sing their psalm.

5 If we ourselves have found, lo! others seek;
If we ourselves be strong, see others weak;
If we ourselves rejoice, other hearts bleed;
Still "smoking flax" Thou seest and "bruised reed."

6 Men tempted, fall; Lord, let not us be proud,
In passion judging and with accent loud;
Forbid that on our lips aught else be found,
Than "sav'd by grace" and grace that did abound.

7 The best man, Lord, but man is at the best;
O may this lowly thought high thoughts arrest!
Knowing for chief of sinners Thou dost plead;
E'en for the "smoking flax" and "bruised reed."

331. THE THREE SISTERS FAITH, HOPE, AND LOVE. 1 Cor. xiii. 13. 8s.

1 Ye linked three Faith, Hope, and Love,
Fairest of Graces from Above!
O that I might within me find
Your heav'nly trinity enshrined!
  E'en Faith, that clings unto the Cross;
  With Hope, that looks beyond the sky;
  And Love, that counts all things but loss,
  To win the rest that is on High.

2 Anoint our eyes, that we below,
The walk of Faith, not sight, may know;
Midst fiercest storms Hope's anchor cast,
And still in Love our Lord hold fast;
  E'en Faith, that clings unto the Cross;
  With Hope, that looks beyond the sky;
  And Love, that counts all things but loss,
  To win the rest that is on High;

3 If we must bend beneath our load,
Think on Thy Covenant, O God!
Help that we ne'er from Thee remove;
Sustained by Faith, and Hope, and Love;
  E'en Faith, that clings unto the Cross;
  With Hope, that looks beyond the sky;
  And Love, that counts all things but loss,
  To win the rest that is on High.

4 Guard us, we pray, once-tempted One,
That Satan boast no conquest won;
Thou Who upon Thy Cross did'st bleed,
Knowest all graces that we need;
  E'en Faith, that clings unto the Cross;
  With Hope, that looks beyond the sky;
  And love, that counts all things but loss,
  To win the rest that is on high.

5 And Thou, O Spirit, who dost strive!
To keep our death-drawn souls alive;
Grace with Thy greatest gifts impart,
Faith, Hope, and Love in ev'ry heart;
  E'en Faith, that clings unto the Cross;
  With Hope, that looks beyond the sky;
  And Love, that counts all things but loss,
  To win the rest that is on High.

382. FAITH, HOPE, AND LOVE. 6s. 1. Cor. xiii. 13.

1 I BLESS Thee, Lord, for FAITH,
That rests upon "He saith;"
I bless Thee, Lord, for HOPE,
Strong with all fears to cope;
I bless Thee, Lord, for LOVE,
In globe of light doth move,

2 I bless Thee, Lord, for FAITH,
Sustained by Thy breath ;
I bless Thee, Lord, for Hope,
Which sees where others grope ;
I bless Thee, Lord, for LOVE,
Grace every grace above.

3 I bless Thee, Lord, for FAITH,
Winner of many a wreath ;
I bless Thee, Lord, for HOPE,
Reality not trope ;
I bless Thee, Lord, for LOVE,
May my life still approve !

4 I bless Thee, Lord, for FAITH,
That sings in vale of Death;
I bless Thee, Lord, for HOPE,
Heav'n's own helioscope;
I bless Thee, Lord, for LOVE,
Make holy, Holy Dove!

5 O Saviour, give Thy love,
That I shew FAITH, HOPE, LOVE ;
Yea, may the gracious Three
Ever be found in me;
Meetning for heav'nly rest ;
Of the " white robe " possessed.

383. LOVE. 7s.

"*The greatest of these is love.*" *1 Cor. xiii. 13.*

"*Let brotherly love continue.*" — *Hebrews xiii. 1.*

1 O LORD, grant that we may shew
As we 'mongst our fellows go :
That like Thee, we sympathize
Where'er on any sorrow lies ;
Whose and what, Lord, we would prove
By still more true Christian love.

2 Sign, sweet and infallible,
May it in our bosom dwell !
And as perfume, day by day,
Word and deed heart-change bewray ;
Whose and what, Lord, we would prove
By still more true Christian love.

3 Poor, we would compassionate,
Give a hand, not hold high state ;
Weakest we would gently shield,
Even when to sin they yield ;
Whose and what, Lord, we would prove
By still more true Christian love.

4 Sad hearts — in their sorrowing
We would have their story bring ;
Lost — ay, tho' as Prodigal,
To their Father back would call :
Whose and what, Lord, we would prove
By still more true Christian love.

5 Vile — we would touch resolute,
Unafraid touch will pollute ;
Guiltiest — lead to the Rood,
Pleading still the mighty blood :
Whose and what, Lord, we would prove
By still more true Christian love.

6 In each man, Lord, we would see
Precious soul most dear to Thee ;
Fellow-sinner, and no worse,
Like grace freeing from " the curse ;"
Whose and what, Lord, we would prove
By still more true Christian love.

7 Build up, Lord, the mystic wall,
With Thy stones, or large or small ;
Let one temple all combine,
Each with each and all as Thine ;
Whose and what, Lord, we would prove
By still more true Christian love.

384 SEEN THOUGH UNSEEN. 8s.

"*When I see the blood.*"— *Exodus xii. 13.*

1 O GOD, too often I am weak
Alas ! so weak I cannot speak
The thought that like a shadow falls
Upon my soul and me appals,
And even hides the mighty Rood ;
But Thou dost say " *I see the blood.*"

2 O God, too often I of Thee
Lose sight : but never Thou of me ;

Yea, when I walk in deepest fears,
Thou dost draw nigh and light appears ;
Though from my heart is hid the Rood,
Yet Thou dost say " *I see the blood.*"

3 O God, too often I confess
I mourn in lightless loneliness ;
Fearful and faint because that I
Cannot my Saviour's face descry ;
No vision of the uplifted Rood ;
But Thou dost say " *I see the blood.*"

4 O God, too often I do doubt
No way from Sin's maze finding out ;
Ah ! then Thou placest in my hand
The "scarlet thread," and dost command ;
Seen or unseen I trust the Rood,
Guided by this, " *I see the blood.*"

385.   CHARACTER.   8s.
Acts of the Apostles xx. 32 : 1 Cor. iii. 10.

1 BUILD thee up CHARACTER, young man
Society may bless or ban ;
Lay thy foundations strong and deep,
For tempests over thee will sweep ;
Begin with Christ— give Him thy heart,
To fashion by His gracious art.

2 Thy Christianhood be no mere creed
By Calvin, or by man decreed ;
"Your life be hid with Christ in God ;"
On that lay no dogmatic load ;
But be it thine to "grow in grace"
By walk of Faith beneath His Face.

3 In homely moral qualities
Lie grandest possibilities :
At all costs and whate'er befall
Stand by THE VIRTUES one and all ;
Be truthful, pure, upright, and brave,
But aye a man — no abject slave.

4 Build Thee up CHARACTER, young man
Society may bless or ban ;
Falsehood abounds and all chicane ;
Conscience is oft put on the strain ;
Be thou still "faithful unto death"
And Thou shalt win th' unfading wreath.

386.   THE HEART AN ALABASTER BOX
OF OINTMENT FOR JESUS.
St. Matt. xxvi. 7.   8,8,7,7.

1 "Box of alabaster" broken
Mary's gift, and Love's sweet token ;
Fragrant ointment on His Head ;
Fragrant more the tears she shed.

2 Lord, my heart each day be filling
With sweet grace 'bove flowers' distilling;
By Thy gentle might then break,
And a Mary's "box" it make.

3 Unto Thee, by Faith, still clinging,
Lord, my broken heart I'm bringing ;
All my "ointment," cries and tears,
Born of mingled hopes and fears.

4 Soft the words by Jesus spoken
Of the "box" of ointment broken ;
May He o'er my broken heart
Whisper peace and heal its smart.

387.   GARMENTS OF SALVATION.   8s.
Isaiah lxi. 10.

1 "My God, my God," on Thy vast loom
Thou weavest threads of bliss and doom ;
These luminous and livid those,
But clear design through all there goes.

2 No body-garment 'tis, Lord Christ,
Thou thus dost weave in love unpric'd ;
But clothing for the soul, as still
Thou Thy great purpose dost fulfil.

3 Alas ! too oft is "sackcloth" worn,
When careless walk leaves me to mourn ;
But lo ! anon to me is giv'n
The blood-bought "white robes" of Heaven.

4 Lord ! I would put my garment on,
Which on the Cross for me was won ;
Thy robe of whiteness dipp'd in red
By Him who ev'n for me, has bled.

5 With praise I fill my grateful lips :
O let no cloud my joy eclipse !
With prayer I bow before Thy Throne,
Thou pleadest Saviour for Thine own.

388.   Desire and Power.   8.9.8.9.
   1 *Peter* ii. 2.3.

1 With the desire, Lord, give the power
   To follow Thee where'er Thou leadest;
   With Thine own strength do Thou me dower,
      Aye feeding me as Thine Thou feedest.

2 With the desire, Lord, give the power
   To work and witness in my "calling;"
   Thy courage, Lord, upon me shower,
      As Thine own soldier me installing.

3 With the desire, Lord, give the power,
   That while myself I'm consecrating;
   I may be found each day and hour,
      Thy holy footsteps emulating.

4 With the desire, Lord, give the power,
   All suffering for Thee still daring;
   As comes success, or dark clouds lour,
      Thy chequer'd life, Lord, gladly sharing.

5 With the desire, Lord, give the power,
   To lend as Thou art to me lending;
   Where'er the shiv'ring needy cower,
      May I be found still freely spending.

6 With the desire, Lord, give the power
   To walk this sin-scarr'd earth in whiteness;
   To wear fair Purity's white flower,
      Touch'd with a gleam of Heav'n's own brightness.

7 With the desire, Lord, give the power,
   Yea, lead Thou me unto perfection;
   The overcoming life devour
      In me each hindering affection.

389.   Finding Fault.   *Galatians* vi. 1.
   7s.

1 Gentle be in finding fault,
   Speak not as thou would'st assault;
   Oh be soft, and low, and plead,
   And "like to Christ" intercede;
   Thus thou shalt most surely win,
   And break the hard bonds of sin.

2 Gentle be in finding fault;
   Seek thou not Self to exalt;
   Be thou sympathetic still,
   Even to most wayward will;
   Kindly words have a strange power
   Tears from dry eyes to make shower.

3 Gentle be in finding fault
   Brother! Did'st thou never ha't?
   Recollect what once thou wast,
   That from grace comes all thou hast;
   Then thou tenderly wilt seek,
   Aye, the true right word to speak.

4 Gentle be in finding fault;
   Season thy rebuke with salt;
   Drive not thou to dark despair
   Souls of the Lord Christ are heir;
   By Thy Faith and Hope and Love,
   Draw to Him in Heaven Above.

390.   Restfulness.   6s.
   Ps. cxvi. 7 ; cxxxii. 8.

1 Dwell in my heart, dear Lord,
   That I may rest in Thine;
   Fulfil Thy tender word,
   Come show Thyself as mine.

2 I ache for Thy sweet peace,
   Thy peace to comfort me;
   O wilt Thou cause to cease
   This numbing misery.

3 Dwell in my heart, dear Lord,
   That I may rest in Thine;
   That my first joy restor'd,
   I may with Thy light shine.

4 Bruis'd like the bruised reed,
   Reach hither, Lord, Thy hand;
   To succour me, make speed;
   Thou dost me understand.

5 Dwell in my heart, dear Lord,
   That I may rest in Thine;
   Like fragrant ointment pour'd,
   And better than "new wine."

6 Calm me as Thou art calm,
   O Blessèd Saviour dear ;
  Put in my mouth a psalm,
   Thy "still small voice" to hear.

7 Dwell in my heart, my Lord,
   That I may rest in Thine ;
  Belovèd and ador'd,
   That I no more repine.

391.   FEAR AND NOT FEAR.   8s.
Job xiii. 21 ; Isaiah xii. 2.

1 I AM afraid, O Lord to fear,
   Yet not to fear I am afraid ;
  Spirit of God, grant me to hear
   Thy guiding word, Thy strength'ning aid ;
  As oft within I look, I fear,
  But when I tremble Thou art near.

2 Outward and upward, Lord, I gaze,
   Then all my heart's fears pass away ;
  My mouth again Thou fill'st with praise ;
   As, all in all, on Thee I stay ;
  As oft within I look, I fear,
  But when I tremble Thou art near.

3 And yet, O Lord, there will come still
   Tremors and starts of inner dread ;
  This deathful body me doth fill
   With achings by Thee to be led ;
  As oft within I look, I fear,
  But when I tremble Thou art near.

4 Fill me, O Christ, with perfect love,
   Then all my fear shall be cast out ;
  Brood Thou in me, O Heavenly Dove ;
   Firm-strength'ning Faith an'conqu'ring Doubt ;
  As oft within I look, I fear,
  But when I tremble Thou art near.

392.   UNCLOTHED.   *2 Cor. xii. 2 ?*

1 My naked soul without a load
  The Spirit in me "shed abroad"
  Plunges into the deep of God.

2 Infinity is o'er my head ;
  Infinity is round me spread ;
  Light shadowless within me shed.

3 Partaker of a life divine,
  A full-proportion'd stature's mine ;
  Lord, more and more within me shine.

4 This vision, Lord, is it mind-trance?
  Yet laud for the swift-piercing glance,
  Which penetrates as sunbeam's lance.

5 Thou Giver of grace to each one,
  When shall my life on earth be done ?
  Unclothèd to be cloth'd upon.

6 I bow me low before Thy feet
  Enthron'd above the Mercy-seat ;
  O Christ ! with me a sinner treat.

7 My naked soul without a load
  The Spirit in me "shed abroad"
  Plunges into the deep of God.

393.   IMPERFECTION.   8.7.8.7.8.8.
Philippians iii 12.

1 Humbl'd but not surpris'd, O Lord,
   Sin still I find prevailing ;
  Humbl'd, but not dishearten'd, Lord,
   Hopeful, e'en whilst bewailing ,
  Behold, "just as I am," I come ;
  Forgive my sin in all its sum.

2 Humbl'd, but going not away,
   My Saviour Thee forsaking ;
  Humbl'd, but daring still to pray ;
   Thy "BLOOD" unto Thee taking ;
  Behold, "just as I am," I come ;
  Forgive my sin in all its sum.

3 Humbl'd, but seeking grace to win
   The vict'ry in temptation ;
  Humbl'd, but bearing me within
   Thy words of consolation ;
  Behold, "just as I am," I come ;
  Forgive my sin in all its sum.

4 Humbl'd, but by Thy Spirit's Hand
   Still showing me Thy pureness ;
  Humbl'd, but 'fore Thy Cross I stand,
   Aye, clinging to its sureness ;
  Behold, "just as I am," I come ;
  Forgive my sin in all its sum.

STRENGTH WITH LIGHT—INFIRMITIES.

394.   Strength with Light.   8s.
  1 *Chron. xxix. 12.*

1 O Lord! wilt Thou with light give strength
  That I may overcome at length?
  Long I have seen, known, yea, believ'd,
  But ah! how little have achiev'd!
  More light give Lord, with strength of will
  By DEEDS my knowledge to fulfil.

2 O Lord! Thy red steps ever show
  And cause my grateful heart to glow;
  That hating sin and loving good -
  ILL in Thy gracious strength withstood;
  I may, my Saviour, "keep" THE WAY
  That leadeth to Eternal day.

3 O Lord! I mourn Earth so attracts;
  Mourn that "this life" me so distracts;
  Ev'n when I fain would upward soar
  Lo! Faith's wings flag: Lord Christ, restore   [strong—
  My "first love's" strength—by Thee made
  That I may break forth into song.

4 O Lord! look on me as I lie,
  The "flesh" still claiming mastery;
  Like to the veining of the marble,
  Or sob of nightingale's sad warble;
  Lo! Sin all interpenetrates
  And as "Backslider" me instates.

5 O Lord! wilt Thou, with light, give strength
  That I may overcome at length?
  Alas! I, weak and wayward, find
  My heart is yet to ILL inclin'd;
  O Lord! let Thine omnipotence
  Safe-guard me in my ev'ry sense!

395.   Longing.   *Ps. xlii. 1.*   7s.

1 Aching with a thousand wants
  My heart, Lord, for Thy heart pants;
  Weak and pain'd and in unrest,
  Thou alone can'st calm this breast.

2 "Broken cisterns" ah have prov'd
  To which, in my thirst, I mov'd;
  Pour, Lord, as 'fore Thee, I stand,
  "Living water" from Thy hand.

3 "Bread of Life" wilt Thou bestow,
  That in its strength I may go?
  Fed as with the bread of Heav'n,
  Daily grace for each day giv'n.

4 Lord, forbid I e'er rebel—
  Murmuring like Israel;
  With Thee, my God, for my guide
  O let me not "turn aside."

5 Constant, as Thou dost me bless
  May I cross Life's wilderness;
  And, all strife and trouble past,
  Canaan safely reach at last.

6 Then, Lord, on the heights of bliss
  I all achings shall dismiss;
  Faithful Thou unto Thy Word
  I'll be ever with the Lord.

396.   Infirmities.   8s.
Gal. vi. 2; St. Matt. viii. 17; St. Luke xi. 46; Romans xv. 1.

1 *Bear with thyself*, as Christ has borne;
  Let not thy sin leave thee forlorn;
  With others bear, as Jesus bears;
  More potent than is wrath, are tears.

2 *Bear with thyself*, tho' sin and grace
  In strange sad conflict thou dost trace;
  Remember that like unto all,
  Thy sad heritage is "THE FALL."

3 *Bear with thyself*, as child of God
  Subm'ssive kiss His chast'ning rod;
  With others bear, that they may be
  In tender sympathy with Thee.

4 *Bear with thyself*, yet lowly lie
  As o'er thy weakness thou dost sigh;
  With others bear, who may still show
  The signs and seals of the great woe.

5 *Bear with thyself*, but still aspire,
  Thy Faith, Hope, Love, a flame of fire;
  With others bear, nor e'er despair
  Upon God "casting all thy care."

6 *Bear with thyself*, no "hard thoughts" think
 Because thy heart doth in thee sink ;
 With others bear, whose falt'ring lips
 Tell that their FAITH is in eclipse.

7 *Bear with thyself*, "false witness" shun
 'Gainst work of grace within thee done ;

With others bear, seek not to boast ;
 Christ came to "seek and save the lost."

8 *Bear with thyself*, 'twill not be long
 Till sighs and groans shall change to song;
 With others bear, who God's Hand feel,
 Nor 'gainst the vilest thy heart steel!

8. Work, Workers, and Witness.

397. CHRISTMAS. *St. Luke ii. 1-20.*
8.8.7.7.

1 How I love to read the story
Radiant with heaven-born glory;
Telling of the Saviour born,
On this glad day—Christmas morn.

2 Burst the clouds in flaming angels
Bringing to men song-evangels!
"*Peace on Earth, good-will to men,*"
Priceless now as it was then.

3 Shepherds o'er their flocks night-watching,
Great celestial voices catching;
Guided by the wondrous word
Went to hail their infant Lord.

4 Wise men, song of joy up-raising,
Still upon His bright star gazing;
From the East expectant came;
Putting Israel to shame.

5 On this day to Earth came Heaven;
Earth to bask in Heaven's rays given;
Jesus was in Bethlehem born
On this glad day—Christmas morn.

6 Lord! we have to make confession,
Looking for Thine intercession;
That those who bear not Thy Name
Us surpass who make the claim.

7 Hearts enlarge, so that warm-glowing
Midst cold of these ice-winds blowing;
We love show to poor and lorn,
On this glad day—Christmas morn.

398. WORK WHILE IT IS DAY. 8.6.

1 Kings xx. 30-40; St. John ix. 4.

1 THE iron is hot for the striking;
Do, man of God, thy part;
O weigh not disliking or liking,
Speak from a burning heart.

2 Speak; for the Harvest now whitens,
In, man of God, and reap;
For he, who dark souls enlightens,
Is gath'ring Christ's "lost sheep."

3 Speak; men around thee are dying;
Forth, man of God, to save;
Hark, captive spirits are sighing
For rest, this side the grave.

5 Speak out the old Gospel story,
Steep'd, man of God, in pray'r;
And Thou shalt, one day, in glory
Find Christ was with thee there.

6 The iron is hot for the striking,
Do, man of God, Thy part;
O weigh not disliking or liking,
Speak from a burning heart.

399. ANGELS. 10s.

"*Are they not all ministering spirits?*"—
Hebrews i. 14.

1 As I read to-day in the Holy Evangels,
The golden words writ of God's blessèd angels;
I find myself humbled that I should be
So lacking their burning agility;
So lacking their patient humility.

2 When the mission of love was laid on them
To publish the great news of Bethlehem; [Birth]
How swiftly they stretch'd out their wings for Earth!
And broke into song o'er the mighty [mirth.
Re-kindling bright hopes and inspiring

3 When a starvèd beggar by wayside died;
A beggar! yet dear to THE CRUCIFIED;

While no one on earth for his poor corse
  cared ;   [were guard ;
For his blood-wash'd soul the angels
                      [prepar'd.
To bear him on lustrous wings were
4 When the dead Redeemer in tomb was
  laid ;   [made ?
Who willing doorkeepers for Him were
The angels of God, all shining with light;
Watching till the " Third Day" burst
  from the night,
To tell the story of His risen might.
5 When a servant of Christ was bound with
  chains,
And left in a prison t' endure all pains ;
  The word being giv'n, a great angel
    came
  And set him free from his suff'ring and
    shame ;
  That the "glad tidings" he might
    proclaim.
6 When came to St. John the Apocalypse,
What glorious words fell from angel lips !
  Exultant revealing their enthroned King
  To triumph and glory, shall all things
    bring ;   [sting.
  Despoiling the grave and Death of their
7 I too would seek the swift angels to
  follow :   [hallow?
Lord of all angels, lo ! wilt Thou me
  I fain would emulate their holy zeal ;
  I fain would their glad obedience feel ;
  My forehead, like theirs, Thy holiness
    seal.

400.   Count one for Christ. 12s.
" *Here am I, send me.*" *Isaiah vi. 8.*
1 Never speak a hard word, if you can
  speak a soft ;
Softest words go farthest, as you will
  find out oft ;
Never give a cold look, when you may
  give a warm ;
A kind thing done unkindly, loses half its
  charm.

2 Never turn your back upon a good old
  friend made poor ;
For the friend in him remains, where'er
  has gone his store ;
Never scanty coppers dole, when you
  might spare a pound ;
A generous gift will often cause some
  poor faint heart to bound.
3 Never " take up ill report " but ever let it
  lie :
By lifting, wings you give it, round and
  round to fly ;
Never listen to a secret, whoe'er it may
  bring ;
Whisper'd honey'd words sheath oft direst
  deadliest sting.
4 Never shrink from duty, man, if it your duty
  be ;   [free ;
Go yourself and do it, seek not yourself to
Never shun heroic speech, that proves
  that you're a man,
Come there praise or come there blame,
  blessing come or ban.
5 Never tell a falsehood whatever be the bribe ;
Truth will always conquer—soon pass off
  jest and jibe ;
Never use profane words—most senseless
  of all sins ;
Rev'rent, pure and truthful speech ! that is
  what aye wins.
6 Scorn to be a coward, who cravenly
  stands by,
When ill tongues our blessed Lord seek to
  crucify ;
Never be ashamed to count always one for
  Him ;
Nor the lustre of the name of " Christian"
  dare to to dim

401. Every Christian bound to be a
            worker.
" *Let him that heareth say Come.*" *Revelation xxii. 17.* 8s.
1 O Lord, Whome'er Thy grace has blessed,
Causing Thy Name to be confessed ;

Wilt Thou now quicken them to see
That each one service owes to Thee.

2 O Thou Who on the Cross did'st die,
On Whom the whole world's sin did lie;
Renew in all its tenderness
How Thy redeeming love doth bless.

3 Enkindle in our hearts such flame
As shall consume all coward shame;
And send us forth with burning love
The might of Thy red cross to prove.

4 Hast Thou not laid on one and all
Still "Come" to say, and still to call
On "whosoever will," to find
Pardon and peace in Thee combin'd.

5 O Lord, inspire us with fresh zeal,
To think and do, to know and feel;
To rally to Thy servants' aid,
Ne'er of the World's "loud laugh" afraid.

6 The time is short, and life is flying,
And all around us souls are dying;
Stir up, O Lord, each heart and will,
And with Thine Own compassion fill.

7 O Lord, Whome'er Thy grace has bless'd,
Causing Thy Name to be confess'd;
Wilt Thou now quicken them to see
That each one service owes to Thee.

402.   KINDNESS IN GIVING.   8s.

*2 Corinthians viii. 4: "Gifts without the
giver are bare."   J. D. Lowell.*

1 *Gifts without the giver are bare:*
As wanting sunshine is the air;
Alas! for the sad rarity
Of even Christian charity
Transfigured with sympathy,
Forth-beaming from warm lip and eye;
With a bright look and kind word;
And all "for the sake of" the Lord.

2 Seeking selfish immunity
From Despair's importunity,
You may fling to thin clutching palms
Your silver or your gold for alms;

But a copper, with pleasant smile;
Will drop as a soft fragrant oil;
Sweetly the common air perfuming;
Hope's dim dying lamp reluming.

3 *Gifts without the giver are bare:*
You will The Christ's own blessing share;
If amid the suffering and lowly
You will walk in His footsteps holy;
Counting no house however mean
A place where you may not be seen;
It is not for us to stand aloof,
Since He is found 'neath poorest roof.

4 O do not in your dignity stand;
Forth, and grasp you a brother's hand;
Recognizing our common kin,
Ay, and our common human sin;
Feeling the possibility
That in the most errant soul may lie;
'Twill bring you blessing and not snare:
Gifts without the giver are bare.

403.   "GOD BLESS YOU."

2 Corinthians iv. 15.   8.8.7.7.

1 Earn "God bless you!" O my Brother!
Had you not yourself a mother?
Know that however defil'd
He she is somebody's child.

2 Earn "God bless you!" O my Brother;
Your flame of ruth do not smother;
Your heart-promptings quick obey;
Chill may come if you delay.

3 Earn "God bless you!" O my Brother;
Reckon it not for a bother;
Kind deed do or kind word speak;
You may heal heart like to break.

4 Earn "God bless you"! O my Brother;
Never act you by the weather;
Forth, e'en on the bleak wet night,
To bear some poor dark heart, light.

5 Earn "God bless you"! O my Brother!
In one way or in another;
Brighten a white face of woe;
You'll do good beyond you know.

182   GO, NOT SEND.

6 Earn "God bless you!" O my Brother,
    Ev'n amid worldly cares' pother;
    Hie you on with willing feet;
    Than music it is more sweet.
7 *Repeat St. 1.*

404.   "IF WE CAN'T ALL GATHER A SHEAF, LET US ALL GLEAN AN EAR." —ELIZA FLETCHER.   *St. Matthew xxv. 15–28.*

8,8,8,8,6,6.

1 If we can't all gather a sheaf,
    Let us all seek to glean an ear;
  It is not for all to be chief,
    Or to hope for a great career;
  Some higher, some lower;
  You reaper, I sower.

2 If we can't all gather a sheaf,
    Let us all seek to glean an ear;
  Life is made up of joy and grief,
    Of the blooming and the sere;
  Some higher, some lower;
  You reaper, I sower.

3 If we can't all gather a sheaf,
    Let us all seek to glean an ear;
  Life fades like the fading leaf;
    To-day as He calls, let us hear;
  Some higher, some lower;
  You reaper, I sower.

4 If we can't all gather a sheaf,
    Let us all seek to glean an ear;
  Opportunity, like a thief,
    Slips away, and leaves us in rear;
  Some higher, some lower;
  You reaper, I sower.

5 If we can't all gather a sheaf,
    Let us all seek to glean an ear;
  Our abiding on Earth is brief,
    Let us all work in holy fear;
  Some higher, some lower;
  You reaper, I sower.

6 If we can't all gather a sheaf,
    Let us all seek to glean an ear;
  It is not for all to be chief,
    Or to hope for a great career;
  Some higher, some lower;
  You reaper, I sower.

405.   GO, NOT SEND.   7s.

* *Pure religion and undefiled before God and the Father is this, to visit the fatherless and widows in their affliction.*— *St. James i. 27.*

1 With thy kindness go, not send;
  Going doth fresh kindness lend;
  Howe'er kindly it be meant
  There's a dull chill in what is sent;
  Kind word dipp'd in a kind smile
  Will pain'd heart of pain beguile;
  And thy "visit" in poor room
  Scatter-light-like—gath'ring gloom.

2 Hearest thou of widow, left,
  Of her strong bread-winner 'reft;
  Of her children fatherless;
  Of her little store made less;
  Hie thee hither now, my brother,
  Thy gift send not by another;
  "Visit" pay—and not in haste;
  Time thus hallow'd is no waste.

3 Hearest thou of fellow-man
  For the right, plac'd under ban;
  And there riseth in thy heart
  A desire to take his part;
  Get thee to him, and thy hand
  Plac'd in his, there by him stand;
  Thus thou shalt indeed befriend
  Far beyond aught thou can'st SEND.

4 With thy kindness go, not send;
  Going doth fresh kindness lend;
  For wrong'd, suffering and poor,
  Look of love is half their cure;
  One true throb of human feeling
  All a brother's heart unsealing;
  So you will reach that within;
  High and low are thus made kin.

5 How transfiguring is a look!
  Heart leaps up to heart; and shook
  Are a hundred prejudices,
  Yea sullen heart it entices;

LIBERALITY—KNOWN AND UNKNOWN.

And there dieth out the rage
Born of heartless patronage;
That flings kindness as an alms
Careless of a proud heart's qualms.

406. USING. *St. Luke xvi. 10.* 5s.

1 Sow thy seed, not store
If thou would'st have more;
Sown—the Lord it keeps;
Stor'd—waste in it creeps;
Sow—do not refrain;
Store—'twill not be gain.

2 Even so, O Lord,
Writ 'tis in Thy Word;
He who God's gifts spends
Unto the Lord lends;
He will full repay,
Nor will long delay.

3 What thou gettest share
To all—ev'rywhere;
Be it light from Him
That doth the sun dim;
Swiftly it impart,
With a loving heart.

4 Is it still more grace
'Neath His shining face?
Hie thee, with low voice
Make some one rejoice;
Carry word of cheer
That will chase all fear.

5 Hast thou gotten wealth,
Hold it not in stealth;
Scatter riches, gold;
Ne'er let it be told
Thee it grippeth fast,
None to Christ's poor cast.

6 Search them out, and see
Wheresoe'er thou be;
How thou can'st devise
Heart-soft'ning surprise;
To cheer sad and faint
Ah! Lord Christ, Thy saint.

7 *Repeat St.* 1.

407. LIBERALITY. 8s.
1 *Cor. vi.* 19-20; *Philemon* 19; *2 Cor. viii.* 2.

1 BLUSH, O my soul, that thou should'st be
Not yet from love of lucre free;
That the Lord Christ's measur'd demands
Find thee still holding back thy hands;
What did "the World" cost thee, my soul,
Ere thou on Him thy sins didst roll?

2 How oft hast thou in prayer and song
Avouch'd thou dost to Christ belong?
Hast thou not, feeling thy heart burn,
Said, thou can'st ne'er give meet return?
What did "the Flesh" cost thee, my soul,
Ere thou on Him thy sins did'st roll?

3 The blood-red flag shall ne'er be furl'd
Until the Gospel fill the world;
Choose thou thy part, nor from it move,
Thou ow'st it to redeeming love;
What did "the Devil" cost thee, soul,
Ere thou on Him thy sins did'st roll?

4 How scant and measur'd are our gifts!
Each on the other duty shifts;
Upon ourselves we lavish, spend,
And paltry nothings His cause send;
What cost it Him to save thy soul
Ere thou on Him thy sins did'st roll?

5 Blush, O my soul, that thou should'st be
Not yet from love of lucre free;
That Christ's all-reasonable demands
Find thee still holding back thy hands;
"Things liberal devise" my soul,
As thou on Him dost thy sins roll.

408. KNOWN AND UNKNOWN. 10s.
2 Cor. vi. 9.

1 THERE are flowers that grow in sunniest light,
There are flowers that grow in deepest shade;
There are flowers that ever are in men's sight,

There are flowers that hide, as tho'
    afraid ;
But in light or in shade, or seen or
    concealed,
To THE GARDENER all are clearly revealed.

2 Ev'n so, O my God, dost Thou deal with
        men ;
    Placing some in the forefront and light
        of day ;
    Placing some to the back, outside the
        world's ken ;
    But each is so placed that Thou hast
        Thy way ;
    Lord, this I would see, and my humble
        post fill,
    Whether known or unknown; bring it
        good or ill.

3 Thy servant of old in poignant self-blame,
    Tho' wearing a crown and in purple clad;
Saw in meanest post not a touch of shame,
    But "door-keeper" would be, and that
        right glad :
Give me, O my God, thus lowly to be,
Yea, give me Thine Own sweet humility.

4 Most gracious art Thou to use us at all ;
    Unworthy the best in Thy name to
        speak ;
    Yet in gracious love Thou dost tenderly
        call,
    And service of each one of us Thou dost
        seek ;
    Grant that, self-emptied and fill'd with
        Thee,
    We may work as Thou send'st—contentedly.

409.   SIMULATION. *James ii. 16.   6s.*

Quid est nisi miserabilis insania ? Nam eo magis eis movetur quisque, quo minus a tabibus affectibus sanus est; quamquam cum ipse patitur, miseria, cum alii compatitur, misericordia dici solet. Sed qualis tandem misericordia in rebus fictis et scenicis? Non enim ad subveniendum provocatur auditor, sed tantum ad dolendum invitatur; et actori earum imaginum amplius favet, cum amplius dolet.—ST. AUGUSTINE, Conf., lib. iii. ii.)

1 I WOULD not merely grieve,
    I also would relieve ;
    For 'tis a per'lous art
    That seeks to act a part ;
    All playing with our tears
    Enervates, yea, and sears.

2 Emotion deftly stealing
    The luxury of feeling
    As drawn from scenes on stage,
    Or found on Fiction's page ;
    Tempestuous or still,
    Sure subjugates the will.

3 I would not merely grieve,
    I also would relieve ;
    For 'tis a per'lous art
    That seeks to act a part :
    All playing with our tears
    Enervates, yea, and sears.

4 Lord, hear me as I plead ;
    All feelings change to deed ;
    Let not mere scenic woes
    Be all my conscience knows ;
    Send me with Christly feet
    Real suffering to meet.

5 I would not merely grieve,
    I also would relieve ;
    For 'tis a per'lous art
    That seeks to act a part ;
    All playing with our tears
    Enervates, yea, and sears.

6 "Real suffering" of men
    Ay tho' in vilest den ;
    "Real suff'ring" where'er found,
    Nor let aught me astound ;
    "Real suffering," that I
    Shew active sympathy.

7 I would not merely grieve,
  I also would relieve;
  For 'tis a per'lous art
  That seeks to act a part;
  All playing with our tears
  Enervates, yea, and sears.

410. NEVER DESPAIR. 10s.

"*We are perplexed but not in despair.*"—2 Cor. iv. 8.

1 *Never despair;* whilst there's life there is hope;
  God's mighty love with the vilest can cope;
  Tell the "old story" in love and in prayer;
  Tell it believingly—*never despair.*

   Chorus. Glory! glory! glory
              Hallelujah!
        For the Gospel story,
              Hallelujah!
        That telleth of the Cross,
        Redeemer of man's loss!
              Hallelujah!

2 *Never despair;* whilst there's life there is hope;
  Rescue the perishing e'en on Doom's slope;
  Lift up the Cross and in Christ's Name dare;
  Praying and working, thou'lt *never despair.*

3 *Never despair;* whilst there's life there is hope;
  God's love in Christ is a truth not a trope;
  Forth and proclaim His great mercy to share,—
  Pardon for all men, and *never despair.*

4 *Never despair;* whilst there's life there is hope;
  Seek out the "lost" as in darkness they grope;
  Shout the glad tidings, to all, everywhere;
  Jesus has died; therefore *never despair.*

411. ERRING. *Titus iii. 2.* 8s.

1 Speak gently to an erring one,
  E'en if a deed of shame be done;
  For else you but exasperate,
  Perchance turn anger into hate.

2 We see the deed and instant blame
  But not how hard it is to tame
  A heart to sin that has not died,
  A rebel will unsanctified.

3 Be ours in love to sympathise,
  Nor stare with hard self-righteous eyes;
  Forgiven ourselves, let us forgive,
  Knowing 'tis thro' His death we live.

4 The softer word has deeper power,
  The sunny face than looks that lour;
  To draw, not drive; not scourge, but melt;
  Ah! We must show that we have felt.

5 Have felt of sin the fearful stress;
  A guilty heart's sad loneliness;
  Have felt the anguish and relenting;
  Ah! stopping short of true repenting.

6 O Brothers! Sisters! on our guilt
  We need the awful blood once spilt;
  That let us feel, and ne'er will we
  Austere to guiltiest, vilest, be.

412. UNSHARED PLEASURE 10.8.10.8

1 John iii. 17.

1 Pleasure is only half-pleasure unshared;
  O forth then, my brother, share thine;
  Pleasure when shared is as treasure prepared,
  Excelling aught drawn from the mine.

2 Pleasure is only half-pleasure unshared;
  Earthly or heav'nly it is so;
  Those who for Christ have most nobly dared,
  This passion unselfish forth-shew.

3 Never would I seek to know joy alone ;
   I would not receive to retain ;
 O to o'erflow to all sad hearts that moan,
   Such o'erflow is not loss but gain.

4 Place me, O my Lord, 'neath Thy touch
     that thrills ;
   Wilt Thou, O wilt Thou me melt ?
 Give me the power Thine Own arm fills,
   To impart all the grace I have felt.

413. Missed. *Psalm xlv. 17.* 6s.

"*I should not like to die and never be
missed.*"—Bella Cooke *in 'Rifted Clouds.'*

1 I would be miss'd when gone,
    I would not—my life done—
  Have no eyes wet for me,
    No hearts touch'd tenderly ;
    No good of me confest;
  Dead—and yet never miss'd.

2 For self to live and die,
    Our home our boundary;
  To do no kindly act
    Seeking to break Sin's pact ;
  To lead no soul to Christ;
    So—we shall not be miss'd.

3 To care for the Lord's poor,
    Pleading His promise sure ;
  To win the wandering back,
    To His footprinted track ;
  To patiently keep tryst ;
    Ah ! thus we shall be miss'd.

4 Only thy pleasure seek,
    Mindless of sad and weak ;
  Go dress, and drink, and eat ;
    Thine own soul madly cheat;
  Scorning the love unpric'd,
    So—we shall not be miss'd.

5 The grace of God infus'd,
    And we of Him still us'd ;
  Found true in word and deed ;
    Like Him to intercede ;
  Nor till the end desist,
    Then, then we shall be miss'd.

414. Humble Usefulness.
"*Arise, shine!*" *Isaiah lx. 1.* (*Cf. St.
Bernard De Gradibus humilitatis, c. 1.*)

1 Lord ! Not as lightning but as light,
      Seek I to be ;
  To shine serenely, Lord, not smite,
      Constrain Thou me :
         Hear me, O Lord,
         I plead Thy Word.

2 My Lord, I covet not the breath
      Of grand renown,
  But rather that which lies beneath
      A blood-bought crown :
         Hear me, O Lord,
         I plead Thy Word.

3 I'd wear such, Lord, in simpleness ;
      Not great, but good ;
  I'd do good in all silentness,
      Even to the rude :
         Hear me, O Lord,
         I plead Thy Word.

4 Fain would I hold, if but small cup,
      To thirsty lips ;
  Fain would I shine but to light up
      Some soul's eclipse :
         Hear me, O Lord,
         I plead Thy Word.

5 Lord, I would lead one soul to Thee,
      Make one rejoice ;
  I fain would one sad heart set free
      By my low voice :
         Hear me, O Lord,
         I plead Thy Word.

415. Peu et Bien ("Little and Well.")
—Francis de Sales. *Jer. xlv. 5.*
6s.

1 'Tis little thou can'st do ;
  Great things are for the few ;
  But what thou dost do well ;
  It in the end will tell :
      Peu et bien.

2 The little 'neath God's eye
  O'ertops the seeming-high ;
  The little may expand -
  Like seed sown in good land :
      Peu et bien.

3 Whate'er thou dost do well ;
  It in the end will tell ;
  The little deed or thought
  Be to "fine issues" wrought :
      Peu et bien.

4 The little is God's rule,
  Man's boastings to befool ;
  Behold the silver rain !
  Behold the fruitful grain !
      Peu et bien.

5 Whate'er thou dost do well ;
  It in the end will tell ;
  The little word of Faith
  Has saved a soul from Death :
      Peu et bien.

6 The little deed of love
  Has rais'd sin's mire above ;
  The little burst of prayer
  Has nations set a-stir :
      Peu et bien.

7 Whate'er thou dost do well ;
  It in the end will tell ;
  The little tears in eyes
  Have been Christ's own surprise :
      Peu et bien.

8 The little kindly act
  Has been potential fact ;
  The little gracious look
  Strong life-long hates has shook :
      Peu et bien.

416. Frailty. *St. Matt. xii. 20.* 6s.

1 I was a bruised reed,
    Pluck'd from the common corn ;
    Play'd on, rude-handled, worn ;
    No one of me took heed.

2 But Thou, O God, cam'st near,
    Thy look serene and meek,
    Touch soft— no ire to wreak—
    Thou my poor plaint didst hear.

3 Now in Thy praise sonorous
    O faint I am and slight !
    Yet in the song-fill'd night
    I join the mighty chorus.

4 I was a taper smoking,
    By the tramp'd footway lying ;
    The last red glimmer dying ;
    Smoke my thin flame was choking.

5 But Thou, Lord, didst pass by,
    And in Thy nail-mark'd hand
    And with Thy breathing bland
    Would'st not my spark let die.

6 O praise to Thy great grace,
    If I a little shine !
    And now that I am Thine,
    Lord, grant me some low place.

417. "Forgive Her, and don't give over trying." Walter Besant ("Children of Gibeon," B. ii. c.)
"*Until seventy times seven.*" — *St. Matthew xviii. 22.* 9s.

1 "Forgive, and don't give over trying ;"
    In spite of thanklessness and lying ;
    In spite of promise madly broken
    Ev'n when the word is scarcely spoken :
      "*Forgive, and don't give over trying.*"

2 "*Forgive, and don't give over trying:*"
God's patience think of, not thy sighing;
Forgiv'n thyself, how much thou owest!
But "sev'n times" is t' his thou shewest?
"*Forgive, and don't give over trying.*"

3 "*Forgive, and don't give over trying:*"
Remember souls all round are dying;
O welcome shame and penitence!
Be gentle ev'n to insolence;
"*Forgive, and don't give over trying.*"

4 "*Forgive, and don't give over trying:*"
Sore-aching hearts aloud are crying;
Backsliding follows close repenting,
But e'en in hardest comes relenting;
"*Forgive, and don't give over trying.*"

5 "*Forgive, and don't give over trying:*"
His lures the Tempter's ever plying;
Like Christ embrace them in your pity
And weep as He wept o'er "*the* CITY;
"*Forgive, and don't give over trying*"

6 '*Forgive, and don't give over trying*':
Let not your scrutiny be prying;
Be generous, sympathetic, tender,
"Rejoice in hope" however slender.
'*Forgive, and don't give over trying.*'

7 '*Forgive, and don't give over trying:*'
Time — life — how they are flying, flying!
Still grasp soil'd hands eyes upward casting;
This word 'Forgive' is everlasting;
'*Forgive, and don't give over trying.*'

418. "GOD BURIES HIS WORKMEN BUT CARRIES ON HIS WORK." JOHN WESLEY.
2 Peter i. 15. 7s.

1 WORKMAN after workman dies,
And unfinish'd their work lies;
Our hearts fail, our hopes suspire
Yea, in Thy sweet service tire;
Fainting in our weaken'd way,
Scarcely able ev'n to pray;
O my God fresh FAITH us give!
Workmen die, but Thou dost live.

2 Workman after workman dies,
This Thy Church, Lord, sorely tries;
As in tears she stricken stands
Sadly missing "vanished hands,"
Strenuous wills, and bravest hearts
Ready aye to take their parts;
O my God, fresh TRUST us give?
Workmen die, but Thou dost live.

3 Workman after workman dies,
Often in extremities;
Just when at their very best,
Consecrate to Thy behest;
And their hallow'd ministry
Binding hearts in unity;
O my God, fresh HOPE us give?
Workmen die, but Thou dost live.

4 Workman after workman dies,
Passing from Earth to the skies;
Leaving fellow-workers weak,
Other workers far to seek;
Motive, inspiration chill'd,
Future with black clouds all fill'd;
O my God, fresh LOVE us give?
Workmen die, but Thou dost live.

5 Workman after workman dies
'Midst our anguish, 'midst our sighs;
And as when a fell'd tree falls
The vast vacancy appals;
Smitten dumb, we can but look
Lord, to Thee, and to Thy Book;
O my God, fresh STRENGTH us give?
Workmen die, but Thou dost live.

6 Workman after workman dies,
And unfinish'd their work lies!
But their work is Thine, O Christ;
Thou wilt keep Thy pledg'd tryst;
Still Thy promise-word observe
Send new workers Thee to serve;
O my God, fresh ARDOUR give?
Workmen die but Thou dost live.

7 Workman after workman dies;
Whence do come these mysteries?

Living Jesus, Thou know'st all,
By no chances these befall;
Earth below as Heav'n above
Compass' round is with Thy Love;
O God, wilt fresh GRACE us give?
Workmen die but Thou dost live.

410.   LIFE SUFFICIENT.   7s.
Job vi. 1 ; xiv. 14.

1 LIFE is longer than it seems;
  Longer than a vain World deems;
  He Who measureth out our span,
  Worketh not by chance but plan.

2 Life is longer than it seems;
  Nor compacted is of dreams;
  Noble deed and noble thought
  By the grace of God enwrought.

3 Life is longer than it seems;
  Catcheth on Earth heav'nly gleams;
  Rul'd not by our hours or years,
  But by movements of the spheres.

4 Life is longer than it seems;
  It with all "fine issues" teems;
  For lo "sons of God" are giv'n
  Even here the "days of heav'n."

5 Life is longer than it seems;
  Tho' it floweth as swift streams;
  Ceaseth not its motion, till
  It doth its great course fulfil.

6 Life is longer than it seems;
  For, lo! Jesus it redeems;
  When God gives a work to do,
  'Tis DONE, be days more or few.

7 *Repeat St. 1.*

421.   LIFE NOT TOO HARD.   7s.
Romans viii. 28.

1 LIFE is hard, but not too hard,
  When from Thee, Lord, not debarr'd;
  Sure conquest o'er circumstance,
  Thro' Faith's hand and eagle glance.

2 Life is hard, but not too hard;
  Saviour! I all fears discard;
  Thee I take now at Thy word;
  Take Thy word to Thee, O Lord!

3 Life is hard, but not too hard;
  If blows fall, Lord, I them ward;
  With strong heart and dauntless brow
  As Thy grace doth me endow.

4 Life is hard, but not too hard;
  Even when the "vessel's" marr'd;
  Thou Great Potter steppest in,
  Clarifying from all sin.

5 Life is hard, but not too hard;
  Thou, Lord Christ, my guide and guard;
  Still would I upon Thee rest,
  Or strong, or weak, or opprest.

6 Life is hard, but not too hard;
  Thanks, Lord, for Thy great reward;
  Thou, Lord, leavest not alone
  Who seek Thee upon Thy Throne.

422.   'SHE HATH DONE WHAT SHE COULD.'
St. Mark xiv. 8.   8s.

1 "*She hath done what she could,*" Christ said :
  On the sweet words have millions fed;
  For lo! deed of love illum'd stands,
  Held high to the light in His Hands.

2 "*She hath done what she could*" not much,
  But see how it rounds 'neath His touch!
  Until as the fair star of Eve
  It shines—ne'er her mem'ry to leave.

3 "*She hath done what she could*" her gift
  This great truth to us doth uplift;
  That FAITH which is rooted in LOVE,
  Most of all doth the GREAT HEART move.

4 "*She hath done what she could*" for Him,
  And no time shall e'er her act dim:
  Catch up the word, O heart of mine,
  Forth, and make it pattern of Thine."

5 "*What she could*" this is all He ask'd;
　The Lord's children are ne'er o'ertask'd;
　Be it ours — as we can — to serve;
　The Lord's heart — like her — we may nerve.
6 "*She hath done what she could*" — and lo!
　The fragrance thro' the Earth doth go;
　"*She hath done what she could*" — O worth
　That demands Heaven's praise to set forth!

423. Highways and Hedges.
St. Luke xiv. 23. 8s.

1 A GREEN lane hedged with milk-white May,
　Fragrant with breath of fresh-mown hay;
　Rosy children amongst the mows;
　A field dotted over with cows;
　Far, far up in the blinding sky
　Larks — specks of mystic melody;
　An old woman in old red cloak,
　Gleaning faggots 'neath woodman's stroke
　Pair'd lovers half-hid by a stile
　In loving chat with winsome smile;
　A mile off — the grey church spire —
　Vane burnish'd like flame of fire:
　　　Thanks, Lord, for such pleasant scene,
　　　English of English, I ween.

2 Foxgloves with pink and pendant bells,
　Fairy music hid in their cells;
　Ferns that their crosiers uplift
　Where soft the dim green light doth sift;
　Blue hyacinths on wavy banks
　That with all garden beauty ranks;
　Tangled amidst the beetling rocks,
　Dog-roses — safe even from the flocks;
　A beck fair glinting past the sedges,
　With pebbled streaks by the low edges;
　Wee white clouds in an azure sky —
　Like flock o' sheep charmingly:
　　　Thanks, Lord, for this nook of Thine,
　　　Inviolate by care divine.

3 Ev'n so, O Lord, in hidden nooks,
　Where the World's hard eye ne'er looks;
　Away behind the rush and roar
　Of the great City's throngs that pour

Day by day in their mad pursuit
O' pleasures — oft as Dead-Sea fruit;
I come upon pure Youth and Beauty
Sweet-following in Christly duty;
Now caring for Thy sick and old,
Now speaking words richer than gold;
Praise and prayer and uplifting spell,
Of tireless love unspeakable:
　　Thanks, Lord, for bright lives like these;
　　O to stir up hearts at ease!

424. No Retreat.
Revelations ii. 25-26. 10s.

1 The trumpet of Christ ne'er sounds a retreat;
　Or be it danger, or be it defeat,
　For still our Great Captain shouts high
　　and clear,
　Stand firm, my soldiers, stand, lo! I am
　　near.

2 The trumpet of Christ ne'er sounds a retreat!
　His watchword is forward whatever we
　　meet;
　Be devils our foes, or be our foes men,
　Be strong in the Lord and at them again.

3 The trumpet of Christ ne'er sounds a retreat;
　Midst clamour, confusion and hurrying
　　feet,
　Ye Knights of the Cross fear ye not nor
　　faint;
　Let no throb of cowardice you attaint.

4 The trumpet of Christ ne'er sounds a retreat;
　Be it ours, fellow-soldiers, each other to
　　greet;
　High-hearted resolve beat in ev'ry breast,
　Trusting the Lord to do all the rest.

5 The trumpet of Christ ne'er sounds a retreat;
　All bloodless His battles yet by blood
　　made meet
　Aye pulling down strongholds of Satan
　　and sin,
　And predestin'd peace for the World to win.

425. "IF YOU WANT A THING WELL DONE YOU MUST DO IT YOURSELF." — *Longfellow*—"*Courtship of Miles Standish.*" *James i. 27.* 6s.

1 "If you want thing well done
   You must do it yourself;
  A good cause is half-won,
   And, shunn'd many a shelf,
  When, your heart all a-flame,
   You go forth in Christ's name.

2 Mere giving of money
   To those you command
  With voice sweet as honey,
   Whilst 'tis dropp'd in their hand,
  Is not that which He did;
   Be your cry "God forbid!"

3 If you want thing well done
   You must do it yourself;
  A good cause is half-won,
   And, shunn'd many a shelf,
  When, your heart all a-flame,
   You go forth in Christ's name.

4 Let the 'Easy Way' smile;
   Easy, oft is the 'Broad,'
  'Narrow' choose 'gainst all guile;
   'Tis *the* Way The Christ trod,
  Let Society mock,
   'Tis but foam on the rock.

5 If you want thing well done,
   You must do it yourself;
  A good cause is half-won,
   And, shunn'd many a shelf,
  When, your heart all a-flame,
   You go forth in Christ's name.

6 'Go,' not 'send,' is His word;
   Forth then, Brother, thyself;
  Well may gird on his sword,
   Hohenzollern, or Guelph;
  Fight with your own right hand,
   One for Christ, with Christ stand.

426. ENDURING TO THE END. 7s.
"*To Him that overcometh will I give.*"—*Revelation ii. 7.*

1 Lo! we read in Gospel story
   That the FIGHT precedes the GLORY;
  Glory none, without the fight;
   And no right like conquer'd right.

2 Ah! the error's old, yea hoary,
   That without THE FIGHT seeks glory;
  So to seek the truth you wrest;
   By "enduring" only blest.

3 Look! how the great sea is froary;
   Symbol of divinest glory;
  Tempest-toss'd, and then the calm;
   E'en so conflict ere the palm.

4 Not the Fight madd'ning and gory,
   As is won the world's poor glory;
  But strong Faith and a strong Will
   The Lord's purpose to fulfil.

427. WORK AND REST. *1 Corinthians xv. 58.* 8s.

1 *He resteth best who worketh best:*
   Lord! be this in me manifest;
  Give grace that I may work for Thee
   By Thine Own "glorious liberty";
  Yea toil nor ever, Lord, be tir'd,
   By Thy thrice-holy love inspir'd.

2 *He resteth best who worketh best:*
   O Christ! give me this gracious rest!
  The rest of conscience and of faith,
   Sustain'd by Thy quick'ning breath;
  The rest that comes of each day done
   A-witnessing some victory won.

3 *He resteth best who worketh best:*
   Lord! wilt send more this to attest?
  Alas! alas! only the FEW
   Seek Thy example to renew;
  Alas! alas! fitful and weak
   Is all the work we do or seek.

4 *He resteth best who worketh best:*
   Lo! Thine own dearest thus are blest;
   Thou the Great Worker on Thy Throne
   Who Lab'r's dignity didst own ;
   Help us to see, and know, and feel
   That without work, rest is not weal.

5 *He resteth best who worketh best:*
   From North to South, from East to West;
   Lord! Thou art calling us to fear,
   Lest the World's cries we do not hear ;
   Ah! aching hearts and wilder'd brains
   Are longing for the Gospel's strains.

6 *He resteth best who worketh best:*
   O Christ, come swift! be my heart's guest ;
   Yea, make all hearts Thy dwelling-place;
   And into deeds transmute Thy grace ;
   Lift Thou us up and send us forth
   Still—still to tell Thy Cross's worth.

428. UNADVISED SPEAKING. 8s.

1 Lo! Wit is wine of human speech ;
   It sparkleth and wins froth of praise;
   But 'ware, it too lands in the ditch,
   Ev'n when the "loud laugh" it doth raise.

2 Put guard, my brother, on thy lips ;
   'Tis silence that in gold is drest ;
   The rash word oft its user trips ;
   And speech is silver at the best.

3 But when THE MASTER comes and calls
   That we for Him shall witness be ;
   We must "take heed," or on us falls
   The word of doom, "asham'd of Me."

4 Still, let us act and speak with thought ;
   Grace ever seeking to be true ;
   None e'er in vain for Him have sought
   Who walk beneath His Faith-seen Face.

5 *Repeat St. 1.*

429. PRAYING AND WORKING. 7s.
   2 Cor. vi. 1.

1 PRAYING work and working prayer
   So would I be kept from care ;
   Active ever, Lord, for Thee,
   Thou active ever in me.

2 Praying work—for vain to serve
   Unless Thy grace doth me nerve ;
   Working prayer—for vain to speak
   Unless I do that I seek.

3 Blessed Jesus, touch our wills
   With uplifting touch that thrills ;
   Blessed Jesus, guard our hearts
   From the World's ensnaring arts.

4 Be our prayer no idle breath ;
   Be our work not all beneath ;
   Be our prayer a laying hold ;"
   Be our work unpaid by gold.

5 Nearer Thee, Lord, and more near
   That I may no longer fear ;
   Grant me this and I shall know
   To work and pray, pray and go.

6 *Repeat St. 1.*

430. THE LORD'S HANDMAIDEN. 6s.
   Ps. lxxxvi. 16 ; cxvi. 16 ; St. Luke i. 38.

1 "*The handmaid of the Lord:*"
   It is a fragrant word ;
   Writ in a Christ-full psalm
   That falls like unto balm
   Upon a bruised heart,
   Aching in its keen smart.

2 "*The handmaid of the Lord :*"
   Sweet key-note 'midst discord :
   Crown'd David's mother she,
   Accepted now we see ;
   In covenant great and sure,
   Holy—submissive—pure.

3 "*The handmaid of the Lord:*"
Strike ye, strike high the chord;
Handmaid—no more her own;
Handmaid—God on heart's throne;
Handmaid—in the Lord found,
And to the dear Lord bound.

4 "*The handmaid of the Lord:*"
What cheer it doth afford!
Removing words of blame;
Removing words of shame;
All grace to her abounding,
Satan and Sin confounding.

5 "*The handmaid of the Lord:*"
Thou O Lord God ador'd;
Walking beneath Thy Face,
Holy by Thy free grace;
Unto Thee consecrate,
Upon Thee still to wait.

6 "*The handmaid of the Lord:*"
By His great love restor'd;
Sin now put far away,
Led into light of day;
Kept still in Hope and Faith,
Fulfilled each "He saith."

7 "*The handmaid of the Lord:*"
May such Thy Church afford:
That in all sweetness seen,
Walking in Heaven's own sheen;
They may draw hearts to Thee
By flawless purity.

430.   TEARS AND SWEAT-DROPS.   8s.

"*Tears cost us less than sweat, and it is our sweat that the inexorable sentence demands from us.*"— FREDERICK OZANAM ("*Letters*" by Coates 1886.)

1 True tears lo! are thrice-lovely things
As aught of which the Poet sings;
Mercy's jewels that she puts on
In her tender compassion;
Grief's one adornment that she wears,—
Purest white, and heart-cradled tears.

2 But none the less these sweat-drops call
For our thanksgivings as they fall;
Born of hard toil for "daily bread"
That many mouths still may be fed;
Or of the strong deep-brooding brain,
Meditative of "higher strain."

3 Tears often on mere eyelids lie
Some eyelids are scarce ever dry;
Tears are apt to be at command,
By those who yet heart-harden'd stand;
Alas! tears may be frivolous;
Ah! even deadly treacherous.

4 But these swart sweat-drops speak the truth,
Whether on Age's brow or Youth;
They tell of lowly duty done,
Of a long honest day's wage won;
Or witnesses are to deep thought
Into God-fearing action wrought.

5 Tears come quick and as quickly go;
Slightest touch and they overflow;
Tears that are true are eas'ly seen—
Alas! in few and far between;
Sweat-drops cannot like tears deceive
Or play tricks in what they relieve.

6 Sweat-drops that come on the tann'd brow
Tho' they do not as our tears glow;
Yet have a glory of their own
In highest estimation;
Brothers! of sweat-drops have no fears,
Sweat-drops may be finer than tears.

431.   RIGHTS AND DUTIES.   10s.

Romans xiv. 27.

1 There are no rights except those built on duty: [beauty
"My Lord, my God," me grant to see the
Of holding power that I may quietly serve,
Nor e'er from Thee—Thou Great Exemplar swerve.

2 No love to man unless thro' love to God:
"My Lord, my God," wilt Thy love "shed
abroad?"
That I with Thy true sympathy may feel,
For woes and suff'rings Thou alone can'st
heal

3 With Thine Own purity me, Lord, endow;
"My Lord, my God," my one IDEAL Thou:
That Body, Soul, and Spirit consecrate,
All sin I may with perfect hatred hate.

4 Breathe Thou within me Thy life-giving
breath; [death;
"My Lord, my God," to die Sin's gracious
I place me as I am in Thy pierc'd hands,
Rule me as sea Thou boundest by the sands.

5 So shall I witness, live, and work for Thee;
Partaker made of Thy serenity!
A pilgrim going forward to my Home;
But on my way, to all, still saying "Come."

6 Repeat St. 1.

432 KEEP AT THY POST.
Zacharias: St. Luke i. 5-25. 7s.

1 ZACHARIAS, saint of old,
Has his story sweetly told:
Dumb and deaf, he yet remain'd
And his priestly post retain'd;
Clos'd his ears and clos'd his tongue,
None the less he censer swung;
And all holy rites appointed,
Telling of the Great Anointed;
Ceaseless day by day he serv'd,
Nor from single duty swerv'd.

2 O my soul, the lesson learn,
Nor from post of duty turn
When afflictions thee assail,
And accustom'd succours fail;
Weak and silenc'd, still attend
Where thy Lord doth blessing send;
He will keep alive thy hope,
In His time thy mouth will ope;
He Who loosen'd His saint's tongue
Thine will fill with sweetest song.

433. LABOUR AND REST—REST AND
LABOUR.
St. Mark vi. 31. 7s.

1 *After labour rest is sweet;*
And rest makes labour meet;
Rest of tir'd brain, or feet.

2 *After labour rest is sweet;*
Labour rough or labour neat;
In the cold or in the heat.

3 *After labour rest is sweet;*
Labour indoors, or in street;
Active, knowing life doth fleet.

4 *After labour rest is sweet;*
Soft-un'ravelling ev'ry pleat,
Care doth into the brow eat.

5 *After labour rest is sweet;*
Gracious gift 'midst world's deceit;
Of which none can poorest cheat.

6 *After labour rest is sweet;*
Lord! to Thee I make retreat;
Thy words are no vain conceit.

7 *After labour rest is sweet;*
When heart-cradling night doth greet
Christ's own from the mercy-seat.

8 *After labour rest is sweet;*
Each day bright with some good feat;
Wherein Love and Pity meet.

9 *After labour rest is sweet;*
Shepherd-Saviour Thy sheep bleat;
Wilt Thou all their foes escheat?

10.*After labour rest is sweet;*
Lord! Send lab'rers 'midst Thy wheat;
Gathering to Sin's defeat.

11.*After labour rest is sweet;*
Restful toil Lord I entreat;
Strengthen'd by Thy heav'nly 'meat.'

12.*After labour rest is sweet;*
And rest maketh labour meet;
Rest of tired brain, or feet.

434. GOD'S "LITTLE ONES." 7s.

"*Is this......a small matter, that thou hast slain* MY CHILDREN, *and delivered them to pass through the fire.*" (*Ezekiel xvi. 28*) (Cf. *Ps. cvi. 37.*)

1 Israel upon the plain
  'Bove the wails and cries of pain
  Of their little children slain;
  Heard this low and sad refrain,
   " *My* children ! *My* children !"

2 Lo ! 'midst horrors that appal
  Soft and sweet the words do fall,
  From the Father of us all;
  His Own PEOPLE to recall :
   " *My* children ! *My* children !"

3 Ah ! 'Tis not thing pass'd away
  That no longer need affray;
  For all thro' long night and day
  " Little ones" are still a prey :
   " *My* children ! *My* children !"

4 Pale as Spring's first snowy flower
  Shiv'ring thro' the sleety shower;
  Our own English children cower
  'Neath abus'd parental power;
   " *My* children ! *My* children !"

5 Dark the secrets that are found;
  Crimes that demons might astound;
  Helpless babes fell'd to the ground,
  Bleeding oft with many a wound :
   " *My* children ! *My* children !"

6 Homes — worse than a wild beast's lair:
  Breathing foul infected air;
  Hunger-bitten, cold and bare;
  Shrinking, tremulous with fear;
   " *My* children ! *My* children !"

7 Open Lord ! our sealèd eyes,
  To the GUILT that on us lies;
  Lest the day of Grand Assize
  Bring to us a dread surprise.
   " *My* children ! *My* children !"

8 Laud, Lord, for the noble Few
  Who to Thy great charge are true,
  Grappling with the hellish crew;
  Bringing them to England's view:
   " *My* children ! *My* children !"

9 Save our "little ones," O Lord !
  Ev'n if Thou make bare Thy sword;
  At all costs Thy help afford;
  Lo ! We plead Thy promise-word:
   " *My* children ! *My* children !"

435 YES. 8s.

Joshua xxiv. 15-24.

1 Be *brave*, my Brother to say ' Yes,'
  Let cowards flee when dangers press;
  Like Joshua in the days of old
  Tell on whose side thou art enroll'd.

2 Be *strong*, my Brother, to say ' Yes,'
  Let men thee ban, or let them bless;
  Yield not to changing circumstance
  But be a MAN, unmu"d by CHANCE.

3 Be *true*, my Brother, to say ' Yes,'
  Stand forth by no constraint or stress;
  Bring out thy words straight from the heart,
  Take thou a stand and fill thy part.

4 Be *prompt*, my brother, to say ' Yes '
  Amidst abounding wretchedness;
  The call of God to help obey;
  Men perish while thou dost delay.

5 Be *bright*, my Brother, to say ' Yes,'
  Dipt in a smile, our words caress;
  Stand not apart or patronize
  Look straight into thy fellow's eyes.

6 Be *kind*, my Brother, to say ' Yes,'
  Not alms alone, with Love's impress,[bine;
  Look — tone — hand-grasp, let these com-
  Round these ev'n hardest hearts will twine.

7 Be *meek*, my Brother, to say ' Yes,
  Be patient still with wilfulness;
  Soft patience conquers where wrath fails ;
  He's victor most who least assails.

8 Be *sweet*, my Brother, to say 'Yes;'
 A haughty temper doth oppress;
 "Not easily provok'd" is still
 Our watchword by The Master's will.

436.   LITTLE HELPERS.   7s.
 "*There were with Him certain other little
 ships:*" *St. Mark iv. 36.*

1 "*Little ships*" of Galilee
 Fair ye must have been to see,
 Like a flock of birds, wind-driv'n,
 Haven seeking, haven giv'n.
2 "*Little ships*," your story old,
 Fit is to be 'graved on gold;
 For it tells us how that ye
 Follow'd Jesus lovingly.
3 "*Little ships*," ye bear us word
 From Christ Jesus our dear Lord;
 That like you we too may go
 Where HE is and love HIM so.
4 "*Little ships*" of Galilee,
 Made like you would we now be;
 'Neath His watchful care abide;
 Fearless then whate'er betide.
5 "*Little ships*," saw ye HIM rise
 And in calm naught could surprise,
 Hush the wild waves and the winds:
 By a word their fury binds?
6 "*Little ships*," across the gloom
 Flash'd the FACE doth all illume?
 Were ye in the splendor caught
 When the miracle was wrought?
7 "Little ships" where'er ye bore
 Heard ye 'bove the storm-wind's roar
 His "still small" yet mighty voice,
 All hearts making to rejoice?
8 "Little ships," bright fancies breed
 As of you we sweetly read:
 Whilst THE TWELVE were all alarm'd
 Ye went on your way unharm'd.
9 "*Little ships*," not great be ours;
 Suited to our childhood's powers;
 Prizing our fresh early years,
 Hasting not to our careers.
10 "*Little ships*" of Galilee,
 Still sail ye o'er that fair Sea;
 Ye will live till TIME departs
 In all children's loving hearts.

437.   THE TEN COMMANDMENTS. 8.4.
 Exodus xx.

1 No longer thunders Sinai's LAW;
  But stand in awe
 All ye that think the great "Ten Words,"
  Those flashing swords —
 Have blunted aught of their sharp edge;
  And vain allege
 Them now to be effete and gone—
  Their mission done.
 Nay verily, they be strong still;
  Declare His Will:
 Nor ever shall their force be spent,
  God spoke, God sent.
2 Methinketh that in sooth 'twere well —
  I ring a bell —
 If this stone-ey'd, brass-throated Age
  Would re-engage
 In deepest study of THE LAW:
  Time's greedy maw
 Has swallow'd much, but this still stands,
  And still commands:
 Ah! Conscience indestructible
  Will loud rebel,
 When the brave old moralities
  By glozing lies
 Are cunningly explain'd away,
  Things of a day.
3 Laud, O my God, for Thy great grace
  By which we trace
 Thy RIGHTEOUSNESS at rest in LOVE,
  That still did move
 With JUSTICE on straight lines, yet saw
  The *Holy Law*
 Strong; and a clear way open laid —
  Of SEERS pray'd;
 Whereby man's utmost guilt and loss
  Are by the CROSS
 Remov'd, yea, the vast World redeem'd,
  But Law esteem'd;
 Our RACE set free from Sin's vast load
  By Son of God.

10. Christian Views of Death and Eternity.

433. OUR DEAD FIRST-BORN AND OTHER TWO LITTLE ONES.17

1 THE Lord gave us a first-born child ;
'Twas as if Christ had on us smil'd
In His sweet holy infancy ;
When beneath his young mother's eye
He lay in purest innocence,
Creature almost too fair for sense.

2 How his coming knit our two hearts
Into one, that now nothing parts !
How our love leapt up to new being,
Deeper, finer far than all seeing !
As before the GIVER we knelt,
Brokenly utt'ring what we felt.

3 O ! day by day the little thing
Caus'd to us hourly wondering ;
Day by day life's strange mysteries
Flash'd on us from his azure eyes ;
Rose-red lips, and a rippling smile
That austerest might well beguile.

4 By-and-bye came—not without awe—
His first word, naming his "mam ma;"
And sure signs of the dawning mind
'With winsomeness of feeling join'd ;
Quick responses to word or look,
Clear as e'er any printed book.

5 Thus still our FIRST-BORN grew and grew
Till almost Heav'n on Earth we knew ;
Crept enticingly on the floor ;
Chas'd a bright sunbeam o'er and o'er;
Little new words still added daily,
That his fond mother knew right gaily.

6 Tokens that a 'live soul was there,
Enrich'd of faculty, and rare
Fore-gleamings of intelligence,
From Thee Above, and not from hence :
And O the tricksome pretty ways
That forming character bewrays!

7 Ah ! It was too too bright to last !
Soon our sunshine was overcast;
More sudden than the fading flower
Bedrabbled by the chilly shower ;
Sickening, our sweet darling lay,
Life—how swiftly !—ebbing away.

8 O the sad mystery of pain
Binding an infant in its chain ;
With subtleties inscrutable
As might have been contriv'd in hell;
I own it, my poor faith was shook
'Fore my child's suff'ring, pleading look.

9 How fears arose ! and how fears fell !
The wearying struggle who may tell ?
He tost on his bruis'd mother's knee
In anguish that 'twas hard to see ;
Moan, and thirst, and O burning hands !
With words e'en Love not understands.

10 It came at last: the wee wan face
Chang'd as by celestial grace ;
A shadow pass'd across his brow,
One long last look, and now and now
Our FIRST-BORN lay before us dead,
Our hopes united, shattered.

11 Long years have come ! long years have gone !
Since that day of desolation ;
And still our hearts are left forlorn,
And others followed our FIRST-BORN;
Yet sweet light on their mem'ry lies :
Parents of children in the skies.

12 *Parents of children in the skies :*
This turns discords to harmonies ;
Tho' here by darkness we are tried,
Luminous is the other side ;
Less of Earth, the more of Heaven—
Christ's Own consolation given.

439. *Submission — Our First-Born.*
8,8,4,8,8,4,8,8,4,4,4.

1 How very small! and yet how great,
E'en in this life's novitiate
   A little Child!
Perill'd and frail, as op'ning flower
Beaten by sleet in windy shower,
   On lonesome wild;
But "kept" by Jesus, strong and sure,
If foes assail or tempters lure
   In onward years:
   So hush my fears;
   Stay, heart, thy tears.

2 Scarce more than toy this tiny hand;
Scepter'd anon, I see it stand
   In gentle might;
These lips rose-red that know no speech
Undying truth may one day teach;
   Strong for the right;
This head crown'd with its golden hair—
Like sunshine's gold — Faith's eyes declare,
   Will yet be shewn
   To be a throne,
   That God will own.

3 O cradled sleeper! as I pray
I mark how o'er thy sweet face play
   Shadow and shine;
I may not seek to lift the veil
Of years — His word can never fail;
   It is divine;
So trusting all to Him, I take
My child to CHRIST, and no more ache;
   Safeguard him, Lord;
   Fulfil Thy word,
   That I have heard.

4 Ah! In the same year he was sent
Our FIRST-BORN the "far journey" went
   To the Unseen:
And our two hearts were bleeding left
To pine, as if of all bereft;
   The might have been
All shatter'd — hopes far-stretching lost;
We tempest-driven, on wild sea tost:

Incarnate Love,
We look Above;
Heal Heav'nly Dove!

410. SORROWFUL YET REJOICING.
2 Cor. vi. 10. 7s.

1 SING, Believer, and rejoice;
Listen to His conquering voice;
He His mighty work has done,
And abides "The Living One;"
Death hath no dominion now;
See all crowns upon Christ's brow.

2 Having died, He dies no more;
Sing Believer, and implore
That He will anoint thine eyes
To behold, beyond the skies,
All thy lov'd ones with Him blest
In the "Everlasting Rest."

3 *Earth to earth and dust to dust*
Stands illumin'd by Hope's trust;
O Believer, child, not slave,
Tremble not before the grave;
He has pass'd it and return'd;
He keeps safe all thou hast mourn'd.

4 Sing, Believer, and rejoice,
Listen to His conquering voice:
He His mighty work has done,
And abides "The Living One,"
Death hath no dominion now;
See all crowns on Jesus' brow.

441. A CHRISTIAN'S DEATH-BED.
Philippians i. 23, and Psalm xxiii. 4.
8,8,8,8,8,8,7,7.

1 WHEN I upon my death-bed lie,
And mystic film bedims my eye;
Lord Jesus, wilt Thou by me stand,
And place in mine Thy guiding Hand?
That walking thro' the gathering dark
I may to Thy "still, small voice" hark:
   O my God! me not forsake,
   But let me with Thee awake.

2 If Memory " old sins " re-charge,
  Thy mercy wilt Thou not enlarge?
  If conscience presses on me guilt,
  Wilt Thou not shew me Thy Blood spilt?
  If the Great Tempter me assail
  May I be clad, Lord, in Thy mail;
     O my God! me not forsake,
     But let me with Thee awake.

3 Thou know'st, Lord, the valley of Death;
  Thou know'st the pain of lab'ring breath;
  Thou know'st the sinking heart's alarms
  Thou know'st how frail all mortal arms;
  Be Thou near by in that dread hour,
  And keep me by Thy gracious power:
     O my God! me not forsake,
     But let me with Thee awake.

4 So shall I place me in Thy care;
  Vouchsafe that I may ne'er despair;
  Serene and peaceful be my sleep
  As those whom Thou in love dost keep;
  O give me glimpse of th' open door,—
  The life of joy for evermore:
     O my God! me not forsake,
     But let me with Thee awake.

442. THE DYING CONQUEROR.   9.5.
2 Timothy iv. 7.

1 I AM going from dimness to light;
  I am going to daybreak not night;
  I am changing Faith's walk for sight;
     Laud! Holy Saviour!

2 Praise, O my God, 'tis not a hard fight;
  Thou hast giv'n the vict'ry and the right;
  Thou dost me to Thy Right Hand invite;
     Laud! Holy Saviour!

3 I am in "perfect peace," not in fright;
  I am girded, O God, by Thy might;
  Thou the Last En'my on cross didst smite;
     Laud! Holy Saviour!

4 Thou, O God, gav'st the heart contrite;
  And my life to Thine Thou didst unite;
  Thou hast promis'd the robe of white;
     Laud! Holy Saviour!

5 On my spirit Hope's vision looks bright;
  Thou hast put fears and doubts all to flight;
  Ah! I triumph death in thy despight;
     Laud! Holy Saviour!

6 I am going from dimness to light;
  I am going to daybreak not night;
  I am exchanging Faith's walk for sight;
     Laud! Holy Saviour!

443. CROSSING TO THE OTHER SIDE.   8s.
"Let us pass over unto the other side."—St. Mark iv. 35.

1 *Pass over to the other side:*
  I hear! O Lord, be Thou my guide;
  Thou bidst me go, and go with Thee;
  Lord, I believe, but keep Thou me;
  I list Thy call, I grasp Thy Hand,
  Me safe on " other side " to land.

2 *Pass over to the other side:*
  I give it meaning still more wide;
  'Twas but to pass across the Sea,
  Holy, transfigur'd Galilee—
  But Thou dost seek we should decide
  With Thee, Lord, ever to abide.

3 *Pass over to the other side:*
  Yea, Lord, whatever me betide;
  Ne'er would I go or come alone,
  I bow me low before Thy throne;
  " Lo! I am with you " let me hear;
  So shall I cast away all fear.

4 *Pass over to the other side:*
  O Lord, in Thee I do confide;
  And as when Thou the call didst give
  By Thy divine prerogative;
  As " little ships " then with Thee went,
  Grant all I love be with us sent.

5 *Pass over to the other side:*
  And " safe into the haven glide "—
  The haven on the sunny shore;
  To know or toil or storm no more;
  This is, dear Lord, the hope we cherish;
  That none of Thy redeem'd can perish.

444. Longings for Departure.
*Deut. iii. 23-25 (Cf. xxxiv. 1-4); Philippians
i. 23.*   78

1 O "Let me go over," Lord,
 To Thy "goodly Land" on high;
'Twas Thy servant's pleading word;
  Lord, wilt Thou again deny?
O I weary am, and weak;
  All the "outward man" decaying;
Suffer me, that I may speak,
  Send me Death, long long delaying.

2 Lo! I see the Jordan flowing,
  Down the over-shadow'd dale:
And beyond are Heav'ns walls glowing,
  As Faith's hand draws back the veil;
O, blest Lord, my heart is aching,
  For Thine Everlasting Rest;
Life-strings one by one are breaking;
  Help, help, Lord, I am opprest!

3 O my Lord, "let me go over"
  To Thy "goodly Land" on high;
See my fainting spirit hover
  Spreading forth its wings to fly;
Hold me not, O King anointed,
  With soft kiss call me away;
I have liv'd the time appointed;
  "If thou wilt" O say me "yea."

4 Lord, forgive if 'tis unruly
  Thus to yearn for going home:
Thou, dear Saviour, knowest truly
  How such longings o'er us come;
For Thine Own Name's sake release me,
  From this languor and sharp pain;
Thou my only Lord, can'st ease me;
  I plead, that "to die is gain."

5 O "let me go over," Lord,
  To Thy "goodly Land" on high;
Thy kind touch to me accord,
  That shall shut my glazing eye;
By the Cross I make my dwelling;
  Lord on Thee I place my sin;
Take me over Jordan's swelling,
  Blood-bought crown and robe to win.

6 O "let me go over," Lord,
  To Thy "goodly Land" on high;
'Twas Thy servant's pleading word;
  Lord, wilt Thou again deny?
O I weary am, and weak;
  All the "outward man" decaying;
Suffer me, that I may speak;
  Kind Death come, long long delaying!

445. Mi Dissɛ: "Non Cercar, L'ho
Sotterato!" (Tuscany: Disperati.) 18
                                          1 Cor. xv.

1 *Seek him no more: I've laid him 'neath the
  earth:* [mocking mirth;
Nay, Nay, O Death, surcease thy
Not "him" but his—the poor worn robe
  of clay—   [away.
That only thou hast marr'd and put

2 I look not on Earth's level low, but Heav'n;
  I know whom I believe, by His grace
  given;   [art;
I know that thou, O Death, discrown'd
Nor fear thy scoffing; no, nor yet thy dart.

3 *Seek him no more; I've laid him 'neath the
  earth:*
A lie it is of unbelieving birth;
Last Enemy! Thy sword put in its sheath,
Thou touchest since Christ died—but
  mortal breath.

4 Thou, Living Christ, Whom lowliest may
  trust,   [our dust;
The soul is Thine, not Death's; and ev'n
Death! Where's thy sting? where Grave
  thy victory?   [sky.
Our lov'd are not 'neath earth but pass'd to

5 *Seek him no more; I've laid him 'neath the
  earth:*   [mocking mirth;
Nay, nay, O Death, surcease thy
Not "him" but his—the poor worn robe
  of clay—
That only thou hast marr'd and put away.

446. The Good Die Not.

"Mortality swallowed up of life." — 2 Cor. v. 4.
"Passed from death unto life." St. John v. 24.
"Your life is hid with Christ in God." Colos. iii. 3.   8.6.8.6.8.8.

1 The good die not ; they but undress
　And lay them down to sleep ;
They wake anon in blessedness ;
　Ev'n whilst for them we weep ;
Let Faith ascend within the vail,
Nor as disconsolate still wail.

2 The good die not ; He went before
　A mansion to prepare ;
And if we only could thus soar,
　We should not shed a tear ;
Laying aside their chrysalis
Bless'd are they in that Day of His.

3 The good die not ; but disappear
　For the Lord's "little while :"
Let us now watch ; the day draws near
　Shall close the brief exile ;
In hope and patience let us wait ;
Soon will unclose the Golden Gate.

4 The good die not ; an ampler life
　Is theirs where they have gone ;
No more of sin, or grief or strife,
　Can vex His haven'd one ;
"Life more abundant" their reward :
Not lying dead 'neath daisied sward.

5 The good die not ; they but undress
　And lay them down to sleep;
They wake anon in blessedness,
　Ev'n whilst for them we weep;
Let Faith ascend within the vail,
Nor as disconsolate still wail.

447. Death Dethroned.

1 Cor. xv. 55-57.   8.6.8.6.

1 Death ! Men to Thee no longer bow,
　Nor as thy abjects stand ;
There is no crown upon thy brow,
　No sceptre in Thy hand.

2 Thou art dethron'd two thousand years,
　By Him The Crucified ;
Thou, born of sin ! Thou King of fears !
　Didst die when Jesus died.

3 Thou touchest now but mortal breath ;
　The soul Thou dost not touch ;
And, e'en a little child, O Death !
　Before Thee need not crouch.

4 For He, the Prince of life, bids sing ;
　"No evil will I fear ;
Thy rod and staff will comfort bring,
　When Death to me draws near."

5 We needs must grieve, we needs must weep,
　For lov'd ones gone before ;
But ah ! in Christ, they do but sleep,
　The Day will them restore.

6 O praise and thanks unto the Lord,
　Who having died arose ;
We rest upon His mighty word ;
　Our heart no terror knows.

7 Death ! Men to thee no longer bow,
　Nor as thy abjects stand ;
There is no crown upon thy brow,
　No sceptre in thy hand.

448. No More Death nor Pain.

Revelation xxi. 4.   7s.

1 Aching heads and aching hearts,
In Earth's homes and in Earth's marts ;
Wasted ones, ah ! slowly dying ;
Unknown ones in anguish lying ;
Shatter'd frames in hospitals ;
Sick ones shelter'd by white walls ;
Sweet as song to these the strain
Heaven knows " *no death nor pain.*"

2 Aching heads and aching hearts,
   In Earth's homes and in Earth's marts;
   Grave's corruption ante-dated,
   Death in lifetime e'en instated;
   Labor'd breathing, sleepless nights;
   Ashen colour that affrights;
   To these the soft words pertain,
   Heaven knows "*no death nor pain.*"

3 Aching heads and aching hearts,
   In Earth's homes and in Earth's marts;
   Mothers wistful and heart-broken,
   By hope-quenching word, just spoken;
   Sons and daughters nigh distraught,
   That for dearest can do naught;
   To these comes like "latter rain,"
   Heaven knows "*no death nor pain.*"

4 Aching heads and aching hearts,
   In Earth's homes and in Earth's marts;
   Nerves unstrung and quivering,
   Burning pain and shivering;
   Human skill, a mockery;
   Yet, for long they do not die;
   Ah! What cheer to these, and gain,
   Heaven knows "*no death nor pain.*"

5 Aching heads and aching hearts,
   In Earth's homes and in Earth's marts;
   Lord! bestow on us we pray
   Thine Own tenderness, to stay
   With the sufferer, and with heart,
   And with hand and patient art,
   Bear with us for sweet refrain,
   Heaven knows "*no death nor pain.*"

6 Aching heads and aching hearts,
   In Earth's homes and in Earth's marts;
   How shall we sufficient show
   What for years of health we owe?
   Grant us, Lord, our strength to give,
   To Thee, and for Thee to live;
   Nor the lowliest task disdain;
   Heaven knows "*no death nor pain.*"

449.   No More Pain. [19]

". . . *"neither shall there be any more pain." — Revelation xxi. 4.*   10.4.

1 There came to me, as o'er the late-mown grass
   Heav'n's tender rain;
   A "still small voice," that from Above did pass —
   "There — no more pain:"
   Then, as I woke, it seem'd an angel note
   Of heavenly song;
   That in His pity great, He caus'd to float,
   My way along.

2 "There — no more pain;" O Saviour, soft and sweet,
   The holy phrase!
   And now I come to Thee with tired feet,
   Full thanks to raise;
   That thus Thou tell'st I shall not always lie
   Pained and weak;
   But that, Thy purpose wrought, I by-and-bye
   My chain shall break.

3 Thou know'st the suff'rings of this weary frame,
   My sleeplessness;
   Thou knowest through long years the searching flame
   Of my distress;
   Lord, give me patience still to watch and wait,
   Or long or short;
   Be it for Thee, not me, to fix the date
   To enter port.

450.   The Christian's Gain By Death.

"*To die is gain.*" — *Phillip. i. 21.*   8s.

1 A noble life hath noble end,
   Its sunset glory Heav'n doth lend;
   And dying saint doth oft attain
   Assurance, that *to die is gain.*

2 Wondrous the privilege to know,
  The "closer walk" with Christ below ;
  But soft and sweet as Summer rain,
  The gracious word, *to die is gain*.

3 Growing in knowledge and in grace,
  Still running in the Christian race ;
  The child of God runs not in vain,
  The prize awaits, *to die is gain*.

4 Using all "talents" to him given ;
  Forgiving, as himself forgiven ;
  Blood-wash'd by Love from ev'ry stain—
  This is his joy, *to die is gain*.

5 Honour to live and work for Christ ;
  For transient toil reward unpric'd ;
  But grander far with Him to "reign,"
  Approving that *to die is gain*.

6 Increase, not decrease, Death will bring ;
  The ransom'd soul shall upward wing ;
  No longer girt with galling chain ;
  To find in truth, *to die is gain*.

7 To sinless air, effulgent skies,
  Expansion of all faculties ;
  To re-clasp loving hands again :
  Praise to the Lord! *to die is gain*.

8 For ever pure, for ever blest,
  How may the rapture be exprest !
  O this shall be our glad refrain,
  To die is gain! to die is gain!

451. Christ With Me Or I With Christ.[20]   10s.

1 *If I am spar'd, then Christ will be with me ;
  If I am not spar'd, I shall be with Christ ;*
  I bless thee, saint of God, for thy sweet
    words ;
  I place them in my treasury unpric'd.

2 Feeble and worn, how often do I feel,
  That my poor life may end at any day ;
  Strangely it lengthens out, and I remain ,
  Ready, please God, either to go or stay.

3 How many who began life's march with me
  Have long long since gone to the other
    side !
  How many, who still live, live without God!
  Whilst I do know Him and in Him abide.

4 White flakes are falling on my aging head,
  And deepen'd lines cross and recross my
    brow ;
  I cannot think to-day as once I thought ;
  But ne'er lov'd Jesus more than I do now

5 The ties that bind me to this Earth are few ;
  My heart ascends where my best treasures
    lie ;
  I wait His final summons full of hope ;
  Yet fain would be at rest with Him on
    high.

6 *If I am spar'd, then Christ will be with me,
  If I am not spar'd, I shall be with Christ;*
  I bless thee, saint of God, for Thy sweet
    words :
  I place them in my treasury unpric'd.

452.   Not Dead, But Just Beginning To Live.

*Billy Bray (secundus) Haslam's "Life from
   Death."*

1 " Death ?"   " Nay, beginning now to
    live ! "
  Thanks, O my God, that Thou did'st give
  This word of cheer by dying saint
  Resting on Thee, when low and faint.

2 "Death?" "Nay," he said, with glazing
    eye,—
  They thought that he had gone on high—
  " Beginning now to live," he sigh'd,
  " Henceforth to live "—and then he died.

3 O glorious truth of holy faith !
  O blessed triumph over death !
  To die's to live, and die no more,
  With Christ, safe on the shining shore.

4 Be mine, Lord, — for 'tis Thine to give —
This word, "beginning now to live;"
When worn and weak I dying lie,
Let no film hide Thee from my eye.

5 Death?" "Nay, beginning now to live!"
Thanks, O my God, that Thou didst give
This word of cheer, by dying saint
Resting on Thee, when low and faint.

453. THE TEAR-DIMMED LAMP. 6s.

*"There shall be . . . boys and girls
playing about the streets." Zech. vii. 5.*

1 I HAD a dream that wafted me far up to
  the CITY OF GOLD:
Before me walls of jasper flashed and a
  crystal river rolled;
And O most real dream it was! For all I
  saw, as plain
As when I look on the landscape green,
  thro' my trellis'd window pane.

2 Most glorious was this heav'nly sight, most
  wondrous was the throng;
Lo! myriads on myriads walked the shining
  streets along;
I yearning, gazed, until there came a sweet
  soft mist of tears
But not of sorrow, for the scene still'd all
  my anxious fears:

3 Lo! lo! I saw in one radiant square,
  marching in song-led tramp,
Ten thousand bright young children, each
  holding a slender lamp.
O fair were their sweet faces! O winsome
  was the sight!
O wondrous was the vision from the holy
  Land of Light!

4 Far, far on gleam'd the twinkling line, and
  I gazed upon each one;
At length, with start of wonder, I beheld
  my own dear son:
Amaz'd, heart-bruis'd, I looked and looked

—*his* lamp seemed going out;
I cried a cry of anguish keen — of agonizing
  doubt:

5 "O Willie dear, my own lov'd child! oh,
    tell me what means this!
Each lamp but yours burns brilliantly. — O
    are not you in bliss?"
He met my eye, he heard my cry, he
  named me by my name:
"O mother! how can *my* lamp shine,
  since *your* tears dim its flame?"

6 Then I awoke, but ne'er again for my lost
    boy to weep:
I praised the Lord, Who thus lit up with
    joy my weary sleep:
'Twas but a dream of the night, I knew;
    yet blessing it brought to me,
For thoughts of the *tear-dimmed lamp* aye
    keep my heart from murmuring free.

7 O mothers all, I tell you my dream, to
    reach out a helping hand,
As wistful, childless, desolate, in your
    great grief ye stand;
Ev'n now look up to the CITY OF GOLD, and
    in the line of light,
By faith see there your dear ones playing,
    nor *dim their lamps so bright*.

454. TEARS BUT HOPE.

*"She goeth unto the grave to weep there."—
St. John xi. 31 (Cf. xi. 26.)* 6s.

1 WE weep amidst our graves,
    But fear thee not, O Death;
  We are not now thy slaves,
    To speak with bated breath:
  Here, even here, we sing;
    Our loss to Christ we bring.

2 Our hearts thou bruisest still,
    And plungest us in grief;
  But 'tis our Father's will,
    And thus we seek relief;
  We look beyond the skies,
    Not where the poor dust lies.

3 We miss, we muse, we mourn,
   And shall unto the end;
  Lord, unto Thee we turn;
   Thy consolation send!
  We know Thee, Living One,
   And all that Thou hast done.

4 The ties of Earth grow less,
   As lov'd ones from us go;
  But ties of Heav'n increase
   By increase of our woe;
  O, Thou Incarnate Love,
   Lift us to Thee Above!

455. Soothing Thought. 10s.
St. Peter v. 10.

1 Another yet another young life goes;
  Again and yet again falls in the strife;
  Ah! I must own my FAITH shakes 'neath such blows;
  My anchor'd HOPE is cut as with sharp knife;
  But, lo! there comes to me a "still small voice"
  Bids me no longer mourn but aye rejoice;
  I caught it even as my dear ones died—
  Life is completed on the other side.

2 Fair blossoms were just rounding into fruit;
  Their INTELLECT—with glimpses of bright power;
  HEART—open as the day, not involute;
  And CONSCIENCE still unsullied as a flower;
  But, lo! there comes to me a "still small voice,"
  Bids me no longer mourn, but aye rejoice;
  I caught it even as my dear ones died—
  Life is completed on the other side.

3 On this our Earth but genesis of things;
  'Tis still thus seen, and so it aye shall be;
  All broken fleeting—as a bird on wings;
  O Lord! thus day by day do we not see?
  But, lo! there comes to me a "still small voice,"
  Bids me no longer mourn, but aye rejoice;
  I caught it even as my dear ones died—
  Life is completed on the other side.

456. Christ in the Under-World. 7s.
Acts of Apostles ii. 27-31; Ps. xiv. 10; 1 Peter iii. 19.

1 DEAD! Upon the Cross suspended,
  Christ to SHEOL is descended,
  In the under-world proclaiming
  Satan's throne shatter'd—him shaming;
  Everlasting purpose wrought,
  Redemption by His blood bought.

2 Patriarchs! Seers! Saints Him greet,
  Low-adoring at His feet;
  All fulfill'd they had foretold
  In the far back days of old;
  Jesus—His supreme work done;
  Jesus—His full triumph won.

3 Burning hearts and glowing lips
  Welcome the apocalypse;
  From First Man to latest son
  Rejoice o'er the completion;
  Ring from earth and ring from heav'n
  Joyous songs by God's grace giv'n.

4 Face of calm and high-borne palm!
  Jesus brings all-healing balm;
  Eyes of light and hand of might;
  Jesus! Thy Love infinite!
  Prize-crown'd race! O words of grace!
  Heav'n made aye man's dwelling-place.

5 "It is done"—on Earth below;
  "It is done" all Heav'n doth know;
  "It is done" 'tis heard in Hell;
  "It is done" loud let it swell;
  Pass'd appointed "forty days"
  He ascends 'fore THE TWELVE's gaze.

457. Resurrection—The One Unopened Grave. 8s.

None who has seen the Last Judgment of Beato
Angelico da Fiesole in the Academy of the Fine Arts
in Florence ever can forget its awesome realism in the
long avenue of open and empty graves terminated with
the stately tomb of Christ, which alone is closed,
because it has nothing to give up. A thrill passes
through the spectator as he gazes and reflects. St.
Luke xxiv. 5.

1 Lo! the great DAY OF DAYS is come,
 That shall men's probation sum;
 Peals the last trumpet shatt'ringly,
 Taro' land and sea where'er graves be.

2 Stirreth the universal Earth;
 From dust again MAN leaps to birth;
 Innumerable as the sands [stands.
 Our whole RACE 'fore the White Throne

3 One grave alone does not unclose
 To wake the sleeper's long repose,
 The tomb of Christ from Third Great Day,
 Forever ceas'd to hold its prey.

4 Christ is THE JUDGE ev'n as He said—
 Judge of the living and the dead;
 All numberless the dead arise,
 But Christ descendeth from the skies.

5 One grave alone does not unclose
 To wake the sleeper's long repose;
 The tomb of Christ from Third Great Day,
 Forever ceas'd to hold it's prey.

6 Now, the Eternal Purpose wrought,
 All—all are to Last Judgment brought;
 The graves yield up their ancient trust;
 Alive most secret-hidden dust.

7 One grave alone does not unclose
 To wake the Sleeper's long repose,
 The tomb of Christ from Third Great Day,
 Forever ceas'd to hold its prey.

8 And, lo! above his tomb is seen—
 Like pointed flames in bick'ring sheen;
 Bright angels bow'd before "the place"
 O, eyes rais'd to THE JUDGE'S FACE.

458. The Resurrection. 5s.

St. Matt. xxviii. 8-10; St. Luke xxiv. 19.

1 "We have seen the Lord:"
 O transcendent word!
 He is now alive
 Who with Death did strive,
 On the "bitter tree"
 Rais'd on Calvary;
 Yet, and in the tomb
 Made bright all its gloom;
 Light of life THE LORD:
 O thrice-precious word!

2 "We have seen the Lord:"
 O hope-giving word!
 That the women brought
 When "The Twelve" they sought;
 "We have seen the Lord:"
 O joy-bringing word!
 Jesus' "work" all done,
 His great vict'ry won;
 "We have seen the Lord:"
 O heart-calming word!

3 "We have seen the Lord:"
 O love-kindling word!
 All fulfill'd He said;
 Truth established;
 "We have seen the Lord:"
 Bearing no sharp sword;
 But sweet as before,
 Or more and still more;
 "We have seen the Lord:"
 O faith-working word!

4 "We have seen the Lord:"
 O wonder-upbuilt word!
 That all hell confounds;
 Gospel that astounds;
 "We have seen the Lord:"
 We have Him ador'd;
 He the LIVING ONE
 Returns to His Throne;
 "We have seen the Lord:"
 Tell the mighty word.

59. O DEATH WHERE IS THY STING. —
1 Cor. xv. 55. 8.8.8.8.8.

1 They wrong thee O grace-changèd Death,
   To whom the hard task is given
Ceaseless to stop our mortal breath ;
   'Tis thy pale hand leads us to Heav'n ;
      Men do thee wrong, O SILENT
         Death !

2 No longer enemy but friend,   [weep,
   Thou now dost weep with those who
As " Jesus wept," and peace dost send ;
   " So gives He His belovèd sleep : "
      Men wrong thee, O STILL-FOOTED
         Death.

3 Thy touch is touch of ruth not hate ;
   Thy heart doth thrill to anguish'd grief ;
The Cross thou liftest in high state,
   To staunch sin's wounds with sweet
      relief ;
         Men do thee wrong, O GRACIOUS
            Death.

4 Withdrawing from this earthly life
   Thou takest to pure Land of Light ;
Ending all Sin's turmoil and strife ;
   Soft, thy inexorable might :
      Men wrong thee O CHRIST-
         SERVING Death.

5 From fading to the never-fading ;
   From few to many thou dost take ;
From loads our bruisèd hearts o'erlading,
   Thou as at one bright bound dost
      shake ;

      Men do thee wrong, O GENTLE
         Death.

6 *In* Christ, thou bringest us *to* Christ,
   To tired feet and hearts giv'st rest ;
I would with thee keep grateful tryst ;
   Like lost child, aching for His breast ;
      Men wrong thee, O BENIGNANT
         Death.

460.   GLORY TO GLORY.   8.8.9.9.
2 Cor. iii. 18.

1 With " holy boldness " I draw near,
   For God, Thy grace casts out all fear ;
      I come with upward gaze unquailing,
      Not as the angels, my eyes veiling.
2 With " open face " I Thee behold,
   As in Thy precious word foretold :
      Thy "glory " in " a glass " reflecting ;
      Yet humbled, Lord, my flaws detect-
         ing.
3 Laud, O my Saviour, for that grace
   That " changes " me, so that I trace
      Thine own " image," from grace to
         glory—
      Ah ! 'tis Redemption's " old, old
         story."
4 Dwell in me, Lord, that I may see
   Myself " transform'd," made like to Thee ;
      I plead my dear Redeemer's merit ;
      Fulfil Thine office, Holy Spirit.

461.   TYPES OF RESURRECTION.
Acts of the Apostles iv. 2.   10s.

1 ALL round about are types of Resurrection
   To meditative and anointed eyes ;
Lord, give to me Thy heavenly direction,
   That I thus look on green Earth and
      blue skies.
2 Behold ! awaking from dead Winter's arms
   The Spring is with us, all a-thrill with
      life ;
Trees seeds roots now deliver'd from
      all harms
   With numbness, cold, and darkness long
      at strife.

3 Behold! from death to life rises the seed
  Overtly sown in the Spring-furrow'd field
  Or drawn forth from the ancient cere-cloth
      weed,
  Waes the grey pyramids their dead
      upyield.

4 Behold! upon a rose a butterfly,
  Bursting from chrysalis with rich-stain'd
      wings;
  Like creature not of Earth but of the sky
  In the fair dower of beauty that it brings.

5 Behold! the chemist, how with subtlest
      cunning
  Fetching forth pureness from impurity;
  Foul it goes in;—a touch, and swiftly
      running
  All is celestial white and clarity.

6 Repeat St. i.

462. GONE BEFORE. *St. Luke viii. 42.*
(Willie, James, John, and Grandpapa.)

1 Thou cam'st, Death, to us again and again,
  Filling our eyes with tears, our hearts
      with pain;
  As out of cradles and " the old arm chair,"
  Thou ledst our lov'd ones down thy unseen
      stair.

2 But ah! Thou wast the ambassador of
      Love;
  Didst not lead down but up to realms above;
  Thou stoppedst but their faint and labouring
      breath;
  The Lord of Life o'er-matched thee, O
      Death!

3 Thou cam'st, Death, to our home again
      and again,   [pain;
  Filling our eyes with tears, our hearts with
  As out of cradles and " the old arm chair,"
  Thou ledst our lov'd ones down thy unseen
      stair.

4 Away! Away! on mighty gleaming wings
  Each soul redeem'd his angel to God brings;
  Thou marr'd'st no more, O Death, than the
      poor dust,
  And that the Soul will claim again we trust.

5 Thou cam'st, Death, to our home again
      and again,   [pain;
  Filling our eyes with tears, our hearts with
  As out of cradles and " the old arm chair,"
  Thou ledst our lov'd ones down thy unseen
      stair.

463. ROSES ON OUR FAMILY GRAVES IN BLACKBURN CEMETERY. 6s.
St. Matt. xiv. 14.

1 Roses, bright'ning our graves,—
  Red as the blood that saves;
  Sweet messages ye bring,
  Yea, make our hearts to sing;
  Ruddying 'neath Summer's breath
  Symbol ye to our Faith,
  Of great life-words He spake
  Tenderly for our sake.

2 Roses, bright'ning our graves,—
  Red as the blood that saves;
  Glist'ning in the soft rain,—
  Yours are tears bring no pain;
  Ye in the sunshine smile—
  Lo! smiles that know no guile;
  To bruised hearts such charm
  As e'en Griefs stings disarm.

3 Roses, bright'ning our graves,—
  Red as the blood that saves;
  Your buds full sweetly blow
  As tho' it were to show
  BLOWN FLOWERS ON OTHER SIDE,
  Our faithlessness to chide;
  To fade—how tenderly!
  Exhaling fragrantly.

4 Roses, bright'ning our graves,—
  Red as the blood that saves;
  Alas! we still must weep
  O'er lov'd ones here who sleep;

ROSES ON OUR FAMILY GRAVES IN BLACKBURN CEMETERY

But Hope's tears, like yours pure,
The more our hearts assure,
That their dust here is kept
By Him, on Earth, who wept.
5 Roses, bright'ning our graves—
Red as the blood that saves;

Ye speak home to our hearts
With art that knows no arts;
For ye our graves illume,
Robbing them of their gloom;
And ye lift thoughts Above,
To Garden of His love.

11. Praise, Prayer, and Season-Thanksgiving.

A godly peasant home in Scotland: 1824 onward.

Our home consisted of a "but" and a "ben" and a "mid room," or chamber, called the "closet." The one end was my mother's domain, and served all the purposes of dining-room and kitchen and parlour, besides containing two large wooden erections, called by our Scotch peasantry "box beds," not holes in the wall, as in cities, but grand, big, airy beds, adorned with many-coloured counterpanes, and hung with natty curtains, showing the skill of the mistress of the house. The other end was my father's workshop, filled with five or six "stocking frames," whirring with the constant action of five or six pairs of busy hands and feet; and producing right genuine hosiery for the merchants at Hawick and Dumfries. The "closet" was a very small apartment betwixt the other two, having room only for a bed, a little table, and a chair, with a diminutive window shedding diminutive light on the scene. This was the Sanctuary of that cottage home. Thither daily, and oftentimes a day, generally after each meal, we saw our father retire, and "shut to the door;" and we children got to understand by a sort of spiritual instinct (for the thing was too sacred to be talked about) that prayers were being poured out there for us, as of old by the High Priest within the vail, in the Most Holy Place. We occasionally heard the pathetic echoes of a trembling voice pleading as if for life, and we learned to slip out and in past that door on tiptoe, not to disturb the holy colloquy. The outside world might not know, but we knew, whence came that happy light as of a new-born smile, that always was dawning on my father's face; it was a reflection from the Divine Presence, in the consciousness of which he lived. Never in temple or cathedral, on mountain or in glen, can I hope to feel that the Lord God is more near, more visibly walking and talking with men, than under that humble cottage roof of thatch and oaken wattle. Though everything else in religion were by some unthinkable catastrophe to be swept out of memory, or blotted from my understanding, my soul would wander back to those early scenes, and shut itself up once again in that Sanctuary Closet, and, hearing still the echoes of those cries to God, would hurl back all doubt with the victorious appeal, "He walked with God, why may not I?"—John G. Paton, *Missionary to the New Hebrides: an Autobiography* (1889), *pp.* 10-12.

PRAYER.

464. PRAYER. 7s.

"Praying always."—Ephesians vi. 18.
"Pray without ceasing."—1 Thessalonians
v. 17.

1 For the praise that we may bring,
 For the thanks that we may sing ;
Lord, we bless Thy gracious Name,
And the privilege would claim ;
Making " grave sweet melody,"
Like to the redeem'd on High ;
 But, Lord, threefold thanks for Prayer —
 The heart's white-wing'd messenger.

2 Joy—must sing, with a full heart ;
 Peace—its deepest rest impart ;
Love—rejoices most in praise ;
Hope—basks in its sunny rays ;
Faith is valiant and is strong
As it sets its fears to song :
 Yet, Lord, threefold thanks for Prayer—
 Loving Saviour's minister.

3 When the heart is bruis'd and sore,
 Sin prevailing more and more ;
When the waves of sorrow dash
And all things we trusted crash ;
When help needed, none is there,
O how priceless then is Prayer !
 Yea, Lord, threefold thanks for Prayer—
 Of all blessings harbinger.

4 When the mystery of things
 Leaden darkness o'er us flings ;
When the tempter doth assail,
And his darts have pierc'd our mail ;
When in helplessness we lie,
And can only moan or sigh ;
 Then, Lord, threefold thanks for Prayer —
 Darkest things interpreter.

5 When the body sick and low
 Makes the soul like sickness know ;
When with weak and wav'ring will
Unrest doth the bosom fill ;
Thou Who break'st not bruisèd reed,
How doth prayer our succour speed !
 O Lord, threefold thanks for Prayer—
 'Twixt both worlds, blest traveller.

6 When some testing crisis comes,
 That our destiny up-sums ;
When upon us there doth lour
Our whole life's decisive hour ;
When to choose right, we must dare,
O how luminous is prayer !
 Therefore threefold thanks for Prayer—
 In Faith's battles arbiter.

7 When the world is like to win,
 Conscience heard not 'midst its din :
When Earth's joys with syren spell
Seek our graver thoughts to quell ;
And we yearn to burst the chain,
Flee to prayer we must amain ;
 Dear, Lord, threefold thanks for Prayer—
 Strong 'gainst ev'ry sophister.

8 When on this side, we would know
 How in holiness to grow ;
And upon this sinful Earth
Reach full stature of " new birth;"
Holy Ghost, our hearts possess ;
Fill us with all Righteousness ;
 And, Lord, threefold thanks for Prayer,
 Free—always—and everywhere.

9 Prayer—that breathes serener air ;
 Prayer—that lightens every care ;
Prayer—that strengthens when in pain ;
Prayer—that snaps our strongest chain ;
Prayer that comforts when we sigh ;
Prayer that brings home by-and-bye ;
 Thanks, Lord, threefold thanks for Prayer,
 Of our soul's life register.

465. THE WRESTLING AT JABBOK. 8,7.
Genesis xxxii.

1 Jacob, Lord, by Jabbok wrestled ;
  Wrestled until break of day ;
While men in their calm sleep nestled,
  God! He met Thee in the way ;
He the power of prayer must prove,
Wrestling with Incarnate Love.

2 Half of Earth, Lord, half of Heaven ;
  Was the wrestling of that night ;
Strangest conflict ere was given,
  Man to put his God to flight ;
" Let me go " — Thy pleading word ;
Vain, till Thou hadst blest him, Lord!

3 Thy saint, Lord, by Jabbok wrestled ;
  Wrestled until break of day ;
While men in their calm sleep nestled,
  God! He met Thee in the way ;
He, the power of prayer must prove,
Wrestling with Incarnate Love.

4 Victor in the mystic striving,
  Ne'ertheless he wounded was ;
His importunance forgiving,
  Yet Thy hand did o'er him pass ;
Touching sinew till he halts,
Lest too high his triumph vaults.

5 Thy saint, Lord, by Jabbok wrestled ;
  Wrestled until break of day ;
While men in their calm sleep nestled,
  God! He met Thee in the way ;
He, the power of prayer must prove,
Wrestling with Incarnate Love.

6 Thou, soul, to Thy Jabbok led,
  Would this wrestling thou would'st dare!
Leaving, yearningly, thy bed,
  Sspending nights in anguish'd prayer ;
" On my strength lay hold," saith God,
Ev'n as when this Earth He trod.

436. SUSTAINED PRAYER. 8s.
St. Luke xi. 12.

1 O Lord, I read with prickèd heart, [pray ;
  How Thou did'st through the long night
And how Thy saints let nothing thwart,
  Their sacred prayer-hours, day by day.

2 Alas ! O Lord, I find it hard
  Truly to pray for one half-hour ;
'Gainst wand'ring I keep watch and ward,
  But soon—too soon—temptations lour.

3 O Lord, I read with prickèd heart, [pray ;
  How Thou didst through the long night
And how Thy saints let nothing thwart,
  Their holy prayer-hours, day by day.

4 Teach me to pray, Lord ! and bestow
  Thy Holy Spirit's chastity ;   [glow,
Control my thoughts, make my heart
  Yea, hold me in Thy sanctity.

5 O Lord, I read with prickèd heart, [pray ;
  How Thou did'st through the long night
And how Thy saints let nothing thwart,
  Their sacred prayer-hours, day by day.

6 Shew me myself, and all I need ;
  Shew me Thyself, and all Thou hast ;
" Thou wilt not break the bruisèd reed ;"
  Thy mercy as Thy love is vast.

7 O Lord, I read with prickèd heart, [pray ;
  How Thou did'st through the long night
And how Thy saints let nothing thwart,
  Their sacred prayer-hours, day by day.

8 Shew me the riches of Thy Book ;
  Shew me each promise faithful kept ;
Turn on me Thy heart-melting look,
  That I may weep as Peter wept.

9 O Lord, I read with prickèd heart, [pray ;
  How Thou did'st through the long night
And how Thy saints let nothing thwart,
  Their sacred prayer-hours, day by day.

10 Give me to know of Pray'r the joy ;
   Give me to know its holy strength ;
   O let not aught my heart decoy,
   That prayer-possessed I be at length.

467. Restraint in Prayer. 8s.
Proverbs iv. 12 ; Micah ii. 7 ; Job xv. 4.

1 I find it hard, O Lord, to pray ;
  This hardness fills me with dismay ;
  For, O my God, were I Thy child
  Within Thy Fold, not on the wild ;
  Sure "Abba Father," swift would come ;
  Not earthly thoughts or thoughts that
      roam.

2 I find it hard, O Lord, to pray ;
  Scarce have my poor words died away,
  Than steals o'er me a strange forgetting;
  Some worldly care my heart besetting ;
  Till 'tis as if I had not pray'd,
  Or ne'er my burden on Thee laid.

3 I find it hard, O Lord, to pray ;
  Idle and vain this to gainsay ;
  Alas ! my God, 'twere counterfeiting
  My own benumbèd conscience cheating
  To go to Thee wearing a mask,
  And not desiring what I ask.

4 I find it hard, O Lord, to pray;
  My weary case 'fore Thee I lay ;
  O wilt Thou touch me with Thy fire,
  E'en if it be in holy ire ;
  That quicken'd by Thy Spirit's might,
  I may o'ercome in this sore light.

5 I find it hard, O Lord, to pray ;
  My nay is yea, my yea is nay ;
  I cannot steady heart or eye,
  Know not the sweet pain of a "cry ;"
  Feel as tho' all were words, words, words,
  Less prayerful than the notes of birds.

6 I find it hard, O Lord, to pray ;
  For sin and Satan me waylay ;
  I throw myself upon my knees,
  But a cold heart my prayers will freeze ;
  Forgive, O Gentle One, forgive,
  Thy "Spirit of adoption" give.

7 I find it hard, O Lord, to pray ;
  I lack the graces that up-stay ;
  Alas ! there come world, flesh, and devil,
  All the distracting powers of evil ;
  O gracious Saviour, of Thy power
  Pour out on me Thy Spirit's dower.

8 I find it hard, O Lord, to pray: [ray ?
  Wilt Thou send forth Thy quick'ning
  That shining on Thy Holy Word,
  Thy promises may me afford
  Fuel to feed my Love's low flame,
  And bow me low in meek-fac'd shame.

9 I find it hard, O Lord, to pray ;
  Before myself I stand at bay ,
  I know, I feel how much I need ;
  How I owe all to Thee did'st bleed ;
  For a brief moment comes a glow,
  The next as 'twere a fall of snow.

10 I find it hard, O Lord, to pray ;
   O God, my God, Thy power display !
   Thou Who Thyself on mountain's heights,
   Pray'dst on and on through the long
       nights,
   Bestow Thy staying grace on me,
   To prove Prayer's blessed agony.

11 I find it hard, O Lord, to pray ;
   Wilt Thou my tempters far affray ?
   Be they within, be they without ;
   Born of my fears, or born of doubt ;
   Control my will, lift up my heart,
   Thine Own sweet secret, Lord, impart.

12 I find it hard, O Lord, to pray ;
   For ever I do lose my way :
   Lo ! darkness comes, distrust, distress ;
   Yea, comes distracting wilfulness ;
   Lord Christ, take Thou my heart of stone,
   Subdue, and make it all Thine own.

"PRAYED, AND SPAKE THE SELFSAME WORDS."

1 I find it hard, O Lord, to pray;
   This hardness fills me with dismay;
For, O my God, were I Thy Child
Within Thy Fold, not on the wild
Sure "Abba Father," swift would come;
Not earthly thoughts or thoughts that
   roam.

468. "PRAYED, AND SPAKE THE SELF-
SAME WORDS" (GREEK): *St. Mark xiv. 39.*
7s.

1 *Prayed and spake the self-same words:*
O the cheer that this affords!
To the soul that oft may be
In its dark Gethsemane,
Wordless all as though struck dumb:
For no longer will words come,
Or will come but brokenly,
Chok'd with moaning or lorn cry.

2 Thus, O Christ, proud Satan's hour
O'er Thy spirit once did lour,
When, in dark Gethsemane
Prone, in deepest agony;
Thou, the cup of trembling held,
While Thy mortal flesh rebell'd:
Prayed, and spake the selfsame words:
O the cheer that this affords.

3 Even so, O Lord, to-day,
When we more and more would pray;
When wave-tost and tempest-driven
We lift up sad eyes to Heaven;
When alone, we sadly moan,
Tearless as insensate stone;
O the cheer that this affords!
Prayed, and spake the selfsame words.

4 Pity us, O Lord, and see
In our dark Gethsemane,
When some looming dread event
Fills us with astonishment;
And alas! we can but cry
"O my God, let it pass by!"
Prayed, and spake the selfsame words:
O the cheer that this affords.

5 In our lone Gethsemane
Helpless, Lord, we cry to Thee;
Still again, and yet again
Quick comes back our poor refrain;
The oft-utter'd same request,
Of our aching, humbled breast;
O the cheer that this affords!
Prayed, and spake the self-same words.

6 At Thy feet, my life I lay,
Even though Thou should'st me slay;
I my sin can never tell—
For it is unspeakable;
O my God, I moan to Thee,
Wilt Thou mercy have on me?
Prayed, and spake the self-same words:
O the cheer that this affords.

7 Yet, Lord, wilt Thou give to me
In my dread Gethsemane;
When some threat'ning trouble near,
I ask succour while I fear
Thine Own Spirit me to bless,
With Thine Own meek "Ne'ertheless?"
O the cheer that this affords!
Prayed, and spake the self-same words.

469.   THE "SHUT DOOR."   8s.

St. Matt. vi. 6.

1 WHEN worldly cares and troubles press
And head and heart feel sore distress;
O God, my God! my "shut door" brings
Such calm as taketh out their stings;
Thy Hand—like mother's on my brow—
Me blesses even as I bow.

2 When path of duty hidden is,
And I know not or that or this;
When as the Night without its stars—
Darkness my going on debars;
Lord, to my "shut door" I retreat;
Light beameth from the Mercy-seat.

3 When in the fierce strain of the world,
  Sharp, fiery darts at me are hurl'd;
  Which tempt me still to acquiesce
  In ways I dare not ask Thee bless ;
  Ah! In my "shut door" I get power
  To stand firm in the evil hour.

4 When by long sickness "ta'en aside,"
  I, worn and weary, must abide ;
  Dread thoughts will come and me oppress
  As I sit in my loneliness ;
  But for my "shut door" I should be
  Plung'd darkly in despondency.

5 When by the stress of circumstance
  I can see no deliverance ;
  When Faith's lamp burneth dim and low,
  That I a doubter almost go;
  There comes to me Thy "still small voice"
  And in my "shut door" I rejoice.

6 Lord, when Thy Face upon me shines,
  And my heart on Thy heart reclines ;
  When I, within, have "perfect peace"
  And from all turmoil sweet release;
  In my "shut door" without alloy
  I find me singing out my joy.

7 I thank Thee for the House of Prayer ;
  By grace, I will "forsake" it ne'er;
  I thank Thee, too, for Family-prayer
  That sanctifies Home's daily care ;
  Thrice thanks for "shut door" where alone
  Each his own secrets maketh known.

470. PRAYER IS THE DEW OF FAITH.
MRS. L. H. SIGOURNEY. 6.7.7.7.

1 Thessalonians v. 17.

1 *Prayer is the dew of Faith :*
  True what this sweet Singer saith ;
  Only thus shall we keep strong ;
  Only thus sing Faith's bright song.

2 *Prayer is the dew of Faith :*
  Gently falls as on parch'd heath ;
  Brightening the sere and green
  With touch of beauty between.

3 *Prayer is the dew of Faith :*
  Bringing oft sweet after-math ;
  Freshening, yea vivifying ;
  Quickening e'en what is dying.

4 *Prayer is the dew of Faith :*
  Coming by the Spirit's breath;
  God of grace, Thy grace fulfil,
  Moulding our will to Thy will.

5 *Prayer is the dew of Faith :*
  True what this sweet Singer saith ;
  Only thus shall we keep strong ;
  Only thus sing Faith's bright song.

471. PRAYER FOR PURITY.
Ephesians v. 8 ; 2 Cor. iv. 6. 9.9.8.8.

1 Lo! The DAWN in unsullied whiteness—
  Shadow of the Almighty's brightness ;
  Far-streams along the Eastern skies,
  "Bringing all Heav'n before mine eyes."

2 Seem to flash - as in great days olden—
  "Walls and towers" of JERUSALEM GOLDEN;
  Yea, I catch gleam of angel wings
  Speeding to Earth in burning rings.

3 Light of light, wilt, for Jesus' merit
  Make luminous my aw'd spirit ?
  That walking closer with my God
  My faith be aye a shining road.

4 Alas ! Morn's skies are swift beclouded—
  Ev'n the imperial sun is shrouded ;
  Thou the UNSHADOW'D, keep me near,
  Then cloud or sun, I shall not fear.

5 Child of the Light - by Thy grace given
  I yearn for riddance of Sin's leaven ;
  O Christ of God, in gentle might,
  Speak the great word, "*Let there be light.*"

6 The purity of this fair morning -
  Celestial glory Earth adorning ;
  Be it with me, Lord, all the day,
  Nor ever suffer me to stray.

7 Lo! The DAWN in unsullied whiteness —
 Shadow of the Almighty's brightness ;
 Far-streams along the Eastern skies
 " Bringing all Heav'n before mine eyes."

472. *" No more, no more."*—*2 Cor. xii. 2.*

Os.

In these churches Philip was often surprised by such an abundance of spiritual consolation that, unable any longer to endure so great a fire of love, he was forced to cry out " No more, Lord, no more," and throwing himself on the ground, he used to roll up a it, as though he had not strength to endure the vehement affection which he felt in his heart; and again he would vehemently cry out, " I cannot bear so much, my Lord, I cannot bear so much, Lord : for see I am dying of it."—BACCI's Life of S. Philip of Neri of the Oratory.

1 " No more, no more, O Lord ! "
 Thy LOVE, like flaming sword,
 Cleaveth my heart in twain
 With a delicious pain :
 Withhold, O Christ ! withhold !—
 Forgive if I'm too bold.

2 " No more, no more, O Lord ! "
 Or double grace afford :
 My very flesh cries out
 Even as loud I shout ;
 Thy gifts, O Lord, refrain
 Or 'fore Thee I am slain.

3 " No more, no more, O Lord ! "
 Thou seest how each chord
 Of harp of thousand strings
 Touch'd by Thy Spirit, flings
 Me into ecstasy ;
 Yea Lord, I die, I die.

4 " No more, no more, O Lord ! "
 Thou of all Heav'n ador'd ;
 Too shallow is this heart
 To fill so great a part ;
 Lighten, my God, the strain
 Of this delicious pain.

5 " No more, no more, O Lord ! "
 Till I have cross'd Death's ford ;
 When by Thy merit sole
 I shall Thee full extol ;
 My heart enlarg'd, and I
 Citizen of the sky.

6 " No more, no more, O Lord ! "
 Until in sweet accord
 Body and soul are one
 After the great " Well done,"
 Upward I then shall soar,
 Surceas'd " No more, no more."

473. *" LUX IN TENEBRIS."*

(On a painting by Sir Noel Paton, engraved by James Fa d.)

1 My way is long, and rough, and dark ;
 Crags frown above it, steep and stark ;
 And ghostly shapes the darkness haunt,
 That ev'n the boldest needs must daunt ;
 But soft as day-dawn on the hills,
 The Lord Christ His great word fulfils,
 " Lux in tenebris" (" Light in darkness.")

2 From Thee, my God, I had stray'd far ;
 With Thee and Truth at strenuous war ;
 Against Thy strife of Love I strove,
 And still away from Thee would move ;
 I stifled conscience, dimm'd Thy light ;
 In very truth a child of Night ;
 " Redde Lucem" (" Restore the light.")

3 How long Thy patience ! and how sweet
 In foll'wing my departing feet :
 How slow Thy wrath 'gainst me to burn !
 How tender, seeking my return !
 How conquering Thy gentle might !
 Thou still did'st shine and did'st not smite:
 " Lux in tenebris."

4 I praise Thee, Lord, that thus it is ;
 I praise thee, Lord, for hope of bliss ;
 Still, darkness comes upon my path ;
 Still, throbs and stings, dread of Thy wrath;
 But guiding, guarding, left or right,
 Gracious Thou hold'st me, child of Light :
 " Lux in tenebris."

5 I lay in pain upon my bed,
   While thro' the Vale of Shadows led ;
   O then how sweet with morning rise,
   To turn my heavy-laden eyes
   To Jesus, standing nimbus-crown'd,
   With a lost maiden He has found
     "*Lux in tenebris.*"

474.   FAMILY PRAYER.   8s.

Jeremiah x. 25.

1 HOMES of Britain! Stately, lowly,
   None in the wide world more PURE ;
  Kept of Thee, O God Most Holy,
   By Thy covenant strong and sure ;
  That Thy blessing still commands,
  Where a Family-altar stands.

2 Homes of Britain! Stately, lowly,
   None in the wide world more BRIGHT ;
  Kept of Thee, O God, Most Holy,
   Lum'nous thro' Thy shining light ;
  For to shine Thou giv'st commands
  Where a Family-altar stands.

3 Homes of Britain! Stately, lowly,
   None in the wide world more GLAD ;
  Kept of Thee, O God, Most Holy,
   Sanctifying ev'n the sad ;
  For Thy joy Thou dost command
  Where doth Family-altar stand.

4 Homes of Britain! Stately, lowly,
   None in the wide world more BLEST ;
  Kept of Thee, O God, Most Holy,
   As on Thy true word we rest ;
  For Thy grace Thou dost command
  Where doth Family-altar stand.

5 Homes of Britain! Christian homes!
   Still may prayer in you abound!
   Daily as the sweet call comes,
    May all on their knees be found!
  Foremost nation 'midst all Lands,
  Where the Family-altar stands.

475. CHRIST JESUS MY CRUCIFIED LOVE.
Galatians v. 24.   8s. *Beato Angelico Da Fiesole.*

1 *Christ Jesus! my crucified Love,* [move;
   Thy red wounds hardest hearts might
   Much more this heart, of grace new-born,
   'Fore them must be with anguish torn.

2 *Christ Jesus! my crucified Love,*
   E'en now upon Thy Throne Above,
   Thou bearest radiant scars, nor yet
   Thy "glorious shame" doth e'er forget.

3 *Christ Jesus! my crucified Love,*
   My love enable me to prove ;
   Going about still doing good,
   Under the shadow of Thy ROOD.

4 *Christ Jesus! my crucified Love,*
   Ne'er may I seek from Thee to rove ;
   Or dark, or rough, or long the road,
   Still would I go where Thou hast trod.

5 *Christ Jesus! my crucified love,*
   Give me to strive as Thy saints strove;
   With sin without, with sin within,
   That I the final conquest win.

6 *Repeat St.* 1.

476.   THE ALL-RULING FATHER.
Romans viii. 15.   7s.

1 THOU, "my Lord, my God," to me
  Givest "glorious liberty ;"
  Now I see, I feel, I know
  Thou all things dost guide below ;
  NOTHING THAT THOU HAST NOT SEEN ;
  Nothing trivial, nothing mean ;
  Nothing dark or involute,
  Ruling by laws absolute ;
  But a Father's heart o'er all
  That marks ev'n a sparrow's fall.

2 Thou, "my Lord, my God," to me
  Givest "glorious liberty ;"
  I can trust Thee now, my God,
  Yea, when Thou dost wield Thy rod;

Ev'ry stroke Thou dost inflict
Gracious is — aye, when most strict ;
Prescient is Thy large forethought
Into gifts and graces wrought ;
Far above our poor contriving
As above our wilder'd striving.

3 Thou, "my Lord, my God," to me
Givest " glorious liberty ; "
Thou to me a Father art
When to Thee I yield my heart ;
Sovran Lord, but all in love
As the end doth still approve ;
Silent, yet all-hearing aye
Who their burdens on Thee stay ;
Thou hast spoken by Thy Son ;
Thou hast promis'd His "Well done."

4 Thou, " my Lord, my God," to me
Givest " glorious liberty ; "
Oft like Joseph speaking " rough"
Thine Thou givest sharp rebuff ;
Disappointments sore, and pain
And such pressure, and such strain
As their heart-strings seem to break
And their FAITH and HOPE to check ;
But thro' all, Thine come to feel
Darkest cloud will light reveal.

5 Thou, "my Lord, my God," to me
Givest " glorious liberty ; "
Wilt Thou keep me thus serene
As upon Thee still I lean ?
Wilt Thou with Thy strength me nerve
That I ne'er shall from Thee swerve ?
Wilt Thou build me up in trust
Thou dark problems wilt adjust ?
Father, hear—I am Thy Child ;
Keep me near Thee undefil'd.

477. WINTER. 8s.
Genesis viii. 22.

1 TEMPESTS of wind and rain are here,
Cold is the rain, yea cold is all ;
Darkest, saddest time o' the year ;
Winter reigns in wild carnival.

2 The days are short, the nights are long,
The ways are rough, the skies are dim ;
Save Robin Red-breast, the birds' song
Is hush'd ; stars shine as seraphim.

3 Far over street, and field, and hill,
Oft falleth the snow's ghostly white ;
The East-wind, keen-tooth'd, works its will
And Earth's manifold life doth smite.

4 Rich folks sit by their fire-side blaze,
Shielded from harms others befall ;
The poor their plaintive voices raise,
And Thou, O God, doth hear their call.

5 For, " God o'er all," 'tis not by chance
Cometh successive Seasons four ;
Thou rulest o'er all circumstance,
Thou carest or for rich or poor.

6 Tempests and winds, and snows and cold,
Thou sendest in unchanging love ;
Thy goodness cannot half be told,
As Thou dost onward all things move.

478. SPRING.
Genesis vii. 22 ; i. 14. 8s.

1 THE clouds are passing from the sky
Over East and West gray turn'd to blue ;
Save for white spots that tenderly,
Like flocks of sheep, come into view.

2 Like flocks of sheep, come into view
Holding the treasure of soft rains ;
The Earth is quickening anew,
Life strong-throbbing in all her veins.

3 Life strong-throbbing in all her veins,
Shewing in field and wood and wold ;
Daisies are wearing their red-tipt stains,
And butter-cups their shining gold.

4 And butter-cups their shining gold,
Amid the grass where couch the cows ;
The shepherds lead their flocks to fold,
And active all within the house.

5 And active all within the house,
For, lo ! the SPRING bright dances in ;
And none may laggard be or drowze
But the Year's tasks of love begin.

6 But the Year's tasks of love begin,
  Giv'n, Lord, by Thee, to each and all;
  Keep us, we pray, from ev'ry sin;
  Month in, month out, nought ill befal.

7 Month in, month out, nought ill befal;
  The Winter past the green Earth smiles,
  And seems on all of us to call,
  Strength'ning for duty, sweet'ning toils.

8 Strength'ning for duty, sweet'ning toils;
  God for the Cov'nant, cov'nant keep!
  Protect us 'mid the World's soft guiles,
  Be near us waking or asleep.

9 Be near us waking or asleep;
  With Thine Own "perfect peace" us fill.
  It is the Spring! mild South winds sweep,
  And hark! the cuckoo on the hill.

479. Summer—A Metrical Medley.
  Psalm lxxiv. 17.

1. The early trees are leafing;
  The birds their nests are reefing;
  The fragrant flowers are blowing,
  For bees full honey stowing;
  The hay's green waves are swaying,
  The South Wind o'er them playing;
  Brooks 'neath the greenwood shewing,
  In shine and shadow flowing;
  Skies one dome of flawless blue;
  Air as crystal-clear as dew.
    Summer is here! Summer is here!
    Lord of the Seasons! Thou art near.

2. Wealth of bloom
      the May decking;
    Golden sunshine
      all flecking;
    Lambs running
      on the meadows,
    Sportive with
      their own shadows;
    Cows amid
      the grass resting
    Look with large eyes
      unmolesting;
    Children on banks
      glad reclining,
    Daisies fair
      with rushes twining;
    Young hearts
      in lanes courting;
    Love and Purity
      consorting.
    Summer is here! Summer is here!
    Lord of the Seasons: Thou art near.

3. The corn-fields are yellowing,
  Wheat and barley mellowing;
  Wains are barn-ward creaking
  As tho' our thanks bespeaking
  For coming Autumn golden,
  Fulfilling cov'nant olden;
  Men's hearts a-gladdening
  Lifting off their saddening;
  All intermingling voices
  Telling how Earth rejoices:
    Summer is here! Summer is here!
    Lord of the Seasons! Thou art near.

4. All these riches thus outpour'd,
  Be Thou Lord, by all ador'd;
  Fill'd with joy, fill'd with brightness,
  Help us walk in robes of whiteness;
  While the glad birds are winging
  Tune Thou our hearts to singing;
  While flowers are incense sending
  May our praise and prayer be blending;
  While the bees are going, coming
  Let us work unite with humming:
    Summer is here! Summer is here!
    Lord of the Seasons! Thou art near.

480. Harvest Festival; or, Joy in Harvest. 7s.

1. God of Harvest, from of old
  Thy great Cov'nant is extolled;
  Summer! Winter! Autumn! Spring!
  Still unfailing Thou dost bring:
  Now before Thee, Lord, we come,
  Joyous o'er our Harvest-home.

2. Thou didst watch the ploughèd field
   That the scatter'd seed might yield;
   Clouds and dews, and shine and shower,
   Thou didst give in plenteous dower :
   Now before Thee, Lord, we come,
   Joyous o'er our Harvest-home.
3. O it is a beauteous sight
   To see 'neath Thy gladd'ning light;
   Golden corn and mellow'd wheat
   Laid abundant at our feet:
   Now before Thee, Lord, we come,
   Joyous o'er our Harvest-home.
4. Yards and barns are brimming o'er;
   Hold for man and beast full store;
   Lord, wilt Thou receive the praise,
   That with bounding hearts we raise?
   Now before Thee, Lord, we come,
   Joyous o'er our Harvest-home.
5. But as we united call
   At our Harvest-festival ;
   Fill us with heart-searching thought
   For the little we have wrought:
   As before Thee, Lord, we come,
   Joyous o'er our Harvest-home.
6. Lord, alas! how few the sheaves
   That our year's work with Thee leaves !
   And yet, Sun of Righteousness,
   Thou hast shone on us to bless!
   Now before Thee, Lord, we come,
   Joyous o'er our Harvest-home.
7. God of Harvest, from of old
   Is Thy faithfulness extolled;
   Summer! Winter! Autumn! Spring!
   Still unfailing Thou dost bring:
   Now before Thee, Lord, we come,
   Joyous o'er our Harvest-home.

481.   FLOODS IN HARVEST.   6s.
(Composed in view of desolating floods in Lancashire and in Yorkshire and Cheshire, in mid-harvest.)
Jeremiah vi. 21-25.

1 The skies are thick with clouds,
   The clouds are black with rain ;
   The fields are drench'd with floods ;
   Bogging the lab'ring wain ;
   O God ! why all this waste ?
   Wilt not to rescue haste ?

2 The Land laugh'd to the sun ;
   The sun laugh'd to the Land ;
   Wav'd harvest, gold and dun,
   But now all sodden stand ;
   O God ! why all this waste?
   Hear us, O Lord, and haste.

3 Plenty for man and beast,
   Lies 'neath these pit'less showers ;
   North — South and West and East,
   The "great rain" all devours ;
   O God ! to us make haste,
   Arrest this frightful waste.

4 Is't as in days of old,
   That we do Thee forsake ?
   Is't as of Israel told,
   Thy COVENANT we break ?
   Save us with gracious haste
   To "sanctify" this waste.

5 We would, Lord, lay us down
   In penitence and shame ;
   We have deserv'd Thy frown ;
   Forgive for Thy Great Name !
   O God ! 'tis awful waste ;
   To help and save, make haste.

6 Behold, O God, Thy "sign"
   Belting the tumbling skies ;
   Ah, Thou art still benign ;
   We lift our sw'mming eyes;
   O Lord ! look on this waste,
   And to our succour haste.

482.   LATE AUTUMN.   7s.
1 Lo! mantled green drop the leaves
   Littering beneath the eaves ;
   Robin hops on window-sill,
   Picking strewn crumbs with deft bill:
   Livid sky and low horizons;
   All the fens distilling poisons:
       Late Autumn 'tis in the North ;
       Heralds of Winter, race forth.

2 Ah! "In huts where poor men lie"
   Who may tell the misery?
   Toils unceasing, wages scant,
   Ever face-to-face with WANT;
   Clamorous "little ones" and wife,
   Giving edge to the sore strife:
      Late Autumn 'tis in the North;
      Heralds of Winter, race forth.

3 Ye to whom the Seasons bring
   Naught of struggle or of sting;
   As ye count your blessings o'er
   Kindly think of God's own poor;
   Christ is near; and lo! HE knows
   Hearts from which compassion flows:
      Late Autumn 'tis in the North;
      Heralds of Winter, race forth.

4 It is not true life, to live
   "Three score years" mere fugitive:
   Fill them with kind thought and deed;
   Let your hearts for suff'ring bleed;
   For by light'ning others' cares,
   Ye 'receive' Christ unawares:
      Late Autumn 'tis in the North;
      Heralds of Winter, race forth.

5 Kindness still goes far to hush
   Waves of passion as they rush;
   Wild is the revolt 'gainst those
   Who their eyes shut to POOR's woes;
   Brothers, forth and know the worst.
   Lest upon ye vengeance burst:
      Late Autumn 'tis in the North;
      Heralds of Winter, race forth.

483.   EARTH IS NO DESERT DREAR.
7.8.7.8.

1 O beautiful is our Earth,
   Though shadows of blackness mar it!
   O radiant is our mirth,
   Though tremblings of sadness jar it!

2 As grows the rose on the thorn,
   Is the blessing above the wrath;
   For Jesus the curse hath borne,
   And lifted the shadow of death.

3 I would not live alway here,
   My Home is in Heav'n above;
   But Earth is no "desert drear,"
   A-glow in the light of His love.

4 O beautiful is our Earth,
   Though shadows of blackness mar it!
   O radiant is our mirth,
   Though tremblings of sadness jar it.

434.   EVERY Fête HAS A TO-MORROW.--
Alexander Vinet. Eccl. xi. 9. 8.8.7.7.
1. *Every fête has a to-morrow:*
   See thou sow not seeds of sorrow;
   Seeds that spring from bitter roots,
   Fecund with all baleful fruits.

2. True and pure be all thy pleasures
   As thy conscience to thee measures;
   If from Him thou would'st withdraw
   Know they're evil - stand in awe.

3. *Every fête has a to-morrow:*
   Light of joy will shadow borrow;
   Action base, and the base thought
   Heart flee—by THE SPIRIT wrought.

4. O be not by FAIR sin "taken!"
   'Tis asp, be it from thee shaken;
   Lures to tempt—tempts to betray,
   Yea, thy very soul to slay.

5. *Every fête has a to-morrow*
   That doth pierce 'twixt "joint and marrow";
   Never let thy retrospect
   Thy heart growing cold detect.

6. God the Lord doth will thy gladness;
   Seeks not Thou should'st walk in sadness;
   Only, that as "child of light"
   Thou live ever in His sight.

7. *Every fête has a to-morrow:*
   Yet thy soul this need not harrow;
   God, thy God, benignant is,
   Brightening thy way to bliss.

12. National Hymns.

485.   For our England.

Deuteronomy iv. 7.

1 God of our Fathers! Thou hast blest
This island-empire of the West;
From age to age inviolate,
Still keep it strong in high estate;
Home of the free, and free-men born;
Charter, ne'er by proud tyrant torn.

2 God of our Fathers! Thou hast blest
This island-empire of the West;
Invaders vain their flags unfurl'd,
Our England from her shores them hurl'd;
It was not luck, it was not chance,
Preserv'd our great inheritance.

3 God of our Fathers! Thou hast blest
This island-empire of the West;
Early Thy Gospel shed its light;
Early the Cross approv'd its might;
And now no land beneath the sun
For Jesus Christ so broadly won.

4 God of our Fathers! Thou hast blest
This island-empire of the West;
Never has England wanted men
To take the field, or hold the pen;
Great deeds of finest daring done;
Supremest books, surpass'd of none.

5 God of our Fathers! Thou hast blest
This island-empire of the West;
Bards! Thinkers! Workers! aye renown'd,
And by the round world's homage crown'd;
Thro' Thee, our islands have sent forth,
To mould the forces of the Earth.

6 God of our Fathers! Thou hast blest
This island-empire of the West;
With riches such as beggar Ind,
Or fables in romance we find;
And power to such circumference
As shadows forth Thy Providence.

7 God of our Fathers! Thou hast blest
This island-empire of the West;
Increasing millions speak our tongue
The grandest ever said or sung
May past experience chastise!
Each generation be more wise.

8 God of our Fathers! Thou hast blest
This island-empire of the West;
My country! O may England's might
Stand ever strong to guard the right!
May poverty and crime surcease,
And Heaven lead in the reign of Peace!

486.   For England.

*On reception of Burmah, New Guinea,
South Africa, recently.*

1 My native Land! I see thee stand
   The mightiest of nations known;
O God! command, with lifted Hand,
   That deathless shall be her renown;
But, Lord, we seek Thee so to bless,
   That we may grow in righteousness.

2 My native land! Noble the band
   That aye have thy great makers been;
Thy sea-wash'd strand, doth still expand,
   Till ne'er was such an empire seen;
O grant, my God, that being great,
   The right we love, the wrong we hate.

3 My native Land! Thou dost demand
   From all thy children—sons and
To understand that like the sand, [daughters
   Which holds in check her tidal waters;
Each shall seek to keep her name,
   Untouch'd of cruelty and blame.

4 My native Land! The reprimand
   By God to His Own Israel spoken;
When with strong Hand, by Moses' wand,
   Proud Egypt's heavy yoke was broken;
Let it still thunder to our heart,
'Thy God has made thee what thou art.'

FOR SAILORS—AFTER A STORM AT SEA.

5 My native Land! I see thee stand
　Mightiest of nations known;
O God! command, with lifted Hand,
　Deathless shall be her renown;
But, Lord, we seek Thee so to bless,
That we may grow in righteousness.

487.　For Sailors.　*Psalm lxv. 5.*　5s.

1 O God of the Land!
　I place in Thy Hand,
　Wife, children and all;
　　Do Thou them safe keep
　　Whilst I'm on the Deep.

2 O God of the Sea,
　I look unto Thee;
　Our ship wilt Thou guard
　As Thou hast declar'd?
　　By day and by night
　　Keep me in Thy sight.

3 O God of the Land!
　Who dost all command,
　May my dear ones still
　Thy good word fulfill;
　　All cares on thee cast,
　　Come quiet or blast.

4 O God of the Sea!
　Look Thou upon me;
　Preserve Thou my lips
　From all profane slips;
　　Temptations beset;
　　I'm apt to forget.

5 O God of the Land!
　Before Thee I stand;
　Me and mine defend,
　All needed help send;
　　At home or abroad,
　　Be Thou still our God.

6 O God of the Sea!
　Our Guardian be;
　Come tempest or calm,
　This shall be our psalm:
　　The Lord He is near,
　　What ill need we fear.

488.　A Christian Sailor's Hymn at Sea.　7s.

1 Sailing on and on all day,
　Sailing on and on all night;
　I am with Thee Lord alway;
　Thou with me, in love and might;
　Come there storm or come there calm,
　Thus I sing my evening psalm:
　　'I with Thee, and Thou with me.'

2 Sailing on and on all day,
　Sailing on and on all night;
　Home and dear ones far away;
　But Thou'rt near them—all is right;
　Come there storm or come there calm,
　Thus I sing my evening psalm;
　　'Thou art near, I will not fear.'

3 Sailing on and on all day,
　Sailing on and on all night;
　Knowing not what happen may,
　Yet Thou knowest—that gives light;
　Come there storm or come there calm,
　Thus I sing my evening psalm:
　　'I with Thee, and Thou with me.'

4 Sailing on and on all day,
　Sailing on and on all night;
　Hard my work, but I obey,
　Ever Lord, as in Thy sight,
　Come there storm, or come their calm,
　Thus I sing my evening psalm:
　　'In Thy sight, thro' day and night.'

5 Sailing on and on all day,
　Sailing on and on all night;
　Thou, O Lord, art still my stay;
　Danger cannot me affright;
　Come there storm or come there calm,
　Thus I sing my evening psalm:
　　'I with Thee, and Thou with me.'

489.　After a Storm at Sea.　*Psalm cvii.* 29-30.　8s.

1 God of my life! God of my life!
Thro' fiercest winds and waves at str'fe;
Thro' week-long fogs in ghostly gloom—
Reverberating thunder's boom;

IN THE "DESIRED HAVEN" SHIPWRECK.

Thou hast us brought back safe to land,
The sea "in hollow of Thy Hand."

2. God of my life! God of my life!
In deepest stress Thy help is rife;
The lab'ring ship's sudden-rent sail,
The quiv'ring masts 'fore driving gale;
Thou hast us brought back safe to land,
The sea "in hollow of Thy Hand."

3. God of my life! God of my life!
As tho' the Cyclone held a knife,
Thy edgèd cold the dim air froze;
Or sleep or food none of us knows;
Yet Thou hast brought us safe to land,
The sea "in hollow of Thy Hand."

4. God of my life! God of my life!
I thought of home, of children, wife;
But land! ev'n when by tempest driv'n,
Shone clear and steady light from Heav'n:
And Thou hast brought us safe to land,
The sea "in hollow of Thy Hand."

490. IN THE "DESIRED HAVEN."
Psalm cvii. 30.

1 From utmost end of Earth I cry,
To Thee O God, my God Most High;
By day and night still onward sped,
Our good ship is safe anchorèd.

2 Lord, Thou hast sent us fav'ring gales;
Lord, Thou hast fill'd our spreading sails;
Lord, Thou hast prosp'rous voyage giv'n,
Aye lighting us with light from Heav'n.

3 O God, my God, I pray that Thou
Would'st hear me as I pray that Thou
On board, on shore, where'er I go,
That I am Thine, help me to show.

4 Alas! too soon, Lord I forget
Mercies and perils I have met;
O wilt Thou keep them in my mind,
That each day grateful may me find.

5 From utmost end of Earth I cry,
To Thee O God, my God Most High;
By day and night still onward sped,
Our good ship is safe anchorèd.

491. THE SEA. 8s.

1 Thou hast a voice, O thou great Sea,
That might be the strong voice of God;
But how dread were man's misery,
If only thus th' Almighty spake;
His soul with terror white should shake,
And look for his uplifted rod.

2 Thund'ring upon a thousand shores,
With pulse-beats, like a human heart;
There comes such cry amidst thy roars
As maketh mortals prostrate bow
A-hushed and awed, with throbbing brow:
For thou, O Sea, thrice-awful art.

3 Not thus, O not thus, God doth speak,
But stilly as in days of old;
Not thus the hardest hearts doth break;
Like breeze of eve He softly breathes—
His vengeful, furbished sword He sheathes,
Is it not in the Gospel told?

4 It is told, O "my Lord, my God,"
And as I turn me to Thy Word
I bring to Thee all my sad load;
Thy voice so sweet, so soft and low,
O let it into my heart go;
Ah! Jesus, Thou art still our Lord!

492. SHIPWRECK. *2 Cor. xi. 25.*
7.7.7.6.9.4.

1 The sea is up, and under
Quick go the shuddering ships;
Loud booms the fire-seam'd thunder;
Sky black as in eclipse;
O Jesu! hear Thy suppliants' cry,
For Thou art nigh.

2 Wave on wave in whiteness breaks,
Weighing down the moaning deck;
And beneath is whisper'd, "Leaks
Gain on us: O vain to check!"
O Jesu! hear Thy suppliant's cry,
For Thou art nigh.

3 Sails and cordage—all are gone;
  Crashing down, the masts o'erwhelm;
 O my God, leave not alone!
  The ship will not obey the helm:
 O Jesu! hear Thy suppliant's cry,
  For Thou art nigh.

4 Vain—ah vain! yet not in vain,
  As near to Heaven by sea as land;
 Lord! to Thee I turn in pain,
  Grasp me with Thy saving hand:
 O Jesu! hear Thy suppliant's cry,
  For Thou art nigh.

193.   THE MINER'S SONG.

    Gen. v. 29; 2 Thess. iii. 10.

DEEP down in the dark and rock-walled Earth,
Where minerals—God's gifts—have their birth;
All lying there through time untold,—
Coal—iron—lead—tin—silver—gold:
We miners work in the lone black night,
Yet oft by grace we're children of light:
  Aye trusting the Lord, tho' danger is nigh,
  Safe-guarded of Him, our God Most High.

Each man has his post, and ours is the mine,
Not merely of chance, but of order divine;
He Who plac'd His stores there most clearly foresaw
Men's hands and men's toil must these stores forth-draw;
We miners work in the lone black night,
Yet oft by grace we are children of light:
  Aye singing praise and thanks to the Lord,
  We're restful through resting on His Word.

3 How wondrous the treasures our Earth contains!
How wondrous the working our God ordains!
The shadow of risk o'er every hour,
But still beneath His protecting power;
We miners work in the lone black night,
Yet oft by grace we are children of light:
  Aye looking up even thro' the dark,
  And knowing the Lord to our cry will hark.

4 So we calmly commit us to Thy keeping,
Whether we're toiling or quietly sleeping;
Whether above, Lord, or down below,
We are strong in Thee wherever we go:
We miners work in the lone black night,
Yet by grace we're oft the children of light:
  Our hands soiled and hard now, but by-and-bye
  We shall pass beyond the bright blue sky.

13. Old and New Year Services.

494 LOOKING BACK—OLD AND NEW YEAR. 10s.

1 Lo! On God's loom, the OLD YEAR hangs complete,
 Woven of joy and grief, of hope and fear;
 Once more within the House of God we meet,
  To wait for and to welcome the NEW YEAR.

2 Now, ere the OLD YEAR passes out of sight,
 Its blessings manifold we would recall;
 Mercies and troubles, mix'd of dark and bright,
 Its number'd days have brought to each and all.

3 For some, sweet chains, two hearts in one have bound,
 Making the house of life the house of love;
 New "little ones" in some glad homes are found,
 Bringing to Earth the light of Heav'n Above.

4 Our boys and girls have ripen'd and have grown;
 Bless God for all now walking "in the Way;"
 Much of His "good seed" has in them been sown;
 The dear Lord keep them till life's closing day.

5 Grey hairs, not unperceiv'd, are here and there
 On some of us—first flakes of Age's snow;
 Changes and chances, meet us everywhere;
 Our Father's daily discipline below.

6 Alas! We miss lov'd faces here to-night,
 Familiar faces, seen on Earth no more;
 But not for ever gone; The Lord of Light
 Said, "Go up higher to the golden shore."

7 Oh! To be watching for that solemn hour;
 Lord Jesus, make Thy Truth, Thyself more dear;
 Now fill us with the Spirit's living power,
 And we shall dare to welcome the NEW YEAR.

495. ONWARD—UPWARD—HEAVENWARD.

Tune—Rutherford's 'Immanuel's Land.'

1 ONCE more grey Time the Warder
 Shouteth his midnight cry;
 "Behold! The Old Year dieth,
 The New Year draweth nigh!"
 Lord, we would catch the summons,
 But with no pulse of fear;
 God's messenger we hail him;
 God's voice thro' him we hear.

2 O shew us now Thy glory,
 Thy beauty and Thy grace;
 Yea, lift upon us, waiting,
 The splendour of Thy Face;
 That 'neath the radiant vision,
 We onward still may go;
 Ascending, aye ascending,
 Until our pathway glow.

3 O fill us with deep longings,
 For better than "new wine";
 Thy peace, that never changes,
 The joy Thou givest Thine;

Bestow on us Thy fulness,
   Thy purity, Thy love;
That, like to Thee in all things,
   Our Home may be Above.

4 Our mouths attune to praises,
   Howe'er our faith be tried;
Our hearts, still keep Thou tranquil,
   Whatever may betide:
That thus in sweet communion,
   Our daily duty done;
We each may win the palm-branch,
   And each receive the crown.

5 The Past lies now behind us;
   On it be pardon seal'd;
The Present is around us,
   The Future unreveal'd;
Or long, or short our lives be,
   We place us in Thy Hand;
O Jesus, guide and guard us,
   Unto Thy blessed Land.

496.   THE NEW YEAR BORN.
Tune—"O how He loves," Sankey's S.S. 125

While together we are singing
   Ere New Year morn;
Lo! The midnight bells are ringing,
   For New Year born;
Tidings far and near forth-flinging,
Of the Old Year upward winging;
Of the New Year's blessings bringing;
   The New Year born.

Lord, as low before Thee kneeling,
   This New Year Morn;
Prayer and praise our vows re-sealing,
   This new Year born;
Fill us with all ho y feeling;
Thy blest Spirit o'er us stealing;
Thy great love afresh revealing,
   To weak and worn.

Back we look, and on us rises
   This New Year morn;
Vision of Thy Love's disguises,
   This New Year born;

Even losses proving crises,
Blessings 'gainst our dark surm'ses;
And our suff'rings sweet surprises;
   Rose on each thorn.

4 On we look, ourselves exhorting,
   This New Year morn;
Red-cross knights, with Thee cohorting,
   This New Year born;
Thy Cause, heart and hand supporting;
World nor flesh consent extorting;
While to Thee is our resorting;
   Glad or forlorn.

5 Shine, Lord, on our ignorances,
   This New Year morn;
Give us Faith's anointed glances,
   This New Year born;
Rule us Truth not circumstances;
Trusting Providence, not chances;
Meekness grow with sure advances,
   Let who will scorn.

6 Be our spirits calm or riven,
   This New Year born;
Peaceful living, or storm-driven,
   This New Year morn;
Be it good or ill us leaven;
Graces rip'ning, sins forgiven,
Bring us near and nearer heaven,
   Each New Year morn.

497.   ANOTHER YEAR.
   Tune—Wells, 7's.

1 Awe, and Hope, and Trust, and Fear
Meet before the unknown Year;
Whether long or short our path,
Christ, our Lord, the secret hath;
Long or short, Lord, let it be
As it seemeth best to Thee.

2 Come then grief, or loss, or pain,
As we onward march again;
Bear away upon its wing
Mercies, or new mercies bring;
May the Year we enter on
Holy be to every one!

3 Nearer, Lord, to Thee we cry,
  Living ever 'neath Thine eye;
  Liker Thee we yearn to grow,
  Temples of Thy grace below;
  That possessing and possest
  We may as Thine Own be blest.

4 Use us, Lord, each day to serve,
  Never from Thy Way to swerve;
  Use us, Lord, some work to do,
  Brave, or good, or right, or true;
  Use us, Lord, Thy truth to speak,
  On Thy Day, and all the week.

5 Faithful in a little, may
  We still keep the "narrow way";
  Light of glory on us shine,
  Making earthly lives divine;
  Light of duty on us break,
  Doing all for Jesus' sake.

6 Awe, and Hope, and Trust, and Fear,
  Meet before the unknown Year;
  Whether long or short our path,
  Christ, our Lord, the secret hath;
  Long or short, Lord, let it be
  As it seemeth best to Thee.

498. A NEW YEAR'S HYMN.   7.7.8.8.
  Tune—German Hymn.

1 Gone the Old Year, come the New,
  Lord, we would our lives review;
  'Neath Thy Throne of Grace adoring,
  Our imperfect PAST deploring.

2 Gone the Old Year, come the New,
  Lord, we would unto Thee sue;
  In the PRESENT swiftly gliding,
  Thou, O Thou, be our abiding.

3 Gone the Old Year, come the New,
  Lord, we would to Thee be true;
  Thro' the FUTURE onward moving,
  Keep us by Thy sweet reproving.

4 Gone the Old Year, come the New,
  Lord, with more grace us endue;
  In Thy cross, behold our token!
  Seal the words that Thou hast spoken.

5 Gone the Old Year, come the New,
  Lord, we seek Thy nurturing dew;
  Past and Present, Future, all,
  Trust with Thee, whate'er befall.

499. TRANSIENT AND PERMANENT.

1 Men's live come and men's lives go,
    Still the fragile flowers blow;
  Think my soul, what meaneth this!
    Soft admonishment I wis:
  Fragile may the strong outlive;
    'Tis thy God's prerogative.

2 Men's lives are but brief we see,
    While for centuries grows the tree;
  Think my soul, how once again
    Warning comes, like a refrain;
  Life of man not here complete,
    See life's fulness in Christ meet.

3 Few years to the grave must bring,
    Still the blithesome birds will sing;
  Think my soul, ere that "too late"
    Greet thee at Death's iron gate;
  Ever live that when thou'rt gone
    Thy kind deeds shall still live on.

4 Lords of broad lands disappear,
    Brooks remain and gleaming mere:
  Think my soul, and look above,
    And thy heart from Earth remove;
  That, when e'en the sea is dried,
    Thou, redeem'd, one shall abide.

5 If we but for this life live,
    —Changeful, hard and fugitive—
  Flower and tree, and land and brook,
    Bear unto us all rebuke:
  Live in Christ, and thus be heir
    To all ages, HERE and THERE.

500. THE JUDGMENT.—*Rev. vi. 12-17.*
  8.7.8.7.

1 Day of Judgment! Day of Terror!
    To the Christless in their gloom;
  Lo! It bursts in sudden horror—
    Dawn of dread and day of doom.

THE JUDGMENT.

2 Thro' the awful darkness flashing,
  See the Great White Throne appear;
Hark! While flaming walls are crashing,
  The last trumpet smites each ear.

3 Lo! In haste the Heaven fleeth,
  From that Face like to the fire;
And beneath, the strong Earth heaveth;
  Who shall stand before His ire?

4 Black the sun—of light forsaken;
  Red as blood the lab'ring moon;
And the stars—like figs storm-shaken—
  On the shudd'ring Earth are strewn.

5 O the anguish! O the crying!
  "Mountains falling, on us fall"!
O the terror! O the sighing!
  "Shaking rocks, O hear our call!"

6 Every eye beholds Him splendent,
  They who scorn'd and they who loved;
Seraphim around attendant,
  Sheep and goats apart have mov'd.

7 O the tremour! O the clangour!
  O the cow'ring and amaze!
As THE LAMB in holy anger
  Shows the LION'S lightning gaze.

8 Who are these with peaceful faces?
  Who are these who softly sing?
Ah! The blood-bought in their places,
  As they soar on starry wing.

9 Who are those in ashen pallor?
  Eyes averted, clenchèd hands?
These? The LOST in woe and dolour
  Plunging to hell's burning strands.

10 Day of Judgment! Day of terror!
  To the Christless in their gloom;
Lo! It bursts in sudden horror—
  Dawn of dread and day of doom.

14. The life-story of Jesus Christ our Lord.

A Sacred Cantata. "A name which is above every name." Philippians i. 9.

*** I indulge the "Pleasures of Hope"—may they not wholly prove "Pleasures of Imagination"!—that some capable and sympathetic Composer, will arrange these Celebrations of the chief incidents in the life of our Lord to music worthy of such a Celebration. I have not come up to my own Ideal I feel. Nevertheless I cherish a hope that, just as it is this Cantata will some day find its own Oratorio.

1. BETHLEHEM.
1 Timothy iii. 16.

BETHLEHEM! O Bethlehem!
 Judah's fairest coronet.
Bethlehem! O Bethlehem!
 Still upon thy green ridge set;
Angel feet these fields have trod;
 Heav'nly light has o'er them stream'd;
When th' Eternal Son of God—
 Child of Promise—on men beam'd;
Star of th' East, the sages leading—
 Of the manger not asham'd—
Lowly shepherds their flocks feeding;
 Mightiest birth of Time proclaim'd.
 Bethlehem! O Bethlehem!
 Of all hallow'd spots, the gem.

2. NAZARETH.
St. Mark vi. 3; St. John i. 46.

NAZARETH! O Nazareth!
 Couch'd like bird in hollow'd nest.
Nazareth! O Nazareth!
 Light of glory on thee rest!
Tho' a name of evil holding,
 Here was brought 'The Undefil'd';
Like a dove a serpent folding,
 Here grew up 'The Holy Child';
Toiling for a workman's bread,
 Carpenter in village small;
Thrice ten years away had sped,
 Ere Thou heard'st the supreme call.
 Nazareth! cross-like we see,
 Thy stain'd name from all stain free.

3.   THE BAPTISM.

St. Matthew iii. 13; (and vv. 14-17).

O THY Baptism! O Thy Baptism!
  Sinless One! O Man divine!
Why Thy Baptism! Why Thy Baptism!
  Ah! for sin that was not Thine.
Hark! the testimony given,
  '*This is my beloved Son*';
While descends from cloven heaven
  The Dove, sealing what is done.
Christ! Thou wast my Substitute!
  This rite hallow'd was for me;
I draw near with rev'rent foot,
  This myst'ry of grace to see.
    O Thy Baptism! Cleanse me, Lord,
    By Thy mighty, quick'ning word.

4.   THE TEMPTATION.

St. Matthew iv. 1-11; Hebrews iv. 15.

(*Rev. Vers.*)

QUARANTANA! Quarantana!
  Where the tempter dar'd his worst.
Quarantana! Quarantana!
  Lone and lorn, like place accurst.
O my Saviour, Thou wast tempted!
  Thyself proved our ev'ry snare!
From no searching flame exempted!
  Of no testing unaware!
Felt Sin's force; its sudden seizure;
  Felt Sin's terror; felt Sin's pain;
Felt the anguish of Sin's pressure;
  And as "tempted" dost remain.
    Quarantana! Bless His Name.
    Still "well knoweth He our frame."

5.   GALILEE.

St. Mark i. 14.

GALILEE! O Galilee!
  Lustrous Sea, and plains, and hills!
Galilee! O Galilee!
  Name that yet the World's heart thrills.
Gone, God's Israel from thee now,
  Where the Law from Sinai fell;
But Thy "Mount" lifts loftier brow;
  Lord, Thou hast the mightier spell.
Great words spoken by "the Lake,"
  Forth o'er all the Earth have gone;
Nor shall cease men's hearts to shake
  Till Redemption's work be done.
    Galilee! Capernaum!
    Terrible shall be your doom.

6.   JUDÆA.

St. John iii. 22.

O JUDÆA! O Judæa!
  Sweeter name than note of birds.
O Judæa! O Judæa!
  Thou did'st hear His tend'rest words.
"Wounded man" by road-side lying,
  "Fig-tree" spar'd and "graff" in "vine";
Priceless, too, "the shepherd dying":
  These, O favor'd Land, were Thine!
Who may seek to tell their story?
  Who may gauge their gentle power?
Who may reckon up their glory?
  As the Gospel's richest dower:
    O Judæa! deed and word
    Link thee, deathless, with "The Lord."

7.   SAMARIA.

St. John iv. 4 et seq.

O THOU fair Samaria!
  Diadem of Palestine.
Glorious Samaria!
  Thy first beauty still is thine.
Vine, fig, olive on hill side,
  Flocks, and herds in dale and fell;
Thy great memories abide;
  Bethel! Shechem! Jacob's Well:
Words of portent—words of blessing—
  By the Master spoken there;
God no more a House possessing,
  Lo! to be found ev'rywhere!
    Country fair! a woman's fame,
    Gives to thee undying name.

8. MIRACLES.

Acts of the Apostles ii. 22.

MIRACLES! O Miracles!
 The most heartless hearts ye move;
Miracles! O Miracles!
 Words of pity, deeds of love:
Came the deaf—anon they heard;
Came the dumb—a touch, they spoke;
Came the blind—saw with a word;
 Dead were brought, and lo! they wake!
Devils ev'n were subjugate.
 Ne'er came one Thou did'st delay;
 Ne'er came one who came "too late;";
 Ne'er was need that said Thee nay:
  Miracles of gentle might,
  Ye Him crown with stars of light.

9. PARABLES.

St. Mark iv. 2.

PARABLES! O Parables!
 Food for heart and food for mind.
Parables! O Parables!
 Barb'd yet soft as the South wind.
Wisdom—such as mocks the Sages;
 Grace—full of all sweetest ruth;
Love—that widens down the ages,
 From the 'Way,' the 'Life,' the 'Truth.'
'Lost Sheep'—'Lost Coin'—'Lost Son'—
 How they set the Gospel forth! [all,
Nor shall cease their gracious call,
 Till 'tis heard by the round Earth.
  Parables! before all eyes
  In you Christ's heart open lies.

10. PUBLIC MINISTRY.

St. Matthew iv. 17.

MINISTRY! O Ministry!
 God in Christ and Christ in God.
Ministry! O Ministry!
 Love's soft hand holding the rod.
Words of deepest wisdom speaking;
Works of might, with mercy join'd;
All His wandering sheep still seeking;
 Ceasing not until He find.
His Own Twelve preparing, training,
 '*He went ever doing good;*'
His whole life but a detaining,
 Till He shed His awful blood.
  Ministry! O Ministry!
  Gaz'd at with a swimming eye.

11. PHARISEES.

St. Matthew xxiii. 13-17.

PHARISEES! O Pharisees!
 Awful His rebukes to you.
Pharisees! O Pharisees!
 Heart-o'erwhelming; but how true!
Still reverberates His 'Woe,'
 The far centuries along;
Bends Hypocrisy, how low!
 None the less keen falls His thong
Mask'd falsehood, but a cloak,
 Howe'er grand, or deftly worn;
Sharper, heavier the stroke,
 And inexorable scorn:
  Pharisees of later day,
  Fit ye tremble with dismay.

12. PUBLICANS.

St. Matthew xi. 19; xxi. 13.

PUBLICANS! O Publicans!
 The great heart of love ye knew.
Publicans! O Publicans!
 The great heart of love knew you.
Scorn'd, malign'd, ye to Him crept,
 Laying there your burdens down;
Laden, weary, as ye wept
 Lo! a welcome, not a frown!
Well He understood your grief,
 Well He felt your shame and ban;
With sad words ye sought relief,
 Soft as tears His pity ran.
  Publicans! 'tis Gospel still;
  Turn to Christ whoever will.

13. THE MULTITUDES.
St. Mark xii. 37.

MULTITUDES! O Multitudes!
 Hedge and highway forth did send.
Multitudes! O Multitudes!
 Ah! They felt Who was their Friend.
Rabbi proud caught up his skirt;
 Priest pass'd on with look askance;
Reck'ning 'common people' dirt;
 Bearing ever scornful glance.
'Gladly' hung they on His lips;
 'Gladly' clasp'd His outstretch'd hands;
Led from 'neath their long eclipse,
 Lo! Light shines as He commands.
Multitudes! He lov'd them all!
 His, a universal call.

14. A LITTLE CHILD.
St. Matthew xviii. 2-5.

LITTLE Child! O little Child!
 That the Saviour 'took' and bless'd.
Little Child! O little Child!
 Who such fame has e'er possess'd?
To the World's great heart up-taken
 Thou art an unchanging Child;
And the truth abides unshaken—
 Taught by Him 'The Undefil'd'—
That no Child may be forbidden
 To be 'brought' unto 'The Christ';
In parental hearts 'tis hidden,
 Sacred as the Eucharist.
 Little Child, that still lives on—
 A perpetual benison.

15. PRAYERS OF JESUS.
St. Luke vi. 12 and St. John xvii.

PRAYERS of Jesus! Prayers of Jesus!
 Sweet the thought that Jesus pray'd.
Prayers of Jesus! Prayers of Jesus!
 All our wants on Him were laid.
On the lone Mount when men slept,
 Lo! The Saviour on His knees!
Ere Storm on His foll'wers leapt,
 He their peril knows and sees;
And when shadows round Him closing,
 Told of His approaching 'hour';
Mid all evil interposing,
 For His Own He sought 'all power.'
Prayers of Jesus! Still He prays—
 Thought that all our fear allays.

16. THE LORD'S PRAYER.
St. Matthew vi. 9-13.

O THE Lord's Pray'r! O the Prayer!
 Golden-worded, tender, sweet!
O the Lord's Prayer! O the Lord's Prayer!
 For all human need complete!
Child-lips say it, maidens fair;
 Dewy youth and manhood strong;
Age it loves, even to white hair;
 'Tis to all as gracious song.
Yes, "Our Father"— who may tell
 The sad hearts it has inspired?
Mem'ries old, lay their sweet spell,
 When hope has well-nigh expired.
 The Lord's Prayer, to mankind given,
 Lifts mankind from Earth to Heav'n.

17. JERUSALEM.
St. Mark xiii. 49.

SALEM! O Jerusalem!
 Ruin'd now as He forespake.
Salem! O Jerusalem!
 Lov'd well still, for Jesus' sake.
Oft thou heard'st His burning speech;
 Oft did'st see His mighty life;
Oft thy heart He sought to reach;
 Oft He held a gracious strife;
Warning, pleading—all in vain!
 Stretched to thee His hand's appeal;
Awful tears—like thund'rous rain—
 The great heart of Love reveal.
 O thyself thou did'st condemn!
 Salem! O Jerusalem!

18.   BETHANY
 St. Matthew xxi. 17.

BETHANY! O Bethany!
 Sweet to hear the tender sound.
Bethany! O Bethany!
 Where a home my Saviour found.
Hearts of love receiv'd Him there;
 Hands and feet to serve Him set;
When the evening cool'd the air,
 And He cross'd green Olivet.
Lazarus, Mary, Martha, three
 Star-names aye to shine appointed;
And that Mary, who, in thee,
 Her dear Lord and ours anointed.
Bethany! O Bethany!
 Sweet Thy very name to me.

19.   THE TRANSFIGURATION.
 St. Matthew xvii. 1-8; St. Mark ix. 2-8.

O MOUNT TABOR! O Mount Tabor!
 Crownèd hill of Galilee!
O Mount Tabor! O Mount Tabor!
 Heav'nly splendors flash'd o'er thee.
Son of Man—veilèd His 'glory,'
 Now He shines forth Prince of Light;
As foretold in psalm and story,
 In effulgence of His might.
Moses now within 'the Land'—
 And Elijah, homage pay;
As beside THE CHRIST they stand,
 'Talking' of the awful day.
 O Mount Tabor! to 'the Three,'
 Mighty, wondrous memory.

20.   THE ANGER OF CHRIST.
 St. Mark iii. 5.

WRATH of Christ! O wrath of Christ!
 When 'watch'd' Pharisee and Scribe.
Wrath of Christ! O wrath of Christ!
 His sweet 'healing' met with gibe.
Holy that transcendent 'look,'   [through;
 As He search'd them through and
'Blindness of their hearts' Him shook;

All their evil thoughts He knew.
From the mass He each one singled,
 As 'the man' stretched forth his hand;
Wrath and grief in His heart mingled,
 Whilst He gave the great 'command.'
 Wrath of Christ! Lo! it shall burn
 'Gainst all who the Gospel spurn.

21.   THE WITHERED FIG-TREE.
 St. Matthew xix. 17-22; St. Mark xi. 12-14, 20-24.

WITHER'D fig-tree! Wither'd fig-tree!
 Guerdon of His gentleness.
Wither'd fig-tree! Wither'd fig-tree!
 Blighted thou that He might bless.
Hoary-headed man, neglecting
 The great words of saving love;
Rabbi, Scribe, their Lord rejecting,
 Spite of 'witness' from Above;
With one word each had lain dead,
 And beyond—O awful doom!
But by love and pity led
 He still strove that they might 'come.'
 And so smote a fruitless tree;
 Not a man, with destiny.

22.   JESUS WEEPING.
 St. John xi. 35; St. Luke xix. 41.

JESUS Weeping! Jesus Weeping!
 How it knits His heart to ours!
Jesus Weeping! Jesus Weeping!
 Stainless tears as dew on flow'rs.
But like lightning sheath'd in rain,
 Awful were the tears He shed;
Burden'd was his heart and brain;
 Each great tear from deep wound bled.
"Jesus wept" at Lazarus' grave,
 And o'er doom'd Jerusalem;
His vast love would all men save,
 Nor does He the worst contemn.
 Jesus Weeping! Human woe
 Still to 'Man of Sorrows' go.

23. THE KING.
St. Matthew ii. 1-2; St. Luke ii. 8-14;
xix. 36-38.

BLESS the King! O Bless the King!
  Gleam on Olivet that fell.
Bless the King! O Bless the King!
  As old Seers and Psalmists tell.
Multitudes His praises sang,
  Palm-boughs strewn upon His way;
In words that o'er Bethlehem rang,
  When had dawn'd th' appointed day.
King of kings He was indeed,
  As His herald had proclaim'd;
But, our Victim, He must bleed;
  King, who may with Him be nam'd?
    Bless the King! shout earth and sky;
    Comes the Kingdom by-and-bye.

24. THE LORD'S SUPPER.
1 Corinthians. vi. 23-25.

TH' Eucharist! The Eucharist!
  Lowly meal yet heav'nly feast.
Th' Eucharist! The Eucharist!
  Dear to greatest and to least.
On the night of utmost trial,
  When Gethsemane was near;
Traitor's kiss and friends' denial;
  Cross of shame and piercing spear;
Thou did'st give these symbols holy
  Of Thy Sacrifice and Love;
Spread'st a Table for most lowly;
  Antepast of bliss above.
    Holy Supper! Blessèd rite,
    May it still all hearts unite.

25. JESUS SINGING.
St. Matthew xxvi. 31.

JESUS Singing! Jesus Singing!
  Dear the record, '*Jesus sung;*'
Jesus singing! Jesus singing!
  Tho' His heart felt sharpest pang.
Bread and wine, a sacred token
  For His people He had giv'n;
And, with words pathetic, broken
  Their ' offence ' to the ' Eleven;'
And to Simon soft fore-telling
  Of his sad ' denying ' fall;
Yet His pard'ning love up-welling
  By a ' hymn ' made festival.
    Jesus Singing! Bless His Name,
    Joy and Grief together came.

26. GETHSEMANE.
St. Matthew xxvi. 36-56.

AWFUL, dark Gethsemane!
  O! my Saviour there I see
In the dread Gethsemane!
  Kneeling in His agony.
Broken words release imploring,
  Cup of trembling in His hands;
Bloody sweat in great drops pouring;
  Stealthy step of brutal bands;
Staves, as 'twere to ' take a thief;'
  Traitor-kiss; and Three who slept.
Guilt, my guilt! O grief, my grief!
  Swift-successive o'er him swept.
    Who Gethsemane may sound?
    Mystery, as sin profound.

27. THE ARREST.
St. John xviii. 12.

"THEY went backward;" "They went backward;"
  Caesar's soldiers, "to the ground."
"They went backward;" "They went backward,"
  Stranger sight was never found.
Simple words of Jesus spoken,
  '*Whom seek ye?*' thus laid them low;
Their strong Roman breasts were broken,
  As though He had struck a blow.
Touch omnipotent was there;
  Yet touch only—not to kill.
Great self-choosing Sufferer,
  Thou wast 'taken' by Thy will.
    "They went backward," and still, Lord,
    Sheathest Thou Thy glitt'ring sword.

28. GABBATHA.

St. John xix. 13.

GABBATHA! O Gabbatha!
 Scene of guilt and scene of shame,
Gabbatha! O Gabbatha!
 Love sees thee with heart a-flame.
Lo! before the judge He standeth,
 Whilst he says, '*Behold your King!*';
But malignant scorn demandeth,
 '*To the cross*' the Just One bring.
Crucify Him! Crucify Him!
 Yell a thousand vengeful throats;
And the Prince of Darkness by Him,
 O'er his nearing triumph gloats.
Gabbatha! These all unite
 Infamous, thy name to write.

29. THE PRÆTORIUM.

St. Mark xv. 16-20.

O SAD, sad Prætorium!
 Hall of scourging, scoff and jest.
Gloomy, base Prætorium!
 Where they mock'd '*God manifest.*'
Soldier's cast-off mantle o'er Him,
 Crown of thorns on bleeding brow;
Striking, spitting, they adore Him
 Tongue in cheek, with insult low.
Flash forth, Lord, Thy glittering sword,
 Smite these mockers—all Thy foes;
Nay, He bears the'r maddest word;
 Forward to the cross He goes.
Justice seat! To thee we turn,
 And our hearts within us burn.

30. BEARING THE CROSS.

*St. Matthew xxvii. 31-32 ; St. Mark xv.
 19-21 ; St. Luke xxiii. 26.*

O His Cross! Bearing His Cross!
 Lo! God's Son! Was not earth rock'd?
O His Cross! Bearing His Cross!
 Jesus struck, spat on, and mock'd.
Strength divine He will not wield;
 High and deep His woe's tide swelled.
No one near His Lord to shield?
 Only one—and him 'compelled.'
Truly man, O Christ, Thou wast,
 Fainting, falling in the street;
Yet the 'work' on Thee was cast,
 Came from Thee flawless, complete.
O His Cross! O Saviour mine,
 Light our cross compar'd with Thine.

31. CALVARY.

St. Luke xxiii. 33-43.

CALVARY! O Calvary!
 Consummation of all crime.
Calvary! O Calvary!
 Thy dark mount in dread I climb.
On the cross my God they raise,—
 Type fulfill'd and prophecy,—
Callous-hearted there they gaze,
 Thro' His darken'd agony.
There He hangs 'twixt Earth and Heav'n,
 All man's sin upon Him lies;
Lo! the dying thief forgiv'n,
 Bounds with Him to Paradise.
Calvary! O Calvary!
 All thy agony for me!

32. DENIAL AND FORSAKING.

*Denial, St. Matthew xxvi. 69-75; Forsaking.
 St. Matthew xxv. 56.*

O DENIAL and Forsaking!
 Dark the page on which we read.
O Denial and Forsaking!
 How the heart of Love did bleed.
Warn'd and pray'd for by The Master,
 Peter! how couldst thou so fall?
And as deepen'd the disaster,
 How forsake Him could ye all?
Mystery of God and man!
 Sinless one by sinful taken;
Depths no mortal eyes may scan,
 By His Own 'denied,' 'forsaken.'
O Denial and Forsaking!
 His great anguish greater making.

33. THE GRAVE. *St. Matthew xxvii. 57-60.*

SILENT Garden ! Silent Garden !
 Holy mem'ries round thee shine.
Silent Garden ! Silent Garden !
 Where is there a grave like thine ?
There with tears the Lord they lay;
 Darken'd hopes and 'bated breath;
To awake the Great Third Day,
 Silent conqueror of Death.
Chosen ones ALIVE Him saw;
 Wond'ring, heard Him when He spoke;
His work 'finish'd' without flaw,
 Gospel light in glory broke.
  Silent Garden ! We must weep,
  But, laud for that holy sleep.

34. THE RESURRECTION. *St. John xi. 25.*

RESURRECTION ! Resurrection !
 O strong, gracious, lustrous word !
Resurrection ! Resurrection !
 Triumph of the Saviour-Lord.
Into Death's realm, lo! He went,
 And in tranquil sleep there lay;
But rose then omnipotent,
 When had come the Great Third Day.
Not in haste but calm and still;
 Folds His grave-clothes and steps forth;
Ev'ry promise to fulfil;
 Guerdon—a redeemèd Earth.
  Resurrection ! Last foe Death,
  Touches now but mortal breath.

35. EMMAUS. *St. Luke xxic. 13-32.*

EMMAUS ! O Emmaus !
 Memorable 'walk' was thine.
Emmaus ! O Emmaus !
 Faith and Love hold thee for shrine.
Two disciples on that Eve,
 With hope quench'd, went on their way;
Christ 'drew near' and saw them grieve;
 Sought their sorrow to allay,
By deep great words from 'the Word,'
 Mingling Suffering with Might;
But they knew not 'twas their Lord,
 Till He vanished out of sight.
  Each He gave a burning heart !
  Lord ! like fire to me impart.

35. THE SCEPTIC : ST. THOMAS.

St. John xx. 24-29.

O ST. THOMAS ! O St. Thomas !
 Great thy record, and yet sad.
O St. Thomas ! O St. Thomas !
 Who can all read, and be glad ?
Walking not by faith but sight,
 Trusting only eye and hand .
Treating 'witness' with despite,
 Wouldst not as Believer stand.
Christ was pitiful, and came —
 Shew'd Himself and all His signs ;
Gracious, putting thee to shame,
 Winning worship that still shines.
  'Lord, my God !' was thy great word,
  As once more thou knew'st the Lord.

37. RESTORATION OF ST. PETER.

St. John xxi. 1-17.

O ST. PETER ! O St. Peter !
 Great thy fall, but great thy rise.
O St. Peter ! O St. Peter !
 Tears were mighty in thy eyes.
Once more at thy Master's word,
 Thou art come unto 'the Lake' ;
Lo ! new vision of the Lord,
 Thy first fervour doth awake ;
Stepping fearless on the sea,
 Seeing Him upon the shore ;
The great heart forgiveth thee
 Thee again He will restore.
  Three times yearning love is mask'd,
  As thrice 'Lov'st thou Me' He ask'd.

38. THE GREAT COMMISSION.
St. Mark xvi. 15.

MIGHTY Charter! Mighty Charter!
  Given by the Risen Lord.
Mighty Charter! Mighty Charter!
  Ev'n the Lord's supremest word,
The round world before Him lay;
  For that world, this one command;
Go—and I'm with you alway.
  Send it out o'er ev'ry Land;
Down the ages it has gone,
  Nor shall cease until Earth, won,
At His cross shall ransom'd rest.
  Mighty Charter! Great Commission!
Till this Earth be Christ possession.

39. THE ASCENSION.
Acts of the Apostles i. 9.

O ASCENSION! O Ascension!
  From the old familiar path.
O Ascension! O Ascension!
  But in love and not in wrath.
Leading them o'er Olivet,
  His full 'secret' they have shared.
Promise-words—like jewels set—
  For 'departure,' have prepared.
Very God, He climbs the sky,
  Lifting up His hands to bless;
Kneel th' Eleven adoringly,
  Then 'return' with joyfulness.   [eyes,
  Th' 'cloud' receives Him from their
As they gaze in meek surprise.

40. THE GREAT WHITE THRONE.
Revelations xx. 11

GREAT White Throne! O Great White
    Throne!
  Sculptur'd of the dazzling light. [Throne!
Great White Throne! O Great White
  Bursting on my ravish'd sight.
Jesus, I behold Thee pleading,
  Giver of The Spirit's dower;
For the guiltiest interceding,
  Shewing forth Thy saving power.
'*Many crowns*' upon Thy head,
  Thine all pow'r on Earth, in Heav'n;
All in all time to Thee led,
  All their sin in Thee forgiv'n.
    Great White Throne! To gaze we dare;
    JESUS, Thou art seated there.

15. Nature's Field of Cloth of Gold.

Nature's Field of Cloth of Gold.

It is told of the great Linnaeus, that when he first saw a many-acred English moor covered with full-blossomed gorse (Scotice whin), that he knelt down and gave God thanks for bringing him to a country that could show him such a spectacle of beauty. I have named just such a spectacle—combined with broom— Nature's Field of Cloth of Gold; albeit only at a great distance, may the tinsel of the historic Field, be compared with the workmanship of Him Who is at once the Great Gardener and the Great Weaver.

From earliest and (in a sense) life-long associations this Field of Cloth of Gold holds an innermost place in my deepest and sacredest memories. For thither as a boy (almost child) I was wont to retreat, and all alone work out problems that perchance prematurely be denied.

The little incident of the Linnet, which was the motive of the poem, is a pathetic Fact.

In the Book of Fame enroll'd
Shines THE FIELD OF CLOTH OF GOLD;
Chroniclers with fervid rage,
Making luminous the page.
  But more rich than Ardres hoar
Lo! upon a billowy moor
Whin and broom in interfold,
NATURE'S FIELD OF CLOTH OF GOLD,
With an ever-changing splendor
Such as Summer makes attend her.   10
  But this Field of Cloth of Gold,
Whose brief tale shall now be told —
If to tell be mine the skill,
And the Reader listen will —
Lieth not in sunny France,
Or in page of old Romance :

'Tis a wood-enring'd retreat
Couching at Demyat's feet;
Where the Forth its coil unwinds
And the hill and valley binds;   20
On a gently sloping hill,
Gleaming bright with many a rill;
Vocal with all singing birds —
Clear as ever human words —
While the sunshine, gold on gold,
Shimmers far across the wold;
With all subtleties of shadow
Dappling dale and down and meadow,
As holds Fancy's heart in thrall,
Making Fairy Festival :   30
  Nook, as at Creation's date,
Kept of God inviolate.
  There I've watched at break of day
Till a-hush, I could but pray;
There I've watched in blaze of noon,
All the landscape in a swoon;
There I've watch'd in gloamin grey
Closing on my homeward way;
There I've watch'd 'neath shining stars
 Plough, Orion, Venus, Mars;   40
There I've watch'd in ghostly light
When the moon shed mystic light;
There I've watched both soon and late;
And my Muse, I were ingrate
If, with mem'ries I recall,
My heart's gratitude were small.
  As a Youth I climb those hills,
In their loneliness that fills

Eager heart and seething brain
With such thoughts as come again: 50
Problems stern, Faith even wounding,
Reason high and sense confounding,
And deep mysteries astounding.
　Yearnings 'O that God would speak
And His awful dumbness break'
Dark suspicions God was dead
And no more the great world led ;
Achings after dear ones gone ;
Purpos'd action left undone;
Aspiration unfulfill'd ; 60
Passionate heart-ardours chill'd ;
Life rul'd but by circumstance ;
Destiny a thing of chance ;
Soul by fleshly cravings riv'n ;
Fir'd of Hell, unkept of Heav'n ;
Falsehood conquering the Truth ;
Pitilessness mocking ruth ;
Fools still heaping up their wealth ;
Busy toilers grudg'd e'en health :
　These th' enigmas that me smote 70
As amidst those hills remote
I on my life's threshold stood
In Youth's ever-changing mood.
But as mists before the sun
Scatter, being shone upon ;
When I couch'd again within
Shadow of the broom and whin
Then I found God lov'd His child ;
Patient still when I was wild.
　Thou wast in the solitudes 80
Breathing sweet beatitudes ;
Thou, God, led'st me by the hand ;
Mad'st me on '*The Rock*' to stand ;
Guarded'st me from paths of death ;
Did'st breathe in me Thine Own breath ;
And to-day 'twere long to trace
All Thy love and all Thy grace ;
And Thy goodness manifold
In that FIELD OF CLOTH OF GOLD.
　This fair leaf of nature's book 90
Torn out was -
　　　　　I've undertook

To set it in a lowly rhyme
To live perchance in after-time ;
(As wee fern lives when great trees fall
Or daisy meek survives the wall ;
Or little bird that sings its song,
Tho' magnates join the shadowy throng :
All the modesties of Nature
Kept still by the Great Creator
Beautiful and permanent ; 100
His own constancy them lent).
　Ne'er was known who was to blame—
'Twas in sooth a deed of shame
If it planned was, and meant—
May it have been accident !
Jets of smoke and tongues of flame
Sheep-boys saw with loud exclaim ;
But no ear was there to hear
Or to bring deliv'rance near :
Helpless, aimless they look'd on 110
At the sad destruction.
　Flames went creeping o'er the ground
Sere and brown ferns all around;
Stealthily quiver'd in the grass;
Gleam'd at edge of the morass;
Leapt the dell within, smoke-sheath'd,
In an awful beauty wreath'd;
Shewing as 'twere crests of gold,
As the red waves bick'ring roll'd;
Fiercely mingling shine and gloom,
As they bore a certain doom ;
Higher, higher, on and on,
As in vengeful passion.
　Ah ! Sweet birds in skurrying crowds,
Sought the coolness of the clouds ;
And the myriad creatures small
Forth from their concealments crawl:
Pitiful to see their strait,
Scorch'd their homes and desecrate.
　Scatter'd blooms in showers of gold 130
Which the ruddy sparks enfold ;
Stems erect and tall were blacken'd
Not an instant the flames slacken'd ;
Till as in fair temple, all
Slender pillars 'gan to fall;

Ah! like God's carv'd work of old,
Fell my FIELD OF CLOTH OF GOLD.
Streams! did ye with fire complot
That ye now o'erflowèd not?
Had ye but your torrents lent 140
In this mournful exigent,
No such spoiling had been told
Of my FIELD OF CLOTH OF GOLD.
  And, ye Clouds! where were your rains—
Pour'd destructive on the plains—
Why, why, in this fateful hour,
Came ye not with saving shower?
  When the Fire had done its worst—
O deed cruel! deed accurst!
For it was a very shrine 150
Holy as e'er House divine—
I took my solitary way
The sad havoc to survey:
Spectral 'neath the moon's wan ray,
All was gone, save here and there
A broom-stem besmirch'd and bare.
  Cynic! Tears were in my eyes:
Let your chill heart feel surprise!
As I turnèd me to leave
Through long after-years to grieve 160
For the fell destruction wrought
In my scene of purest thought
When my Faith and Hope were shook,
And thro' dark to Heav'n I'd look,
Or would rest upon "The Book";
A sight I saw that struck my heart
E'en as through me had run dart—
In the crown of a broom-stem,
Like despoilèd diadem,
Scorch'd, begrim'd, behold there lay 170
A LINNET'S NEST.—
              Naught do you say?
Ah! But in that tiny round
Such pathetic thing I found
As in chains of tears me bound;
Such a miracle of love
Pointing me to Him Above;
Such a tender martyrdom
As would strike a scoffer dumb:
Linnet's nest, and lo! its brood

Living, and a-gape for food; 180
Which, alas! none to them brings:
SAV'D BY THEIR DEAD MOTHER'S WINGS.
Scorch'd and burnt e'en to the bone
Till almost a skeleton;
There she lay her brood above
Self-devoted in her love.
  Call ye this instinct, I pray,
Far from human love away?
'Tis thankless lie I protest;
In that tiny heart did rest 190
Such a spark celestial
As I here shall dare to call
LOVE—that should make us more lowly,—
Love most beautiful, most holy.
  Think of what that LINNET bore
Yet away it would not soar!
Think of terror of the light
Flaming o'er it on that night;
Think what stirring at its heart
As it felt the fiery smart; 200
Think what power within that breast
Held it in its blazing nest.
  No! The problem is not solv'd
When you instinct have evolv'd;
Clearest choice and will were there,
Fervid love and almost pray'r;
Touch of God was on that bird
True as e'er in His seers stirr'd.
  Here I find, tho' involute,
His great law of love; and, mute, 210
Reason of it not, but feel
It may God's Own heart unseal;
E'en as law that rules the ocean
Rules the dewdrops in their motion.
O Love! vast as God is vast;
Yet in tiniest Linnet cast.
  And so FIELD OF CLOTH OF GOLD
Lie in my heart's inmost fold!
Mem'ries of now far-off years
That I'll carry to the spheres; 220
Tenderest associations
That 'midst life's exacerbations
Calm me—as a mother's hand—
And a victor make me stand;

Aye shall make thee consecrate
Till my life's concluding date ;
And that little martyr-linnet
(*Let the world see nothing in it*)
Still to my heart sweetly sings,
Kindling such a love as brings   230
Me before the King of kings ;
Moving iridescent fancies ;
Prescience as in heavenly trances ;
When the body left behind
The soul soars, and mind to mind
Rais'd on high b' Imagination
See the destined restoration,
When, through all God's great creation,
Shall go forth the mighty word
As He girds His glitt'ring sword ;   240
That no longer SIN shall reign,
Or redeem'd Earth longer stain ;
Or hold men in longer thrall
By demoniac carnival ;
But that Truth and Righteousness
The whole race of man shall bless ;
And the groaning of the creature
Shall surcease ; and ev'ry feature
Of the long slow agony
Pass away from Earth and Sky ;   250
When the wonder of ' the BLOOD,'
Shed upon the ghastly rood,
Shall assert itself ; and then
Come salvation to all men.
  Drop of water is ;
Grain of sand, behold it is
Of the substance of the shore
Checking ocean's bellowing roar ;
Beam of light is light as true
As in sun itself we view :   260
  Even so a Bird's small breast
Where such strength of love did rest
Holding her fast in her nest ;
God's Own glorious love revealeth,

And to our own heart appealeth ;
That His love shall be a power
To uphold in Danger's hour ;
That His love shall us up-bear
Thro' all trial and all fear ;
That His love shall sanctify   270
True to live and true to die ;
That His love, cast in the mould
Of the FIELD OF CLOTH OF GOLD,
Shall enfold us with the beauty
Born of brave fulfilléd duty.
  So there come swift sudden startings,
And inevitable dartings ;
Shoots of immortality,
Witnessing SOULS do not die,
But have home beyond the sky ;   280
Wondrous introspective glances
Poignant as the sunbeam's lances ;
Conscience steadying the will ;
Aches that set the heart a-thrill ;
Longings to be "cloth'd upon,"
And to hear His great "Well done !"
  Thing of Past, O golden Field !
Still thou livest, still dost yield
Mem'ries indestructible ;
Deeper joy than words can tell ;   290
Joy which only music showeth
As heart-searchingly it floweth,
And to deepest spirit goeth ;
Wov'n in substance of my life,
Now in calm and now in strife ;
Steeping me in light supernal,
Lifting up to God Eternal :
  CHRIST shall yet be King of Men,
And all Earth shall rule again ;
Upward still our race shall move   300
To the watchword "God is love !"
  Quickly dawn this glorious Day !
All may speed it on its way.

16. "Sunny Memories" of the "Dead in Christ;."
An Elegy.

⁎ *The following poem was privately printed in, [Month] 1889, but the 100 copies of which the issue consisted, were so rapidly taken, to my regret, as not a few of friends could not be supplied. I reprinted it in my "Three Centuries of Hymns," and I am glad of the opportunity now given to republish it. Though a personal Elegy, the consolations or 'teachings given,' have wide application. The title of the original instalm, thus ran—"Elegy Sacred to the Memory of John M'Dowall, Esq., only son of David M'Dowall, Esq., J.P., Dublin, and my beloved brother-in-Law, who died suddenly on 1.?.?, 1889, aged ??. By the Rev. Alexander B. Grosart, D.D., LL.D., St. George's, Presbyterian Church of England, Blackburn, Lancashire. ?. Only 100 copies printed for private circulation." (?? pp. 15.) This Elegy has been finally revised.*

Oh! Surely they are all in error
Who still name Death, the King of Terror;
The enemy of enemies
From whom each one instinctive flies :
O! Surely they have never seen
Dead face like this:—
  A heavenly sheen
Lies on it, like an angel's kiss,
Who would assure us of his bliss ;
A sweet, heart-calming tenderness
(For this the dear Lord I do bless) 10
Breath'd in the pathos of erst brightness
Now melted into marble whiteness
Of the shut eye-lids and shut lips :
O! It is an apocalypse
Straight from the mighty heart of God
Disburthening our grief's great load.
  I see no touch of marring change,
But rather transformation strange ;

A light as of Christ's glory shining,
Or nimbus his white brow entwining, 20
His still and noble face refining ;
Telling us that no hand of mail
With cruel blows sought to assail,
But the thin veil, soft-raised, not rent,
Lo! he to sudden glory went :
Accepted in the Well-Belov'd,
And so by gentle touch remov'd ;
Touch gentle as of gentlest sleep
To tired eyes that vigil keep;
As quiet as in cups of flowers 30
Comes dew in the dim twilight hours ;
Or a wing-weary bird to rest,
Low flying in the purpling West.
No langour of disease or pain,
No wrenching as of iron chain,
But with a painless swift release—
Ah! The dear Lord's Own "perfect peace.'

Hush! hush! my heart! for he is found
By Death, not smitten down, but crowned;
Cloth'd with a brighter dignity,   40
As if in his benignity
He would ennoble him, and bring
Sweet solace to our sorrowing;
Witness to cleansing of all sin,
Ev'n Christ's own purity within;
Yea, witness to His "Grace abounding"
And the "Last Enemy" confounding;
Witness that in His fresh mid-life,
Remov'd from this our earthly strife,
He has a nobler post to fill
With finer work and finer skill;
His call came like a whisper'd word,
That his ear and his only heard,
When with a look of bright surprise
As he a-list'ning did arise;
Wide his soul's wings, snow-white, expand-
And him all safe with Jesus landing. [ing;
Again I turn, again I gaze,
'Rapt in a rev'rent still amaze;
Lo! Mid the tempest of our weeping,
How tranquil is our brother sleeping:
My brother! thy whole heart was mine;
Nor less I wot, was my heart thine.
We sore shall miss thee, O belov'd;
And missing thee be unreprov'd
Of the Lord Christ, Who called thee hence:
Who knows the poignant influence
That aye was thine, whilst yet alive;
Who knows how hard 'tis still to strive,
With motive and with impulse gone,
In our bleak desolation.
O rip'ning harvest, all rain-drenched!
O! numerous hopes now all quench'd!
O anchors strong all rudely wrenched!
'Twas pitiful to see strong men,
As they again and still again
Upon their young dead master gaz'd;
And brokenly with tears him praised.   80.
They lov'd him well, and the grey head
Of agèd sire deep honourèd.
Alas he will be missed by many,
Waifs, scarcely car'd for by any:

(Altho' the Christ's own heirs of glory)
Ah! how he listened to their story,
And sent each one away light-hearted,
His own pure brightness aye imparted.
O holy grows the darken'd room
For Christ's great word doth it illume; 90.
Reminding us as we relook —
Our hope undimmed, our faith unshook,
That here not he, but his, doth lie,
Himself pass'd far beyond the sky.
As still with tear-steeped eyes I turn,
And grief-smit heart within doth burn;
Behold a vision visits me,
And, lo! all "glorious things" I see—
The temple of a soul redeem'd,
Full richly furnished, as beseem'd   100
A MIND, deep, strenuous, and high,
And moulded into symmetry;
Fill'd with rare knowledge and resource—
Soft as the light with lightning's force;
Clear, penetrative, pois'd, and keen
As the upleaping flame, I ween;
A HEART, large, fervid, sensitive,
And passion only fugitive,
Still loving, gracious, tender, true—
Such as I've seen in very few.   110
Shrine of all sweetest sanctities,
And of Love's own sincerities.
Alas! hid there the weak link lay,
That all our rich hopes doth affray;
The dark and mystic chain of being
Was sudden snapp'd beyond our seeing.
His CONSCIENCE—a thrice holy thing—
Red shield borne true before the king;
And steadfast in fine rectitude,
To crooked ways never subdued.   120
WILL resolute, and aye decisive;
His speech strong, ready, and incisive;
Rare Scottish humour, Irish wit
That sharp and shatt'ringly did hit
All falsehood, and hypocrisy,
With its fair-painted mask awry.
Fell swiftly the undaunted blow
Against all craven and all low;
A nature to "fine issues" touch'd,

And that integrity avouch'd ;   130
Eyes steely blue, and aye steadfast,
Such as keen and levell'd looks did cast,
As we see arrows in the bow,
When loos'd and to their marks they go.
His FOREHEAD wide and prominent,
Such as to strong men still is lent ;
His MOUTH, firm-lipp'd, curving, and sweet,
Wrath and swift ruth in them did meet ;
His HANDS as tap'ring as a woman's, [man's
And yet staunch, strong for any foe —   140
But enemy he never had
Saving the base, the vile, the bad ;
And even among those who err,
No enemies found ever were ;
Ne'er said he with disdainful brow—
" Lo, I am holier than thou !"
He, pure himself, naught fear'd of taint,
Unlike your Pharisaic saint ;
A genuine hand-grasp, look, and word –
Sincerest servant of the Lord.   150
His inner life was reticent,
But ever with the outward blent ;
In such a subtle union
As maketh words and music one ;
Reflective of the closer walk,
But shunning loud and fluent talk.
Upon his knees, with love and awe,
When none but the Great God he saw—
The life of God and Jesus hidden—
Therefore, all human boasting chidden. 160
In all his friendships true as steel,
So that he made you always feel
Your joy was his, and of your care
He still must take an equal share.
If by mishap a man was down,
Crush'd by Society's cold frown ;
And ev'n if, wand'ring far astray,
He had forsook the narrow way,
Yea, plung'd deep into Sin's black mire ;
He still had pity in his ire.   170
He had a gentle word to speak,
The bruised reed he would not break.
Both strong and tender like his Master,
He lent a kind hand in disaster.

O brave is he who bravely thinks,
And the brave word with brave deed links;
Tho' two or three against the world,
Yet none the less his flag unfurl'd,
Eager to take a foremost place,
Tho' the world count it a disgrace.   180
Thus Freedom's charters have been won—
Thus epoch-making deeds are done—
Kind is he who his own self goes
With all the kindness he bestows ;
And with a sympathetic look,   [Book."
With warmest heart-words from " the
His kindness doubles, and awakes
In hearts forlorn a force that shakes
All dark'ning fears, bewild'ring doubt,
And then the light of God beams out. 190
His was no empty sending alms,
Or pence flung into empty palms.
O good he is whose goodness knows
Still naught of boasting, but aye shows,
That rooted in humility,
He groweth in his sanctity.
He went about as did the Christ,
And close with Him kept holy tryst.
Alas ! my brother. Thus he stood !
Brave still, and kind, and simply good, 200
Under the shadow of the rood :
Ne'er fell from him or gibe or jest,
Cheek of pure maiden would molest ;
And never ribald word or sneer,
To wound or stain a shrinking ear ;
A good RED KNIGHT of old romance,
Whatsoever the circumstance,
Aye clean in thought, and clean in feeling,
A pure and gracious heart revealing,
All, God the Holy Spirit sealing.
  Oh he loved all God's living things,
That go on feet, or fly on wings;
He lov'd to tend the tinted flowers,
Or in the sunshine, or in showers;
Deep pondering the hidden cause,
Of growth, and change, and secret laws
By Darwin shewn—that prince of sages—
Working down the distant ages.
And he had deft and cunning hand,

To make ideas great forthstand;
As swift as thought his pencil ran,
To trace invention, sketch out plan,
Or with most rare art-faculty,
Dash off a likeness, by-the-bye,
With rapid touches, quaint and sly.
Books much, not many, he had read,
Slowly and musingly, when led
As captive of great Thinker, Singer,
Or whosoe'er was a truth-bringer.
 But was there nought of fault in him?
Nothing this brightness that could dim?
Ah! he was mortal; therefore flaw'd;
But me Death's most pure touch has aw'd,
Has soften'd, so that now I see
Him from each fault and flaw set free.
Yes, free from every mortal stain,
As he is free from mortal pain -
As dross falls from the cleansèd ore;
As Science kills the deadly spore;
As shadows fade before the light;
As stars most beautify the night—
So do I see him clarified
By sweet ruth of *The Crucified*.
Lo! Sinful, but a sinner sav'd,
In the vast crimson fountain lav'd.
Soul-grace the body bright enfolds,
And to its own pure beauty moulds—
A common face transfiguring,
With that light which no sun doth bring;
Yea, giving it such goodly grace
That the soul's self you see, not face.
But when the body too is fair,
And doth the fair soul's beauty wear,
Now God's own image is restor'd,
As at the first by His great Word.
 'Twas thus with him that we lament—
A body fair to fair soul lent,
For its fine-fitting instrument.
 O! surely they are all in error,
Who still name Death the King of Terror!
The enemy of enemies —
From whom each one instinctive flies.
O surely they have never seen
Dead face like this!—

A heav'nly sheen
Lies on it; yet, alas! we must
Soon (O too soon!) say "dust to dust."
And him the grave must quietly keep
Till he again shall rise from sleep,
On the most awful day appointed,
When Christ the Lord—our King anointed
Shall as the Judge of all the Earth
Us summon to a mightier birth.
Behold! Thrice-wondrous transmutation!
Behold! Fear's sweetest refutation!
O! Jesus Own sweet salutation!
Death in the Lord, turned to a friend,
Us thus benignly home to send,
So that the grave will not receive
Our lov'd, for whom we aching grieve;
Only the garment that he wore;
The mortal flesh alone, no more.
 Lo! Father, mother, in old age
Advanc'd far in their pilgrimage,
Think wistfully, his race now run,
Of all he was to them as son;
Their staff so strong to lean on broken,
Dread anguish never to be spoken.
Fond Sister! to her only brother,
And all in all to one another—
She, too, is left heart-sad, alone—
Her pride, her joy in him, all gone.
 I may not, dare not, seek to tell,
For, oh! it is unspeakable,
What as true husband, father be
E'er sought (of Christ's great grace) to be,
The brightness of his happy home
Firm-anchor'd, all unus'd to roam;
Aye finding truest, deepest joys
Amidst his wife and bonnie boys;
Still chatty, kindly, always pleasant,
If speaking or to peer or peasant.
 Ah! all our hearts are stricken, sore,
Who here shall see his face no more.
 Now we will plant upon his grave
The fairest flowers that fragrance have—
The lilies of the valley pure,
Sweet snowdrops, violets that allure
The Spring's first breath, and a fair cross

Enwrought of daises white, and moss
Gold-speck'd, and the bright maiden-hair
With ivy wreaths so debonair;
And at his head the love-red-rose
That theo' all-changing seasons blows.
There like the red leaves wavering by,
The Robins shall sing pensively,
Clear-warbling their pathetic lay,
Sweet still as in our childhood's day;
And far up in the blinding sky,
The larks shall trill their minstrelsy—
One half of earth, one half of heav'n,—
The rarest singer to man given.
He lov'd them both so tenderly,
'Tis fit that they his grave be nigh.
 Ah! hearts of never-changing love,
Oft hither yearningly shall move;
For through our poor lives' "little while,"

Fond Mem'ry's lamp shall ne'er lack oil.
Still mourning, yet as those who know
He lives above though lost below.
Gone Godward to his heav'nly mansion;
Gone Christward for his soul's expansion;
Gone Godward to th' eternal sureness;
Gone Christward to th' eternal pureness;
Gone to his everlasting rest —
No longer search'd for but possess'd;
Gone—and all mystery left behind,—
Unsullied light in Christ to find;
Gone, with fell sin no more at strife,
Now enter'd into glorious life; [grasp'd,
The white robe worn, the palm-branch
His brow by blood-bought crown enclasp'd;
Life's battle fought, the vict'ry won, [Done."
And heard the dear Lord Christ's "Well

17. In Memoriam—Thomas Ashe, M.A.

(Died December 18th, 1889; interred in Sutton Churchyard, near Macclesfield.)

Alas! Alas! is Ashe to disappear [fear?"
"Without the meed of some melodious
A master-spirit, is there to be none
To tell an English Singer true, is gone?
  'Twas mine to know him, and 'twas mine
    to love ;
To know him was to love him; nor reprove
Can I myself that I stand even now
In deepest reverence, with bared brow.
In heart of hearts of friends, he will lie
    shrin'd,   [twin'd :
With, finest, keenest, subtlest mem'ries
Late ages yet shall pilgrim visits pay ;
Upon his grave my simple wreath I lay.
And if "Songs Now and Then," "Songs
    Here and There,"
Should die ; sad-hearted, I must needs
    despair
That any Singer of our day shall live,
Or name or fame be else than fugitive.
His "Edith," "Lost," and "Found," on to
    "All's Well,"
Are wov'n of stuff men do not buy or sell;
Nor less "Marit,"—of dainty fancies
    wrought ;   [sought ;
"Fair Women," too, that Chaucer had be-
"Hildegarde"—"Plectrude"—"Yseult"—
    starry three,
Born daughters all of immortality ;
With many things of thrice-perfected art,
Flower-fair, shell-fair, with which Time
    ne'er shall part.

He was a Thinker from his earliest days ;
Yet never was he one to lightly raise
Perplexities, or feeblest faith to shake ;
The problems came to him, and he must
    make
Effort to pierce to their most inner core ;
Now plumbing deep, and now, how he
    would soar !
You gaz'd and listened as a-hush, you saw,
'Neath Clouds of Glory, old Seer's faith and awe;
That light of glory in his brooding eyes
Which is not earth-begot, but of the skies.
He had the child's heart, but the strong
    man's brain ;
Before The Man supremest, he would rein
His chafing thoughts, and say, "I'll bide
    His time ;"
Then how he warbled of the ampler clime.
  He was a Reader, aye reflective, slow ;
Read much, not many ; in the books that go
T' enrich the brain, as live blood from the
    heart ;   [part
Elect books and great-thoughted ; chiefest
Of this our England's mighty heritage,
That to all times and climes flings down the
    gage
To none on earth yielding supremacy ;
Great Chaucer—Spenser—Milton—in
    our sky   [soul'd, august ;
Bright stars, with Shakespeare, mighty-
And Bacon—Browne and Hooker—that
    no dust

IN MEMORIAM—THOMAS ASHE, M.A.

Can ever dim. How eloquent he grew
As with mellifluous cadences, he drew
The FUTURE vast of our great English
   tongue—
Of all speech mightiest, or said, or sung :
And how diviner is the sov'reignty
Of these immortals that uncrownèd lie
Than of mere titled rulers ; intellect [deck'd.
And goodness far beyond mere purple-
O it made tumult in one's blood to listen ;
Yea tears—inevitable tears—would glisten
When he discoursed of England's worthies
   bright: [height
And led us on, and up to some peak'd
Of reasoning, or song, or deathless deed;
Giving to each and all distinctive meed.
How bounteous-fed was his full MEMORY !
How ordered its vast stores' so that his eye
Seem'd to o'erlook all he had ever read
Or known, until we stood astonishèd.
A SCHOLAR ripe was he ; for rung on rung
Had he climbed up, till at his girdle hung
The keys of many languages, whose lore
He held with fine reserve; and would explore
Another and another—yet all wore
In modesty: so that you had to bring
Sharp pressure ere he would wide open fling
His wondrous spoils of learning, or bewray
Such learning as is rare at this late day.
He was a GENTLE MAN of the old style:
Free from pretence, as he was free from
   guile ;
Shy, lonely, self-contained, until there came
Another —and but one —of kindred frame:
How then, as 'neath the ice the torrents
   roar,
Sparklingly his hid musings he would pour
In musical yet piercing monotone;
As reading a Greek chorus, or his own,
Or grappling with some problem social
Or politic-ecclesiastical; [paint ;
A still-remembered landscape he would
Or character, in phrasing rich and quaint,

Whether it was some hero or some saint.
He was old-mannered, yet as blithe as boy
Ere the "fine gold" of youth has got alloy.
Out-spoken, fervid, but aye sadly mute
To scandal-monger—base and involute.
You felt his hand-shake as a benison;
The sun that day upon you warmer shone.
I may not speak of deeper things and great;
To memory they still are consecrate.
His blue eyes kindling, quivering of his lips,
You saw the Seer of the Apocalypse.
But most of all this noble sp'rit was set
To wear an English Poet's Coronet. [most
A few green leaves or simplest flowers, the
He sought ; far, far from him was it to
   boast ;
But none the less, half awed, he inly felt
That he the Maker's dower, held, to melt,
To elevate, and write immortal things ;
With dulcet touch that when it writeth sings,
And you catch lustre as of angels' wings.
Pathetic now his " Apologia;"
Sad-sweet, yet fragrant, as with cassia :—
"O my poor flowers dead in lap of Spring,"
We read, and soft tears to our eye-lids
   bring ; [cry—
And its half-sobbing and dove-mourning
"Yet I must still go singing till I die :"
Upon his cheeks and in h s eyes the flame
That tells of singer's aching for pure fame;
If only he might hold a worthy place
'Mongst poets of the mighty English race :
Nor England, shalt thou wrong this son of
   thine ; [mine
As men draw gold, long-hid, forth from the
Shall lovers of true poesy find here
" Brave translunary things," and hush'd
   draw near,
To read the name of ASHE—a knightly soul,
And a "sweet singer," beyond Time's con-
   trol.
Hail and farewell ! " This side idolatry"
I lov'd thee, and without thee heart-bruis'd
   sigh.

PAIN.

We know that the whole creation groaneth and travaileth in pain together until now—Romans vii. 22.

Said Lillo to Romola ... "I should like to be something that would make me a great man, and very happy besides—something that would not hinder me from having a good deal of pleasure." "That is not easy, my Lillo. It is only a poor sort of happiness that could ever come by caring very much about our own narrow pleasures. We can only have the highest happiness, such as goes along with being a great man, by having wide thoughts, and much feeling for the rest of the world as well as ourselves; and this sort of happiness often brings so much pain with it, that we can only tell it from pain by its being what we would choose before everything else, because our souls see it is good. There are so many things wrong and difficult in the world, that no man can be great—he can hardly keep himself from wickedness—unless he gives up thinking much about pleasure or rewards, and gets strength to endure what is hard and painful. My father had the greatness that belongs to integrity; he chose poverty and obscurity rather than falsehood. And there was Fra Girolamo—you know why I keep to-morrow sacred; he had the greatness which belongs to a life spent in struggling against powerful wrong, and in trying to raise men to the highest deeds they are capable of. And so my Lillo, if you mean to act nobly and seek to know the best things God has put within reach of men, you must learn to fix your mind on that end, and not on what will happen to you because of it. And remember, if you were to choose something lower, and make it a rule of your life to seek your own pleasure and escape from what is disagreeable, calamity might come just the same; and it would be calamity falling on a base mind, which is the one form of sorrow that has no balm in it, and that may well make a man say,—"It would have been better for me if I had never been born!" (GEORGE ELIOT: Romola 'Epilogue').

1 Oh mystery of PAIN,—
   Strong even FAITH to strain,
   Yea LOVE itself to stain!
   Oh mystery of PAIN!

2 Is it of Heav'n or Hell?
   A blessing or a spell?
   Is it paean or knell?
   Thy secret who may tell.

3 Thou all-pervading PAIN?
   (Unseen electric chain
   (Stretching o'er land and main;
   Pulsing from foot to brain).

4 Inherited disease,—
   As one in children sees;
   Leaves the heart ill at ease,
   Even when upon our knees.

5 PAIN has strange instruments,
   Which HOPE, sad-ey'ed, assents
   Are awful,—and laments,
   With dark presentiments.

6 And yet, "my Lord, my God,"
   The Spirit "shed abroad"
   Relieves th' unmeasur'd load;
   Makes bloom and fruit the rod.

   As to ripe grain the flail;
   As blow unto the nail;
   As frost to blossom pale;
   As to wind the bulg'd sail;

8 So is PAIN in God's care,
   Deliv'rance, and not snare;
   Bringing blessing un'ware;
   This is seen ev'rywhere.

9 Love overruleth all;
   To whoe'er on Christ call;
   A veil, and not a pall,
   Across our Earth doth fall.

10 How vast the range of PAIN!
   Abundant as thick rain
   That spoils our Autumn grain,
   Full sowing all in vain.

11 Yet it is not of CHANCE,
   Nor of mere circumstance;
   But man's inheritance:
   Clear shewn unto Faith's glance.

12 Why PAIN? That it may warn,
   That we more caution learn;
   Lest we for evil yearn:
   Ah! only grief to earn.

13 As friction in machine
    Calls SKILL to intervene, —
    So PAIN when rightly seen,
    As on Christ's breast we lean.

14 PAIN circleth the least child,
    That it be not beguil'd,
    Nor by temptation foil'd ;
    Uninjured—only soil'd.

15 Lo ! Drawn by bick'ring flame
    The child seeks to play game:
    PAIN telleth him his blame—
    Flushing his cheek with shame.

16 EVIL, the young attracts,
    But quick PAIN God enacts
    Stern penalty exacts ;
    For breaking of HIS pacts.

17 So that the smart awakes,
    And from base purpose shakes;
    As, conscience-struck he aches,
    And the monition takes.

18 Why PAIN ? Life to safe-guard,—
    Life sweeter far than nard ;
    Threat'ning danger to ward,
    That the soul be not marr'd.

19 Why PAIN ? That it may give
    Key-note how man shall live
    Up to's prerogative;
    Not rul'd by fugitive.

20 Why PAIN ? To fill with awe
    Before all-present LAW,
    And us to kneeling draw;
    Owning our every flaw.

21 That PENALTY we see
    In Earth, and sky, and sea;
    And ever wakeful be,
    From our tempters to flee.

22 Why PAIN ? To shew the root
    Of SIN's death-dealing fruit,
    And that FIRST LIE refute;
    In God's strength resolute.

23 PAIN is a subtle thing;
    Hides honey near its sting;
    And makes forlorn heart sing,
    As Christ doth His peace bring.

24 The cruel scourge and jail,
    Made not apostles quail,
    But all with songs to hail,
    Bright clad in Faith's strong mail.

25 PAIN is the cord that ties
    Our hearts to the blest skies,
    In true self-sacrifice ;
    Shewn Love's anointed eyes.

26 Sacrifice is the flower
    Of all man's moral power,—
    Nurtur'd as by soft shower;
    God's finest richest dower.

27 But sacrifice means PAIN,
    Means wearing of a chain ;
    Nor vilest to disdain,
    Or helping to restrain.

28 Sacrifice—born of LOVE,—
    Heroes, martyrs, approve;
    Vibrates to Christ Above,
    As our hearts to Him move.

29 Through PAIN, far upward drawn,
    As from NIGHT leaps the DAWN;
    Of bliss we hold the pawn,
    Trampling upon DOUBT's spawn.

30 PAIN, by touch of God's Hand,
    Makes callous hearts to stand
    Aw'd, by His reprimand,
    And His correcting wand.

31 Saul, taken in the way,
    Sharp-wounded, smitten lay—
    Oh ! blessèd, holy fray !
    Anon, behold him pray.

32 PAIN sifts the chaff from wheat;
    PAIN truth detects, and cheat;
    Till we it grateful greet,
    And the Lord makes us meet.

33 As furnace-fire refines,—
   Only the dross calcines;
   PAIN proveth, and then shines,
   And " perfect peace " inshrines.

34 PAIN, well-borne, nerves the heart
   To play a noble part;
   To DARE, whate'er the smart,
   'Gainst ev'n thick-coming dart.

35 If conquest thou would'st win
   In strife 'twixt grace and sin;
   Seek PAIN'S keen discipline:
   Christ breaks its javelin.

36 Would'st thou chant victor's song
   Then "*suffer* and be strong";
   Strength cometh, soon or long,
   Nor wilt thou suffer wrong.

37 PAIN trains to patience oft,
   Till not proud word that scoff'd
   Falleth—but meek and soft,
   As still rain on the croft.

38 PAIN is the salt of life,
   With all " fine issues " rife,
   Howe'er with sense at strife,
   Yea and wielding edg'd knife.

39 It is not in caprice,
   Or as of joy to fleece,
   Our PAIN and woe increase;
   Christ suffers no false peace.

40 We in His footsteps tread;
   Led ev'n as He was " led;"
   Be not astonished,
   But Hope's own bright tears shed.

41 Steadfast endurance lifts
   'Bove darkest cloud that drifts;
   And of its hurts PAIN sifts,
   So that the pressure shifts.

42 By PAIN COMPASSION thrills;
   Christ's law of love fulfils,
   And medicines all ills,
   Until HOPE sweetly trills.

43 PAIN mitigates our fear,—
   No PAIN, the end is near;
   We moan ev'n thankful hear,
   As voice from Heav'n's own sphere.

44 As sweetest, fairest rose
   On sharpest spines oft blows;
   So JOY may spring from woes,
   Far deeper than World knows.

45 Seekest thou sympathy
   With those in PAIN that lie;
   Know thyself Christ's "strong cry,"
   In the Garden's agony.

46 Thus heart to heart is knit,
   So that if one be smit
   Lamp of RUTH swift is lit;
   Lighting up darkest pit.

47 PAIN holiest souls has prov'd.—
   Long-lasting not remov'd;
   Shewing they most were lov'd,
   Blessing with grief inwov'd.

48 Not PAIN, but PAIN well-borne,
   With patience and not scorn;
   Ne'er leaves a heart forlorn,
   Or no rose for the thorn;

49 The CROSS interpreting,
   The Gospel minist'ring;
   Till to our Christ we cling,
   And our ALL on Him fling.

50 Thro' PAIN are charters won;
   From "bleeding sire to son";
   Suff'ring great deeds has done,—
   Greatest aneath the sun.

51 O Lamb of God, all PAIN
   Smote THEE upon ROOD slain;
   So came Redemption's gain;
   FAITH and LOVE'S glad refrain.

52 As Horeb's Bush illum'd,
   Burn'd glorious unconsum'd,
   Be PAIN to me perfum'd,
   Yea, and victory plum'd.

PAIN.

53 Jesus! Thy crown of thorns
Than golden more adorns—
Tho' the great world still scorns,
All PAIN to glory turns.

54 PAIN ne'er is of God sent
But for admonishment;
Purpose with suff'ring blent,
That the WILL may be bent.

55 Our eyes to see are dim,—
Ay, eyes of seraphim;
Avaunt, ye devils grim!
The secret is with Him.

56 Hidden, but ne'er unjust—
O God! help me to trust,
Bow'd 'fore Thee in the dust;
Submissive to Thy "must."

57 Who in Thy wisdom rare
Weav'st darkest threads or fair,
As Thy true ones can bear;
Leaving none to despair.

58 Nor may we doubt at all
Whate'er doth us befall,
GOOD o'er ILL triumph shall,
And all men on Christ call.

59 Sorrow shall change to mirth;
The long travail of Earth
Heralds a mighty birth,
That shall feed the World's dearth.

60 Lo! The glad day shall burst
When Earth—a sick child nurs'd—
Shall be no more PAIN-curs'd;
Hell, smitten at its worst.

61 O Holy Spirit, I
Lift unto Thee my cry;
All my PAIN sanctify;
Pleading 'fore Thee I lie.

62 Lo "Comforter" is Thy Name!
In my PAIN Thee I claim;
Put Thou not me to shame,
Alive keep my Faith's flame.

63 Join'd in Thy Glory, Lord,
Fulfil Thy gracious word,
Thy PAIN and mine accord;
So finer joy afford.

64 Deeper love, Christ, impart;
Thine Own Love fill my heart;
All murm'ring this will thwart,
With skill beyond all art.

65 O Thou THE CRUCIFIED
By grace to Thee allied;
All fear is falsified;
All PAIN is sanctified.

18. For Youth and "Little Ones."

THE SNOW-STORM.

A SNOW-STORM that, in the far north of Scotland, came suddenly down during the month of May—an especially bright and pleasant May—is still remembered as "the May Snow-storm." Many incidents of it have been transmitted. One that seems to me exceedingly pathetic and beautiful thus authentically runs:—"On the night in question a poor widowed woman, carrying in her plaided bosom a sickly infant, was making her difficult way home across a lonely moor, and down a deep glen. Setting out in the early 'gloamin'' (twilight), she struggled against the unexpected storm with a brave heart, and reached the middle of the glen. At this point she was still a good two miles from human habitation and her own home. Worn out, she strove to find a sheltering place for her infant, that relieved of her tender burden, she might push forward for help, and return. On the instant, a flash of lightning that vividly illumined the entire horizon, must have shown her a great rock, that at the base of it had a 'cleft' far away under. Hither she crept, and, stripping herself of all possible of her own clothing, she put her babe in there. All who knew her said this would be done with prayer. And so once more she faced the terrific snow-storm; hail, and mist, and rain combined inscrutably. She cannot have gone many yards from the rock when she must have swooned and fallen. In the morning her body was found by the villagers. As they were engaged lifting the corpse, a low, feeble wail caught their ears. Listening again, again it reached them, and the "cleft in the rock" was found, and the poor woman's infant safe and warm. It need hardly be said that the dead mother was borne softly home and decently interred; nor that the orphan found kind friends. The sorrowful sequel is, that the child grew up to be a particularly rough, wayward and bad boy; so much so that he well nigh broke the heart of the good woman who, for his godly mother's sake, had adopted him. He became notorious for every kind of wickedness. Again and again he was in gaol, and once was sentenced to seven years of penal servitude. At last he enlisted in a Highland regiment, and shared the lights and shadows of a soldier's life. He went through the Crimean war. At Inkerman (it is believed) he lost a leg, carried off by a cannon-ball. While in the hospital at Scutari, the Past came back to him, and his childhood's story, of how his mother had saved his life at the cost of her own, when she placed him in the lightning-revealed "cleft of the rock;" and he showed meltings of heart. It so happened that while thus softened, one of the hospital nurses (a lady) one evening sang Toplady's "Rock of Ages." It had a thrilling effect upon (as all thought) the dying soldier. As he sobbed and moaned, the sweet singer told him of redeeming love and of salvation to the uttermost. He narrated to the lady-nurse, in turn, his infant escape. He recovered, and was discharged, and sent back to Scotland. Tragical to say, the emotion and convictions of the hospital-bed passed away; and spite of his being a cripple, and otherwise wounded, he ran his old course of drunkenness and profligacy, his pension payment-time being habitually a week of debauchery. Circumstances led him to revisit his birthplace. Nobody remembered him there, and he knew nobody. On the Sabbath he made his way to the village "old churchyard," that he might see his mother's grave. It was one sheet of 'gowans' (daisies), for the excellent woman's memory was a holy thing thro' four generations. He was greatly moved. He went into the church. Lowly and unadorned, the 'kirk' (Secession now United Presbyterian) was none the less a House of God. The very gospel of the blessed God was preached—grandly, fully preached within it. The closing hymn—strangely and yet not strangely—was again Toplady's "Rock of Ages," by which the Spirit of God had ten years before spoken to the old soldier. It came upon him with startling and awing distinctness, giving resurrection to forgotten feelings and forgotten days. He sank down in the pew, and "wept bitterly," wounded of Him who alone can heal. It was the turning-point of his life, everlastingly. He cast himself just as he was, "a poor sinner and nothing at all," on the infinite mercy, and infinite patience, and infinite love of the Lord Jesus, as his very own Saviour; and after a sore conflict found "perfect peace." He survived for at least other five years, and gave evidence of the Divine heart-change in a touchingly lowly, penitent, abased, devout life. In a ripe old age, when his head was like the driven snow, and when he was really a fine-looking old man—standing, as he did, six feet two inches—he was laid in his mother's grave. There he "sleeps well." The double recurrence of Toplady's hymn, "Rock of Ages," as resting on his own child-deliverance in the "cleft of the rock," is only another proof of how much stranger truth is than the most imaginative fiction. I have tried to put the incident into verse, as told to me (for there are variations as well as parallels elsewhere located) with only a little colouring in the frame-work.

Part I.

1 'Tis the old sweet-breath'd month of May;
  Leaves are grass-green on ev'ry spray;
  Blithe birds singing their roundelay.
2 But swift the sky is over-cast;
  Chilling, destructive, roars the blast;
  Winter returns when it had past.
3 Thick descend with wildering fall
  The ghostly snow-flakes, and a pall
  Spreads over groves erst musical.
4 Dread as e'er December night,
  The tempest rages in its might;
  Putting timorous May to flight.
5 Facing the tempest in its wrath,
  Toiling along the drifted path,
  Lo! a woman—what is't she hath?
6 She bears upon her anxious breast
  A sickly infant in dull rest;
  Weary and worn, haggard, opprest.
7 Groping and struggling on and on,
  Dark, fearing, wistful, and lone—
  Alas! for her affliction!
8 The ground is treach'rous as morass,
  Yet deadly smooth as is the glass:
  How may she hope o'er it to pass?
9 But there is that within her heart—
  A mother's love—that still doth dart
  New life, and courage fresh impart.
10 Low words of pray'r are whisper'd faintly
  With look appealing, sweet and saintly—
  As told in olden legends quaintly.
11 The narrow glen with hail is lash'd;
  The trees together loud are clash'd;
  Mother and babe to earth are dash'd.
12 "O gracious God, show me the way,
  To some near place where I may lay
  At least my child." So she doth pray.

13 There flashed forth then the lightning
   keen,
   And lo! beneath its vehement sheen
   A great rock with a cleft is seen.
14 Forward she staggers, faint and lorn ;
   Into the cleft her babe is borne :
   So she will leave it till the morn.
15 Baried of tender burden, now
   Onward for help, behold her go,
   Right thro' the whirling, blinding snow.
16 Few are her steps : the rain and ice
   Beat in her face and blind her eyes ;
   She swoons —and is in Paradise.
17 With early dawn along the glen
   Come kindly women and strong men ;
   The poor corpse, wan and stark, they ken.
18 Softly they raise the storm-slain one :
   The women weep, the strong men moan
   O'er the dead mother left so lone.
19 But, hark! e'en thro' the furious gale,
   A sound as of an infant's wail,
   Their startled ears doth now assail.
20 They list and list, with all eyes bent
   In ruth and wistful wilderment ;
   To find from whence the sound is sent.
21 Again it came, tho' faint and low ;
   A broken wail, a cry of woe ;
   With a bound they stand the rock below.
22 Folded round is the babe with care ;
   Motherly love has left herself bare
   I' the awful night and the bleak air.
23 The orphan's to the village ta'en ;
   Warm hearts adopt him ; not in vain
   Rose his mother's pray'r thro' the rain.

PART II.

24 Long years have pass'd—the child's a
   man :
   Alas ! a wicked course he ran ;
   Winning not benison but ban.
25 Drunkard and thief, waif of the street ;
   At the hulks seven years complete ;
   The way to hell the path of his feet.
26 A soldier at last, reckless and daring ;
   Heedless of man ; of Evil unfearing ;
   And the devil's own livery wearing.
27 At Inkerman— that terrible day
   As he fought in the bloody fray
   A cannon bore a limb away.
28 Brave comrades, from that carnage wild,
   Carried him, helpless as when a child
   His mother nurs'd him an infant mild.
29 Death shakes his dart before his eyes ;
   For weeks on weeks wasting he lies ;
   Hope is now kindled and now dies.
30 Softly, a lady fair as day,
   Sang 'mid the wounded a sweet lay,
   Cheering them on along their way.
31 Low, tenderly the lady sang,
   The "Rock of Ages," and it rang
   O'er *his* bed, and gave him a pang.
32 Why ? Ah, his own childhood's story
   Came back to him, now he is hoary ;
   Whisp'ring of his mother in glory. [shed,
33 Tears —first tears for long years—are
   Falling on the hospital-bed :
   There is a rainbow overhead.
34 Still " Rock of Ages cleft for me "
   The gentle voice sings clear and free ;
   The old soldier sobs audibly.
35 Oh, 'twas the Spirit striving still
   With His own peace that heart to fill,
   And win the wayward, sin-thrall'd will.
36 Came the lady with gracious look,
   Open'd and read the Holy Book ;
   Till with remorse the soldier shook.
37 He told her of the ' cleft' long ago,
   Which the lightning show'd, and saved
      him so ;   [snow.
   When his mother perish'd that May of
38 Alas! it pass'd as the morning dew ;
   Forth he went his course to renew ;
   Only to wicked impulses true.
39 Oh, 'twas pitiful him to see,
   Old and beggar'd, in misery ;
   Wretched as reprobate could be.
40 Yet ten years now are pass'd, and lo !
   The old man to the old home doth go ;
   But none now care for him, or know.

41 To the old churchyard the old man hies,
  Where his mother in lowly grave lies:
  Her mound is spangled with day's eyes.
42 The heart is touch'd; and once more tears
  Fall thick and fast, as mem'ry bears
  The old man back to his infant years.
43 Into the House of God he goes;
  Bows his head: the Spirit knows
  And on that harden'd heart He blows.
44 Praise and prayers to heav'n ascended:
  The old man's trembling accents blended;
  God's blessing on the Word descended.
45 Oh, not by chance it was that then
  Sweet "Rock of Ages" rose again—
  Heaven's echo from the snowy glen.
46 And now at last the thing is done;
  Now the grand heart-change is begun;
  Now the prodigal is a son.
47 The dear old hymn was us'd of the Lord,
  To be His Own converting word;
  Piercing the heart as with a sword.
48 The old man humbly loves to tell,
  How far he stray'd, how deep he fell;
  How the Spirit strove and sav'd him from
49 Yea and oft of the "cleft" he speaks [hell.
  And the big tears still wet his cheeks,
  And "Rock of Ages" his old heart breaks.
50 Now in white-hair'd serene old age,
  Pass'd five more years; we may presage
  A calm close to his pilgrimage.
51 And in the "cleft" he is secure, [endure:
  Long as "The Rock" Himself shall
  O blessèd refuge! sweet and sure.

THREE BIRTH-DAY GIFTS TO A LITTLE GIRL.—A LIFE STORY.

Four decades ago, when I was young,
A fair girl I knew, and of her sung
In many a rapt and yearning rhyme,
To music of Love's golden clime.
And now when we are both growing old,
I grudge her story should not be told.
  My head is grey, and alas! my hand
Reft of its first cunning to command
Such dulcet strain as to her is due,
Seeking to tell only what is true.
Yet I fain would try (tho' all unskill'd)
To utter memories wherewith I'm filled.
  God bless her! when a sweet young child,
She led me to Him, the undefil'd; [words,
Drew me and drew me, with tender
As sweet as the notes of singing birds:
O how may I hope my debt to tell,
For (ah me!) it is unspeakable!
  Lo! now I see her, a radiant girl,
With gold-red locks in many a curl;
And eyes of blue, that in me awake
Thoughts of Como, its sky and its lake;
Then O the charm of her dimpling cheeks!
A doméd brow, that a MIND bespeaks,—
Latent subtlety and gentle power;
Her lips rose-red, and with such a dower
Of pearly teeth, and soft-sculptur'd chin,
As enkindles rapture without sin.
  Fairest of children out of Heaven,
It was her birthday; her age was sev'n.
Father and mother unto her brought
A gold Moss-rose, in pot finely wrought;
Sooth 'twas a thing of beauty, and
Made still more beautiful, in her hand.
'Tis sweet to-day to recall her look,
As carolling like a hidden brook,
She kissed her thanks, and with a trill
Set her birthday gift i'th' window-sill
Of her own room. (I chanc'd to be there
And I saw all by good fortune rare).
  Came the Spring to prank its tender leaves; [eaves;
Came the whisp'ring winds under the
Came the Summer's sunshine, and its rain
Tap-tapping upon the window pane;
Came the Autumnal mellowing dews,
With blooms and buds, of all changing hues: [night,
'Twas the last thing she look'd at each
The first she look'd at with morning light.

Two dainty buds that soon came, she gave
Father and mother; the third I have.
(Faded long since; yet to my old eyes
'Tis beautiful still just as it lies;
E'en if it be turned all to dust,
Into my coffin it goes, I trust.) [strong!
One night a tempest ah! swift and
Rag'd for hours upon hours; and along
The land and the sea, work'd havoc sore;
Wrecking what ages could not restore;
A vast-boled oak of a thousand years
Fell; and the tall Light-house off the meres.

Our fair Child heard it not, nor awoke
Until the morning upon her broke:
(So He gives His beloved sleep—
Tranquil and soft and dreamless and deep).
She soon went to see her rose-tree fair,
To cull a bud for a Cottager—
(A lowly widow, white-hair'd and frail,
And one to whom THE CHRIST says ' All hail!') [blown,
She gave a start; for away 'twas
By the whirling storm, and to ground thrown.
My poor Child had a lump in her throat,
As together her wee hands she smote;
And rush'd into the back yard, to find
Her rose kill'd by the pitiless wind.
Broken, and soil'd, and wither'd, it lay,
Filling the dear young heart with dismay;
Dismay and grief, and her eyes with tears—
(O blame her not: remember her years).

Beneath a tree sat father and mother,
Talking o'er the storm with each other;
And fond love-light enkindling their eyes
They plan for their Child, a sweet surprise.
Anon little Maud drew near; her face
Of her grief shewing pathetic trace—
With a shy look of unconscious grace,
She told her brief story of the Rose;

How the bad storm wind, last night, with blows
Had out of its place her gift flower shak'n
And its life in all its sweetness, taken;
Broken her pot and the laden stem—
(It might have been Beauty's diadem):
The poor young heart gave way; and she hung [tongue.
On her mother's heart, with falt'ring
Father and mother led her away
Across the meadow, to where there lay—
Like white wee clouds of a Summer's sky
That the shepherd-star folds charmingly—
Of sheep and of lambs, a comely flock;
One lamb 'neath shadow of a rock.
Prettily prettily there it couch'd,
As tho' expectant, I had avouch'd,
That *her* pet-lamb it was meant to be—
Could a sweeter mistress Lamb e'er see?
Pointing to the o'ershadowing stone,
" The lamb is yours, Maud, and yours alone; [take,
This for your welcome eighth birth-day
And grieve no more for your Rose's sake."
Thus father and mother tenderly,
Sought their sweet Child's heart-sore tears to dry;
'Twas indeed a charming birthday gift:
Spotless as ever the virgin drift:
-The drifted snow that so softly fills
The sunless clefts of lonely hills.
Then, with great open eyes of wonder,
Her heart quick-throbbing her breast under; [for me?
Maud answer made—" What! the Lamb
O is't possible that this can be?
A real live lamb and all my own
To play with as my companion?
Oh thanks, you are most good and kind,
Thus my heart's rose-sorrow to up-bind."
'Twas a pleasant sight for all to see,
The Child and Lamb on the daisied lea;
Racing and chasing at Morning's dawn,
Over the meadow, over the lawn.

I'm sure bits of sugar oft were miss'd ;
I'm sure again and again they kiss'd ;
Racing and chasing with boundless mirth,
Like creatures scarcely of sinful earth.
 Alas! alas! again Sorrow lour'd,
And a second storm of anguish shower'd
On poor little Maud. Early one morn,
Half-hidden 'midst the yellowing corn,
Her Lamb lay dead.
                  O 'twere hard to tell
This trouble fresh that to Maud befell!
And hard to see o'er her wan face pass
—Like shadow over the shining grass—
Her look of pain—half of terror born,
As she felt how sharp was this new thorn.
   Words would not come ; but close to
        her breast
Her poor dead Lamb she passionate prest;
And with alternating tear and moan
Sate motionless as a fixed stone. [Child,
   Father and mother sought out their
In her loss grieved ; and with words mild,
Soft, gentle, loving, shared her grief,
Seeking again to bring her relief.   [see
"O look, dear Maud, look ; and yonder
Better far than any Moss-rose tree ;
Better far than Lamb, or aught can be ;
Look, dear, take that for ninth birth-day
     gift ;   [lift."
And once more in brightness your face
   She heard their voices (rather than
      words)
Like skilful hand touching tender chords ;
Raised her pitiful tear-fill'd eyes
(Soft as the azure of rain-dimm'd skies)
And waited. And then again they spoke,
And in on her melting sorrow broke ;
Pointing her to their own Baby-boy,
Who lately brought to their home new joy.
   Cradled 'neath a wide-bough'd Cedar
      tree,
Cooing and gooing right merrily ;
There he was, her sweet baby-brother
(Very miniature of his mother).
   She look'd and re-look'd, but felt as tho'

It were only adding blow to blow
Thus strangely to put aside her woe.
   "O father, mother, dear Hubert take
For my new birth-gift, and of him make
Treasure, in place of my Lamb and
   Flower
That I've been robbed of in evil hour ?
Never, oh never ! It may not be !
How little he is surely you see ?
My poor dead Lamb, after me would go,
Calling 'ma! ma! ma!' (Maud you
   must know),
And run me a race ; and oh, how sweet
Was the patter of his jetty feet !
And soft note of his innocent bleat ;
But Hubert"——
                  On the instant she felt
Her sisterly heart within her melt ;
Saw that indeed her baby-brother
Far better was than one or other
Of former Birth-gifts.
            Then up she sprang,
Now all-forgetting her double-pang,
Sweet and gracious words the while she
Full lavishing on the cradl'd boy [sang ;
The swift bright current of her fresh joy.

   Once more the bright sun above her
      smil'd,
And day after day the Child and Child
Together play'd, and lov'd, and grew
As flowers beneath Heav'n's nurturing
   dew.

   Two Lambs they were of the Shep-
      herd's fold
From their chrism-birth 'mongst His Own
   enroll'd ;
And oh ! fair picture it was to see
Them run together in fearless glee.
   But what is this that a Poet sings ?
Of one whose young heart keen sorrow
   wrings ?
Listen, oh ! listen ; for it doth tell
As sad grief as e'er did bosom swell :

THREE BIRTH-DAY GIFTS TO A LITTLE GIRL.—A LIFE STORY.

"O! ever thus from Childhood's hour,
I've seen my fondest hopes decay; /200
I never lov'd a tree or flower,
But 'twas the first to fade away.
I never nurs'd a dear gazelle,
To glad me with its soft black eye,
But when it came to know me well,
And love me, it was sure to die.
Nor too—the joy most like divine
Of all I ever dreamt or knew,
To see thee, love thee, call thee mine.—
O mercy! must I lose that too." * /210

Ev'n so was't now; for the story of old,
Is ev'ry day, and still must be told.

Fever came with its burning finger,
And through long days and nights did
    linger; [brow,
Pressing sharp and keen, the throbbing
Parching the tongue, life-pulse sinking
    low, [ebb out,
Now Hope would rise high and now
Alternately with fear and with doubt;
Sometimes child-prattle and bright'ning
    eye, /220
Seemed to assure 'No! he will not die';
But the next moment, all rack'd with pain
And every feature on the strain,
Each bonnie wee cheek, with purple flush
Like a flame that ever did up rush; 10
Burning within with a smother'd rage,
As if a mortal war it would wage
In his body's tiny citadel,
Where Beauty with Innocence did dwell:
Oh such was the bitter agony, 230
One almost long'd that the child would
    die.

Prayers went up from hearts believing,
Quiet submissiveness achieving;
For the Child's life, if that were the best;
Or failing it, to give His Own rest.

The sun was setting, the after-glow
Shone into the room (I see it now);
A light of glory fell on the bed,
And a nimbus crown'd the infant head;

Transfiguring fair the changing face, 240
With splendor as of a heav'nly place:
Paling as paled the pallid West:
Sudden the great eyes clos'd, and then
    'drest
Now to go to the Golden City,
So pass'd he to Infinite Pity.
Oh how may I dare again to tell
The shadow dark that on Maud now fell;
The terrors of anguish 'gan to swell!
Oh 'twas awful on her grief to look
As over the wee dead face she shook; 250
All consolation now refusing,
With her wild eyes and words, accusing—
"You gave me the Rose that storm
    o'erthrew; [slew;
You gave me the Lamb which Autumn
And then you gave me a dearer one;
But my baby-brother too is gone:
All that I ever have loved have died."
Here my Maud broke down, and wildly
    cried—
Her words thick-coming importunate,
In uttermost grief disconsolate,—
"O mother, give me something that I
May love and love, that will never die."
Most meetly were the sad words spoken,
Yet, sweetly sad; and sure a token
That the dear Lord was about to deal
With that bruised heart, its wounds to
    heal;
The wounds that Sorrow in her had made
In His Own sweet Child—our little maid.
Tenderly father and mother spake,
Making all their own their Child's heart-
    ache;
They told her soft and low His story,
From manger-crib to final glory; [love
Then whisper'd how "there was One to
Who ne'er, no ne'er from her would
    remove;
One—and His Name too was from a Rose,
The crimson Rose that on Sharon blows;
Yes, and 'the Lamb' was also His Name:
Lamb of the dread sacrificial flame;

---

* The Fire-worshippers in Lalah Rookh.

And He* yes, is our 'Elder Brother';
Never has there been such Another;
Love Jesus, Maud, and He ne'er will die,
Love Him, and He'll take you to the sky,
When your pilgrimage on earth is done,
The battle fought and the vict'ry won."
Once more with rounded eyes of wonder
The Child quiver'd the sweet words under;
Uplifted her mouth them both to kiss,
Sobbing soft, "O this is bliss of bliss!
With Jesus now I will leave my smart.
To my Jesus now I give my heart;
All, all to Him give, THE UNDEFIL'D;
If He will have me a sinful Child."
   And thus the THREE BIRTH-DAY GIFTS
     withdrawn;
The Rose in its pot and Lamb on lawn;
And then sweet Hubert, the Baby-boy,
Her latest and greatest birth-day joy;
Successive, being all sanctified,   [died:
Won the dear young heart to Him who
Won it; and on, from that very hour
Such was in her heart His gracious power,
That day by day she still sweeter grew,
Until she stood 'mongst the chosen few
Who on this the hither side attain
That life of God, which most die to gain;
Pure the purity of its whiteness!
Radiant its unearthly brightness!
For through her long and varying years
Maud has liv'd for Christ, and now she wears
Like to a silver crown, her hoar hairs,
Found still in the way of Righteousness: 310
O MY DEAR GOD, 'KEEP' HER AYE, AND
                           [BLESS.

STORY OF THE LOST SHEEP.

*That would not go into the fold, but which
ran in when her lamb was taken and borne
within. A message to mourners.*
It was a Shepherd and a sheep:
The way was long and rough and steep;
And by the closing of the day
That none of all his flock might stray,
He guided them into green fields,

That thickly wooded mountain shields:
Foot-sore some and well-nigh dead
All the flock within was led.
"All the flock?" Nay counting o'er
The shepherd found there was one more. 10
  He scann'd all round with troubled face
But missing one he could not trace,
He grudg'd to lose it, and still hop'd
To find; when, lo! where downward slop'd
A ferny bank, 'bove a running stream
That caught the sunset's crimson beam,
He saw the LOST ONE; and quick-hasting,
—Its instant peril clear forecasting—
Sought to lead it into the Fold
And shelter it from Autumn's cold.
But 'twould take no heed to his call,
Running back and back; until all
His skill and patience naught availing
Neither his dog nor crook prevailing,
He must leave it—leave to perish
If he his flock would guard and cherish.
  But as he turn'd away to go,
There came a lamb's bleat, soft and low,
As though to him it were appealing
And another LOST one revealing.   30
  Swift as thought he bounded back,
Sprang 'mongst the ferns, and on the track,
Lo! a lamb—the Sheep's lamb—was seen
Shiv'ring in the East Wind keen.
Most carefully he took it up,
As he might a full-brimm'd cup,
Or his own tir'd little child
Found asleep on the moorland wild:
And all gently bore it down—
But he goes not now alone,   40
Wistful eager to him goes
That *Lost Sheep*—her lamb she knows,
The shepherd marks her, and moves on
Assur'd his rescuing work is done.
  The gate is reach'd and open'd wide,
And he places wee lambie inside;
Plaintive it bleats and looks around
Its mother joins it at a bound:
And now the Flock is within the Fold

As sets the sun in red and gold.   50
  Ah! Fathers and mothers my story I tell
Of what this Shepherd once befel,
When all in vain he sought to bring   15
His SHEEP within the green fields' ring,
That I perchance may speak to your heart
As, achingly, dumbly under the smart
Of the loss of child or children belov'd,
To depths of despair you are almost mov'd;
Doubting accusing a Saviour's love,
Or that our Father reigns Above.   60
  What, if you've compell'd Him so to take
Your child or children for your own sake?
What if to win you to turn to Him   [dim?
Your hearts are made sore and your eyes
What, if having tried and tried in vain
Your hearts' allegiance to Him to gain:
What—oh, what! if by a hundred ways,
Met only with long and longer delays,
He yet has fail'd to conquer your will
And you live only for this life still;   70
He has call'd child or children hence
In His most gracious beneficence?
That dear one or dear ones being there
You may run in after, their bliss to share?
The wilful sheep that yet lost would be
Ran in to her lamb as you've heard from
      me;
O Fathers! mothers! the dear Lord grant
That over you the angels may chant
That led by your own little child
You are now seeking Christ, all undefil'd;
Then earthly loss will be heav'nly gain   [80
And soon you will see all your LOST ONES
      again.

THE LITTLE MAID AND LITTLE LADS OF
          HOLY SCRIPTURE.

I.—*The "Captive Little Maid" of Naaman's
      Wife.—2 Kings v., 1-14.*

1 NAAMAN, in his pride of place,
    Wears a sad, beclouded face ;
    Why in pomp and high estate
    Is he thus disconsolate?

He is fill'd, alas, with anguish ;
A foul leper he doth languish—
Lo! a leper white as snow,
Life-blood all corrupt below.

2 'Tis a "captive little maid"
    Lists to what at Court is said ;
    And it makes her very sad,
    But anon she's strangely glad ;
    For—a child, but "taught of God"—
    What if she may lift the load
    That so presses on her lord,
    If to him she might bring word.

3 Knows she how in her lov'd Land
    Prophets great before God stand ;
    Speaking in His mighty Name,
    While His goodness they proclaim
    For their body and their soul,
    Who on Him their sorrow roll :
    'O God! that my lord were near
    Thy Elisha—holy seer.'

4 'Twas but prattle of a child,
    But thro' it, to heal, God will'd ;
    They her words to Naaman bring,
    Light of hope administering ;
    They inspire resolve to go
    And prove whether it were so ;
    And, by gifts of gold, to buy
    Cure of his dread LEPROSY.

5 Needeth not the tale to tell ;
    Shrin'd within us it doth dwell ;
    How thro' humbling, sharp rebuke
    He the prophet's counsel took ;
    Dipp'd in Jordan—and lo! there
    Found his foulness disappear ;
    And he stood all undefil'd ;
    Pure as flesh of little child.

6 Sweet 'tis that our "little maid"
    Brought to the great lord such aid ;

Honour 'twas, by her small voice
Heart of leper to rejoice;
From her own bright Land far taken
Faith in God still kept unshaken.
English children, will ye see
[illegible]

2.—*The "little lad" who bore Jonathan's*
arrows.—1 *Samuel* x.x., 17-23: 35-40.

7 'Tis a vivid INCIDENT,
Strong-lin'd, yet with pathos blent;
David great, and Jonathan
With their two pure hearts made one;
When the friend would shew his friend
What Saul's acting did portend;
Good or evil being proclaimed
By three arrows deftly aim'd.

8 "Little lad" the quiver bore
At Ezel by the woodland hoar;
And his royal prince attending
All obedience sweetly lending;
Running still with footsteps due
Where the arrows onward flew;
That as past the mark they fell
David's message they might tell.

9 "Little lad," he did not know,
Quickly running to and fro,
That he us'd was of the master
Thus to shield ONE from disaster;
All unconsciously he wrought
Nor of hidden meanings thought;
Only working out his part,
But, beneath, a gracious art.

10 'Tis no old Judaic fable,
But a truth of God still stable;
Has its teaching for to-day
If to heart we will it lay:
"*Little lads*" *would ye but [illegible]*
(*Whether ye do ought or speak*)
Sweet obedience aye to yield,
Reason given, or conceal'd.

11 *Oft in [illegible] ye little [illegible]*
Why or here or there ye go;
It may be a little thing
As the arrow from the string
That the little lad was sent
To bring Lord's intent;
[illegible] be it done
He it is Who bids you run.

12 "*Little lads*" *the secret learn,*
As ye would God's blessing earn;
Do the thing " laid to your hand "
Though you may not understand;
Be it word or be it deed,   [meed;
You will gain the Lord Christ's
Ah! unconscious influence
Stronger is than seen by sense.

3.—"*Little Samuel*" *and his* "*little coat.*"
    1 *Samuel* II., 18-19-26.

13 Beautiful the story still
Told of Shiloh on the hill,—
Heaps on heaps of ruins now,
Yet it keeps Time's after-glow.
Samuel, a little child
In his ephod undefil'd;
And by mother's own hands wrought,
Yearly came his " little coat."

14 Vision of the " little lad "
THERE by shatter'd gate I had;
Reading, I was taken back,
Tracing all along the track
Of his mother's willing feet
As she brought her off'ring meet;
THERE, across the plain it wound
Till it reach'd the holy ground.

THE "LITTLE LAD" WITH THE "FIVE BARLEY LOAVES."

The "little lad" with the "five barley loaves" and "two small fishes."—St. John vi, 5-14.

15 In the hush of eve I sate
By the fair scene captivate;
'Twas again a place for prayer—
Hallow'd—for the Lord was there;
'Twas again a place for praise,—
Voice of EVENING HYMN to raise;
While the "little lad" was seen
All transfigur'd in Heaven's sheen.

16 English mothers, [illegible]
Win you, listen to my [illegible],—
'Hannah and her little [son],
And the "little coat" she [made];'
Let it give YOU your [illegible]
Faith, it's [illegible] that [illegible] fear,
Do YOU to the Lord Christ [illegible]
And your child unto Him [illegible]

17 English mothers, let me plead!
As of Samuel ye [illegible]
And that yearly "little coat"
Which his mother to him brought;
You will [illegible] the Lord [illegible] [made]
Your "little lad," [illegible] of them
Servants of the Lord Most High—
[illegible]

18 [illegible]
[several illegible lines]

19 Multitudes to DESERT come
The DISCIPLES would send home;
But THE MASTER tenderly
Would their hunger satisfy;
But, lo! first THE TWELVE to prove
Question to them He did move;
"Bread enough where shall we buy
Such vast numbers to supply?"

20 ANDREW'S quick eye noticed had
In the crowd a "little lad;"
And so, answering, told his Lord
"That a lad had with him stor'd
Barley loaves five—peasants' bread—
With two fishes." "But," he said,
"What are these amongst so many?"
As well almost not have any.

21 JESUS speaks—"Bring them to Me:"
(Wistfully they wait to see
What will come of His command
Yet, obedient, 'fore Him stand):
The throngs order'd on the grass,
Over all a hush doth pass,
Whilst with lifted hand He prays
And life to the bread conveys.

22 "Little lad," thy store was small,
But behold a miracle!
Five loaves now five thousand fill
Not a child left hungering still;
Thronging multitudes all fed
While they ate and wondered;
Benediction to them giv'n,
As if bread sent down from Heav'n.

23 "Little lad," he little knew
That his store, so poor and few,
Should thus be so multiplied
As FIVE THOUSAND satisfied;

THE SLAVE-MARTYR.

But he was there—nor shall die
Story of his ministry;
Who he was is all unknown;
None the less his Lord shall own.

24 *[stanza too faded to read reliably]*

25 "Captive little maid," thy fame
Outlasts those of once great name;
"Little lad" of Jonathan,
Still thou runnest as thou ran;
Lo! Samuel's "little coat"
Is of stuff immortal wrought;
"Little lad" whose store Christ blest
A nimbus doth thee invest.

[two faded lines]

The Slave-Martyr who in the Coliseum drew a cross on the floor, dipping his forefinger in his own flowing blood.—Revel. xvii., 6. Hebrews xii., 4.

1 SMITTEN to the bloody ground
In the COLISEUM's round,
A young Christian martyr lies
In his mortal agonies;
Slain on Roman holiday—
The foul murder they call 'play';
But before falls the death film,
While blood streams from every limb,

Lo! a CROSS in dust he draws—
Sign that even Pagan awes.

2 Noble was it in that SLAVE,
Secret of his HOPE to grave,
"*Tho' He slay me I will trust*;"
Holy One, Thou wert his trust!
And who in this far on day
To our tribute will say 'Nay'?
Or whose bosom does not swell,
This old MARTYRDOM to tell?
Christian slave, whom Christ made free,
Luminous thy memory.

3 So, too, in the Catacombs,
Lighting up their ghostly glooms,
Lie dear saints of God, whose lives
In no 'Calendar' survives:
Yet in the "Lamb's Book" are set,
And the great 'Well Done" shall get:
'Crook' and 'Crown' and 'Palm,' and
 'Cross'
Their graves graciously emboss;
"*Tho' He slay me I will trust*,"
From our lips again doth burst.

4 Wilt Thou, Lord, in these soft days,
In our bosoms 'searchings' raise?
Few are striving "unto blood,"
Greatness counting to be good:
Suff'ring Saviour, to us give
Grace to live as Thou did'st live;
Bearing witness, strong and brave,
Thro' same strength Thou martyrs gave;
Nor e'er may we know despair;
For Thy Cause still all things dare.

HOLY SCRIPTURE.

1 "MY LORD, my God," thanks for Thy
 WORD,
Wherein Thy LAW flames like a sword;—
But 'tis to guard "the tree of life,"
Us arming to meet SIN and STRIFE.

2 Thanks for the men of burden'd eye,
   Who spoke for Thee in PROPHECY;
   Clear-seeing the far-off event;
   Daring to speak wherever sent.

3 Thanks for the great deep-hearted
     PSALMS—
   Each song that stirs — each song that
     calms;
   Simple—as notes of birds in woods;
   Grand—as the far-resounding floods.

4 Thanks for the GOSPEL OF THY GRACE,
   That in Thy LATER WORD we trace;
   The LAW and PROPHETS all fulfill'd;
   Sweeter than sweet from all distill'd.

5 Now "Jesus only" is our PEACE,
   As He brings us the great release;
   Sum of all PROMISE and all HOPE,
   First star in the wide Heaven's cope.

THE BIBLE.

St. John v. 39.

1 When God's Word thou readest, *pause*—
   God's Word that most heedless awes;
   As sea estuary fills,
   Slowly read—with hush that stills.

2 God's Word see thou *reverence*,
   As thou gatherest the sense;
   Faith and Hope and Love combine;
   See thro' human the divine.

3 God's word, *conscience-rul'd*, regard,
   Ever keeping watch and ward;
   Thy law, make it, by free choice;
   Listen to its "still small voice."

4 God's Word as thou readest, *trust*—
   Holy — tender — gracious — just;
   As turn-sol to the sun turns,
   See that His light in thee burns.

5 God's Word ever *hopeful* read:
   His BLOOD ample for world's need;
   Cry thou that He all men bless,
   Clothèd in His righteousness.

6 God's Word *mindfully* search thou,
   Lifting up a dauntless brow;
   This sword valiantly still wield,
   Conqu'ror, thou shalt hold the field.

7 God's Word read thou *Spirit-taught*;
   Self-dependent be in naught;
   He Who as its Author shone,
   Thee and it illumes alone.

8 God's Word consecrate *with prayer*,
   "Casting on Him all thy care;"
   Heart's desires like flames ascend,
   As thou prayer and praise dost blend.

9 God's word read as *seeking Christ*,
   Keeping with Him holy tryst;
   Ev'ry page as thou dost read,
   Ponder that thou mayest plead.

THE LIGHT OF THE WORLD.

"*The beauties of Nature show us God's love; but there is no voice in them that can speak words of comfort to the wounded heart. Brilliant as are the starry spheres, there to no star that could lead a benighted soul is God.*"—T. T. LYNCH.

1 ONE star alone
    That e'er has shone
   On paths men trod,
    Them led to God—
   The shepherds old
    By angels told,

THE LIGHT OF THE WORLD.

To Bethelem.—
And guided them,
To where there lay
'Mongst oxen's hay
The CHILD divine—
Round Whom did twine
Great words of truth,
Great words of ruth,
From holy seers
Of far-back years—
"God manifest"
As lowliest.
  Lo! It did glow
And onward go,
Till manger o'er
(Crib! O how poor!)
It standeth still;
Lo! all the hill
A-blaze with light
Of angels bright,
That gospel bring
As clear they sing—
"Peace on the Earth
By this GREAT BIRTH":
  While "wise men" bow'd
And as they vow'd,
Rich off rings made,
At His feet laid:—
Bright "gold" and "myrrh";
And that, to stir
Still deeper thought
Of man blood-bought—
"Frankincense" sweet,
Which once did meet
On altar pyres'
Atoning fires.
    O wondrous sight!
    O mystic light!

2 One star alone,
That e'er has shone
On paths men trod,
Them led to God
For now man's load
In heart's abode,

Too awful is:
Too far from bliss;
Life's sea so dark—
Flood without ark;
His sky so drear,
So fill'd with fear,
That wilder'd soul
Needs there shall roll
In on his heart,
By gracious art,
A keener light,
With finer sight:
No light e'er giv'n
From mortal heav'n;
No brightest star,
Of all that are,
Has beams to send,
Or guidance lend,
That will suffice
To open eyes.
  Sin-dimm'd and weak,
Ah! we must speak,
Yea to Christ cry,
That He be nigh;
Us still to tell,
'Gainst Earth and Hell,
Of His great light
For soul's black night;
Of Him the Guide,
And none beside;
Of Him Who meets,
And darkest greets,
With beaming Face,
And words of grace;
That darkness flies
From dimmest eyes.
    O soul of mine!
    His light be thine.

"———BUT SOME DOUBTED."
   St. Matthew xxviii. 17
1 The Lord Who died now lives
Lo! Burst the Grave's strong gyves;
Fulfill'd the great Third Day
Death no more holds his prey;

Th' ELEVEN welcome HIM —
His Face the sky doth dim;
Joyous they Him adore
Again by the Sea-shore ;
All their dark fears are routed;
But still we read " *some doubted.*"

2 Them to condemn we shrink,
As all perplex'd we think:
Fain would we find excuse
Rather than them accuse;
But there are the sad words.
Piercing sharp as edg'd swords;
To them we're driven back
With twist as of the rack ;
And read, not that they shouted,
But, griev'd, this, that " *some doubted.*"

3 Ah ! Like ship cast on shelves
The 'doubt' was of themselves ;
That, their dear Master gone
And they left all alone
Fail they must. But His lips
Speak words that end eclipse;
Telling that from that hour
Center'd in Him all power;
The Tempter had them flouted
And thus we read *"some doubted."*

4 As Peter sinks in waves
He 'doubts' but Christ him saves ;
Not incredulity
Sent up his pleading cry:
He knew his Master there,
Not thence came his despair ;
But weakness in a heart
Thro' which FEAR shot its dart;
The died-down faith re-sprouted,
He not of those who " *doubted.*"

5 To-day the record comes
And warning in it sums,
Not to ourselves to look —
Else sure our Faith is shook;
But still to know Him risen
From Death and the Grave's prison;

Yes ever-mighty One
Our King-priest on the Throne ;
That, howe'er it be scouted
Erases swift, "*some doubted.*"

A LITTLE BOY'S PRAYER.

1 JESUS, once a little Child,
I am naughty, I am wild;
Jesus, once a little boy,
Mother's bidding be my joy.

2 Jesus, Who pure words didst speak,
Holy words I from Thee seek;
Jesus, Who each day did'st good,
Poor falls, may I not give food ?

3 Thou Who did'st small children love,
Help me daily to improve;
Jesus, Who on cross did'st die,
Help me never tell a lie.

4 Jesus, Who did'st go to Heaven,
I'll come too, my bad forgiven ;
Jesus, wilt Thou near Thee take
This child, for Thine Own Name's sake.
                              Amen.

A CHILD'S SONG-PRAYER AND PRAYER-SONG.

1 LOVING Jesus, I am small,
Yet upon me Thou dost call;
Thou wast once a little Child,
Wept like me, and like me smiled.

2 See, as I place palm to palm;
Pray to Thee, with holy psalm;
Listen to the little prayer
Of Thy little Follower.

3 Keep, sweet Jesus, keep my lips
And my feet from heedless slips;
Keep my eyes and keep my tongue,
That I never may go wrong.

A VERY LITTLE CHILD'S PRAYER.

4 Father, mother, brothers bless,
Sisters, too, with happiness;
Grandmama in old arm-chair;
Grandpapa with whitened hair.

5 Servants all, whate'er betide,
May they still be on Thy side;
All within our happy home
Keep, that none may ever roam.

6 *Repeat St. 1 in full.*

Amen.

A Very Little Child's Prayer.

*** *With reference to the present little hymn, it may be permitted me to recal that Count Agénor de Gasparin was wont to pray for his sick kitten and other creatures of God, as finely told by his biographer, Borel. Parents will agree that ' nasty ' (st. 5, l. 2), though semi-naughty, is just the child's word, and the reader will please remember that the hymn is "a very little child's prayer," not an adult's.*

1 LITTLE Birdies go to sleep
Till the day again shall peep;
Jesus, let the birdies live,
Loving care to them, Lord, give.

2 Bless dear pussy and her kitten,
Do not let them, Lord, be smitten;
Bless my rabbits in the yard;
Them, good Lord, in safety guard.

3 Bless the sheep out on the wold,
Sleeping in the Autumn cold;
Bless my lamb amongst the mows;
Hens and ducks, and all the cows.

4 Bless dear Rover at our gate,
With his supper on a plate;
Bless my pony in his stall,
Let no hurt to him befall.

5 Bless my apple-tree and flowers;
Keep far off the nasty showers;
Bless my bats and balls and kite;
Let no thief steal them to-night.

6 Bless my father, bless my mother;
And dear Jesus, every other;
Me unto Thy bosom take;
All I ask for Jesus' sake.

Amen.

"IT IS ENOUGH TO HAVE DESERVED."

Motto of the Massingberds of Gunly Hall, Lincolnshire, painted on the signboard of the recently opened (1899) "Massingberd Arms," Bournemouth, which is to be used as a coffee palace and temperance club House.

1 "It is enough to have deserved:"
From duty never to have swerv'd;
And never in these days of ease
From "hardness" to have sought release.

2 Now with so much to do for Christ,
Alas! that few with Him keep tryst;
The praise be His if, by grace giv'n,
We have fore-won "well done" of Heav'n.

3 "It is enough to have deserved:"
Caring for fallen and for starv'd,
For this life and for life to come;
Tho' on it all the World be dumb.

4 Still potent are the hosts of Evil
These three—" the World, the flesh, and devil;"
But "stronger" He Who in us is;
Than powers of darkness, powers of bliss.

5 "It is enough to have deserv'd:"
With brave and true hearts by Him nerv'd;
Faithful 'gainst odds, to His appeals
Who win, or fail, our efforts seals.

"DEAD, I SING MORE THAN WHEN I WAS ALIVE."

(Inscription on a violin of Stradivarius).

1 "I dead, sing more than when I was alive,"
More than when I did with the East wind strive;
Lifting my needled branches to the skies
A-thrill with all the greenwood's [harmonies.

2 "I dead, sing more than when I was alive,"
More still since ART has put on me her gyve
And slain me - paradox! yet I'm not slain, [rain.
But still as erst sing—in glad Summer's

3 "I dead, sing more than when I was alive,"
A willing captive—as bees in their hive—
And from my breast—like sunlight in the coal— [roll.
Lo! Subtlest tones all passionate forth

4 "I dead, sing more than when I was alive,"
My soul! Wouldst thou into this secret dive? [still;
Then know our dead in Christ are with us
Their voices—soft and low—the hush'd [heart fill.

5 "I dead, sing more than when I was alive,"
Ev'n so—Death to despair shall not me drive; [keep
"I know Whom I believe," and He doth
My lov'd and loving ones who rest in sleep.

6 "I dead, sing more than when I was alive,"
Precious the quaint old words—and lo! belyve [song;
Fulfill'd are they—dear mem'ries turn to
And cheer me, as life's vale I pass along.

7 "I dead, sing more than when I was alive,"
My gracious Master, wilt Thou not me shrive [gone,
If I humbly have hope that when I'm
I too shall sing—kept from OBLIVION?

DROPPED-OUT NUMBERS OF HYMNS.

_{*} By inadvertance Nos. 109 and 420 have been dropped out in their places. They are to be filled in with the following respectively:—

109. THE FINAL JUDGMENT. 11s.

1 SEE! The word of the Lord of old time given
Is fulfill'd,—— From one end to th' other of heaven,
Lo! The sign of the Son of Man flameth vivid;
WHILST BENEATH GAZE MYRIADS WITH FACES LIVID.

2 'Tis the Last Great Day and the Judge is seated;
His PURPOSE stands fast—all HIS foes defeated;
The trumpet is blown by mouth of archangel;
The dead re-live—to hear doom or evangel.

3 To all who for Saviour THE CHRIST had taken
Not one of them all of his hope is shaken;
"Come, ye blessed"—hark the reverberation,
The sav'd and the damn'd in vast separation.

4 Woe! woe! and woe! like storm-waves uprisen,
Comes the wail of the LOST as they pass to their prison;
Joy! joy! and joy! swells upward adoring;
The song of redeem'd hosts, still Christward soaring.

420. THE STRONGER THAN THE ENEMY.
1 John iv. 4 : 8.8.7.7.7.6.6.

1 To fight the arch-en'my Satan, [man;
Needs more than the strength of mere
Not weapons our arm'ries yield,
But great Faith's God-fashion'd shield;
To quench his hell-kindled darts
Deft-aim'd at our mortal hearts:
   The Lord is on our side,
   No hurt shall us betide.

2 He comes with his vaunts outrageous,
Fond-dreaming but to engage us;
To ANOTHER he must bow,
We stand in the Lord Christ now;
No anvils of earth can forge
The weapons we 'gainst him urge:
   The Lord is on our side,
   No hurt shall us betide.

3 The Lord Christ, than he is stronger,
Then Brothers fight a while longer;
You still may Satan assail,
Yea dinted be your strong mail;
But brave in your FAITH, HOPE, LOVE,
Look stedfast to Him above:
   The Lord is on our side,
   No hurt shall us betide.

4 Then, tempter, fierce and malignant,
Lowly souls by grace indignant
Fear not in strength of the Lord
To draw His great sword "the Word";
Yea turning its words to prayer
Quail to no foe whosoe'er:
   The Lord is on our side,
   No hurt shall us betide.

5 Be not from your REFUGE shaken ;
 By none be your weapons taken ;
 Lo ! the overcoming life
 Is in you for this high strife ;
 Tho' dark and terrible the fray,
 " The Captain" will aye be your stay :
  The Lord is on our side,
  No hurt shall us betide.

6 Soon ye shall be victorious
 Soon earn your rest all-glorious ;
 'Tis but on this earth below
 That Satan abides our foe ;
 'Tis but in this flesh, that sin
 In aught doth victory win :
  Resist still, and anon
  Ye glad shall hear "well done."

For 429 substitute the following—

PRAYING AND WORKING. 2 *Cor. vi.* 1.   7s.

1 PRAYING work, and, working, pray ;
 Christ ne'er to His own says nay ;
 Active ever for our Lord,
 He us all grace will afford.

2 Praying work—for vain to serve
 If His grace do not us nerve ;
 Working pray—for vain to sue
 Unless 'tis that we may DO.

3 Blessèd Jesus, touch our wills
 With uplifting touch that thrills ;
 Blessèd Jesus, guard our hearts
 From the great world's "fiery darts."

4 Be our prayers no idle breath ;
 Be our work not all beneath ;
 Be our prayers a laying hold ;
 Be our work unpaid by gold.

5 Nearer Thee, Lord, and more near,
 Draw us that we cease to fear ;
 Grant us this, and we shall know
 How to work, and pray and "GO".

Repeat St. 1.

NOTES AND ILLUSTRATIONS.

1 Hymn 1, st. 6, l. 4, '*I think of mortal men that hear.*' There can be no denying that it is one advantage of a Liturgy, that not only does the congregation know what the successive prayers will be, but that these prayers are the elect thought and emotion of generations of holy men. Personally, I prefer spontaneous and present-day prayers; but there is the danger of preaching rather than praying, and the temptation to address men rather than God. Happy they who are lifted above danger and temptation alike, and who escaping monotony and formalism, also escape over-familiarity and irreverence.

2 Hymn 2, st. 1, l. 3, '*Paran's pinnacles.*' Those who, like myself, have toiled on dromedary-back across the Sinaitic peninsula in long foreview of Paran, and who have watched this remarkable mountain-mass against the glorious morning and sunset skies, will agree that 'pinnacles' is *the* one word to describe its serrated peaks. I counted upwards of twenty.

3 Hymn 6, st. 4, l. 2, '*burning brand.*' See Zechariah iii. 2. . . . "Is not this a brand plucked out of the fire?" This refers to Joshua, the then high-priest, of whom little or nothing more than this solitary fact seems to be known. It startles one to read such a (metaphorical) question as this in relation to one who filled so august an office as that of high-priest. But when one thinks deeper, it is found and felt to exemplify John Bunyan's idea of "Grace abounding to the chief of sinners." Self-evidently there lay in the forgiven Past in the case of this Joshua such a life as St. Augustine's earlier or Billy Bray's later, which only the conquering grace of God had overcome and sanctified. The metaphor is a singularly vivid and striking one. For it is not fetched from a tree or branch felled simply, or even that barked, peeled and winnowed in the hot sun, or even the long-dried trunk or branch shaped into a fagot or 'brand,' but that **brand** a-blaze

and consuming in the fire. So that the message of gospel is,—near as such a 'brand' under such conditions and circumstances is to destruction, so near had been once Joshua the high-priest. But the gentle yet mighty hand of God had 'plucked' him as it were 'out of the fire.' Myriad instances of such 'redemption' and 'salvation' in extremity, go to attest the breadth and patience of redeeming love.

4 Hymn 19, st. 3, l. 2, "*And 'put' like hatred me within.*" The first promise in Eden was "I will *put* enmity between thee [the Tempter] and the woman, and between thy seed and her seed" (Genesis iii. 15). This 'enmity' to sin is of grace, never of nature. It must be given, must be 'put' in these human hearts of ours by the Holy Ghost. When so 'put' it is sanctified to higher issues, is, so to say, the starting of conversion. With reference to our refrain, be it remembered that it *is 'Our* God' Who is a "consuming fire." Many sentimentalists think it evangelical to talk of and to '*poor* sinners,' and often pronounce individuals to have been 'converted' on merely voluble or emotional words. It is imperative that we hold firmly the sinfulness of sin, the 'abominableness' of sin, and how out and out a righteous God "hates" it and takes an attitude toward it of "consuming fire." I fear multitudes of so-called converts are misled to conceive of God as incarnate good-nature, sublimated, easy-going forgivingness; whereas He is incarnate Love administering righteousness. It will awe and solemnize and prevent light and slight notions of sin to remember these mighty words, "Our God is a consuming fire." Cf. Deuteronomy iv. 22.

5 Hymn 37, st. 3 l, 2, "*And dimness fell on the Great Birth.*" Surely it is extremely remarkable that so stupendous an event as the birth of "God manifest in the flesh," so soon and so utterly passed out of human speech and memory. It is clear that John the Baptist's clarion proclamation of 'The Christ' came with surprise on the nation. Had the 'great birth' been remembered this never could have been, or the wonderful resident in Nazareth have been suffered to live for thirty years in such strange obscurity.

5* Hymn 20, st. 2, l. 1, "*Thou livest though men come and go.*" How pathetic is the contrast between the dead gods of Greece and Rome and the "*Living* God." How touching such a sight as that of the colossal Baal at the foot of Hermon, without a solitary worshipper! And so the Sphinx under the shadow of the pyramids! Not one to do any one of them all slightest homage, their being defunct being universally recognized. When I was at the Temple of the Sun at Baalbec I witnessed a Mahommedan prostrate in prayer, but it was to God not to the erewhile god of the temple. Our God lives on, abiding the "same yesterday, to-day, and for ever." Contrast Jesus Christ as King of kings and still 'reigning' with the brief reigns and final utter severance from the living of all other kings and of all other men, and you get the same result.

6 Hymn 38, "*I will not meet thee as a man.*" The Revised Version reads, "I will take vengeance, and will accept no man;" in margin, '*Or* make truce with Heb. meet. The Authorised Version is a deeper unfolding of the idea, though the Revised Version is more verbally exact. The ground-fact is that outside of Christ as "God manifest in the flesh," God is a vengeance-taking God. St. Paul, in I. Corinthians, xv. 24-25, gives us solemn glimpses of the finality of doom of all who had personally rejected Christ, and how thereupon the Christless must reckon with absolute Godhead.

7 Hymn 126, "*The first Japanese convert.*" Xavier introduced Christianity amongst the Japanese in 1549. There was apparent success given to the illustrious missionary. But in 1637 Japan was closed "for ever" (so the edict ran) to foreigners and to Christianity. Death was the inexorable penalty of any adherence to "the vile Jesus doctrine" henceforth. And so things went on darkly and sorrowfully for long generations. Every one knows the wonderful re-opening of Japan; but perhaps not many have heard of how Christianity was re-introduced. It was by a Japanese noble. One day he saw in the Bay of Yeddo something floating on the water, which proved to be a Bible. He himself did not know what it was, but was told that it was an English Bible that had been dropped from some English or American vessel. His curiosity was excited, and he became eager to know more about the sacred book. He sent to Shanghai for an interpreter. His study of the Bible was blessed to him. He gave himself to the Lord Jesus. In 1857 he was baptized, being the first Japanese convert in modern days. Two others were baptized along with him; and from that time Christianity has been a living and ever-widening and deepening power in this unique island-empire. Thus the seeming chance-found copy of the Bible was the divinely-human instrumentality of giving the great impulse that is rapidly lifting up Japan to a splendid place among civilized nations. Few will disagree that it was worth while trying to commemorate so striking an incident.

8 Hymn 132, st. 6, l. 3. '*Chouse*'—to cheat.

8 Hymn 80, '*I am safe, for Christ holds me, comforted, for I hold him.*' This distinction

between being saved and being in comfort (or "perfect peace") was actually made by a poor gipsy woman to the late Rev. James Robertson, Newington. See his 'Life.'

9 Hymn 143, '*Unworthy*,' '*Unworthily*.' "Whosoever shall eat this bread and drink this cup of the Lord *unworthily* shall be guilty of the body and blood of the Lord." "He that eateth and drinketh *unworthily* eateth and drinketh damnation [condemnation] to himself, not discerning the Lord's body," 1 Corinthians, xi. 27-29. I take the liberty to refer to a small book of mine called "Joining the Church, or Materials for Conversations between a Minister and Intending Communicants." Herein I show the profound difference between 'unworthy' and 'unworthily,' though the words sound so much alike. A grand device of the enemy of souls is to confound the two, and to make the timid, self-accusing intending communicant refrain because of felt personal unworthiness, as though that were designated by the 'unworthily' of St. Paul. To the latest and last every one of us must abide 'unworthy' but "*worthy* is THE LAMB." As being in ourselves 'unworthy' we are invited, charged to 'lay hold' of His worthiness, and the more keenly in so doing we feel our own personal unworthiness the more we do magnify His grace in redeeming us. To eat and drink 'unworthily' is to do so as attaching no real worth to the observance, to come carnally, unmourningly, unfeelingly, unlovingly. But all that is as far as the poles asunder from a lowly, penetrative, abased sense of personal unworthiness. Coming as 'unworthy' we come as the deathfully sick patient to the physician, and there is welcome and blessing; 'unworthily' sure condemnation and peril. But better imperfect, inadequate communion than no communion; better to limp and creep in the way than not to seek the way at all; better to err in trying to obey than certainly to disobey by neglecting or delaying. For further guiding words see above-named Manual, which has had a very large and continuous circulation.

10 Hymn 144, st. 1, l. 10, '*White Jordan*.' The Jordan at 'the Fords' when I was there ran white as milk. It gives a peculiar character to the landscape. Higher up the whiteness was not found.

10* Hymn 147, '*Weeds*' '*waifs*.' "I never understood the parable of the Tares," said Arthur Hamilton to his biographer, "till I found these words in a book the other day: 'The root of the common darnel *(lolium)* or dandelion, with saltpetre, makes a very cheap and effective sheep-drench. It can be applied successfully in cases of fluke.'" (Memoirs, p. 205).

NOTES AND ILLUSTRATIONS.

11 Hymn 159, '*Martyrs of our day.*' Miss Yonge's 'Life of Bishop Patteson'; the various 'Lives and Memorials of Bishop Hannington'; Mr. Ashe's, 'Two Kings of Uganda,' and the recent terrible revelations of Turkish brutality and cruelty in Crete and elsewhere, will abundantly illustrate this celebration of 'Martyrs of our day.' Incidentally Stanley and fully the memoir of the noble Mackay give testimony to the nobility and thoroughness of adherence to Christianity of the converts of Uganda and all over "Darkest Africa."

12 Hymn 194. st. 1, l. 1, '*Pinking*'—turning pink from gold or black. Thomas Hardy thus uses the word: "Get on with your work or 'twill be dark before we have done. The evening is *pinking* in a'ready." ('Dairyman' in *Wessex Tales*—the Withered Arm i), albeit here it may be = contracting *i.e.* darkening.

13 Hymn 203, '*He leads round, but He leads right.*' This came to me so spontaneously on the Sunday morning of the 21st anniversary of my marriage with my beloved wife, viz., 1st May, 1866—1st May, 1877, that I had simply to write it down.

13* Hymn 290, '*Sweet longings.*' Composed on the sands at South Shore, Blackpool, while witnessing a magnificent sunset—a frequent thing there.

14 Hymn 312, '*Love or Death.*' "Death is a bitter thing without the Saviour's love; and love itself were bitter without His Death, inasmuch as that precious death has won that heavenly love for us, without which neither our works nor sufferings could ever win eternal life. The dear Bishop had taken for his motto: 'Ou Mourir, ou Aimer' ['Death or Love'.] He paraphrases it thus: 'Die to all other love, in order to live to Jesus' love, and so not to die eternally, but live in Thy everlasting love, O Saviour of our souls, for ever to sing the song of the blessed! Hail Jesus, Whom I love, Who lives and reigns world without end. Amen.'" And again: "I would either love God or die. Death or love. Life without that love is infinitely more terrible than death." (Bishop of Belley's "The Spirit of S. Francis de Sales," c. ii. 6. xiv.)

15 Hymn 315, st. 1, l. 1, '*Command......*' "Da quod jubes, et jube quod vis."—S. Augustine' Conf. lib. x. xxix.

15* Hymn 337, '*Despair and God.*' I discovered that what I thought was a personal and exceptional experience, another and very remarkable man had also gone through—Arthur Hamilton, B.A. He thus wrote to his Biographer concerning the tragedy of his life, the death by accident of his young Persia-born pupil Edward Bruce: "People talk and write about instantaneous momentary *conversions*. I never realised what was meant till a week ago. Day after day, all that time, I had been filled with gloomy, reproachful, or bitter thoughts of God and the providence which took Edward from me. It was intolerable that he should be swept away into silence, leaving me so worn and hopeless, and, worst of all, so dissatisfied and discontented with the hand that did it,—my vaunted philosophy failing and giving out utterly. I *knew* it was right, but could not *feel* it. But last night as I sat, as I have often done, burning and racked with recollection and regret, a kind of peace stole over me. It was quite sudden, quite abnormal: not that after-glow of hope that sometimes follows a dark plunge of despair, but a gentle firm trust that seemed, without explaining, yet to make all things plain; not ebbing and flowing, not changing with physical sensation or mental weariness, but deep, abiding, sustaining. You may think it rash of me thus, after so short an interval, to write so assuredly of it; but even if I lost the sense (and I shall not) the memory of that moment would support me; "*If I go down into hell, Thou art there also,*" is the only sentence that expresses it. (Memoirs, cxii. pp. 209-210—a wonderful book.)

15† Hymn 372, '*Song of Joy*,' I fear it must be admitted that most of us are quick enough (perhaps) in going to the Lord in and with our sadness and fears, but on the other hand laggard and fitful in going to Him in and with our gladness. In short is it not indisputable that practically we turn our great High-priest into one who will hear 'confession,' probe with morbid casuistry our vileness, but refuse to hear of the "joy of our salvation?" I apprehend it were well if we would get rid of a portion at least of that stereotyping of prayer that makes it *the* right thing to interweave a litany of humiliation and confession and semi-tones of anguish into every approach to the Throne of Grace. It should rejoice us to tell God our joy, to confide to Him our exultant freedom and lightsomeness in Jesus Christ.

16 Hymn 382, st. 5, l. 1, '*Tove*' = passion

16* Hymn 402, st. 1 l. 1, '*Gifts without the giver are bare*.' I draw this refrain from an American man of genius, J. D. Lowell; but the words are proverbial in many languages. I am satisfied that one-half of good-doing is lost by delegation. I have been personally humbled, almost humiliated by the self-evident enrichment of any little kindness by its being done by one's self. Mere sending chills and hurts. We ought therefore to put ourselves to every inconvenience to 'go' rather than 'send,' as elsewhere I sing (Hymn 405). I ask no impossibilities and draw no hard and fast line, but I ask self-denying and generous possibilities. Several of my Hymns carry this burden.

17 Hymn 438, '*Our dead first born.*' William David Grosart, born 25th March, 1867; died 27th January, 1868.

18 Hymn 445, '*Mi disse,*' '*Non Cercar, &c.*' I would refer any reader who cares to the following charming book for many more of these memorable sayings—" Essays on the Study of Folk Songs. By the Countess Evelyn Martinengo-Cesaresco" (1866—Redway, publisher).

19 Hymn 449, '*No more pain.*' This has been printed in unusually large type and mounted on a thick board, to be hung up in sick rooms, infirmary wards, &c. Price, 1/3 per copy, post free.

20 Hymn 451, '*Christ with me and I with Christ.*' The genuine words of an aged, humble, but remarkable Christian.

21 *Life-story*, p. 234, 'The Transfiguration.' See also Hymn 57, st. 1, l. 1. No one who has actually been in the two scenes, and judicially studied the thing on the spot, will doubt that Tabor and not one of the many spurs of (so-called) Mount Hermon was the scene of the Transfiguration. Hermon is a mountain range, and in no manner of way answers to the Evangelist's wording, " bringeth them up into an high mountain apart." Conceding that κατ' ἰδίαν refers to the isolating, or taking aside from the other nine, of the chosen three, it is yet clear that it was a distinctively separate and clearly defined mountain, being designated by ὄρος which is the Septuagint term for the Hebrew הר. The tradition of Tabor is a very early one; for Origen cites from the " Gospel according to the Hebrews," a paragraph which indisputably relates to the transfiguration and Tabor as its scene; and this takes us back to the second century. Two objections have been urged against Tabor, and in favour of Hermon :—(*a*) The conversation (Mat. xvi. 21-28) which preceded the Transfiguration by six days took place at Cesarea Philippi, *ergo* as Hermon rises above it the transfiguration must have taken place on Hermon. But this statement of the case conveniently forgets that the conversation did precede the transfiguration by (at least) six days. Further—it forgets that while the Lord had reasons for shunning Galilee (xvi. 5), it yet is manifest that He must have returned thither in the interval, seeing that immediately after the transfiguration the Lord and the Three are found going from Galilee toward Capernaum, and not from

Cæsarea Philippi (St. Mark ix. 14, 30, 33); (b) Dr. Robinson having shown that there was a fort or citadel on the summit of Mount Tabor at the period, it has been argumentatively inferred that the transfiguration could not have taken place on that summit. But there is no warrant whatever for saying that the transfiguration took place on the 'summit.' I have been up and all round Tabor (as up and all along the mountain-range of Hermon), and its summit, is not peaked or narrow but wide and large, with ample scope for retirement. But if the event be located—as I claim a right to do—not on the summit but on the mountain, the supposed difficulty disappears. The phrasing is that Jesus took the disciples 'up into a high mountain' (εἰς ὄρος); and I can personally testify that there are many dells and groves and solitudes all over Mount Tabor, in any one of which there could have been the utmost seclusion even with a fort and garrison on the summit. I think of like solitudes in the much more limited areas of Edinburgh and Stirling Castles in Scotland.

Two details of fact must also be remembered viz: (1) That it is a good long three hours 'pull' from Cæsarea Philippi to the top of Hermon above it; and that just as to-day many visit Cæsarea Philippi without going higher, it is a mere assumption that because the Lord was there He and the Three climbed Hermon. (2) That Hermon in summit and other side (if not wholly there) lay outside of the Land of Promise and Possession proper; ergo was less likely to have been chosen by the Lord for such a transaction.

Be it further remembered that Tabor is within a few hours easy distance of Nazareth the almost life-long home of our Lord; and hence that nothing could be more humanly natural than His wishing to pay a last visit to the Nazareth district, and to choose His boyhood's playground for the scene of His transfiguration. I place this alongside another later incident, viz., the walk to Emmaus. After examination on the spot I am satisfied that the recently identified Emmaus is certain. Well! it was near to Bethlehem and it adds new pathos to the 'walk' to connect it with a re-visit, a final visit to His birth-place.

Tabor is one of the loneliest, as it is also one of the loveliest of the mountains of Palestine. The panorama visible from its top and sides includes Carmel—scene of Elijah's mighty works—and all the grand scenes of the great Old Testament events of the Elijah period and ministry. Again, how natural to bring Elijah hither and not to remote Hermon. One feels the congruity of the placing him on Tabor. But I lay more stress on the fact that after the transfiguration our Lord is returning through Galilee by Samaria to Capernaum, and that it was no hurried visit but leisurely, over six days at least. A tradition of the second century might have come down through only three or four persons and be easily verified. Since "Three Centuries of Hymns" was issued, I have read Nicholson's "Gospel of the Hebrews." He connects the fragment in question with the Temptation. See p. 75. *Cf.* also his commentary on St. Matthew v. 1., and on Luke ix. 28—hardly convincing but ingenious.

22 '*Sunny Memories*,' p. 244 l. 109 '*True*,'... Repeatedly I use this word in relation to Christian character, work and witness. I do so advisedly, for "*truth* in the inward parts" is what, more and more is needed to tell on the world. There is so much of seeming. See Hymn 340, 'Genuineness.' Perhaps no sadder historic exemplification of the baleful effects of such 'retreat' is imaginable than is presented in that of the monks of Egypt who retired into the "great and terrible wilderness" of Sinai I found a lump in my throat as I explored their numerous cells on Tahouney and neighbourhood; nor am I unwilling to accept the revival of their memory by George Ebers in his "Homo Sum." But none the less we must lay at the door of these retreating monks the withering of the Coptic Church and the dying out of a once living Christianity in Egypt and along the Nile and inward of the "Dark Continent." Had they but stood firm we should not to-day be lamenting lost provinces of Christendom. In st. 2, l. 2, the word 'vile' gives me opportunity to say that St. Paul is not to be held answerable for the '*vile* body' of our Authorised translation and popular theology—read 'the body of our humiliation,' and link it on with His body of His humiliation. The Christian like Christ is here and now emptied of his glory. On this hither side ours is a time of 'humiliation.'

23 P. 270, col. 2, st. 6, '*Belyve*'—immediately or by-and-bye.

"OH! WHAT A BRIGHT DAY TO-MORROW WILL BE."

S. Frances de Chantal (on her deathbed the night before she died).

1 "Oh! What a bright day to-morrow will be":
  For with dawn of morn I Jesus shall see;
  Pass'd 'bove these dim shadows into the light,
  In the LAND OF GLORY where is no night.

2 "Oh! what a bright day to-morrow will be":
  From this "body of death" for aye set free;
  No more to suffer and no more to sin,
  The "House of many mansions" safe within.

3 "Oh! what a bright day to-morrow will be":
  The sweet fore-feeling my heart fills with glee;
  Though slow the long journey, the end now is near;
  Then wonder not that I shed not a tear.

4 "Oh! what a bright day to-morrow will be":
  For blessèd Saviour, I depart to Thee;
  "Rod" and "staff" 'me "comfort," yea, and uphold;
  Farewell! Lo! I see the CITY OF GOLD.

5 "Oh! what a bright day to-morrow will be":
  Look! Holy angels descending for me;
  See ye not? catch ye not gleams of their whiteness?
  My death-chamber luminous with their brightness.

6 *Repeat St. 1.*

OTHER BOOKS
BY THE
REV. DR. A. B. GROSART, BLACKBURN, LANCASHIRE.

☞ Any wishing copies of any of these books, or futher detail on certain of them, may communicate with the Author, enclosing addressed and stamped envelope.

I. ORIGINAL.

I. Small Sins. Third ed., with additions, 16mo., pp. 119. 1s. 6d.
II. Jesus Mighty to Save; or, Christ for all the World and all the World for Christ. Third ed., with additions. 16mo, pp. 204. 2s.
III. The Lambs all Safe; or, The Salvation of Children. 5th ed. 16mo. 1s.
IV. The Prince of Light and the Prince of Darkness in Conflict; or, The Temptation of Jesus ... Cr. 8vo, pp. xxxiv and 360. 5s. (Out of print).
V. The Helper of Joy. Second ed. 16mo. 1s.
VI. Christ the Key-Bearer; or, An Exposition of the Epistle to the Church of Philadelphia. 16mo. 1s. Large paper, with engraving, 1s. 6d.
VII. The Blind Beggar by the Wayside. 32mo. 1½d.
VIII. Representative Nonconformists with the Message of their Life-Work to-day:
   JOHN HOWE, Intellectual Sanctity.
   RICHARD BAXTER: Seraphic Fervour.
   SAMUEL RUTHERFORD: Devout Affection.
   MATTHEW HENRY: Sanctified Common Sense.
   Post 8vo. 6s. Pp. xvi. & 380.

IX. Hanani; or. Memoir of William Smith, Father of George Smith of Coalville. With steel portrait. 12mo. 1s. 6d.
X. Lord Bacon not the Author of the Christian Paradoxes ... Cr. 8vo. 3s. 6d. 8vo. 10s. 6d., with photo. of Herbert Palmer.
XI. Who wrote Britain's Ida? in a Letter to the Lord Chief Justice of England. Cr. 8vo. 1s. 6d.
XII. Drowned: a Sermon. Cr. 8vo. 4d.
XIII. Joining the Church; or, Materials for Conversations between a Minister and Intending Communicant. Pp. 142. 32mo. 1s.
XIV. George W. Child; a Memoir and Message. With steel portrait. 8vo. 1s.
XV. Annotated Bibliographical Catalogue of the Entire Writings of Richard Baxter. Cr. 8vo. 3s. 6d.
XVI. The Chimney Corner; or, Scotland in "Auld Lang Syne," being Stories and Sketches. (Anonymous.) 1s. 6d.
XVII. Leaflets.—152 of the Hymns of "Songs of Day and Night," have been printed separately for enclosure in letters, &c. *List being prepared: also being*

OTHER BOOKS BY REV. DR. A. B. GROSART—*continued*.

prepared, 50 cheap tractates addressed to *professing Christians* on vital matters.

II. EDITED.

. In each case there is a full Memoir drawn from original sources, and notes and illustrations; and, in many cases, specially engraved (steel) portraits, &c., &c.

XVIII. **The Complete Works of Richard Sibbes, D.D.** 7 vols. 8vo.

XIX. **The Complete Works of Thomas Brooks.** 6 vols. 8vo.

XX. **Demonologia Sacra of Dr. Richard Gilpin.** 1 vol. 8vo.

XXI. **Meditations and Disquisitions upon certain Psalms.** By Sir Richard Baker, Kt. 1 vol. post. 8vo. 5s.

XXII. **Memoirs prefixed to Nichol's "Puritan Commentaries,"**—Henry Airay, D.D.—Thomas Cartwright, B.D.—John King, D.D.—John Rainolds, D.D.—Richard Stock—Samuel Torshell—Richard Bernard, B.D.—Thomas Pierson — Samuel Smith; also John Trapp, prefixed to reprint of his great Commentary. See Stephen's Dictionary of National Biography, Encyclopædia Britannica, &c., &c., for many other Memoirs.

XXIII. **Unknown Book by Richard Baxter**—The Grand Question Resolved—What we must do to be saved, 1692. See No. XV. 3s. 6d.

XXIV. **Selections from the Unpublished MSS. of Jonathan Edwards.** 8vo. 7s. 6d. Fine paper, 10s. 6d.

XXV. **The Complete Poems with New Memoir and Vindication, of Michael Bruce.** Cr. 8vo. 3s. 6d. Illustrated, with photo, 4to. 10s. 6d.

XXVI. **The Complete Poems, with New and Full Memoir, of Robert Fergusson.** Cr. 8vo. 3s. 6d.

XXVII. **The Poems of Palmer of Annan,** with Introduction. 12mo. 1s. 6d.

XXVIII. **Selections from Philpot's "Pocket of Pebbles"** with Preface. 32mo. 1s.

XXIX. **The Fuller Worthies' Library.** 39 vols. cr. 8vo, 8vo, and 4to, viz., the Complete Poems of Dr. Thomas Fuller— Dr. Thomas Washbourne— Fulk Greville, Lord Brooke—Henry and Thomas Vaughan (Prose also)—George Herbert (Prose also)—Christopher Harvey—Giles and Phineas Fletcher—Andrew Marvell (Prose also)—Dean Donne —Sir Philip Sidney—Sir John Davies (Prose also)—Joseph Fletcher – Robert Southwell—Richard Crashaw—Miscellanies (4 vols.)

XXX. **The Chertsey Worthies' Library** 14 vols. 4to, viz., Complete Works in Verse and Prose of Nicholas Breton — John Davies of Hereford—Joshua Sylvester—Dr. Joseph Beaumont— Francis Quarles—Abraham Cowley and Dr. Henry More (Verse only).

XXXI. **The Huth Library.** 29 vols. cr. 8vo, 8vo, and 4to, viz., Complete Works of Robert Greene, 15 vols.; Thomas Nashe, 6 vols.;

OTHER BOOKS BY REV. DR. A. B. GROSART—continued.

Gabriel Harvey, 3 vols; Thomas Dekker, 5 vols. (non-dramatic).

XXXII. **The Manuscripts of Sir John Eliot**, never before printed. 6 vols. 4to (for the Earl of St. Germans), viz., The Monarchie of Man An Apologie for Socrates—Negotium Posterorum—De Jure Majestatis, and Letters—Portraits, &c., &c.

XXXIII. **The Poems of Richard James, B.D.** 1 vol. 4to. with engraving.

XXXIV. **The Complete Poems of Richard Barnfield.** For the Roxburgh Club. With engravings, &c. 1 vol. 4to.

XXXV. **Townley MSS.** 1. The Spending of the Money of Robert Nowell of Reade Hall; 2. English Jacobite Ballads, Songs, and Satires. 2 vols. sm. 4to, and l. paper 4to.

XXXVI. **The Farmer Manuscript.** For the Chetham Society. 2 vols. 4to.

XXXVII. **The Manuscripts of the 'Great' Earl of Cork, entitled 'The Lismore Papers.'** For His Grace the Duke of Devonshire. 10 vols. 4to. Never before printed.

XXXVIII. **The Miscellaneous Works of Alexander Wilson, Ornithologist.** 2 vols. cr. 8vo, and large paper. With steel Portrait. 7s. 6d. and 12s. 6d.

XXXIX. **The Early English Poets of Chatto & Windus.** 9 vols. viz., Giles Fletcher—Robert Herrick—Sir Philip Sidney—Sir John Davies. Cr. 8vo, and large paper.

XL. **George Herbert's Complete Poems**, with MS. additions and an original and Full Memoir in the "Aldine Poets." Cr. 8vo, 5s.; also Fac-simile of 1st ed. of 'The Temple' (Elliot Stock), 3s. 6d.

XLI. **The entire Prose Works of William Wordsworth.** 3 vols. 8vo: also private ed. with special illustrations, £1 11s. 6d.

XLII. **The Poems of George Daniel, Royalist.** 4 vols. 4to. Never before printed. With Portrait.

XLIII. **The Poems of Sir Robert Chester.** 1 vol. 8vo; also reprinted by the New Shakespeare Society. *⁎* Much new light shed on Shakespeare.

XLIV. **Occasional Issues of Unique and very rare books.** 38 vols. 4to. *⁎* The rarest of English rarities—from 30 to 62 copies only.

XLV. **The Complete Works of Edmund Spenser.** 10 vols. cr. 8vo, 8vo, small 4to, and large 4to. [Vol X. to come.]

XLVI. **The Complete Works of Samuel Daniel.** 5 vols. cr. 8vo, 8vo, sm. 4to, and large 4to. [Vols. IV. and V. to come]

XLVII. **Large and very fine private steel portraits of Spenser—Milton—Marvell—Otway—George Herbert: Smaller of Leighton (a gem)—Sidney—Wordsworth's sister, &c., &c.**

A LAST REQUEST.

With simplest words of humble faith, me lay
    Within a simple grave;
Above a simple stone—no more I pray—
    Let a white hawthorn wave;
My name, two dates, inscribe alone; and may
    A benediction have
Of some few hearts to miss me when away;
Above my dust, may birds sing, flowers blow
And little children play—nor fear to go.
A. B. G.

FINIS.

D. E. ROTHWELL, ART PRINTER, BLACKBURN.